AND STILL
WE RISE

Feminist Political Mobilizing
in Contemporary Canada

Edited by

Linda Carty

women's
P R E S S

CANADIAN CATALOGUING IN PUBLICATION DATA
Main entry under title:
And still we rise : feminist political mobilization in contemporary Canada
Includes bibliographical references.
ISBN 0-88961-177-7
1. Feminism - Canada. 2. Women in politics - Canada.
3. Women - Canada - Social conditions. 4. Race discrimination - Canada. 5. Minority
women - Canada. I. Carty, Linda E (Linda Eugenie), 1952–
HQ1453.A54 1993   305.42'0971   C93-094362-7

Copyright © 1993 Linda Carty
Cover art: Grace Channer
Cover design: Kok-Kwan Shum
Copy editing: P. K. Murphy

Grateful acknowledgement is made to the following for permission to reprint their
copyright material.
Debi Brock, "Violence Against Women: Strategies for Change" from *Canadian
Woman Studies/les cahiers de la femme*, Vol. 12, No. 1 (Fall 1991).
Diane Driedger, "Discovering Disabled Women's History" from *The More We Get
Together*, Proceedings of the CRIAW/ICREF P.E.I. Conference (Ragweed
Press/gynergy books, 1992).

This book was produced by the collective effort of Women's Press.
Women's Press gratefully acknowledges the financial support of the Canada Council
and the Ontario Arts Council.

Printed and bound in Canada
1 2 3 4 5 1997 1996 1995 1994 1993

Contents

Acknowledgments

A project of this sort is always a collective effort and cannot be seen solely as the editor's handiwork. The members of the Women's Press collective have been truly supportive and committed to the project from its inception to the end, especially those involved in the day-to-day, tedious and difficult tasks of making it happen: Ann Decter, Lois Fine, Heather Guylar, Angela Robertson, Deborah Barretto and Martha Ayim. Their skills and good humour really made the effort worthwhile. Special thanks to the Social Issues Manuscript Group, particularly Chris Gabriel, Angela Robertson and Katherine Scott, who were instrumental in bringing the idea for this anthology to life and provided their insights and support throughout. As co-managing editor of the Press in the early stages of the project, Angela was most diligent in helping with the search for the "right" materials, particularly when we seemed stuck poring over numerous inappropriate pieces. Special thanks also to Ann Decter, whose impeccable editorial skills and keen political insights often brought dreary material alive, while she simultaneously helped manage difficult authors in the most delicate manner. I am very grateful to all these women. Together we do have a lot to celebrate!

I would also like to acknowledge the support I received from the department of Sociology/Anthropology/Social Work at the University of Michigan-Flint while working on this project. Fax, telephone and courier charges alone would have been unmanageable without that support.

Finally, I am grateful to all the authors whose patience and commitment made this anthology possible.

Linda Carty

COMBINING OUR EFFORTS

Making Feminism Relevant

to the Changing Sociality

Linda Carty

The celebration of twenty years of feminist publishing by Women's Press and its contribution to New Wave feminism in Canada has to be assessed with great excitement and at least a little trepidation. Specifically, the excitement revolves around its struggles and accomplishments, for which there is deservingly enormous pride. To date, Women's Press is the only publishing house in Canada founded by whites which has an expressed commitment to anti-racist publishing that is more than rhetoric, that is an applied policy. This commitment led to an entire restructuring of all the collectives in the Press to make them more racially and ethnically diverse and representative of the community. The restructuring was not about seeking representation merely for the sake of representation; it was a commitment to coalition building and anti-racist praxis. Indeed, it has been a long struggle, as the article by Gabriel and Scott so eloquently expresses.

As the Press sought to reorganize, committing itself to a more inclusive publishing policy and practice, those who thought that it was their "baby" — with all the attendant possessiveness that notion includes — felt wounded. The costs of that struggle have been high, but the gains have been enormous. Many thought that Women's Press would not survive; indeed, many who left probably hoped that it would not. One of the most heartening outcomes of the struggle is that, defying all doubts, there *are* white feminists who are committed to working with racial-ethnic women in a relationship of equality. They do not play "shrinking violets" or collapse in tears as they continue to be confronted with the fact that unlearning racism is unending or when they realize that they have to get involved when they are faced with prejudicial or classist behaviour among racial-ethnic[1] women which threatens to get in the way of the goals the Press has set for itself. For white feminists to recognize that gender is not the only or always the primary contradiction in the struggle for women's liberation is simple: they merely need to join the ranks of their many liberal sisters. But to problematize that liberal — "politically correct" — feminism and work towards a more inclusive politics is a challenge that only few are prepared to engage in and fewer still succeed at.

In the broader feminist community, a lot has been accomplished, and while it is indeed important to acknowledge this, it is equally as important to note that a great deal more needs to be done. This anthology gives the reader a brief look at some of the more important developments within contemporary Canadian feminist organizing. We do not present an analytical reflection on the past, nor do we chronicle the struggles within Canadian feminism over the last twenty years. Instead, the articles address different aspects of feminist organizing and take varied approaches. Some articles in this collection provide an historical glimpse into organizing by women we have never heard about; others address issues like AIDS which are now important to feminism but were not twenty years ago. Yet others look at where we are now and where we have to go.

Still, there are issues that some would consider very important to feminism which are not covered in this anthology, and while we make no apologies for their absence, we do acknowledge this. One such absence is the matter of women's reproductive rights. Feminist discourse bursts with analyses of numerous perspectives on this issue. Yet, it was difficult to find a piece that took an integrated approach to this subject. Any feminist analysis of women's reproductive rights must make race and class central to the argument. The struggle for abortion rights for women in Canada, for example, remains largely a white, middle-class affair. Often there is the assumption that racial-ethnic women are not part of the struggle because they are not interested. This is false and based on stereotyped ideas. After all, these women are the women most affected by the state's regulation of abortion. To contextualize the movement appropriately, feminists interested in analyzing the struggle for reproductive freedom, for example, must problematize the absence of racial-ethnic women from the discourse. The issue is not just about masculinized state and its female victims. The latter fit into a varied spectrum and are victimized in various ways. Similarly, feminists who examine the advance of reproductive technologies have to problematize what these mean for poor, racial-ethnic women who suffer infertility but can never afford the costs of invitro fertilization.

There are numerous problems with the manner in which most of contemporary Canadian feminism presents itself, both at the levels of scholarship and of activism. Its persistent taken-for-granted reproduction of whiteness as its blueprint is problematic. Increasingly, First Nations, Black, Asian, Arab, Latina and other racial-ethnic women have been criticizing this narrow perspective as myopic and racialist. But the practice continues. Some of the most mainstream of Canadian academic feminists indirectly acknowledge the whiteness of their scholarship and, as if in defense of it, claim that to add Third World/racial-ethnic women as just another topic in the discourse while that discourse remains grounded in and circumscribed by white ruling relations does nothing. Others stop at the point of adding a statement or two on "difference," or add racial-ethnic women as categories and variables. The problem with both approaches is that they assume there is no way to construct an integrated analysis, one which is more representative of the changing Canadian social structure. Very, very few white Canadian feminists have even made attempts at a more inclusive scholarship or politics. The intransigence on the part of the majority indicates at best a slow growth for Canadian feminism as a whole; at worst it points to stagnation and to a failure to contribute to the dynamic changes occurring at an international level.

We put out the initial call for articles for this anthology well over two years ago. Despite stating that we were in search of articles that consider how race, class and sexuality, within a politics of gender, are related in the specific topics we listed, the vast majority of the first round of articles made no attempt to construct such an analysis. It was clear that the authors were not interested in that approach. A perusal of most Canadian feminist journals points to a similar neglect. Why is Canadian feminist scholarship still not representative of the racial-ethnic diversity in Canadian society? Why the disjuncture between the political battles being fought by the broader feminist community and academic feminist discourse? Why, for example, do we hear so much talk from white academic as well as white non-academic feminists about "women of Colour taking over" national and regional women's organizations and that these women have too much influence in the "women's arm of the state," when in the theorizing this is not an engaged problematic? Why the finger-pointing at racial-ethnic women who are hired in high profile positions, either in state-affiliated agencies or in the state bureaucracy, labelling them as having the "double advantage" of race- and gender-oppressed status when it is clear that they are being hired to represent representation while the social relations of power remain intact, reflecting white hegemony? Why is there nothing in Canadian academic feminist theory about transnational capitalism and its impact on Third World women both in Third World and in the advanced capitalist countries? Why haven't we read about the vast numbers of racial-ethnic women, for example, who have no choice but to be homeworkers for Canadian-based corporations, particularly in the garment industry, which subjects them to super-exploitation?

The answers to these questions lie in the discursive practices of mainstream Canadian feminism and point to its parochialism, making it similar to all other forms of Euro-American feminism. Like the male dominated Euro-American discourse before it, a discourse which characterized the Third World and its peoples and cultures as inferior, so too this white feminist theorizing locates racial-ethnic women in binary opposition to white women. This insidious dichotomy was created as Euro-American feminism attempted to speak in the name of all women while excluding the majority. Feminism on both sides of the Euro-American and Third World dichotomy exists in an oppositional relationship, defining the other as polarities. Even in the Canadian context it is changing the once still picture.

The Canadian landscape is not lily white; it never was, despite First Nations peoples being decimated, then hidden away on reservations. Yet academic discourse, state practices, the construction of knowledge imparted to youth through the curricula and the everyday social interactions giving definition to the society continue to reflect the dominant white relations of ruling while paying lip service to diversity and difference through the organized rhetoric of anti-racism. The ugliness of such cognitive dissonance is beginning to show itself.

The Problem That Is So Hard To Name

> Racism — simple enough in structure, yet difficult to eliminate.... Racism is pervasive to the point that we take many of its manifestations for granted, believing "that's life." Many believe that racism can be dealt with effectively in one hellifying (antiracist) workshop, or one hour-long heated discussion. Many actually believe this monster, racism, that has had at least a few hundred years to take root, grow, invade our space and develop subtle variations...this mind-funk that distorts thought and action, can be merely wished away.[2]

The politeness of Canadian culture can no longer conceal the racism in its fabric, just as that politeness has never lessened the vitriolic effects on the victims of racism. Many racialist incidents once pointed to as typical of the culture south of the border are now acknowledged as very much present in Canada. For example, the U.S.-originated Ku Klux Klan boasts many chapters in Canada, as does Operation Rescue. The difference south of the border is that little about racism is hidden, either from the society itself or from the world.

In Canada it has often been said that unlike in the U.S. affirmative action and comparable worth policies and programs are not legally mandated because the state has always acknowledged that the society is multicultural. As a result, it is asserted that Canada has long had a policy of equality of opportunity built into many of its programs. More recently, in Ontario at least, this line has changed to read that the government's adoption of explicitly anti-racist programs indicates the state's commitment to fighting racism. At no level of state policy however, has there ever been an acknowledgement of institutional racism, either in multi-cultural or in anti-racist propaganda.

Whether at the federal, provincial or municipal levels, the political atmosphere has long been putrid with racialist stereotyping and discrimination. Two years ago, in 1991, the mayor of Toronto, June Rowlands, was elected after having campaigned on an overtly racist platform. Among other things, she called on the Black community to control its youth to help her keep the level of crime down once she was elected.

Some two decades earlier this woman had advocated the sterilization of men receiving state welfare support. Nevertheless, her mayoralty campaign resulted in a decisive victory. Politicians in Canada who dare to espouse inclusive politics run the very real risk of not being elected and of being mistrusted by the majority. Meanwhile, those who talk of keeping minorities in check and of making Canada one nation with one people with one language (implicitly referring to the removal of French as one of Canada's official languages and thereby the domination of the French and surely, by extension, the domination of all racial-ethnic peoples) as does the leader of Canada's Reform Party, find themselves and their party gaining popularity.

The media, electronic as well as print, regularly use racialist language when discussing everything from violence against women to problems in our schools. The most recent and undoubtedly one of the most blatant examples of racism in the Canadian media is exhibited in the March 1993 issue of *Toronto Life* magazine. In an article that claims to analyze the resignation of one of Toronto's prominent social fundraisers from the board of a women's shelter of which she was a founding member the author libels a number of progressive white feminists in the city for their anti-racist work; she also indirectly attacks all racial-ethnic feminists, often using condescending and disparaging remarks when referring specifically to those who were directly or even remotely involved in the struggle about which she writes. It is chilling reading, clearly racist in undertone and often homophobic in its references to the women being attacked. It is all the more chilling to know that something so vile was deemed worthy of publication by one the city's major magazines.

Refusal to acknowledge diversity in the changing social structure and increasing actions fuelled by racist impulses are also reflected in the practices of Canadian organized labour. Recently — and prior to the social contract — the General Motors Oshawa division of the Canadian Auto Workers Union, Local 222, voted to withdraw its support from the Ontario government.[3] In part, many members of the local are disturbed by what they see as the government's favouring of minorities. As the discontent increased, the leadership decided it had to put support for the government to a vote. The vote is significant because of what it represents. The New Democratic Party of Canada (NDP), a party with its roots in labour, formed the Ontario government in 1990. The Ontario NDP came to power with the full institutional support of organized labour in the province. As the government, it has made attempts to diversify representation in many state institutions by opening up avenues and providing opportunities for more women and people of Colour. Although increased representation does not necessarily mean a liberalization of state practices, this perceived intent of the state is too disturbing to many. What the vote of CAW Local 222 conveys to the general public is what many racial-ethnic workers have long understood about Canadian organized labour: it is not exempt from racist principles and practices.

A Myopic Feminism

All these developments have repercussions for the feminist movement. It is important to point out, however, that the spectrum of this movement extends from those whose feminism does not move beyond the element of ideas — academic feminists — through a range of extremists and single-issue promoters to those who make a serious attempt to work ideas and theories into coalition building. The latter travel the most difficult path because the struggle is often arduous, the frustrations many and the gains seemingly few.

At the academic level, feminism has little dynamism because most of what is produced in the academy is far removed from the everyday social relations defining women's lives. There is very little discourse about the state's ruling practices, or about poverty, unionization, AIDS, employment, education or about any other pressing issue, that attempts to problematize the racial-ethnic factor. There is very little discourse that even acknowledges the uniqueness of the social relations of race/ethnicity and their impact on racial-ethnic women. To universalize the experiences of white women, to collectivize them as women's standpoint, is not just short-sighted; it is also ultimately racist.

Much too much of contemporary feminist theorizing in Canada

continues to marginalize racial-ethnic women either by ignoring them or by paying lip service to anti-racist feminism — mentioning racial-ethnic women only then to ignore them. As the racial-ethnic composition of the Canadian population continues to change, academic feminism remains static and less and less representative of the social reality. This clearly stems from white middle-class academic feminists' intense fear of relinquishing any of their ascribed power and is supported by their refusal to acknowledge their disproportionate personal and political privilege in Canadian society. Some argue that for white women to give up power and privilege would accomplish little, since it would not change the relations of ruling within the wider social structure, which is where these privileges get organized. This is a poor excuse for resisting change. At the same time, they do recognize that change is taking place without and inspite of them. Their choice to exclude racial-ethnic women from their theorizing and to ignore the contributions of these women to the struggle for gender equality is a response that entrenches their insularity to the winds of change swirling around them.

The need for feminist theorists to get in touch with the issues that are important to most women cannot be over-stated. In light of the changes taking place in global capitalism at the present juncture, reconceptualizing and rethinking the relevance of our feminist frameworks is not merely an academic exercise but an absolute necessity. The changing nature of capitalism is cause for concern to those of us interested in the international division of labour and its implications for women. The disintegration of the Soviet empire into Western dependencies strengthens the global hegemony of Western capital and its international division of labour and gives transnational corporations control of the cheaper labour power of the world's women. There is a three-tiered structure to women's labour internationally. At the top are white women of the advanced capitalist states, followed by white women of the dependent capitalist countries. Racial-ethnic women, regardless of their geographical location, constitute the cheapest of women's labour.

There are many shifts taking place in the global economy, shifts engineered by the dominant states on behalf of their capital interests, shifts that increasingly benefit transnational capital. These shifts are harming women, particularly through the international division of labour. For example, the internal shift in dependent economies is pushing people to migrate to the advanced capitalist economies, into racialized and gendered categories of work. This pattern sees many racial-ethnic women from Third World countries replacing white women at the lowest levels of employment, whether in so-called women's jobs or in the more gender-integrated segments of the labour force. As white women are able to move up into the higher paying and more prestigious jobs in larger numbers, they are being replaced by racial-ethnic women who find themselves with no opportunities to get out.

These changes in the international division of labour further alter advanced capitalist economies in a way that solidifies white hegemony. Despite gender stratification, this accrues significant power to white upper-middle and middle-class women relative to all other women and even to racial-ethnic men. The relationship between white and racial-ethnic feminists is one of the micro manifestations of the relationship between the so-called Third World and advanced capitalist states which is engendered by the international division of labour. In this relationship women with their origins in the Third World play a particular role of subordination, similar to Third World nation states. This role is determined by the control of resources which allows for the ascription of power. Indeed, it is a relationship characterized by marginalization. This is not to say that such a relationship is predetermined and cannot be changed. The point is that once it is recognized, the inherently unequal relations ought not to be inscribed over and over again by those for whom power and privilege are taken-for-granted resources. Change calls for more than the acknowledgement of power and privilege; it entails a willingness to commit oneself to the struggle and the *actual* sharing of that power and privilege.

Feminists Working Through Differences, Constructing Real Change

Institutionalized rejection of difference is an absolute necessity in a profit economy which needs outsiders as surplus people. As members of such an economy, we have *all* been programmed to respond to the human differences between us with fear and loathing and to handle that difference in one of three ways: ignore it, and if that is not possible, copy it if we think it is dominant, or destroy it if we think it is subordinate. But we have no patterns for relating across our human differences as equals....

Certainly there are very real differences between us... [b]ut it is not those differences between us that are separating us. It is rather our refusal to recognize those differences, and to examine the distortions which result from our misnaming them and their effects upon human behaviour and expectation.[4]

The articles in this anthology transcend the differences that separate white, privileged women from all others. No article attempts to fix the world, or present the quintessential theory, or provide *the* answers. Similarly, to borrow from Audre Lorde, none of the authors, not even those who deal specifically with issues of difference and with the oppression of racial-ethnic women, attempt to "reinvent the pencil."[5] In other words, they do not rehash mainstream white feminism or criticize its inadequacies before getting on to their own project. The articles offer insight into a range of problems and experiences that women struggle with daily, problems and experiences largely ignored in academic feminist discourse. Through this reading, we come to understand the path they are clearing collectively, to construct *real* social change. This anthology goes beyond the politics of diversity and difference to show that it is not our identities or location that create change but our vision for the future. The question we must ask is do we have a vision for the future which can bring all women together in a common politics — the politics of inclusion — fighting for a common cause, for freedom for *all* women regardless of race, colour, class or sexual orientation?

This question is not new. It has been asked numerous times in the past by racial-ethnic and even by white feminists. Many have even suggested how to do more than understand women's differences and how to move beyond them.[6] Yet, in the context of feminism in Canada, it is necessary to address the question again because white feminist theory appears stuck in hegemonic history, incapable of recognizing knowledge outside its Euro-American frame of reference.

Part of what is being celebrated in this anthology is the legitimacy of that "external" knowledge and its deeper relevance and suggestion that we rethink and reconceptualize our social reality. The articles here engage issues that challenge women daily. Collectively, they point to the need for collective struggle and agency to restructure the politics of everyday life, which would then ground a reformulated feminist theory. This is the challenge for Canadian feminism.

So far, white feminists who have heeded the challenge have found their work and contributions largely criticized or ignored by white academic feminists. Furthermore, the significant contributions by many women — organizing on different levels in their own communities, working in coalitions helping women to win power, and fighting against the state — is hardly acknowledged in feminist discourse.

Currently, in metropolitan centres like Toronto, women of varied class and ethnic backgrounds have been working together, with minimal resources, fighting for numerous social causes, many of which should be of central concern to the state but are not. Issues such as AIDS, affordable childcare, wife assault and sexual abuse against women and children have all been pushed on to the state's economic agenda because of the pressure applied by feminist activists who took the initiative because of their knowledge of the painful crises these have become in women's lives. Fighting for these causes is an ongoing struggle for the women who work in the always overcrowded and severely under-funded women's shelters and for women in organizations like Voices of Positive Women, Black CAP, AIDS Action Now or in the coalition fighting women's poverty and in the organizations fighting for the reproductive rights of all women.

The successful efforts of these organizations have come only through the tireless work of the women who have found it necessary to coalesce around issues that indiscriminately affect women. This kind of coalition work constitutes a broader feminism than is represented and possibly even understood by those fashioning academic feminist discourse. Indeed, it is a difficult task to make coalitions work and to succeed at the tasks they set themselves. Feminists involved in these daily struggles do so because they are committed to making life better for *all women*, regardless of race, colour, class or sexual orientation.

The obvious irony when we examine the various factions of feminism — which aspects are relevant to women's everyday world and which merely constitute debates with little more than the intent to disguise race, class and power privilege — is that the feminists who are working in the trenches have little time to reflect on the daily obstacles and hardships they face. The demands of their work compel them to keep going. Yet, those who have the privilege of time for reflection — academic feminists — leave us hopeless because there is no vision of the future in that work. The criticism here is not of ideas *per se*, but of ideas for the sake of ideas, without relevance or roots. This lack of linkages between the theory and the lived experiences of women is very evident in much of Canadian feminist theory. The hope for feminism lies in the work being carried out by the coalitions of women in the trenches.

It is that work which is chronicled in this anthology. Collectively, the articles interrupt hegemonic feminist discourse and challenge its complacency and location with theory that is grounded. They narrate a sociality that is alien to that hegemonic discourse, yet their questions and analyses demand it be held to account. Women on the front lines struggle to keep their causes alive in the face of criticism from the state and sometimes even from their more privileged sisters, many of whom get substantial financial support from the state because of the much less critical approach of their work.

Organization of the Anthology

> We don't have to be the same to have a movement, but we *do* have to admit our fear and pain and be accountable for our ignorance. In the end, finally, we must refuse to give up on each other.[7]

> As women, we have been taught either to ignore our differences, or to view them as causes for separation and suspicion rather than as forces for change. Without community there is no liberation, only the most vulnerable and temporary armistice between an individual and her oppression. But community must not mean a shedding of our differences, nor the pathetic pretence that these differences do not exist.[8]

These passages and this introduction chart the framework of the book. One central theme apparent when we put the pieces together is that feminists fighting a wide range of battles can find unity in political praxis. Collectively, the pieces show us how to combine feminist theory with a practice that calls the state to account and helps women empower themselves.

While there is no central argument here about how the issues addressed are important in all our lives, together the articles contain a strong message about why it is necessary to and how we can work together.

The first section, "Identity, Race and Feminist Politics," addresses some issues of particular political significance to feminism at both the national and international levels. Nahla Abdo questions mainstream feminism about where Arab women fit into its neatly structured paradigms of race and gender, all of which apply stereotyped labels and exclude Arab women. Amy Gottlieb takes on the issue of the state of Israel's oppression of the Palestinian people and allies herself with the Palestinian people in their fight for liberation. Chris Gabriel and Katherine Scott analyze the twenty years of feminist publishing by Women's Press. They look at the birth of the Press, its conflicts, the eventual break in the founding body and the transformation of the Press.

The lesbian roundtable discussion, edited by Ann Decter, together with the articles by Carol Allen and Debi Brock form Section 2, "Politicizing Sex and Sexuality." They address the struggles of lesbian organizing, the problems surrounding lesbian and gay attempts to have their family units acknowledged, and the issue of sexual abuse and its analysis in feminist discourse, respectively.

Section 3, "Recovering Women's Histories" provides an historical look at the organizing efforts of disabled women in Ontario and at the very long history of African Canadian women organizing both in Ontario and in Nova Scotia. In these articles Driedger, Bristow and Hamilton give us a glimpse into the lives of women whose struggles have never before been acknowledged.

Section 4, "The State, Women's Labour and Feminist Struggle," is the longest section. Its six articles address the politics of the state and women's organizing. Donna Goodleaf offers a graphic analysis of the role of First Nation women in the 1990 Oka crisis. Lois Harder examines the child care reform policy in Ontario. Sue Findlay looks at representation and how it is tied to state bureaucratic ruling relations. Jennifer Keck and Daina Green examine pay equity for non-unionized women in Sudbury. Jan Borowy, Shelly Gordon and Gayle Lebans analyze the struggle to organize homeworkers by the ILGWU. And Naomi Wall addresses organizing by the women-and-poverty coalition to bring women's poverty to the attention of the state.

The final section, "Voice, Empowerment and Change," ends with some of the current issues facing feminism. There is a discussion with the NAC executive, a discussion with AIDS activists, reflection on the power of Native women voicing their struggles through their writings, and a look at the disempowerment which racial-ethnic women experience as workers and as clients in women's shelters.

But this anthology can only scratch the surface of what is being done and what needs to be done in women's organizing. So much of feminist analysis remains locked into body and form, while so little explores power and state relations. These latter, however, are precisely what have determined the past and will determine the future. Here we offer something different. We are not celebrating feminism in Canada; indeed, that is too amorphous a term to have meaning. We are celebrating diversity in community struggles and their particular accomplishments. This is the feminism that is relevant for today and tomorrow.

Notes

1. The term refers to all those who are not white, whether or not they define themselves by racial or ethnic origin. In the Canadian context, those of us doing political work have been insistent on naming ourselves: First Nations, Black, South Asian, Chinese, Filipino, East Asian, Latin American, Korean and so on. In reference to our collectivity, we have resisted terms such as "visible minority," terms developed by the state in its attempt to ignore our heterogeneity and to marginalize us by erasing our different histories and cultures and their significance. Usage of the term "women of Colour" acknowledges our ethnic differences, which is why Colour is capitalized, denoting more than skin colour. It indicates a common context, grounded in shared systemic discrimination.

2. Gloria Yamato in "Something About the Subject Makes It Hard to Name" in Gloria Anzaldua, ed. *Making Face, Making Soul: Haciendo Caras* (San Francisco: Aunt Lute Foundation Books, 1990), p. 20.

3. See *The Toronto Star*, March 5, 1993, p. A4.

4. Audre Lorde. *Sister Outsider* (New York: The Crossing Press Feminist Series, 1984), p. 115.

5. *Ibid.,* p. 78.

6. See particularly, Audre Lorde's *Sister Outsider*, specifically her essay "The Master's Tools Will Never Dismantle the Master's House," where she talks about how women can go about discovering their real power to transcend differences and create interdependency, which Lorde sees as "the way to a freedom which allows the *I* to *be*, not in order to be used, but in order to be creative," p. 111. See also, bell hooks. *Ain't I a Woman: Black Women and Feminism* (Boston: South End Press, 1981) and *Feminist Theory: From Margin to Center* (Boston: South End Press, 1984) and Chandra Talpade Mohanty's "Cartographies of Struggle," a critical analysis of a feminism that would move beyond women's common differences, in Mohanty et al., eds. *Third World and the Politics of Feminism* (Bloomington: Indiana University Press, 1991). Mohanty writes about "imagined communities" as one way of doing this.

7. Cherrie Moraga, cited by Barbara Smith, ed. *Homegirls: A Black Feminist Anthology* (New York: Kitchen Table: Women of Color Press, 1983) p. xliv.

8. Lorde, *Sister Outsider*, p. 112.

I
IDENTITY, RACE
AND FEMINIST POLITICS

WOMEN'S PRESS AT TWENTY

The Politics of Feminist Publishing

Chris Gabriel and Katherine Scott

The last twenty years have witnessed the tremendous transformation of the Canadian women's movement from a largely white, middle-class, university-based grouping to a more broadly constituted movement that includes women of different backgrounds and theoretical perspectives. In a process that has been marked by much struggle, women's groups have developed alternative systems of belief and new organizational forms, both of which have attempted to challenge relations of power that exist at the level of broader society and within the organizations of the progressive left.

And there have been successes, notably the 1988 Supreme Court decision declaring the abortion law unconstitutional and other legislative gains in areas such as pay equity, sexual assault and family law. The movement has also challenged the "malestream" trade union movement to identify and address seriously the concerns of working women. In two decades the women's movement has emerged as a significant force in English Canada.

This is not to say that the women's movement has presented itself with a unified voice. Feminists are still fighting systemic inequity; feminists also continue to struggle among themselves and with their political allies to forge political strategies that truly reflect the diversity of experience in Canadian society. Consequently, the movement has struggled within itself over the theory and practice of feminism. This struggle is integral to feminist politics.

This is certainly not a new insight. Politics as self-criticism is an old theme in socialist and in feminist writings. But the struggle evolves as the social, economic and political contexts change. Where one might argue that the women's movement in English Canada grappled with the issue of class and economic disparities in the 1970s, women of Colour[1] challenged the predominantly white movement to take up anti-racism in the 1980s. Women of Colour argued that if feminism is about empowerment for *all* women and improving the conditions of *all* women's lives, then fundamental change is needed within the movement itself.[2]

This article examines how these developments played out at Women's Educational Press of Toronto (referred to in the rest of the article as Women's Press), a non-profit feminist publishing collective. We present this evaluation of where the Press has come from and where it's going from our perspective as two members of the collective. Through a review of two earlier Women's Press anthologies, *Women Unite! An Anthology of the Canadian Women's Movement*[3] and *Still Ain't Satisfied! Canadian Feminism Today*[4] we will demonstrate that the politics of the Press have been neither better nor worse than those of the movement it claims to represent. The Press has slowly — and painfully — come to realize over the past twenty years that its definitions of "women" and "women's issues" have been narrow at best. This has led to the significant and necessary refocusing of its politics and practice. We examine these efforts in the last section of this article.

The Politics of Feminist Publishing

Feminist publishing, indeed publishing itself, has occupied a central place in progressive organizing. Women have struggled long and hard to find a place in public discourse. The lack of access to critical material resources such as printing and publishing has been a significant barrier to efforts to create and disseminate a counter-hegemonic discourse against the dominant patriarchal, racist and homophobic mechanisms of capitalist society. Feminist publishing collectives such as Women's Press have worked to recover women's history, provided women with alternative political views and have generally been part of the organized expression of the movement. As such, we continually need to scrutinize and interrogate them. Whose voices are represented? Whose community? What are the responsibilities of a feminist press to the movement it speaks from and for?

It has been increasingly evident, though not always acknowledged, that the politics of the Canadian women's movement has privileged and continues to privilege the needs and aspirations of white middle-class women. In granting priority to a narrow view of gender oppression the movement relegated a number of "other" women — Aboriginal women, Black women, women of Colour, women with disabilities, lesbians — and their concerns to its margins. The first Press anthology, *Women Unite!*, published in 1972, and the tenth anniversary anthology, *Still Ain't Satisfied!*, are indicative of this type of feminist politics. These two anthologies are significant, not only because they provide an insight into the political orientation of the Press at those points but because they provide a window on the women's movement in Canada in 1972 and 1982.

By the early 1970s, feminist activism — in what came to be known as the second wave of the women's movement — had raised society's awareness of women's issues. Throughout this period, women, both individually and in caucuses across the country, fought to have a say in student organizations, in left political groups, in unions and in the state. It was in this spirit that a group of women from the Toronto Women's Liberation Movement founded a non-profit socialist feminist collective to provide a venue for Canadian women recording and analyzing the lives of Canadian women.

In its founding statement, *The Oscroft Manifesto*, Women's Press members stated, "The Canadian Women's Educational Press was set up in February 1972 in response to a need of women involved in the Women's Liberation Movement for herstorical [sic] and contemporary material on Canadian women."[5] The founders maintained that the domination of the publishing industry by men and by foreign interests actively excluded women's concerns. Canadian women interested in feminist politics were forced to rely on British or American materials. The creation of Women's Press, the first feminist publishing house in Canada, provided an outlet for Canadian women's writing and put the material means of production — the technical skills of printing and publishing — into women's own hands.

Women Unite! managed to capture the grassroots energy and radicalism that marked these early heady days of the second wave of Canadian feminism. Its collective boldly stated:

> This anthology is made up of writings from women who have in some way participated in women's liberation movement in Canada. The movement differs greatly from the middle class women's rights groups which consist mostly of professional and church women. Although the broad basis of both is improvement of the quality of life for women in Canada, the philosophy of the women's rights groups is that civil liberty and equality can be achieved within the present system, while the underlying belief of women's liberation is that oppression can be overcome only through a radical and fundamental change in the structure of our society.[6]

There was also an explicit acknowledgment that the movement was "diverse." However, it is apparent today that the collective's understanding of diversity, and perhaps by corollary the movement's as a whole in the early 1970s, was considerably narrower than ours today. Indeed, Naomi Wall's assessment of this early period notes that women who were actively political in the late 1960s and early 1970s — that is to say white, middle- class women — now approached issues of concern from "diverse *theoretical* bases"[7] [our emphasis]. As a result, liberal, socialist and radical feminists charted different courses for reform and employed divergent political strategies.

And, while *Women Unite!* made no pretext that it was comprehensive, it is evident that a major focus throughout was how to reconcile gender issues and class issues within the context of left nationalism. The collective's understanding of women's oppression is perhaps best summed up by its *Oscroft Manifesto*:

> Many women are now aware of their oppression as a sex, and realize that a fundamental restructuring of society is needed to overcome it. Our oppression is basically economic in nature; most women in the labour force receive lower remuneration than men...[8]

Given its reductive definition of women's oppression and its way of equating diversity with theoretical difference, it is not surprising that the issue of racism among women and outside the movement is largely absent in *Women Unite!*. Indeed, women of Colour are not even acknowledged in *Women Unite!*. As one member recalled:

...there wasn't as far as I know of and I don't know whether there was any debate or discussion or even an awareness of it....it was a period of time when there wasn't much visibility for women of colour. Most of the visibility involved Third World issues because of the war in Vietnam was on so there was some representation of Vietnamese women and some of the struggles in Angola were represented, but they were from a white woman's point-of-view.[9]

The next ten years witnessed the birth of numerous women's organizations which sprang up to pursue, in many instances, single-issue interests such as pay equity, abortion and day care. White women who had cut their teeth in left-wing politics in the 1960s now turned their energies to creating shelters for assaulted women, women's health services, women's union caucuses, publishing houses and other artistic venues. Simultaneously, women of Colour were also actively struggling against sexism, racism and class oppression.[10] Alliances between these two groups had yet to be forged and the mainstream women's movement believed that women of Colour were more interested in issues of race than gender. Consequently, as Das Gupta writes, women of Colour who tried to participate in the women's movement

...experienced great frustration at the unwillingness of most of the predominantly white, Anglo-Saxon women to recognize our concerns as "women's" issues. Our concerns have focused on such areas as social movements in our countries of origin, jobs and racism; that is, on issues of social justice. Some feminists have stated that these concerns represent "an erosion of feminist content," claiming that to talk about political situations was "divisive" and that to chant in Spanish was to use "the language of patriarchy."[11]

By the end of the decade, some white women, Naomi Wall argues, expressed disappointment with the limitations of single-issue politics. There were now questions about how to broaden the base of the women's movement to include, "poor women, working class women, native women and immigrant women." Increasingly, women of Colour were challenging the movement to make the crucial links between racism and sexism. The 1978 International Women's Day in Toronto represented an effort by organizers to include and incorporate the perspectives and concerns of "other" groups of women. Feminist activists now wanted to draw these groups into the movement and to diversify the membership of existing feminist organizations. Wall notes that women's groups, particularly socialist feminist organizations, did develop strong ties with trade union women. They joined them on picket lines and supported demands for equal pay and an end to workplace harassment. But a large number of women's groups were still marginalized from the mainstream white movement. Consequently, Wall asks, "What of poor Canadian and immigrant women, native women and the vast majority of women in Canada who remain outside the movement's existing organizational structures."[12]

In a useful typology, Ann Russo argues that feminists have tended to deal with racism in one of four ways. Some feminists have simply ignored it and continue to work with the same analysis and the same women. Others acknowledge the challenge of racism and attempt to add race and class to their list of issues. This approach often leads to tokenism, and consequently does not advance an understanding of racism as central to feminist theory and practice. In the face of such a scenario, some feminists have chosen to retreat from the challenges that anti-racism poses for feminism, arguing that no response is better than tokenism. And in some instances, women have abandoned feminism as a doomed political project. None of these strategies, according to Russo, contribute to transforming feminism or honestly involve women of Colour.[13] Nevertheless, grassroots feminist politics since the early 1980s remains characterized by these strategies.

The Press's second anthology, *Still Ain't Satisfied!*, offers a case in point. Like *Women Unite!*, it too attempted to offer a chronicle of the women's movement. It presented some of the key areas where women were active. While it may not have matched the grassroots radicalism and raw energy of its predecessor, its publication marks in part some awareness that the women's movement needed to broaden its base. Even so, a review of the articles in this later anthology leaves it clear that a discussion and an analysis of race and of anti-racist politics was not central to either feminist theory as presented in the anthology or to the political issues and strategies that were debated. In this, the anthology reflected the political climate of the women's movement in the early 1980s.

In contrast to *Women Unite!*, the second anthology did attempt to address the differences among women in a section called "Double Oppression." These pieces focused on lesbian, immigrant women and Native women's issues. In particular, Caroline Lachapelle's chapter, "Beyond Barriers: Native Women and the Women's Movement" focused on why so few Native women are in the movement. She wrote:

> Native women perceive their motivation to work as being different from that of white women. White women are often perceived as aspiring to be part of the power system that oppresses native people.
>
> Many native women feel removed from the women's movement because it is seen as primarily a white, middle class movement.[14]

Lachapelle's work underscores both the alienation of Native women from the women's movement and the inability of that movement's goals — premised on a narrow view of gender oppression — to speak to Native women's needs. Race is neither acknowledged or explicitly addressed by the other pieces in the anthology.

In many ways *Still Ain't Satisfied!* provides a concrete example of one of Russo's descriptions of the response of some feminists to racism. In this case race is "added" on to a list of issues. As the editors of the anthology wrote, "We know that all women are oppressed, but some of us experience an added oppression beyond being women"[15] by way of their introduction to the "special interests" of a lesbian, a Native women and an immigrant woman's pieces. This tokenism, and the "othering" of women, allowed the Press and the movement it claimed to speak for to maintain control over what were defined as *the* women's issues.

This type of additive analysis attempts to add oppression such as racism to sexism. It is founded on the following theoretical assumptions:
(i) That racism and sexism are two distinct oppressions that can be separated;
(ii) That all women are oppressed by sexism, but some are additionally oppressed by racism.[16]
The experience of women of Colour, whose lives are profoundly shaped

by the interconnection between race and sex (and other realities), is misunderstood and misrepresented when gender is given priority.

This reasoning also emphasizes and strengthens the position of certain women. There is the notion that there is a unitary or generic experience that can be identified as "woman's experience," independent of race, class and sexual orientation.[17] This "gender essentialism" is posited on the experience of a white, middle-class woman. Dionne Brand captures this when she writes:

> I remember a white woman asking me how do you decide which to be Black or woman — and when. As if she didn't have to decide which to be, white or woman, and when. As if there were a moment that I wasn't a woman and a moment that I wasn't Black, as if there were a moment she wasn't white. She asks me this because she only sees my skin, my race and not my sex. She asks me this because *she sees her sex and takes her race as normal.*[18]

The universalizing of a particular experience — that of a white middle-class woman — and the resulting marginalization of the experience of women of Colour as "double oppression" or "special needs" was questioned in the years that followed the publication of *Still Ain't Satisfied!* Women of Colour increasingly challenged the movement to broaden its base and membership and to integrate an anti-racist position into its concerns. This call was repeated with growing force through the 1980s, both within and outside feminist organizations. An early and decisive intervention was the 1983 publication of the feminist quarterly, *Fireweed*, with its women of Colour issue.[19] Members of the women of Colour guest collective forced *Fireweed*'s white members to "realize just how much power we do wield — the power not only to inform but to silence."[20]

However, the 1986 International Women's Day (IWD) celebration in Toronto is regarded by many as

> ...a turning point for the women's movement insofar as a major oppression faced by immigrant, visible minority and Third World women was generally being recognized by all women and a call was issued to organize against it.[21]

The March 8th Coalition chose "Women Say No to Racism from Toronto to South Africa" as the theme for the day and "invited" women of Colour to join them. The Black Women's Collective responded:

> This Coalition [from] our point of view has organized [only] white women over the last ten years. In selecting this theme [anti-racism], perhaps it was not fully aware of the step it was taking. Simply, it was seeking to organize Black women! Did the Coalition consider how it would have to change in order to do so?…The step of choosing this theme shows interest, shows concern, but it is just a first step.[22]

There were critical political and organizational differences between white women and women of Colour and also among women of Colour. Most significantly, women of Colour challenged the Coalition to demonstrate its commitment to its chosen platform by examining its own internal racism.[23] Women of Colour in effect refused to acquiesce to the role that white feminism had traditionally assigned them:

> ⌐They like us to join them and struggle with them — but just as a symbol.⌐ We don't even have to say anything.…You don't have to say anything as long as they can get a few women of colour and immigrant women out to a demonstration. That's wonderful, because symbolically we've always meant some kind of radical idea.[24]

The link between racism and sexism was put on the agenda of the white women's movement through the struggles around IWD 1986. In its aftermath, some white women acknowledged their own racism:

> From early on in the planning white women were in reaction to women of colour. Our anxiety about the presence of vocal strong women of colour within the Coalition and our eagerness to escape the guilt of racism made us respond defensively as if WOMEN OF COLOUR WERE A THREAT.…
>
> We did not stop to think that without a thorough acceptance by white feminists of our complicity in racism, our adoption of "Say No

to Racism from Toronto to South Africa" would be seen as an attempt to ride on the wave of Third World liberation struggles....[25]

Others joined workshops to discuss racism and the past practices and politics of the movement. Members of feminist organizations also began to look at their groups. And, in general, the uncritical assumption of "sisterhood" and "autonomy" as the basis for feminist organizing was challenged as significant differences among women were laid open and acknowledged. These differences reflected the complexity of power relations in a capitalist, patriarchal and racist society. Efforts to graft the concerns of women of Colour onto a feminist agenda were denounced as inadequate by more and more women.

Politics of Difference

White feminist responses to the challenges of race and class have not generally led to substantial change in the women's movement. The second wave of the Canadian women's movement, as the two anthologies under examination demonstrate, was largely defined by a small community of white women. The problem in large measure is tied up with how this particular feminist political project has developed and been theorized. To different extents, the theory and practice of white feminism have incorporated an understanding of liberation as meaning the transcendence of group difference.[26] In this view equality is measured by the degree to which all people are treated the same. Thus, the ideal society is one where differences based on sex or race are meaningless, where neither political rights, nor obligations and institutional benefits are associated with group differences.

Certainly, the ideal of liberation as the elimination of group differences has been a powerful force motivating social protest movements. As Iris Marion Young writes:

The ideal of universal humanity that denies natural differences has been a crucial historical development in the struggle against exclusion and status differentiation. It has made possible the assertion of the equal moral worth of all persons, and thus the right of all to participate and be included in all institutions and positions of power and privilege.[27]

But, by suppressing group differences in the name of an "ideal of assimilation,"[28] white women organizing within the women's movement, as we demonstrated above, have narrowed the focus of feminist activity to a struggle against patriarchal oppression. Differences among women get ignored or overlooked in order to direct energies into combatting the oppression that women experience because they are women. Feminism framed as a struggle to overthrow women's oppression as women will inevitably fail because no one's life — man or woman — is exclusively defined by gender.

The refusal of white feminism to accept differences among women in effect supports a politics of domination. Challenges are ignored, implicit assumptions are reinforced. The failure to locate the struggle against racism and other forms of oppression at the centre of feminist organizing results in little substantive change for women of Colour. In practice, according to Young, supporting an assimilationist ideal has three immediate negative consequences:

1) For "different" women, the assimilation ideal in practice always implies coming into the game after it is already begun, after the rules and standards have been set;

2) The pursuit of a universal, undifferentiated humanity allows privileged groups to ignore their own group specificity. Point of view and experiences of privileged groups appear neutral and universal; and

3) An assimilationist ideal invariably leads to the [derogation] of groups that deviate from an allegedly neutral standard which in turn often produces an internalized devaluation by members of those groups themselves.[29]

All feminist organizations face these problems in implementing anti-racist strategies. Ultimately, the choice for feminist organizations to develop a "politics of difference" is a political one. Not surprisingly, the debate has been difficult. On the one hand, some feminist organizations have been reluctant to alter their established thinking and practices because of their inability or unwillingness to recognize how racism operates within their groups and concomitantly because they fear change and the loss of power. Other feminists have been caught up in debates about the validity of "identity politics" and the need to mobilize a unified opposition in these dangerous, conservative times. The latter point bears further explanation as the tendency to conflate "identity politics" and the challenge to incorporate "difference" in feminism has derailed the development of anti-racist feminist politics in some instances.

Linda Briskin argues, for example, that the current tendency to identify the self with a particular experience—i.e., being Black or lesbian — "intersects problematically with an over-emphasis on 'experience' inside the women's movement, an emphasis that has been mediated ideologically through the concept 'the personal is political.'"[30] This thinking, according to Briskin, results in the over-arching validation of personal experience which in turn leads to the establishment of an exclusionary set of identifications which becomes a competitive hierarchy of oppressions. As a result, Briskin concludes, a "politics of identity" interferes with open strategic debate and similarly promotes bonding on the basis of shared victimization and exclusion, both of which undermine the possibility of political alliances between feminists.[31]

One gets the sense reading Briskin that she is arguing against the expression of difference because this leads to the fragmentation of the movement and detracts from the feminist political project. We would argue in response that a careful distinction must be made here between support for a "politics of identity" and support for a "politics of difference." We agree that "identity politics" are indeed problematic. As Diana Fuss argues, identity is certainly not "a stable guarantee of a coherent politics."[32] The idea that we can base our politics on our identity needs to be deconstructed and rethought. This is not to say, that the concept of identity is not important; one's sense of self and experience of the world will always shape one's political choice and practice. But as Jenny Bourne argues, we must guard against "the tendency in feminist practice to personalize and internalize political issues ... [which in her opinion] has created a stunted, inward-looking and self-righteous 'politics' that sets its face against the politics out there in the real world."[33]

Critics such as Bourne maintain that we must keep our eye on strategic political struggle. But what of politics? This brings us back to a dilemma where feminists choose to pitch "difference" out with "identity politics" in the name of capital "P" Politics. Diana Fuss makes an interesting point here:

> I must confess that I have become increasingly suspicious of recurrent appeal to "political strategy" or "tactical necessity" in recent critical disputes ... My worry is that deference to the primacy and omniscience of Politics may uphold the ideology of pluralism, for no matter how reactionary or dangerous a notion may be, it can always be salvaged and kept in circulation by an appeal to "political strategy."[34]

Similarly, we would argue that critics of "identity politics" have appealed to Politics in efforts to "get on with the job." Political strategy is very important, but the question we must always keep before us is, "Politically strategic for *whom*?"[35]

In sum, we must be vigilant that legitimate arguments against "identity politics" or an over-emphasis on "the personal is political" do not hinder real efforts to integrate "difference" and the feminist political agenda. While the assimilationist ideal continues to inspire much social, economic and political struggle, marginalized groups within the women's movement are rejecting this "path to belonging." Rather than brushing group difference under the carpet, women of Colour are demanding that the women's movement move the struggle against racism to the forefront, thus creating a movement that acknowledges and resists all forms of structural inequality and privilege in Canadian society.

Collective Politics: Anti-Racist Efforts at the Press

We have argued that the Press's definitions of "women" and "women's issues" — definitions predicated on the experience of white women — have strengthened the position of certain women in the women's movement in English Canada. In this section we will show that this position of privilege has been reinforced by the particular organizational structure developed over the years at Women's Press. This structure inhibited change and ultimately subverted the Press's political goals. Thus, the strategic alliance between women of Colour who challenged the Press to acknowledge difference and those women at the Press who made a commitment to anti-racism and to a new politics also had to confront and expose an organizational power structure.

In the early years of the feminist movement women who were disillusioned with traditional organizing on the Left worked actively to develop alternative organizational forms and leadership processes. The founding members of Women's Press attempted to create alternatives that rejected hierarchy and leadership, emphasized personal experience and focused on collective process.[36] Press members sought to develop a non-traditional, non-hierarchical structure based on consensual decision-making. Each member had an opportunity to perform all the tasks associated with publishing (with the exception of printing); this included editing, typesetting, lay-out and design, marketing, finances and distribution. The structure of the Press in this regard was not uncommon. The early members of the Press exemplified a generation of feminists who were not content to swallow the maxim "the ends justify the means." They and other women struggled to create structures and processes that embodied their ideals for a just and equitable society.

In any organization the key decisions about organizational form, however, are always over-determined by the political analysis and the purpose the organization. As Nancy Adamson, Linda Briskin and Margaret McPhail point out in their book on the Canadian women's movement:

> Organizational structures and processes do not exist for themselves. They have a purpose: to facilitate the political effectiveness of the organization. It is in the context of a particular group's political analysis and strategy that its structure and process must be evaluated.[37]

This said, the organizational structure adopted by the Press in the early years was suited to the purpose and politics of the time. Thus, a small group of white women came together to create a mechanism to foster and spread women's writing, a mechanism that ultimately reflected their own world view and position in society.

Early Press members were committed to two key ideas of the North American women's movement: "the personal is political" and "sisterhood." These ideas served to mobilize thousands of women behind a collective struggle for change. At the same time, the commitment to a singular view of "feminist process" and to a particular and narrow definition of "women" limited the scope of feminist political analysis and constricted the basis for political mobilization and action.

The structure of Women's Press once in place, we believe, served to inhibit change in the organization and ultimately to subvert its political goals. This was evident as early as 1976 when the Press turned away from an open collective format and moved towards a greater focus on business and the market. Paradoxically, this shift away from the political roots of the Press was made easier by the very tenets of feminist structure and process that the founding members embraced in establishing the Press.

The Press, like other feminist organizations of the day, encountered many of the problems inherent in efforts to build alternatives within larger existing power structures. On the one hand, such groups faced and continue to face enormous pressures — notably from the state through funding agencies — to contain and suppress theories, opinions and practices that challenge the status quo. In this explicitly hostile environment white feminists attempted to create personal spaces that reinforced their politics. This included developing alternative "feminist processes" that fostered and validated personal experience and social connections among particular groups of women.

Consequently, many feminist organizations became "an emotional and spiritual home [for white women], a place to feel safe, a place that must be kept harmonious and free of difference."[38] Not surprisingly, these organizational spaces proved to be exclusionary or silenced many women of Colour.

The institution of "feminist process" at Women's Press that embraced the personal over the political and rejected explicit organizational structures such as leadership, led to "a depoliticization of feminist organizational strategies." As a result, process became "separated from political analysis, particular strategies and an identifiable set of organizational norms."[39]

Rejecting a traditional model does not eliminate basic organizational and political questions. Leadership, decision-making, recruitment, the composition of the membership are key considerations for any organization, regardless of political orientation or vision. For example, rotating the chair, administrative tasks, public speaking and organizing did indeed permit some women to learn new tasks associated with democratic leadership. This structure, however, often created an implicit leadership core within the broader group, a focal point of experience and skill that invariably led to tension within the organization when new women could not break into the unacknowledged leadership circle.[40]

This dynamic was played out at Women's Press. As one woman of Colour in the lesbian manuscript group pointed out:

> Women's Press was a more established press; it was larger and the mechanism of controls were more hidden, more subtle and information was extremely hard to get. It is not just women of colour who feel that but any women who are not inside their clique.[41]

The failure to deal openly with these tensions, in no small part exacerbated by a fear of conflict and an inability to deal with real differences among members, and the absence of concrete mechanisms to resolve political differences, inhibited the ability of many alternative feminist organizations, including Women's Press, to grow and change.

By the mid 1970s, the Press was ill-equipped to make the changes necessary to deal with the loss of state funding that had supported six or seven staff positions since 1972. Financial troubles and falling sales after 1975 prompted the Press to reevaluate its operation. The depoliticization that ensued laid the groundwork for the tensions that would split the Press ten years later. A core of members who worked with the Press through the late 1970s attempted to preserve the Press by moving to the mainstream, becoming "more businesslike and professional"[42] in order to secure a larger market share.

As a result, by 1980, a new division of labour and authority emerged. Sales and distribution were contracted out and the remaining publishing functions were reorganized. Where all members of the Press had participated in all aspects of publishing, a division arose between paid staff and members. Paid staff now sought to specialize in certain areas. Non-paid members, on the other hand, who had once worked collectively on each facet of a manuscript, now worked with staff in a new structure, manuscript groups that reviewed each book for publication. Each group focused on a different type of literature.

As the Press expanded in the late 1970s, its decision-making also changed. A two-tier structure emerged. Where once the entire membership had formulated policy and decided what to publish, a smaller group called "the Collective" — made up of representatives from the staff and each manuscript group — took up these responsibilities. Day-to-day administration fell to staff members, leaving the larger issues of policy and publication to the Collective which met on a monthly basis. Power and authority were now largely concentrated in the hands of the paid staff and long-time members.

These changes in and of themselves did not necessarily signify that the Women's Press had abandoned its politics. However, caught up in the here-and-now, in an organization committed to a feminist process that obscured established relations of power, the radical intent of the Press' early politics was diffused. We see this clearly in the 1982 article on feminist publishing in *Still Ain't Satisfied!*. Margie Wolfe, then a member of Women's Press and co-editor of the anthology writes:

> Feminist publishers exist…to guarantee women's liberation a voice. Primarily non-profit, non-commercial collectives, we articulate and promote the concerns of feminism in print. Our ultimate goal is radical social change.[43]

But radical social change for whom?

Wolfe laments that feminist publishing only reaches a narrow audience. This problem stems first, she argues, from the fact that feminist books published in English Canada are not readily available to "immigrants that do not read or speak English" or "Canadians who don't read."[44] Secondly, alternative presses lack credibility with the mainstream public and have little access to mass market outlets such as chain bookstores or supermarkets. Wolfe concludes that the "problems of credibility and anonymity combined are what — perhaps more than anything else — keep feminist publishing marginal."[45] Hence, given limited resources, it is necessary to adopt a more "professional" posture. The only realistic solution, given government cutbacks, increased production costs and an aging volunteer base, according to Wolfe, "seems to be increased sales, securing ourselves by reaching that larger audience women's liberation wants and needs anyways[sic]."[46]

What is immediately obvious from the summary of the problems facing feminist publishing and the solutions presented in Wolfe's article is that the arguments are predicated on an exclusive view of the women's movement, with feminism belonging to one group of women. From this point of view, based on an uncritical understanding of the differences among women and in political practice, one could argue that feminist publishing needed larger and broader audiences of women; whether these women needed this type of feminist press was another question.

Women's Press had by this time adopted a way of working and a structure that effectively excluded many groups of women — including younger women working in the movement — and suppressed dissent. The Press did publish many important and timely feminist books on Canadian women; its work, however, did not touch the broad majority of women. This was not because of problems of credibility or anonymity. Rather, as we pointed out earlier, the theory and practice of feminism in the early 1980s did not integrate the concerns of women who had vastly different experiences of the world. Feminist publishing was marginal to women of Colour, for example, because feminist theory and practice did not speak to these women nor address the centrality of racism in their lives. Instead feminist publishing reflected a commitment to the "ideal of assimilation" discussed above. By extension, efforts to address the concerns of women of Colour, for example, in published works or the promotion of authors were necessarily tokenistic.

Similarly, there was a concomitant failure to examine the basis of white privilege and how the Press as an organization maintained and reproduced existing power relations. Women of Colour presumed that their work was not welcome at the Press. As Makeda Silvera wrote in 1983:

> There are many of us who write, they just don't want to read it; they don't want to publish it. Reading and publishing our work would definitely force white women to look at themselves, at racism and at what has been laid on us for years.[47]

Pressure and tensions built up over the 1980s as women of Colour joined the Press and as some white members engaged in a difficult but necessary reexamination of their own politics. In 1987 the Press came face to face with challenges of racism and exclusion in a public way. Unable to confront or to process the political challenges of women of Colour, a fissure emerged between some members of long standing and other members who were trying, with little success, to change the political orientation of the Press.

The issues raised by women of Colour had to do with power. They reminded the Press that organizational structures and ways of working — even feminist ones — are not neutral. Each step in publishing, from the review and selection of manuscripts to who gets hired, reflects existing relations of power. And at Women's Press white women with established credentials in the feminist community held power. It was not simply the case that women on the collective deliberately excluded or suppressed the opinions of women of Colour or deliberately excluded or suppressed other opinions for that matter. Rather, seemingly small structures and processes served to reinforce the status quo.

Divisions emerged, then, over the political content of the work and over the mandate of the Press, including its accountability to women of Colour. In particular, divisions over the content of and the approval process for a fiction anthology precipitated the widely publicized split in the Women's Press. The struggle revolved around three axes:

1) The idea that racism not only shaped the lives of women of Colour but clearly affected white women who enjoyed the privileges associated with living as whites in a racist society;

2) The structure of the organization that served to reinforce the power of long-time members; and

3) The view of the Press itself as an important political resource in the struggle to eliminate the domination and exploitation of women.

On the first point, white members of the Press struggled to come to terms with their own identities — as oppressor and oppressed. There is a fine line here between exploring and understanding all facets of one's identity in order to strengthen one's ability to forge the alliances necessary to fight for social change and hiding in that identity. The difficulty for feminists, as Mary Louise Adams notes, stems from the tendency to cling to oppression to validate oppositional politics — a position that "divorces us from our own agency and makes it difficult for us to comprehend the ways, subtle or not, we manipulate privilege."[48] At Women's Press some white women tried to skirt the issues of racism by asserting their own claim to oppression, a move made easier by falling back on "feminist process" and reconfirming "the personal is political." In effect, this was to avoid acknowledging and thus having to change structures and ways of working that had excluded women of Colour and had reinforced the authority enjoyed by a few members.

At the heart of the issue, not surprisingly, were differing views on the role of Women's Press in political struggle. We have already argued that the early political goals of the Press had been diluted through its efforts to obtain more financial security and a larger share of the market. The absence of formal mechanisms to record and resolve diversity of opinion, specifically on the very *raison d'etre* of the Press, laid the foundation for the political struggle of 1987 and 1988.

Women of Colour joined the organization as members of manuscript groups and on staff and sought support for an actively anti-racist feminist agenda. As Nila Gupta, a member of the Press at the time, told *Tiger Lily*:

> I am involved in women's writing and writing by women of colour because I feel it is crucial for us to define our lives and to break the hegemony of the existing racism in the publishing industry that either silences our images or produces or constructs racist images about us.[49]

Gupta, other women of Colour in the Press and some white Press members began to challenge the existing power relations at the Press and the very structure and foundation on which they rested. Conflict with the implicit power structures was inevitable.

Women of Colour saw the Press as a political vehicle — one that did not belong to any one group, but one that was not serving the needs of women outside the mainstream white women's movement. In contrast, some long-time members viewed the Press as a haven from which they could pursue their particular vision of women's liberation. There was also a tendency to believe that the Press "belonged" to some members. For some the whole notion of a collective had been lost. As Eve Zaremba writes:

> ....feminist collectives are, as it were, held in trust by those who control them, for the rest of us. This should never be confused with ownership. It's a temporary privilege which cannot be divorced from the duty to manage our resources responsibly.[50]

The challenge put to the Press, by women of Colour and supported by some elements in the Press, also reminded it of its responsibility to the wider women's movement. Unable to reach an accommodation, eight members left the Press, intending to found a new feminist press in Toronto.

That much of the public debate that surrounded the division at the Women's Press over anti-racism focused on the censorship of white women's writing reveals a profound reluctance to examine structural inequalities, specifically those stemming from racism, within the women's movement and on the Left more generally. As Marlene Nourbese Philip noted at the time:

> Racism was the issue that detonated the explosion at the Women's Press; to the exclusion of any other issue, censorship has become the issue that has monopolized the media's attention. Censorship of white writers; censorship of the imagination; censorship by publishers. Censorship in all its myriad forms became, in fact, the privileged discourse.[51]

Within this climate, the majority that remained at Women's Press took up the difficult, complex task of reorganizing the Press around a new political vision. This work has continued since 1988 with marked successes and failures. Incorporating anti-racism and feminism is not just about changing ideas or abandoning stereotypes but about power and control. For the white members of Women's Press this meant giving up control of jobs and resources, of organizational purpose and structure, of political agenda, of style and tradition.

Efforts at Women' Press to implement anti-racism in its policy and practice fall into four broad categories: the political mandate, account-ability, access, and participation and decision-making.

The Political Mandate

At the time of the split in 1988 those members who were advocating a new anti-racist, feminist politics attempted to re-centre the Press around its political mandate. Part of this strategy has been to review the struc-ture and activities of the Press to broaden its political base and to raise the profile of anti-racism in the women's movement. To this end, the Press developed a new publishing policy that explicitly states its intent not to publish materials that the editors find to be classist, racist or homophobic.[52]

Accountability

Developing a new publishing policy was critical in the Press's efforts to make itself accountable to the broader women's communities seeking equality. Establishing clear expectations about the Press's political man-date, its function and role of its membership and staff was a crucial first step in building an inclusive Women's Press and was done in part through consultations with the broader feminist community.

Access

Women's Press has had an affirmative action policy since 1987; it covers full-time, part-time and contract positions. Since 1989 this has developed into an affirmative editing policy for freelancers. Currently, women of Colour occupy one and a half of the four positions on staff. Similarly, efforts have been made to recruit women of Colour to the general membership. After several failed initiatives, Women's Press member-ship is now around fifty percent women of Colour. The Press reexamined its structure and subsequently expanded the ways women can work at the Press. Members can now choose to work in areas other than the traditional manuscript groups that solicit and review potential books. In this way the Press can benefit from the experience of women with an interest in any facet of publishing.

The second area where the Press has attempted to promote greater access is through its affirmative action grants policy. This policy applies principally to the Writers Reserve Program of the Ontario Arts Council. The Press sets aside seventy-five percent of this fund for women of Colour applicants, a group that has had little support as writers in Ontario.

Participation and Decision-Making

Women's Press has reviewed and altered its structure several times in an attempt to make the organization more readily accessible in terms of membership and knowledge and to distribute decision-making power more equitably. The two-tiered structure of the Press has been reorganized. As of this writing, the organization is governed by a Steering Group whose members are directly elected by the general membership, including the staff, at the Annual General Meeting. This group oversees the publishing program of the Press, makes decisions about paid staff and selects manuscripts for publication, based on recommendations from manuscript groups. For a time, strategic direction and publishing policy were debated and established by the whole membership at quarterly membership meetings, but members' energy could not sustain this process.

Women's Press has had some successes, including its new publishing policy and by-laws, its affirmative grants policy and the increased participation of women of Colour at all levels of the organization. There has been a dramatic increase in the number of books Women's Press publishes annually that are by women of Colour, white lesbians and lesbians of Colour.

A great deal of initial energy was expended during and immediately after the division of the Press. In that Women's Press tried to respond to every claim, the explicit focus of its anti-racist work was obscured. The Press, as a result, has been very erratic in challenging feminist thought and practice beyond itself. From 1988 to 1991, more often than not, the Press has been drawn into a defensive position by the mainstream media and other critics rather than articulating and working towards a clear political strategy.

The Press has struggled to implement its new politics for the past five years. Surprisingly, this struggle appears to have reduced the tension between the market and politics. Perhaps the principal difference this time is that the Press has made an express commitment to focus once again on its role as a critical political resource for progressive movements and to make itself accountable to the diverse women's community in Canada. Members remain committed to exploring the implications of a "politics of difference" for feminist practice.

While the Press has tried to respond to challenges by women of Colour in an open and public way much work remains to be done. The changes outlined above represent a starting point, but the Press has a long way to go in ensuring meaningful access for all groups of women.

Looking Forward

> Those who produce the "story of woman" want to make sure they appear in it. The best way to ensure that is to be the storyteller and hence to be in position to decide which of all the many facts about women's lives ought to go into the story, which ought to be left out.
>
> In a racist society like this one, the storytellers are usually white, and so "woman" turns out to be "white woman."[53]

Women's Press has only recently come to terms with the fact that there are many voices within the Canadian women's movement. Unfortunately, for much of the Press's history, as we have illustrated, one voice claimed to speak for all.

The Press has helped to maintain and to reproduce a singular narrative, one which led to inadequate theorizing about women. Recent efforts demonstrate that the Press is engaging in the long, difficult refocusing of its politics to acknowledge differences among women, in the name of a transformative, inclusive feminism.

The challenges posed by women of Colour show that women's experience is mediated by multiple and overlapping determinations. Thus it is necessary to "understand how the conditions of our lives are connected to and made possible by the conditions of other women's lives."[54] For some women this will entail a recognition of how they benefit from a legacy of privileges such as those based on class, race, age, sexual orientation and ability. For *all*, it demands continuous effort to build and strengthen strategic alliances between differing groups of women. Such alliances are not founded on the search for illusionary similarities but are necessarily developed by addressing differences and contradictions and by respecting each other's political positions.

Notes

We would like to thank our colleagues in the Social Issues Reading Manuscript Group — Sheila Block, Ena Dua, Maureen FitzGerald and Lisa Wyndels — and past members Sue Findlay, Marlene Kadar, Rona Moreau, Susan Prentice and Brenda Roman.

We would also like to thank Linda Carty, Ann Decter and Lise Gotell for their many helpful suggestions on earlier versions of this article. Thanks also to Angela Robertson who read our manuscript, with her usual grace and charm, more times than she would like to remember.

1. Drawing on the work of Chandra Talpade Mohanty, we use the term "women of Colour" to designate a "political constituency, not a biological or even a sociological one. It is a sociopolitical designation for people of African, Caribbean, Asian and Latin American descent and native peoples....What seems to constitute women of colour or third world women as a viable oppositional alliance is a *common context of struggle* rather than colour or racial identifications." Chandra Talpade Mohanty in "Cartographies of Struggle." Chandra Talpade Mohanty *et. al.*, eds. *Third World Women and the Politics of Feminism* (Bloomington: Indiana University Press, 1991), p. 7.

2. Ann Russo in "We Cannot Live Without Our Lives: White Women, Antiracism and Feminism" in Mohanty, *op. cit.*, p. 298.

3. Janice Acton et al., eds. *Women Unite! An Anthology of the Canadian Women's Movement* (Toronto: Canadian Women's Educational Press, 1972).

4. Maureen FitzGerald *et al.*, eds. *Still Ain't Satisfied! Canadian Feminism Today* (Toronto: Women's Press, 1982).

5. *Oscroft Manifesto* (Unpublished text, 1972), p. 1.

6. FitzGerald. *Op. cit.*, p. 9.

7. Naomi Wall in "The Last Ten Years: A Personal Political View" in FitzGerald, p. 18. See also Nancy Adamson, Linda Briskin and Margaret McPhail

in *Feminists Organizing for Change: The Contemporary Women's Movement in Canada* (Toronto: Oxford University Press, 1988) and Sue Findlay in "Facing the State: The Politics of the Women's Movement Reconsidered" in Heather Jon Maroney and Meg Luxton, eds. *Feminism and Political Economy* (Toronto: Methuen, 1987).

8. *Oscroft Manifesto,* p. 3.

9. Maureen FitzGerald, cited by Ayanna Black in "Working with Collectives" in *Tiger Lily,* Vol. I, Issue 2, p. 31.

10. For an account of this history, see Tania Das Gupta, *Learning from Our History: Community Development with Immigrant Women, 1958-1986* (Toronto: Cross Cultural Communication Centre, 1986).

11. *Ibid.,* p. 44.

12. FitzGerald. *Op. cit., p. 25.*

13. Russo. Op.cit., p. 301.

14. Caroline Lachapelle in "Beyond Barriers: Native Women and the Women's Movement" in FitzGerald, *op. cit., p. 261.*

15. FitzGerald. Op. cit., p. 232.

16. For further discussion of this point, see Elizabeth Spelman, *Inessential Woman: Problems of Exclusion in Feminist Thought* (London: The Women's Press, 1990).

17. Angela Harris in "Race and Essentialism in Feminist Legal Theory" in the *Stanford Law Review,* Vol. 42, February 1990.

18. Dionne Brand in "Bread Out of Stone" in Libby Scheier, Sarah Sheard and Eleanor Wachtel, eds. *Language in Her Eye: Writing and Gender by Canadian Women Writing in English* (Toronto: Coach House Press, 1990), p. 46.

19. *Fireweed,* No. 16, Spring 1983.

20. *Ibid.,* p. 155.

21. Das Gupta. *Op.cit.,* p. 44.

22. The "Statement of the Black Women's Collective Presented to the Coalition on February 5, 1986." Reprinted in *Cayenne,* Vol. 2, Toronto, June-July 1986 p. 31.

23. See Carolyn Egan, Linda Lee Gardner and Judy Vashti Persad in "The Politics of Transformation: Struggles with Race, Class, and Sexuality in the March 8th Coaliton." Frank Cunningham *et al.,* eds. *Social Movements/Social Change: The Poltics and Practice of Organizing* (Toronto: Between the Lines, 1988).

24. Dionne Brand *et al.* in "We Appear Silent To People Who Are Deaf To What We Say" in *Fireweed, op. cit.,* p. 11.

25. Joanne Doucette and Dawn Heiden in "White Feminist Racism in the March 8th Coalition" in *Cayenne, op. cit.* p. 39.

26. The possible exception is radical feminist thought, which is predicated on a belief in the primacy of women's oppression as women. Accordingly, liberation for many radical feminists lies in establishing separate women-centred alternatives outside the patriarchal mainstream. However, while radical feminism is built on a theory of difference, its central failing is that it does not incorporate an understanding of women as a group divided by race, sexual orientation, class and ability.

27. Iris Marion Young in "Social Movements and the Politics of Difference" in *Justice and the Politics of Difference* (Princeton: Princeton University Press, 1990), p. 159.

28. *Ibid.,* p. 157.

29. *Ibid.,* pp. 164-65.

30. Linda Briskin in "Feminism: From Standpoint to Practice" in *Studies in Political Economy,* No. 30, Autumn 1989, p. 90.

31. *Ibid.,* p. 91.

32. Diana *Fuss. Essentially Speaking: Feminism, Nature, and Difference* (New York: Routledge, 1989), p. 105.

33. Jenny Bourne in "Homelands of the Mind: Jewish Feminism and Identity Politics" in *Race and Class,* Vol. 29, No. 1, Summer 1987, pp. 18-19. Cited in Fuss, p. 101.

34. *Ibid.,* pp. 106-107.

35. *Ibid.,* p. 107.

36. For a discussion of this point, see Adamson, Briskin and McPhail. *Op.cit.,* pp. 234-36.

37. *Ibid.,* p. 253.

38. Harris. *Op. cit.* p. 606.

39. Briskin. *Op.cit.,* p. 95

40. See Jo Freeman in "The Tyranny of Structurelessness" in Jane Jaquette, ed. *Women in Politics* (New York: John Wiley & Sons, 1974). Anne Phillips discusses these problems in her recent book, *Engendering Democracy* (University Park: Pennsylvania State University Press, 1991), chapter 5.

41. Nila Gupta, cited by Ayanna Black, *op. cit.,* p. 31.

42. Lois Pike in "A Selective History of Feminist Presses and Periodicals in English Canada" in A. Dybikowski *et al.*, eds. *in the feminine: women and words: Conference Proceedings 1983* (Edmonton: Longspoon Press, 1985), p. 212.

43. Margie Wolfe in "Feminist Publishing in Canada" in FitzGerald, *Op. cit., p. 267.*

44. Ibid., p. 269.

45. *Ibid.,* p. 270.

46. *Ibid.,* p. 272.

47. Makeda Silvera *et. al.* in "We Appear Silent to People Who Are Deaf to What We Say" in *Fireweed, op. cit.*, p. 11.

48. Mary Louise Adams in "There's No Place Like Home" in *Feminist Review*, No. 31, Spring 1989, p. 29.

49. Nila Gupta, cited by Ayanna Black, *op. cit.,* p. 31.

50. Eve Zaremba in "Collective Trouble" in *Broadside*, Vol. 10, No. 1, October 1988, p. 5.

51. Marlene Nourbese Philip in "The Disappearing Debate: Racism and Censorship" in *This Magazine*, Vol. 23, No. 2, 1989, p. 19.

52. The anti-racist guidelines explicitly state that the Press is precluded from publishing writing:
    - which adopts stereotypes by using generalizations or oversimplifications about a particular group of people;
    - in which a writer appropriates the form and substance of a culture which is oppressed by her own;
    - in which the analysis includes Women of Colour as a supplement to a text, rather than incorporating Women of Colour into the overall content and structure.

53. Harris. *Op.cit.*, p. 589, quoting Elizabeth Spelman.

54. Russo. *Op.cit.*, p. 299.

NOT IN MY NAME

A Jewish Feminist Challenges

Loyalty to Israel

Amy Gottlieb

It has been a decade since I first raised my voice as a Jew in opposition to the policies of the Israeli state. I want to chart the most significant moments of that journey, to look at what brought me to speak out against the occupation of Palestinian land, against the denial of Palestinian history and culture and against the atrocities that are committed daily by the Israeli state in my name.

As a radical and a feminist, one of my first duties is to understand my personal and political location. I have been pushed and fuelled by continuing criticisms of the Western-white-feminist movement's claim to speak for all women and by the contributions of Black, Asian, Jewish, Latin American, African, Arab, Caribbean and Aboriginal women to the development of a politics of location, power and difference. My experience is a complex one. I am a white-skinned, Jewish, middle-class lesbian committed to a revolutionary democratic socialism the world has not yet seen. My personal location embodies both oppression and denial as well as power and privilege in the world. I have been challenged to develop and to integrate anti-racism into my perspective and practice.

This article is part of a much larger collective project that charts the changing consciousness of Jewish feminists through to the development of solidarity consciousness and our capacity to be allies. It traces the increasing inclusion of Palestinian women's voices in the North American feminist movement and the creation of dialogue and active work between Palestinian and Jewish women. The text of this article was inspired by talks that Palestinian activist and educator Nahla Abdo and

I gave at Carleton University on March 4, 1992, on "Breaking the Silences: Palestinian and Jewish Women in Solidarity." Part of what we wanted to explore was how we come from very different places but reach similar conclusions in our words and actions.

During late night discussion preparing for our presentations, we discovered that a controversy about Israel, zionism, anti-semitism and anti-imperialism during International Women's Day 1983 in Toronto had been a significant marker in both our lives. The panel at Carleton was the first time we spoke about the controversy, nine years after the fact.

I locate myself socially for two reasons. First, to indentify the voice with which I speak and the complex social identities that have shaped my experience and my perception of the world. Secondly, I want to use my story as both a tool for self-discovery and for analyzing changing consciousness. My experience is a lesson for me and I hope for others not because it is unique, but precisely because it is not. It illustrates a complex shift in consciousness that is important for Jewish and Palestinian feminists to explore, a shift that can provide us with hope. It offers one way to look at how as feminists we can develop solidarity consciousness and practice it in our lives.

My attempt to link history and autobiography has not been easy — it has sometimes been hard to be big-hearted with my earlier selves. But I realize if I can't do it, how can I discover what drives others to let go of fear, to have the courage to deal with pain and dread?

A Secular Jewish Childhood on the Upper Left Side

One of the many roads that brought me to this place is my biological family road. I grew up as an Ashkenazi Jew in New York. My father was an artist and my mother a fund-raiser and organizer. Both were long-time members of the Communist Party, lived in poverty as children, had Eastern European origins and arrived in the U.S. early in this century. By the time I was born, our family enjoyed the privilege and power of the middle class, though economically our situation was always insecure due to my mother's twenty-one-year struggle with cancer and my father's rejection as a suitable worker by boards of education and other organizations because of his Communist Party membership.

My sense of "otherness" was largely based on the need to hide my parents political affiliation. This was brought home to me by my mother's anxious requests in the late 1950s and early 1960s that I whisper any mention of the Communist Party when out in public. Of course, I had only the smallest idea why she was so distressed, but I relished this well-known secret. It set us apart from the throng of New Yorkers, made us different. On the upper west side of Manhattan being in the Communist Party set us apart more than being Jewish did.

I grew up in a very secular Jewish world where my notion of being Jewish was based more on a fuzzy idea of Jewish culture and history than on celebrating Jewish holidays, going to synagogue or studying Hebrew. The first time I stepped inside the synagogue around the corner was when I was thirteen, when one of my friends was having a Bat Mitzvah. I was never to shul with either of my parents.

In my uptown Manhattan world everybody who was white was Jewish and "other people," the non-Jews, were people of Colour — Blacks, Haitians and Puerto Ricans. My friends were either Jewish or Black. My sense of Jewishness was a sense of being at home in my neighbourhood. I was not an outsider. My Jewishness was embedded in a sense that Jewish people came from Eastern Europe, as opposed to people of Colour, whom I identified as coming from the Caribbean and Africa.

At a political level, I gradually became aware that my parents were critical of Israel and that they had an anti-zionist position, though neither the richness nor the details of that position were very evident to me. I remember my mother saying that her father had gone to build a socialist society in Palestine in the first decade of this century and had left in disgust because of the repression of the Palestinian Arabs. I remember my grandmother speaking about breaking off contact with her brother because he had become part of the World Zionist Organization and was very much committed to Israel as a state.

I remember the Six-Day War in 1967, when I was fourteen, during which Israel forcibly annexed Arab Jerusalem and occupied the West Bank, the Gaza, the Sinai and the Golan Heights. There were endless meetings at our place, people screaming into the middle of the night because a large portion of Jews in the Communist Party couldn't abide the Party line: Israel was wrong to occupy Arab land and zionism inevitably lead to such aggression. Many of these people chose to leave the Party. They left, I understand now, because the war brought to the surface their fears for the survival of Israel. They were swayed by the "victory" of the Israeli state, which was painted by the Israeli government and much of the Western media as the final victory against Hitler. It was a manipulated version of the war and a large part of the Jewish community in North America bought it. My father stood firm, my mother stood firm. They stayed in the party — but huge rifts occurred between Jews and within the Communist Party.

This awareness of my parents' political battles and positions did not push me to figure out my relationship to the state of Israel or to my Jewish identity. I was more interested in organizing against U.S. aggression in Vietnam and in support of the Black Panthers.

My first burning awareness of myself as a Jew occurred when I left New York in 1970 and, two years later, moved to a small city in southern Ontario. It was quite shocking to leave the urban metropolis where I "fit in." It was the first time as a Jew that I understood myself as "other," although it was still very ill-defined. People assumed that I was Christian. When they found out I was Jewish they responded as if I was an unfamiliar fruit or strange breed. I began to comprehend the cultural dominance of white Christianity and I found a predominance of white people who weren't Jews. (Why had I not seen them before?)

There were a number of things that took place before I could deal with my Jewish identity and what that meant to me. One of those was a break with Stalinism soon after arriving in Canada and joining a new revolutionary socialist party which, along with autonomous social movements, was invested by me with the same hope that my parents had in their party. At the same time I was becoming a feminist. And then a year later I came out as a lesbian. This was a time of great personal and political turmoil and change. I found new political and social communities.

The most intensive part of my journey to understanding myself as a Jew came later, and predictably, with a vengeance. There were two events that precipitated the deepening of my consciousness, one very personal and one very political. One was the death of my mother in 1981 and the second, a year later, was the Israeli invasion of Lebanon. These had an enormous impact on my life in very different yet very similar ways.

My mother, in addition to being the central love of my life, represented one of my few living connections to Ashkenazi Jewish culture and history. Her first language was Yiddish and she was steeped in that culture and literature, as was her mother. In her life she had attempted to fuse her different identities, particularly the Communist and the Jewish, without sacrificing either her pride in Jewish history and culture or her communist vision. As I grieved the loss of my mother, I was aware of losing this powerful connection to my Jewishness, an identity that was still undeveloped in me. I went to Paris to visit her mother, to find out my grandmother's story. I searched for my family's history, to uncover the stories, before the European Holocaust, since that time, to find out who had survived and how. I became aware of the pervasive pattern of persecution and hatred of Jews and recognized how that had affected my life and that of every Jew around the world. I began to locate myself as the bearer of a *Jewish* tradition which fought for freedom and against injustice. I began to wear a Jewish star with a labyris in the middle, publicly identifying myself both as Jewish and as lesbian. Each changed because of the other. I immersed myself in writings about what I saw at that point as the persecution and the oppression of all Jews. I read about Jew-hatred and fascism, about the Holocaust and the creation of Israel. And it is important to note that the only Jews that I "saw" were Jews of European origin. They were my focus.

This time gave me a profound grounding and I will always hold on to it. It was very important to claim my place in the world as a Jew — to take pride in my culture, to feel the pain in my history and in the persecution and dispersal of my family. I began to celebrate some Jewish holidays but in an untraditional way, developing along with other Jewish feminists different ways to celebrate our lives. I became more aware of anti-Jewish acts and attitudes and of the pervasive stereotypes of Jews as rich, greedy and pushy.

It was this reforming of my identity and more particularly the invasion of Lebanon that challenged me to deal with my relationship to the state of Israel. My born-again Jewishness led me, as a result of the dominant discourse of nationalism within the mainstream Jewish community, to be protective of Israel and of its right to exist, its meaning for the survivors of the European Holocaust. For the first time, I became hypersensitive to criticisms of Israel. My growing sense of Jewish history and culture brought me face to face with the national consensus within Israel and within the Jewish community in North America — a consensus which linked the survival of the Jewish people with the survival of the state of Israel.

But I also responded to the invasion of Lebanon with shame and a feeling of responsibility. I could not claim neutral ground. For the first time I understood that as a Jew I was considered to be responsible for the policies of Israel. Israeli leaders who spoke about the necessity of the invasion did so in my name, whether I wanted them to or not. And the support of Jews in the North American diaspora for Israel was crucial to silencing opposition and creating a powerful yet unthinking loyalty to the policies of the Israeli state. When I heard about the massacres at Sabra and Shatila (two Palestinian refugee camps) I knew that I had to speak out. I couldn't be complicit in the false consensus that condoned brutal atrocities committed in the name of "security" for Israel.

My angry feelings towards the invasion coincided with my reading of my family's history and of criticism of Israel. I was rediscovering a hidden and often denied perspective within the Jewish community, the anti-zionist perspective. This political perspective had lost most of its adherents and was unfortunately buried and forgotten as a result of the European Holocaust. The anti-zionist current that I saw reflected in my family's history had a vision of fighting the oppression and persecution of Jews, of different kinds of Jews, wherever it occurred. It rejected the idea of an exclusive state and the claims that to survive Jews needed such a state. And it envisioned Jews living side by side with Arabs in Palestine in one state, as my grandfather had.

As I continued to read and to discuss, I became angered at the racist and anti-Jewish policies that Western imperialist nations — the U.S., Canada, Britain and others — had translated into their closed-door policy for Jews trying to escape from the European Holocaust. Despite the Allies' knowledge of the Nazi death camps, virtually no one took a stand; they did nothing to destroy the railway lines, nor did they offer shelter to Jews, gypsies and others who were targetted for extermination. These racist, exclusionary policies put the final nails in the coffin of this anti-zionist perspective. In the face of these attacks both from the Nazis and from the so-called Allies, it became much more difficult to speak against the idea of a separate Jewish state.

I was also angered at the Western imperialist states for creating the whole mess from the beginning, for granting a homeland to the Jewish people on someone else's land. Britain, in particular, saw in zionism an opportunity to build an alliance with a movement which would colonize Palestine and carve out a strategic outpost in the Middle East. I began to see this as a manipulation of both the Jewish and the Palestinian peoples and as setting the stage for constant warfare, expulsions and exploitation.

My developing sense of identity was very contradictory. I was living in a dynamic but paradoxical tension, starting to place myself in history and take pride in my Jewish self. But how could I feel committed to my Jewishness while Israel was invading another country and committing atrocities against another people? I was having difficulty developing and maintaining a sense of myself as a Jew separate from Israel. I was caught in carefully constructed mythologies which equated the survival of the Jewish people and Jewish culture with the security of Israel as a Jewish state, caught between the conflicting views of my born-again Jewish quasi-nationalist self and my socialist-feminist, anti-imperialist self. On the one hand, I felt unsafe as a Jew in the world. Despite the lessons of centuries of persecution and expulsion and the European Holocaust, hatred and fear of Jews remains a potent and dangerous feature of racism in many places. "Another Holocaust is still possible," I thought to myself. And this time the list of endangered peoples threatened would be even longer. "But Jews could be safe in Israel," I reasoned. "That is why Israel is so necessary. Right?" Not really, not for a lesbian or a feminist. And not for someone with my political views. I tried not to think about that too much. One thing I did know: as a Jewish feminist and socialist it was essential for me to respond to the severe repression and oppression of another people whom I felt a connection to and a responsibility for.

I was facing a political dilemma. My consciousness was divided. I faced a moral dichotomy created by the state of Israel. This is a double standard that many Jews in the diaspora confront: outside of Israel the welfare of Jews depends on maintaining secular, non-racial and pluralistic societies, but in Israel we are asked to defend a society in which African and Asian Jews and Palestinians are denied their cultures and their histories. We are asked to defend a society where there is economic exploitation, racism between European "white" Jews and Arab or Black Jews, a society in which the Palestinian is completely the "other" and completely denied, and a society in which the ideal is exclusionary and racialist. This double standard means that to fight for your existence and strength as Jews elsewhere in the world you have to fight *against* the very principles and practices that you are asked to defend in Israel.

Coming Out As Critical of Israel

This was my context in 1983, when International Women's Day was "celebrated" in Toronto. The March 8th Coalition, with its mostly white, socialist-feminist leadership, pushed for the integration of anti-imperialist perspectives into the feminist movement and specifically in the week's events. Three public forums were organized for the week. One addressed "Women's Liberation, Disarmament and Imperialism." Four women spoke, representing different struggles around the globe. Nahla Abdo, a recent Palestinian immigrant, spoke about the struggle of Palestinian women. The forum sparked a lot of controversy and discussion in the feminist movement and in the pages of women's newspapers and magazines. This event was a flashpoint for the feminist movement in Toronto. Similar controversies flared across Canada and the United States.

From the vantage point of my contradictory feelings and consciousness what I remember Nahla Abdo saying was this: zionism is racism; we can't have an International Women's Day without acknowledging our differences and without referring to struggles that divide us; this is not an exercise in false solidarity. She spoke about the violence, the rape, the daily degradation that Palestinian women faced at the hands of the Israeli military. She told us about life in the refugee camps and spoke about the role of Palestinian women in building the social and economic infrastructure central to the Palestinian movement. She spoke of the ways that the Palestinian people were resisting the occupation of their land and history.

I remember my response: I was totally horrified at the brutality and pain she was speaking about. As a Jew, it was almost too hard to hear what she had to say. Because I knew that it was true, I felt shame. I felt supportive of her right to speak, and at some intellectual level, I agreed with her vision of a bi-national state. But I also felt torn. Initially, I felt critical of the forum for being unbalanced, for lacking sensitivity to Jewish women and for not providing a historical understanding for the creation of Israel. I was defensive and fearful. I couldn't manage to maintain my Jewishness *and* support Nahla Abdo. What she said obliterated what I perceived as my identity.

I don't remember whether it was the event that exploded or just my mind. I do know that the forum sparked a debate which was very important for the development of an anti-imperialist and anti-racist perspective within the women's movement in Toronto. There were women who resented Abdo's presence on the panel and charged that she was anti-semitic because she equated zionism with racism. Though these women identified themselves as supporters of the Palestinian struggle, they seemed to feel that she had attacked the Jewish state and the Jewish people and their right to self-determination. I knew I didn't agree with this. There were other women, socialist-feminist primarily, some of whom were Jews, who were supporters of the Palestinian struggle and who were pleased that she was speaking and outraged at the negative responses to her. I wasn't wholeheartedly in agreement with them either. And then there were a few women like myself who were caught somewhere in between.

This was the first time I found myself directly challenged as a white-skinned Jew about my power and privilege *and* my relationship to the oppressive policies of the ''Jewish'' state. It was formative for me as well as for other women. I can see now that for me it was a precursor to the challenge that would come from Black women, First Nations Women and other women of Colour three years later during the organizing for International Women's Day (IWD) in Toronto in 1986. The three years in between continued the momentum, but it was only in 1986 that racism was on the agenda in a very central way in the organizing of IWD, in the theme of the day and the program of events, in the speeches and written material and in the general approach.

I want to address my reactions during IWD 1983. My dominant response to Nahla Abdo's speech was shame. I had begun to speak out but not consistently or wholeheartedly. I was beginning to acknowledge my responsibility, but I also became immobilized with guilt, in much the same way that many white feminists get stuck in shame when challenged about our racism. When challenged about our power we overwhelm the discussion or debate with our sense of powerlessness and therefore avoid any responsibility. When Nahla spoke I became overwhelmed with guilt.

In 1982 I had begun to confront that shame by going public. I joined a number of demonstrations against the invasion of Lebanon and the massacres at Sabra and Shatila. I was beginning to recognize that I did have some power, as difficult as that is to acknowledge or even feel, when confronted both by self-doubt and by the enormity of the system we are struggling to change. I drew on the strength of my past activism and on the history of resistance by my family and my people. I took courage from other Jewish people, particularly women, who were openly critical of Israeli policies. I understood that their strong sense of themselves and their political vision were prerequisites to making that break with others in their community.

My responses to what Nahla was saying in 1983 proved that I wasn't immune to the Jewish community's construction of loyalty to the state of Israel as being totally intertwined with one's Jewishness. I wasn't immune even though my family of origin was openly critical of Israeli policies and the nature of that state. I had a way to go before I could fully untangle my identity and my political perspective from the dominant constructions of Jewish identity in North America.

First, I needed to explore my Jewish identity and culture on a different basis. My survival, much less the survival of Jewish peoples, couldn't be bound up in supporting someone else's expulsion or persecution. A nationalism that excludes others who live in the same territory, that militarizes all social relations and prescribes how to be a Jew, definitely wasn't the answer. I began to see my and our survival bound up in an equally long tradition of fighting for social and economic justice, of fighting against the deadening system of profit, against sexism, homophobia, racism and anti-semitism. This was how the Jewish people would survive — by fighting Jewish oppression and working for social and economic justice. And I realized that the Israeli state, created on the backs of the Palestinian people, was also implicated in this deadening system. The militarism of the Israeli state is intimately linked with the patriarchal, racist and homophobic structures that dominate Israeli society. Not only would I not be safe as a lesbian and feminist in Israel, I also realized that the racist and exclusionary policies of the Israeli state made no Jew anywhere more safe.

Based on this understanding, I was able to "come out" as a Jew who is critical of Israel. I began consciously to separate and differentiate myself from zionism. I rejected the association of Jewish survival with the security and survival of an exclusive Jewish state.

The more I separated myself from the dominant construction of Jewish nationalism, the more my shame turned to anger at the denial and destruction of Palestinian history and culture. Wasn't this what had happened to Jews for centuries? I found myself identifying with the Palestinian struggle for self-determination. I now heard things in a different way and I took the giant step of recognizing that Israel is systematically oppressing the Palestinian people, of recognizing that zionism, whatever one thought of its intention, is a colonial movement.

Armed with a developing anti-racist politics, I further located myself as a white Ashkenazi Jew whose culture dominated and subjugated not only the Palestinian people but also Arab/Mizrachi Jewish people. I began to understand zionism as a national movement of European Jews and that Arab/Mizrachi Jews have been excluded from power, have been subjugated within the Jewish state and within Jewish history. They provide cheap Jewish labour for the Jewish state and they have been and continue to be the victims of racism and poverty. Their Arabness has been rejected and their names changed in an attempt to Europeanize them.

As Ella Shohat, an Iraqi-born Jewish academic and activist, writes in her article "Sephardim in Israel: Zionism from the Standpoint of its Jewish Victims,"

[W]ithin Israel, European Jews constitute a First World elite dominating not only the Palestinians but also the Oriental Jews. The Sephardim, as a Jewish Third World people, form a semi-colonized nation-within-a-nation....the same historical process that dispossessed Palestinians of their property, lands and national-political rights, was linked to the process that dispossessed Sephardim of their property, lands and rootedness in Arab countries (and within Israel itself, of their history and culture).[1]

Jewish women who identified themselves as Sephardic, Arab or Mizrachi challenged me with their writings and in discussion. I started to integrate this learning into my sense of self and into my politics. My white-skin privilege, my European background, was not just a privilege in relation to people of Colour in general, but also in relation to Jews of Colour — Sephardic, Arab and Mizrachi Jews. I recognized that while we all struggle to survive as Jews, Ashkenazi Jewish culture, the Yiddish language and the Ashkenazi part of Jewish history had become "Jewish history." Ladino and other Jewish languages and cultures are barely recognized, understood or celebrated within the Jewish community. We must deal with the racism within our communities, with the way Arab Jews and Sephardic Jews and their histories and cultures have been misrepresented, denied and dominated by Ashkenazi Jews. Jewish history has become the history of the shtetl, the European Holocaust and the history of Israel — all seen through the eyes of Ashkenazi culture. Jews have become a single people in this Eurocentric version of history, while we are many peoples with both different and similar experiences of oppression.

Embracing the Contradictions

As I ventured further on my journey, I started to embrace the contradictions of identity and oppression. I had both to see myself in the role of the oppressor and to take on and feel respect for my culture and history and for the pain in my oppression. This is what it took for me to become an ally of Palestinian people: to acknowledge my places of pain as well as my privilege. And it took time and the support of other Jewish feminists going through similar turmoil.

I think only at that point could I enter into alliances that involved real solidarity. Then I could hear and read about Palestinian experience and feel outrage and anger and the need for action, without feeling small or immobilized by shame or guilt.

A "Balanced" View of History

Let's go back again to 1983. I want to address the need I experienced then for "balance" in the presentation of the Israeli/Palestinian conflict. This notion is a constant in this debate that continues to occupy a tremendous amount of air time and energy. What this need for "balance" excludes is any analysis of power: who has the power to represent themselves and who has the power to deny another people's identity and history. The Israeli state has the military, political and ideological power to deny Palestinian self-determination. In North America, where there is less open dissent within the Jewish community than in Israel, there is a great need expressed within the Jewish communities to balance any presentation of Palestinian history with a Jewish voice in defense of Israel.

As Edward Said says in a February 1992 interview in *Z Magazine*, "Internationally whenever a Palestinian tries to tell a story, to put in a dramatic and realizable way the interrupted story of Palestine and its connection to the story of Israel, it is systematically attacked."[2] I see my own consciousness in 1983 as basically feeding into and maintaining this notion. In the interview, Said speaks about a series of Palestinian documentary films that were to be shown at the Boston Museum for Fine Arts. There was public pressure to stop the films from being shown unless the "other side" was represented on a panel. Edward Said responds, "So we're always the other side of the other side."[3] It's as if Palestinians don't have a history, they just have part of it. This is a denial of Palestinians. They can't represent themselves and their experience on its own or without this constant disruption of the story. The current situation with the Middle East (so-called) peace talks, where Palestinians are only represented through the filter of Israeli rejection and U.S. collusion, is a perfect example of the denial of a people.

Take this issue of balance into another context — the feminist movement. Picture a panel on the history and politics of racism where white feminists are included in order to achieve balance. I draw this analogy because its laughable. But let's seriously look at what it is to experience

Ashkenazi Jews constantly insisting that Palestinian history obliterates Israel.

Representing the "other side," representing the Israeli state as the other side, denies the relations of power between the Israeli Jew, particularly the Israeli Ashkenazi Jew, and the Palestinian Arab. It completely denies that there are relations of power or inequality in those situations. Despite the centuries-long persecution of Jewish peoples, Israel exists as a sovereign state and any Jew from around the world can become a citizen and live in a village that Palestinians were expelled from in 1948 or in a new settlement in the West Bank, constructed on the rubble of a bulldozed Arab village. This "right of return" for Jews does not apply to the Palestinians who inhabited this same land for centuries. This need for representing the "other side" hides the facts on the ground and denies the substantial support (to the tune of $100 billion) from the U.S. since 1948.

This denial of history can also be seen in the original impetus for colonization. The slogan "a land without a people, for a people without a land," sums up the construction of a nationalist and racist ideology which denies that the Palestinian people exist.

In a more contemporary context, the government of Israel has said for a number of years that peace can be achieved if the Palestinian movement recognizes Israel's nationhood. What the PLO believes, what the PLO covenant says, is always raised in this discussion. I've heard a lot of Jewish people say, "They want to destroy Israel, but if they acknowledged our right to exist as a state, then everything would be different." The PLO recognized Israel's existence in 1988 and in effect has said, "You have denied our history, destroyed our culture and taken our land, but we recognize your state. You can have your state and your self-determination for your people in the pre-1967 borders. We want a Palestinian state and self-determination for our people on the West Bank and the Gaza." What has occurred as a result of these compromises on the part of the Palestinian movement? Nothing except a lot of hypocritical statements from the Israeli government about searching for a peaceful solution to the conflict. The burden of proof about who is genuinely interested in peace is always placed on those whom Israel is oppressing. Israel, as a nation, has never made a similar acknowledgement to the

Palestinian people. On the contrary, Jewish settlements in the West Bank and Gaza have increased at such a frightening pace that the political and demographic reality in the West Bank and Gaza has radically changed. By 1992 Israel had expropriated sixty percent of the land in the West Bank and fifty percent in the Gaza. This makes any real discussion about Israeli withdrawal *almost* absurd.

The overwhelming need that many Jews have for recognition and balance is connected to the Ashkenazi Jewish experience of oppression and persecution. More importantly, the state of Israel is constructed on a sense of Jewish powerlessness and fear which is based on many Jews' experience of surviving the European Holocaust. This fear is based on the profound sense that Jews can only be safe with our own people and that the entire Jewish diaspora must eventually settle in our own nation. The tragedy and horror of the European Holocaust is manipulated to create a unified vision of Jewish people with an abiding loyalty to an exclusive state. As Marilyn Neimark writes in her article, "American Jews and Palestine: The Impact of the Gulf War," in *Middle East Report*, March-April 1992, "The fusing of state-people-government was accomplished, in large part, by exploiting the tragedy of the Holocaust and by projecting it onto the Middle East and the Palestinians."[4] Arab hatred of Israel and its policy of occupation, expulsion and expropriation is equated with the Nazis' hatred of Jews. Theologian Marc Ellis writes in *Beyond Innocence and Redemption: Confronting the Holocaust and Israeli Power* about the development of Holocaust theology, a theology that unifies cultural and religious background with loyalty to the state of Israel. The result of this manipulation of the Holocaust has been to push Jewish people, individually and collectively, to become so self-absorbed that any capacity for compassion and solidarity with the Palestinian people is greatly diminished. Ellis writes that for many Jews "Palestinians hardly exist, except as a mass of people threatening the survival of the Jewish people."[5] Palestinians are identified only as menacing characters and always in relation to the central drama of Jewish survival.

The politicized use of the European Holocaust leaves Jews both victimized and victimizing. It exploits our fear, causes us to feel constantly attacked and powerless. This is a fear that holds us hostage, immobilizes us and makes us unable to acknowledge where we do have power. There is no room for change or movement, because no movement goes far enough in allaying our fears. (I see parallels with feminists who sometimes fall into the trap of defining women as powerless and therefore call on the state to increase its power in our lives).

This politicized manipulation of the Holocaust turns it into the experience of all Jews, ignoring that our physical, economic and social locations determined our experience of the Holocaust and World War II. The Ashkenazi experience of the European Holocaust is honoured, while the experience of thousands of Jews in North Africa, who were murdered in concentration camps in North Africa and Eastern Europe, is forgotten. The specific history and oppression of the Ashkenazi Jews is honoured while the histories, cultures and persecution of Arab Jews is ignored. The European Holocaust is constructed as something that only Jewish people own. But we know that there were many other people, including people with disabilities, inmates in psychiatric institutions, political dissidents, gay men, lesbians, Poles, Gypsies and others who died in the camps, who suffered greatly at the hands of the fascists. This manipulation of pain is a liability for the Palestinian people *and* for the Jewish people. It exploits the suffering of Jews and denies the suffering of Palestinians.

Solidarity and Organizing

I did a lot of thinking and talking after IWD 1983. And events in Israel and the Occupied Territories continued to challenge me. The Palestinian intifadah, which started in 1987, provided another important impetus and lesson for Jewish feminists like me. Images of Palestinian women and children fighting back pushed many of us to take a more decisive stand by protesting the massive detentions without trial, the increased settlements in the Occupied Territories, the continuous expulsion and torture of a people. The intifadah crystallized the decades-old challenge to Israeli rule and the women of the intifadah have been central to that struggle. Among Jewish feminists, the intifadah sparked the growth of the women's peace movement (including Women in Black, Women Against the Occupation and the Women's Organization for Political Prisoners), which challenges the occupation of the West Bank and Gaza

Strip within an overall critique of the power relations in the Israeli state. New alliances were also formed between Palestinian women in the Occupied Territories and Israel and Jewish women in Israel. The intifadah, along with PLO recognition of Israel and its demand for a two-state solution, helped to build a majority consensus of nations supporting Palestinian self-determination and resisting the hypocritical stances of Israel and the U.S.

By the time the intifadah started I had a more integrated consciousness. I had rejected a nationalism that obstructs all other contradictions, that covers up and denies differences of sexuality, gender and class, differences between Mizrachi and European Jews, between the secular and the religious. I rejected a zionism that collapses all Jews into a single category of "one people." I began to embrace an understanding of the diversity and distinctness of Jewish cultures.

As I embraced more firmly my family's history and the history of Jewish progressive movements, I began to draw the parallels between Jewish experience and Palestinian experience. It is imperative for Ashkenazi Jews to recognize that in colonizing and displacing the Palestinian people, Jews are committing acts of oppression and expulsion of a people that mirror what has been done to us for over 2,000 years. How can we refuse to see that the actions of the Israeli state against the Palestinian people mirror the history of suffering that Jews have sought to overcome or escape? How can we support these acts? Our power and self-determination cannot be built on the blood of others. We must relinquish ground, ground in the debate and ground in a literal sense — territory. We are forced to look at ourselves and at each other.

I understand that many forms of Jew-hatred still exist and are being fuelled by the economic and political crises of capitalism and "socialism." But why should the Palestinian people have to pay for the oppression and persecution of Jewish people? I have come to understand that in Israel we are confronting a state whose policies have resulted in erasing the Palestinian people from Israel and the Occupied Territories, much as the colonial settlers in North America wiped out the Indigenous population, except for those whose skills and knowledge they could exploit for themselves. While we can debate whether the formation of Israel was necessary in its historical moment, the colonization of Palestine was always wrong in relation to the Palestinian people. Just as Palestinians have become the other side of the other side, they have been made, as Edward Said says, "The victims of the victims"[6] who now have state power. Although we need to be clear that one of the "original sins" was the European Christian anti-semitism and racism against Jewish and Arab peoples expressed through the dominant culture in Western imperialist nations, we cannot deny that the state of Israel oppresses the Palestinians.

Now, ten years after IWD 1983, my journey has brought me angrily and actively to oppose the policies of the Israeli state and to work with Jewish feminist groups, in Canada and Israel, which oppose the occupation of West Bank and Gaza. The more I feel grounded in my complex identities, identities that embody places of oppression and of privilege, the more I can act in a political way. It is important to me that I do not give the impression that this was a linear or a simple process. Far from it. It is filled with contradictions, tensions, the fear of losing community, the creation of new alliances. It is humbling. Some days I feel like I have learned the same lessons over and over again. On others, I know that at each turn I have a deeper understanding and appreciation.

The Jewish Women's Committee to End the Occupation of the West Bank and Gaza (JWCEO) in Toronto is one of the most significant organizations doing this work and deserves specific mention. The JWCEO was created 1989 by a group of women wanting to act as Jews and as women against the Occupation. Many of us had been participating in bi-weekly Women in Black vigils which were organized in solidarity with women in Israel who actively opposing their government's actions in the Occupied Territories. The JWCEO formed to continue this work but also to expand support within the broader Jewish community for a two-state solution, with other Jewish feminists and with Palestinian groups. We hold vigils in different locations in the Jewish community, sponsor educational events and demonstrations. We also hold workshops for Jewish women to explore questions of Jewish identity and oppression, the connections between Jewish oppression and racism and Jewish responses to the Israeli-Palestinian conflict. We continue to organize special events on Jewish holidays and to develop different ways to recognize and celebrate our Jewishness.

During the Gulf War, the JWCEO's ranks expanded because many Jewish women were looking for a place both to oppose the war and to be together as Jews. Our organization was a very visible but solitary Jewish voice opposing the war. We organized Jewish anti-war demonstrations and spoke out at forums and demonstrations organized by the anti-war movement in Toronto.

Now, two years after the Gulf War and a year after the Middle East (so-called peace) talks began, we think that the work of the JWCEO is more important than ever. As the context changes and as much of the Jewish community has been lulled by both the peace talks and the election of a Labour government in Israel, we continue to push for an immediate end to the occupation of the West Bank and Gaza Strip and for Israel to negotiate seriously and honestly with the PLO towards the creation of a Palestinian state alongside Israel.

I feel that I am part of an "alternative" Jewish feminist perspective that is expressed both in writing and in our actions. There are many groups similar to the JWCEO across Canada and the U.S. Some of us organize within the Jewish community, others are in dialogue with Jewish and Palestinian women. We are a diverse network of women in Israel, the U.S., Canada and Europe who have helped our Arab and Palestinian sisters to put Palestinian self-determination on the agenda of the feminist movement. Our words and our actions have also helped the feminist movement confront its racist exclusion of Arab and particularly of Palestinian women and have helped to open up a place for their voices to be heard and respected.

Some Jewish feminists are no longer dominated by narrow constructions of what it is to be Jewish. Criticism of either zionism or of Israel is no longer automatically considered anti-Jewish and anti-semitic within the feminist movement in Toronto. As a result, the silencing of Arab and Palestinian women has diminished somewhat. International Women's Day 1991 in Toronto was an example of this change. The entire day was organized around the theme of self-determination for Aboriginal peoples, Palestinians and Blacks in South Africa. Women from the Palestinian Women's Association and the Jewish Women's Committee to End the Occupation of the West Bank and Gaza marched together that day for the first time, symbolizing our solidarity and common struggle against Israeli policies, despite our different relationships to the feminist movement and our different histories.

The history of Jewish people is intimately tied to the history of the Palestinian people. Unless I can struggle against injustices that are done in my name to the Palestinian people I can never survive as part of Jewish peoples. The answer is not to fear each other or to throw up boundaries around ourselves but rather to engage in solidarity with each other. Through history *and* by force, Jews and Palestinians now belong to the same history. We must heal that history and struggle for self-determination and justice together, while respecting our differences.

Notes

1. Ella Shohat in "Sephardim in Israel: Zionism from the Standpoint of its Jewish Victims" in *Social Text*, Vol. 19/20, 1988.
2. David Barsamian in "An Interview with Edward W. Said" in *Z Magazine*, February 1992, p. 90.
3. *Ibid.*
4. Marilyn Neimark in "American Jews and Palestine: The Impact of the Gulf War" in *Middle East Report*, No. 175, 1992, p. 21.
5. Marc Ellis. *Beyond Innocence and Redemption: Confronting the Holocaust and Israeli Power* (New York: Harper & Row, 1990), p. 30.
6. Barsamian in *op. cit.*, p. 92.

RACE, GENDER AND POLITICS

The Struggle of Arab Women in Canada

Nahla Abdo

The oppression, underdevelopment and degradation faced by the Arab peoples in general and Arab women in particular are historically traceable to the class structure in the region and the latter's position in the world's capitalist system. The image of the Arab in the West is not a new invention. It rather is a product of a long history of the West's alleged superiority over the East. The "manufacturing" — to borrow from Noam Chomsky's famous documentary "Manufacturing Consent" — of such superiority took place during the Enlightenment in the West. The introduction of the Eurocentric sciences, especially the social sciences of the so-called Four Fathers of the West, the role of Western media and Western popular culture, the imperialist onslaught on the Arab world epitomised in the colonial division of the World in the early twentieth century have all contributed to the racist degradation of Arabs.

To survive, let alone be effective, underdevelopment, oppression and racism must be sustained if not reproduced. For that to happen, the collaboration, and in some cases even the unthinking support, of "internal" forces becomes necessary. Not unlike other Third World class structures, the Arab states never lacked oppressors of their own. This list is also long: the installment of puppet regimes, the persistence of military and authoritarian rule, of dictatorship, the rise of forces — fundamentalists and otherwise — resistant to change, and development to hegemonic status.

This article, nonetheless, is not about the oppressive history of internal and external forces in the Arab world, nor is it about stating the obvious. I am not interested in criticizing the entrenched male hegemonic powers of the West, nor for that matter in discussing the oppressive patriarchal rulers of the East. Rather I seek to unravel the complexity of being the embodiment of multiple marginalizations of a society where the hegemonic culture is capitalist, racist and sexist. While being Arab-Palestinian-woman is perfectly normal in three-quarters of the world, this ontological status becomes a problem in North America, including in Canada. She is silenced, ignored and oppressed, not only by structures and institutions, but also by the very social movement whose legitimation is largely derived from its opposition to oppression, namely feminism. In addition to unravelling these complexities, I launch an enquiry into the silence, ignorance and bankruptcy of "inclusive" theory among feminist circles.

What accounts for the marginalization of Arab women's voices in Canada in general and in feminist circles, discourse and practices in particular? Is it because "Arab women cannot be feminists," as some allege? Or is it because Arab women are not "visible," i.e., coloured enough, dark enough or black enough and therefore are not targeted by racism?

Drawing partly on the available literature — which is quite scarce — as well as on my experience as an activist and academic, I will try to look at these thorny questions within the Canadian context.

Racism is about More than "Colour"

There is no doubt that the hierarchy of oppression present in the state system is the product of various elements of power. The most important of these are embodied in the colonial-settler state itself. In the racist politics of the U.S., for example, the dichotomy White-Black sets clear boundaries between two "peoples," excluding in the process many others, most importantly indigenous peoples and Hispanics.

In Canada, due to the persistent struggles of the Native peoples, a different racialized policy has been put in place. Here one finds a hierarchy of oppression/racialization employed in official circles as well as in the print and electronic media, a hierarchy which places the Natives as the "most" affected by racism; the second place is reserved for Blacks and the third for a unspecific category called "people of colour."

These state-imposed hierarchies, instead of being rejected, have tended to be reproduced by feminists, both academics and activists. One can see that the categories "Native" and "Black" are increasingly the undisputed territories for racist subjection; the term "colour" is yet to be decoded. The tendency is to associate the category of "colour" with ethnicity, or culture, occluding in the process the real meaning of racism.

Most often, "blackness," one signifier of racism, is perceived as the only determinant for racism. Racism is identified with "blackness" and as a result is limited to skin colour. Constructing racism as an historically-specific ideology and practice exclusive to colour/race is very problematic, particularly when we recognize that there is no such category as "race" in its pure form. At the practical level, moreover, such a construction renders many "visible minorities" quite invisible and silences the voices of less-coloured or "differently coloured" groups. One group traditionally excluded from the widely held definition of race and colour is Arabs and Muslims (the latter refers to Arabs and to non-Arabs).

The exclusion and marginalization of Arabs and Muslims have not been confined to leftist academic discourse. They are also played out in feminist politics, including those which claim to represent grassroots or community interests. In some feminist discourse, one cannot help but sense a tendency to provincialism, whether through descriptive accounts or through the theoretical remedies produced. A phenomenon I refer to as the "feminist appropriation of the 'authentically and essentially' oppressed" is evident in the following example. In one of my courses a debate erupted over who has historically suffered the most, the Natives or the Blacks! While one student suggested that the Native peoples of Canada have suffered genocide unparalleled in the history of humanity, another argued that the experience of Black Africans is "more bitter and serious" because the latter have no place to go back to even if they wished to. With little or no intervention on my part, this debate was somewhat resolved, with both sides realizing the danger of giving one oppression priority over the other and by both sides recognizing the need for a historical context to situate the different experiences of genocide and oppression-exploitation. The discussion was not over, however; it continued, with other participants joining in, but this time it dealt with the definition of racism.

For some, racism was directly associated with blackness. To be more precise, with blackness as historically rooted in slavery and referring to one part of Africa, Southern Africa, rooted in the loss of culture, land, civilization and all that history involved. This account, which excludes all "coloured" peoples and many Blacks from other parts of Africa, was not well digested by another woman, who argued that racism has also targeted her and her people but not for the same historical reasons. Added to their colour is their culture and religion. For this woman, a recently arrived Somali refugee, the historical-geographical context (past history in particular) was not relevant to her definition of racism. Her country, land, culture and family are still alive and, theoretically, she can go back. This woman, consequently, was asking for a wider definition of racism, one which would account for differing experiences of racism.

Recent immigration policies in Canada suggest that the government's racialized policies extend to cover all or almost all Third World immigrants. Recent racist immigration policies presented by the Minister of Immigration include settling immigrants in specific regions for at least two years and permitting the deportation of landed immigrants if they once belonged to an "illegal" organization. Equally disturbing is the June 1992 survey of public opinion where over fifty percent of Canadians expressed blatant intolerance, to put it mildly, towards Third World immigrants.[1] These policies have significant implications for Third World immigrants involved in national liberation movements and affiliated with anti-imperialist, anti-colonial organizing, such as the ANC and the PLO.

The category immigrant is not homogenous. Not all immigrants are treated as "immigrants." San Juan's differentiation between Third World immigrants and European immigrants [2] is appropriate to the Canadian scene. This differentiation was made very clear in the Minister's defence of policies which opened the gates to Yugoslav immigrants while simultaneously slamming the doors in the face of Somalis. His reasons were that Somalis are a "Nomadic people with little or no family values." Nomadic life is, for the Minister, a state of "savagery or barbarism." It is appalling that the Minister could easily get away with his racist remarks, despite the protests of the Somali community.

The Secretary General of the United Nations, Botrus Ghali, accused members of the UN with ties to the U.S. power structure of being personally against him and for being racist in their overall treatment of the devastation in Somalia. He recognized that the target for racism was not just the African part of the victims but also their Arab or Islamic culture. The same holds for the millions of Sudanese dying of starvation and in internal wars. The racist campaign launched against Arabs and Muslims during and after the Gulf War, while unprecedented in the modern history of North America — at least in its extent, intensity and barbarity — was not just a war tactic or a temporarily useful ideological campaign. The renewal of the long-standing racism against Arabs and Muslims appears to be a major thrust of the so-called New World Order.

The over-publicizing in the pages of a leading Canadian newspaper of the case of one Saudi woman is indicative of this problem. When I first read the front page article [3] on the woman who is claiming refugee status in Canada I applauded Canada's sudden interest in the plight of women living under Muslim laws and oppressed by Islamicist movements. As an Arab feminist who resents patriarchal oppressive laws, even if the latter are packaged with a claim to "preserving identity or culture," I immediately identified with the woman and resented the way she was treated. I first thought interest in the story of one Saudi woman meant that Canada is aware of the repressive Saudi monarchy. To my utter surprise the story continued to occupy the front page — it seemed at the time to occupy the largest media space ever given to Arabs in Canada — I realized that I was reading lines that were not there. My solidarity with the woman became mixed with the need for a context and a framework.

Confronted with the context and history of Euro-American relations with the Arabs, I had to rethink the implications of how this woman's story got reported, particularly so in the aftermath of the Gulf War and the new world reordering of the Arab world. Along with feelings of solidarity I wondered, is this a part of a New World Order hegemonic campaign against Islam? Has the West replaced its old Communist enemy with a new one, Islam? Have Arab/Muslim women become an easy target not only for victimization in their own countries but also as a winning card for Western hegemony?

Feminism is not an abstract category or an empty practice. Feminism begs for context and history. As theory and practice, feminism recognizes that specific political boundaries should not be crossed. The Saudi woman and for that matter most Saudi, Arab and Muslim women suffer from Islam not the abstract and individual private religion but from Islam-the-Law, Islam-the-institution and Islam-the-state.

The freedom of Arab/Muslim women cannot be discussed in isolation from the forces responsible for their oppression. Ironically, neither the U.S. nor Canada perceive the Saudi regime as an oppressor nor as authoritarian. Instead of monitoring human rights violations there, both the U.S. and Canadian governments are racing hard to supply the Saudi state with more machinery for oppression and destruction. Yes, we should keep up the campaign to de-racialize Canadian immigration policies and to convince officials that gender oppression is as abhorrent as political, national and ethnic oppressions. But we must also think globally and realize that the repression of women's rights and of expatriate workers' rights in the Gulf in general and in Saudi Arabia in particular are deemed absolutely necessary by and for the continued reign of the monarchy and for the stabilization of the petro-dollar resources of the U.S.

Making the links between state oppression and women's oppression, through state-sponsored Islam, is fundamental. If the connection between the state and Islam as state power is not made, any criticism of Islam will be hypocritical and any talk on human or women's rights will remain empty. The freedom of the decontextualized "individual" is an empty bourgeois notion.

Where is the feminist voice on Arab and Muslim women, the voice which speaks with and not for? Where is the voice of Arab feminists among the anti-racist voices of "colourism"? And why are Arab/Muslim feminists shunted out of anti-racist feminist debates in general?

To address these questions, I propose that the concept of racism be re-examined and reorganized in an inclusive theory and practice. I do not claim originality for the idea that feminists must reject the view that racism is about colour or that it is to be specifically and uniquely applied to a particular group. Racism, I agree, must be addressed as a totality, one which involves political, economic and ideological exploitation and exclusion no matter which geographical area or skin colour it targets. Racism is the policy and practice of exclusion and oppression, the policy and practice of racialized exploitation. Only when it is defined in these broad terms can feminists claim to have broken the artificial "other-imposed" boundaries.

Racialized peoples, peoples under the yoke of racism, share some common characteristics: their history of Third Worldism (or more properly Two-Thirds Worldism), their history of poverty and imposed dependence and their subjection to colonial-imperialist powers which have rendered them underdeveloped. This colonial legacy remains with Third World peoples even after they acquire "First World" U.S.-Canadian citizenship. And in so far as women are concerned, gender and sexuality have added to their overall lot of oppression and subordination.

But there is no one general theory for racism.[4] Racism is historically specific. It operates on class and gender premises according to the specific ways in which the social, historical, economic, political and ideological are articulated. While for some, blackness in its physical characteristics appears to serve as an important signifier for racism, for others, religion, sexuality (expressed in dress codes, bodily appearance and modes of presentation), social and cultural modes of communication and ways of living, are the signifiers. To understand the racism faced by Arab/Muslim peoples we now turn to one form of racism, known in the literature as "orientalism."

Orientalism: The Male Colonialist Discourse

Despite relentless criticisms, Edward Said's *Orientalism* remains a classic examination of the colonial discourse on Arabs and Muslims.[5] *Orientalism* examines the construction of particular modes of knowledge by the West about the East. It establishes the strong relation between this form of knowledge (Orientalist) and the colonial-imperial powers that have dominated the relationship between East and West.

The institutionalization of Orientalism has, according to Said, enabled the West to reproduce the Orient as a subject of knowledge and power. It has also ensured that any discussion about Arabs/Muslims, whether in academia, popular culture or the media would pass through the Orientalist department or institution. This institution, however, is not just one of the many institutions that liberal democracies pride themselves on having developed. This is "the institution of the institutions." Orientalism informs media, academia and the Colonial Office. The entrenchment of this knowledge in Western circles of power gives it a somewhat hegemonic character. Orientalism becomes a basis for economic exploitation, political domination and cultural superiority over the East.

The bulk of Orientalist-constructed knowledge refers to Arabs and Muslims. The most common denominator is of Arab and Muslims as "Other": they are the backward, the undeveloped and the uncivilized, providing the perfect legitimization for their subjugation. The dehumanization used by the Orientalists varies, depending on the historical circumstance at hand: the French colonization of Algeria, as Alloula,[6] Kabbani,[7] and Ahmad[8] demonstrate, has targeted primarily women. The Iranian revolution, on the other hand, was used to promote hatred against Islam. Islam became associated with terrorism, "with images of bearded clerics and mad suicidal bombers, or unrelenting Iranian mullahs, fanatical fundamentalists, and kidnappers, remorseless turbaned crowds who chant hatred of the U.S. 'the great devil,' and all its ways."[9]

The struggle for Palestinian national liberation and resistance by Palestinians was another major target for Orientalism. "Palestinians," Said writes, "are constructed as terrorist-hijackers, masked killers of airport crowds, athletes, schoolchildren, handicapped and elderly innocents."[10] Orientalism, as a form of cultural imperialism, as a male colonialist discourse and as a manifestation of utter dehumanization, was given full expression before, during and after the Gulf War. Without going into the economic and political reasons for this war or into the dictatorship of the Iraqi regime and its expansionist policies, the most striking dimension on which this war seems to have been fought is that of culture. Two years after the "end" of this war I am still haunted by its Nintendo-style presentation and hopelessly begging to see the human dimension. I am still haunted by the images of jubilation on the faces of American soldiers after every "successful" bombing of civilians. I have not been able to forget the "smart missiles" with their hand-written phrases: "Good Luck" or "That's A Boy" fired at markets, civilian neighbourhoods, at shelters for women and children and at other highly populated areas.

The publication of *Orientalism* and the awareness it generated has produced considerable interest among scholars, West and East, who have begun to enquire further into Western claims for white Christianity (Greek origin) as the so-called roots for today's world, i.e., Western civilization. Important contributions in this area include Martin Bernal's *Black Athena: The Afroasiatic Roots of Classical Civilization*[11] and Samir Amin's *Eurocentrism*. Both authors strip Western social science of its claim to universality and attack its exclusivist Eurocentric and U.S.-centric approach, an approach elitist in nature. Secondly, they assert the contributions to civilization made by African and Asian peoples, including Arabs and Muslims. While using different methodologies and placing different emphases, both works are necessary, reminders of the interdependence and interconnectedness of the world's cultures.

Orientalism is not confined to official circles nor to male discourse on Arabs and Muslims. It has become deeply entrenched in feminist debates on West-East relations.

Orientalism and Racism: The Link

Orientalism is not only about constructed images and forms of knowledge. It is not a work of the imagination or abstractions by some individual, albeit powerful, minds. Orientalism is the product of colonial-capitalist development. The political economy of Orientalism, especially since the First World War, is embedded in the very forces that divided the Arab countries, giving rise to new client states, dismantled existing nations (Palestinians and Kurds, among others) and planted the seeds for a zionist settler-colonial state in the region. Orientalism is part and parcel of economic and political policies and practices. It is *specific, historical and material.*

Orientalism has been used to mean different things. It is used to represent the Arab and the Muslim as the "Other" and has become the predominant discourse about Arabs and Muslims. "Other" here does not mean simple difference, otherwise historically correct and necessary. The "othering" employed by Orientalism intends to show "Others" as inferior and to dehumanize them. Most critical authors since Edward

Said and Bryan Turner have tended to use the term at the descriptive level only. While some of the discussions at that level can be useful in identifying the different forms and representations that Arab, Muslim, and particularly Palestinian, subjects have been assigned, in themselves, these discussions are insufficient to explain the racist substance of Orientalism. To do that, the following analysis focuses on the historical-material and economic-political, the bases for the different ideological forms/representations Orientalism undertakes. To put it differently, the Orientalism we are discussing here is that found in the colonial capitalist policies and practices which have ruled much of the Arab-Muslim East. The Orientalism that concerns us here is the ideology of the colonial-settler powers which occupied, among other Arab countries, Algeria and Palestine and continue to obliterate the human and physical culture of the latter.

In the sense identified above, Orientalism becomes just another form of racism. While the signifiers may vary — sensual, exotic, harem and veiled beauty for the Orientalist and criminal, rapist, hot and exotic for the racist — both Orientalism and racism are similar in that they embody colonial exclusion and capitalist exploitation.

Time and space preclude a detailed analysis of Orientalism in any historically specific case. However, to understand the implications of this ideology for its subjects in Canada, a brief account of Orientalism's history in one Middle Eastern country (Palestine) is worth mentioning here.

Although Arabs and Muslims in general are the victims of Orientalism, the Palestinian people in particular have carried the brunt of this racism. Since late nineteenth century, and particularly since after the First World War and the subsequent imperialist division of the world, the hegemonic ideology which has ruled the Middle East has been zionism, the ideology of the colonial-settler European Jewish class. It was and continues to be the embodiment of racist-Orientalism. Zionism was and continues to be the policy and practice of denial and dehumanization. It has been the policy of destruction (of the indigenous economy, physical culture, family structures…); it is the expropriation of peasants' land, of expulsions, beginning with 1948 exclusion of over seventy-five percent of the Palestinian population to the 1993 expulsion of 415 people;

it is the racial subjugation of Palestinians by the Israeli state and the daily military harassment of Palestinians in the occupied West Bank and Gaza Strip. [12]

The historical and material bases of anti-Arab and particularly of anti-Palestinian racism are often undermined, glossed over or totally ignored while discussing and deconstructing Arab women and men.

Before defining the feminist-Orientalist discourse central to this discussion, a critical observation — a feminist self-warning — in dealing with oppression is in order. Although it is important to be conscious of the "external" colonial, racist oppressor, we must not lose sight of the "internal" structures of oppression. Putting gender above race has been rejected by Black, Arab and other non-Eurocentric feminists. Nor can we put race above gender or above class. Rejecting Eurocentrism as a manifestation of cultural superiority does not mean accepting cultural relativism. The rise of identity politics in the mid- and late-1980s has brought with it a lot of defeatist and rather anti-feminist ideologies. Thus, in "defending" and deconstructing the "self," feminists (particularly academics and intellectuals) ended up substituting the oppression of the "external" with that of the "internal." This has become obvious in the defence of the "family," "the veil," "traditional culture" and Islam. Feminists who say no to Western oppression need to say no to Eastern oppression, be it in Africa, Asia or anywhere else.

Feminist Orientalism and the Subjection of Arab Women

Arab women have been placed at the centre of Orientalist discourse, whether it is debated by, with or among men, or by, with or among women. Sexuality has been central to these debates. On how the whole Orient has been turned into the sexual-sensual, here is Said:

> Orientalism is a praxis of the same sort as male gender dominance, or patriarchy, in metropolitan societies: the Orient was routinely described as feminine, its riches as fertile, its main symbols the sensual woman, the harem and the despotic — but curiously attractive — ruler. Moreover, Orientals, like housewives, were confined to silence and to unlimited enriching production. Much of this material is manifestly connected to the configurations of sexual, racial and political asymmetry underlying mainstream modern western culture, as illuminated

respectively by feminists, by black studies critics and by anti-imperialist activists.[13]

I have chosen this quotation despite Said's having committed the mistake I warned against earlier: giving "internal-Oriental" gender oppression priority over "external" Orientalist oppression. But Said's words
demonstrate how Orientalism, not unlike racism, has largely targeted
women. What differentiates Orientalism from racism is the centrality of
gender and sexuality in the discourse of the former. Orientalist discourse, seen otherwise as the product of the Western imagination, has
been defined as involving "a theory of sexuality in the disguise of a
theory of asceticism." It often perceives the East as the "fantastic, which
is associated with sexual fantasies." [14]

Orientalism has constructed a specific image of the "Other" woman:
she is veiled, secluded, mutilated, over-oppressed, passive and lives in
harems. At the same time, she is the object of exoticism and sensuality,
the veiled beauty. Characteristic of this construction, as Shohat,[15] Alloula
[16] and Kabbani [17] observe, is the totalizing and homogenizing attitude
used by feminist Orientalists. This approach has lumped together different cultures: Turkish, Pakistani, Lebanese, Egyptian, the Arab Muslim, the Christian, the secular...

Orientalist-racist discourse has permeated feminist discourse on
Arab/Muslim women. Western feminism has played a key role in
maintaining and reproducing Arab/Muslim women as the "object-
Other," as "backward" and "over-oppressed" subjects who are beyond
remedy. This is true for various forms of feminism: the official, the
academic and quasi- official, the non-governmental and the activist
non-official. Arab women have endured "double Othering" from the
West, one for being Arab and another for being women. Being Palestinian, one may note, adds another dimension of subjugation. Since the
establishment of the state of Israel, being Palestinian has been enough
to make you a suspect, a terrorist.

Not unlike the genocide inflicted on the Indigenous peoples of the
U.S. and Canada, Arabs, particularly the Algerians and the Palestinians,
have seen the "Frenchification of Algeria" [18] and the "Judaization of
Palestine." [19] While stripping of Palestine of the Palestinians has been

going on since 1920, Algeria has entered the history books as the nation of "one million martyrs," in reference to the number of people killed during French colonialism. But the legacy of racist colonialism is not only about who it "killed off" or what it "finished" but also about how it wanted who and what survived in the colonies to be reproduced. A traditional code of conduct was expected from all colonial subjects; following Western codes of conduct and adopting Western civilization was the "right path to civilization."

Quoting a French feminist on how to "modernize" Algerian women, Marnia Lazreg observes,

> Upon entering tents and bolted doors, [French women] would familiarize Muslim women with our life-styles and ways of thinking... Religion, according to the same was responsible for Algerian women's inability to experience passionate love as French women were assumed to do...The Arab woman lives in limbo...[S]he neither is nor does she feel at home at her husband's. [20]

Another recipe for Algerian women is expressed as:

> [W]e could teach her French, how to sew and run a home...As for the Algerian men...their mental faculties appear to be stunted in the prime of life...men are inveterate liars and display a congenital nonchalance.[21]

The Orientalist/racist construction of Arab women is evident in much of contemporary Western feminist writing. It is no exaggeration to suggest that feminist Orientalism is institutionalized in the U.S. and Canada and at the United Nations and in non-governmental organizations.

One manifestation of institutionalized Orientalism appears in the most recent study undertaken by the United Nations Special Task Force on women. In *Women Power: the Arab Debate on Women and Work*, Nadia Hijab studies the recommendations the UN special committee on women made about Arab women. According to Hijab, unlike the recommendations made about women in Africa, Asia, the Pacific, Europe, Latin America and the Caribbean, the recommendations about Arab women started with a cultural definition of the region. Thus the study immediately defines the framework for any discussion of women in the Arab world today: The "Strategy for Arab women in Western Asia to the year 2000 is based on the heritage of Arab-Islamic civilization and the religious and spiritual values of this region, the cradle of the messages of God which affirm the dignity and the freedom of all human beings in this universe."[22]

The same report dedicates a whole section to the family, while its sections on other regions mention the family to a much lesser extent. It makes the Arab family the core of Arab society: "Priority to the work of women who devote their time to family and home affairs and hence ensure the continuity of generations, the cultivation of values and the transmittal of knowledge and expertise from one generation to another...[23]

Eurocentric feminist writings on Arab women are found not only among liberal and radical feminists but in the writings of socialists and Marxists as well. A debate similar to the debate that erupted around feminist racism or racist-feminism [24]. has emerged between Hammami and Rieker[25] and Mai Ghossoub.[26] This debate calls into question the very Orientalist/Eurocentric nature of socialist and Marxist feminism which continues to locate the oppression of Arab and Muslim women as lying within Islam and its symbol, "the veil." For Orientalist-feminists, the oppression of Arab and Muslim women is inherent in their very culture.

In responding to Amos's and Parmar's challenges to middle-class white feminist racism, Barrett and McIntosh [27] concede that their approach to feminism is Eurocentric in so far as it ignores the struggles of other women, Blacks in particular. They, however, reject the charge of racism. Barrett and McIntosh argue for the need to distinguish between racism and Eurocentrism. The distinction between the two is not useful and is perhaps, false too. Ignorance of Third World cultures — the defense cited by the authors for being Eurocentric and not racist — is undoubtedly in part responsible for producing racism in its many forms. But it is not an adequate defense. An equally if not more important factor is the matter of the power relations between the industrialized developed West and the de-industrialized, dependent and underdeveloped Third World. The power relations between North-South and West-East are what Orientalist, Eurocentric and racist feminists ignore.

The line separating Eurocentrism/ignorance from Orientalism/racism is, I submit, a very fine one, so fine that it fades away when one considers North-South and West-East power relations. It fades away when feminists fail to see the national structures (social, economic, political and historical), on the one hand, and international power structures, on the other, as the material bases for feminist theoretical-ideological constructs.

The bankruptcy of feminist thinking about Arab/Muslim women is vividly demonstrated in the plethora of writing produced about social-historical phenomena such as the hammam (the public or common bath), about saints and sanctuaries and most of all about the harem and the veil. One need only remember that much of this writing is produced under the guise of scholarship and respect for "cultural difference" or "multiculturalism." This writing is obsessed with women as sexual objects. Instead of revealing the contexts for such social-historical phenomena, instead of looking at the social-historical role of the saints and sanctuaries as havens for poor North African women, instead of examining the class character of the harem, instead of exploring the social-economic basis of the hammam, Western feminists have used each in the most anti-feminist ways. As the following look at the veil demonstrates, Orientalist feminists ignore Arab women and turn them into mere constructions or categories.

The profusion of literature on the veil — from both East and West — further demonstrates the feminist obsession with women's bodies as *the* symbol of women's oppression. The debates on the veil are too extensive to be fully considered here. A tradition of deconstructing the Orientalist writing about the veil has flourished in the past decade or so. Feminist critics, Arabs, Muslims and Westerners have already pointed out the superficiality, reductionism and specious universality that most discussions on the veil have involved.[28]

I focus on two issues often ignored by most feminist academics both East and West. The first has to do with academia and the purpose of theory. In 1989 I delivered a public talk, "Feminist Orientalism and the Arab Response," at the Department of Middle East and Islamic Studies of the University of Toronto. The audience split into at least two groups. On the one hand, Arab and Muslim academic women, dissatisfied with my assertion that Arab feminism is alive and well, argued "You cannot be Arab/Muslim and feminist." Feminism, they say is "Western by definition." The second group, composed of radical and Marxist feminist academics (mostly but not solely white Canadians) also split. Some confirmed what the first group was saying, albeit posing the question in the liberal-polite manner: "Can Muslims be feminists?" Others were asking for a more radical approach, one that would condemn Arab men as "the major oppressors." Both Eastern and Western feminists, here, have something in common: the inability to think structurally and to analyze globally. This inability, I submit, is the product of separation of theory and practice; few if any in the audience had direct links with what is happening in Arab women's communities here or in the Middle East.

The second issue is linked to the first. One must not be surprised to learn that who benefits most from the "feminist" debate on the veil are neither the women debaters nor their veiled or unveiled subjects. It is rather the patriarchal forces of Islamicist movements, forces currently quite powerful in the Arab and Muslim world. They include middle-class, educated and sometimes professional men, like the leaders of the Islamic movement Hamas in Gaza and the Islamic Salvation Front, the FIS, in Algeria, men who utilise these debates in promoting their ambition for political power. The reason political movements like Hamas and FIS benefit most from these debates is that, on the one hand, the leadership knows more about the topics in the debates than the debaters themselves. On the other hand, most of these debates were not conducted on the ground with women "undergoing veiling" but rather took place in texts, canons and categories. Adherents of such discourse and deconstruction are more interested in who said what and why, than what do we *do* to bring change. My research in Gaza and my encounters with friends in Canada who undertook the veil during our friendship strongly suggests that veiling comes in response to specific historical challenges.

Feminist Organizing in Canada: The Palestinian Specificity

There is ample evidence to support the claim that beginning with the establishment of the state of Israel on the ruins of the Palestinian people, the latter have become a primary target for Orientalist-racism. Robbed of their national identity and denied the right to their history, Palestinians, especially in North America, are expected to be unheard or to be spoken for or represented by someone else. Arab/Palestinian scholars cannot be "objective;" therefore, it is argued, their struggles have to be presented by Israeli or Israeli-sympathetic U.S. or Canadian academics. Similarly, Palestinian women cannot be feminists, independent, or prolific; therefore the Canadian media must analyze the personality of a Palestinian feminist if and when she is given a chance to speak out.

The treatment of Hanan Ashrawi is a case in point. In a CBC prime-time interview on November 4, 1991, an "expert" on the Middle East was asked to "help us understand the Ashrawi phenomenon." The woman interviewer asked the "expert," "Don't you think that Palestinians now are emerging in a new face [sic]. For example, Hanan Ashrawi. Unlike Arafat [sic], she does not look like a terrorist to us." The "expert," a writer for the *Jerusalem Post,* answered agreeably, "Of course, we don't see, as you mentioned, guerrilla fighters [read terrorists] often [who are] unshaved and [who] can hardly speak English." My initial reaction to this broadcast was, Do I cry or laugh?

You laugh because of the image that such so-called objective journalistic pronouncements conjure up: Hanan Ashrawi — for the satisfaction of Canadian curiosity — being turned turning into a bearded bold man! But laughter is very bitter here.

Orientalist discourse on the Palestinians assumed a more complex form at the turn of the century due to the emergence of new political alignments in the region. These included the British and European Jewish settler-capitalist domination of Palestine, accompanied by a new power ideology: zionism. New economic, political and ideological realities have rendered the Palestinian case a relatively unique one.

A careful examination of zionism as a theory and practice, ideology and policies, reveals the very racist nature and character of this movement which, after 1947, became embodied in the state of Israel. Detailed analysis of the zionist-settler project can be found in a number of works.[29]

The question of why Israel receives often unlimited support from the West has been addressed by various authors. There is a general

consensus among progressives that Israel plays a very strategic geopo-
litical role in the midst of an Arab-Muslim population (to differentiate
it from regimes) historically hostile to Western imperialism. In itself,
however, knowledge is passive unless translated into action, into movement. Most progressive forces in the West, including the feminist movement in general and its Jewish sector in particular have continued to see
Israel as anything but racist, colonialist and genocidal to indigenous
Palestinians. Ironically, for many, Israel is still seen as a bastion of
democracy in the Middle East.

Western feminists in general and Western Jewish feminists in particular have strongly resented criticisms of the state of Israel. To silence
critics, they often equate (consciously or otherwise) an anti-Israeli or
anti-zionist position with being anti-Jewish. When criticisms of the state
of Israel are voiced the speakers are often silenced with cries of anti-
semitism. It is politically correct feminism to be anti-apartheid, anti-
racist, anti-colonialist, anti so many things, but do not touch Israel or
criticize zionism.

What I find most striking in my thirteen years of life and activism in
Canada is what I call the permanent leave of absence taken by progressives and Left academics on the Palestinian issue. From 1979 to the early
1980s I was impressed by the solidarity lent by labour, community
groups, political activists, women's groups and academics in support of
the people of Nicaragua, in anti-apartheid demonstrations and on anti-
imperialist marches. My naiveté led me to believe that oppressed Palestinians might find political allies in the streets of Toronto. This turned
out to be wishful thinking. In demonstrations and protests held after the
1982 Israeli invasion of Lebanon and after the massacres in the Sabra and
Shatila refugee camps, participation by the Left fell between meagre and
almost non-existent. Except for a handful of committed voices, the
community of solidarity radically shrinks when Palestinians are involved.

Recently, I was invited to speak on a panel on the Middle East at a
conference on "Peoples' Movements: A View From the South." In the
fifteen minutes I had, I decided to remind the audience of how the
Palestinians came to be refugees. I discussed the forced expulsions, the
massacres and the rapes committed against Palestinian women and men
and also discussed Israel's systematic policy of obliterating the physical

manifestations of Palestinian culture as a means to deny Palestinians not only the right of return but also their identity and history. In my concluding remarks I added that Palestinians have always told their history as it was but the "world community" chooses not to hear and that today, the history of the massacres of Palestinians is being told by Israeli researchers whose information is based on Israeli Defence Force archives. With this conclusion I thought I would be immune from criticisms of being anti-Jewish. After all, I was quoting Israeli-Jewish and semi-establishment men.

I was wrong. Criticism of my presentation came from two men, both of whom resented what they said was "the lack of objectivity" in my presentation. The man from the floor gave me a long lecture on how to be "objective," while the other man, a panelist, lectured me on the importance of numbers and sources. Ironically, my presentation was the only one based on numbers and sources. I left the conference wondering whether my presentation was "not objective" because I am a woman, because I am Palestinian, or both! My frustration and anger were more at myself for being liberally polite and subduedly tactful.

What I felt I should have done was to stand up and say directly and honestly: "But both of you men are strong Jewish lobbyists for the state of Israel. Both of you have strong ties to zionist ideology. Stories of women's rape — even if the woman herself was a Jew — would not be of interest to you. After all, a women's history is not part of men's objectivity. But again I was silenced, in part by the characterization of Jewish Canadians as "objective," "experts" and "rational," which simultaneously denies these qualities to Arab Canadians, particularly those of Palestinian origin.

A similar, yet more profound experience, came during the March 8th events of 1982. As a panelist on women and anti-imperialist struggle, I took up the struggle of Palestinians against the zionist-settler state. I cannot reproduce the exact wording of my presentation at the time. First of all, more than ten years have passed and computer technology was not yet available to me. Secondly, the debate which my speech seemed to have engendered and the accusations of anti-semitism levelled at me had a grave silencing effect on me. All I wished at the time was to forget what had happened. Partly for these reasons and partly because a full account of the story will be offered elsewhere, only the implications of that experience are dealt with here.

My presentation at the panel focused on the parallels between apartheid and zionism. I analyzed the relationship between imperialism and zionism and the impact both had and continue to have on indigenous peoples and concluded the discussion with a quote from the famous poet Mahmoud Darwish, calling for an anti-imperialist agenda for both Arab and Jewish peoples. The strongest memory I retained about the event is that then, like now, I made a clear distinction between zionism as a colonialist, expansionist ideology and Judaism as a religion. However, as I learned afterwards, my message was not only unheard as it was voiced but also distorted.

A small yet influential group of Jewish feminists heard or thought they heard a different speech than my presentation. As Sherry Gorlick's research into the events reveals, Jewish feminists were themselves divided into those who heard me criticizing the racism of the state of Israel and those who heard me criticizing the "Jewish nation."[30] And while the former thought my presentation was strong and legitimate, the latter heard my presentation as a piece of anti-Jewish hatred. The result was a clear split in the movement, with hard feelings and probably hatred.

My experience, however, was not uniquely Canadian. In almost every international women's gathering Palestinian women have had to wage double if not triple struggles to affirm their identity as Arabs, Palestinians and women. Zionism first entered the global feminist debate in 1975 in Mexico at the beginning of the UN decade for women. The long struggle of the Palestinian people and the uncharacteristically Third World focus of that conference were crucial in winning a victory for Third World women's struggles, including Palestinians. The Conference had called for "the elimination of colonialism and neo-colonialism, foreign occupation, zionism, apartheid, racial discrimination in all its forms...." This victory, while more symbolic than anything else, was not insignificant. Five years later, at the 1980 Copenhagen Conference, the resolution "Zionism equals racism" was kept intact, despite official U.S. and Israeli women's "contempt" at the presence of the Palestinian delegation and despite the sabotage campaign both waged at meetings where Palestinian voices were heard.

The UN resolution,"Zionism is racism," was not to live long though. Seven years before the U.S.-led UN decided to revoke the resolution, powerful forces within "feminist internationalism" or "international feminism" were first to act. A 1985 Heritage Foundation study on "U.S. Policy for the UN Conference on Women," scourged the Copenhagen meeting for "all but ignoring the genuine concerns of women" and argued that these issues had "politicized the conference." They wrote that "an agenda of venomous attacks...had been levelled by extremists...against Israel, S.A., the U.S. and the West in general." Before the Nairobi Conference, Senator Nancy Kassebaum (Republican-Kansas) introduced a bill, later passed by the Congress, that authorized the president to "use every available means to ensure that the final Nairobi meeting wouldn't be 'dominated by unrelated political issues.'" [31] Thus, when one Palestinian woman addressed the Conference, reiterating the UN's position on zionism, the official feminist delegates from Israel, the U.S. and South Africa boycotted the forum and tried to sabotage the meetings. During the Nairobi Conference, Arab women, and Palestinians in particular, found themselves in an alien, bitter and frustrating environment.

Why and how did zionism make its entry into the feminist movement? The argument that feminists could not unlink themselves from global politics is only partially correct. Increasingly, the term "global politics" is undergoing a metamorphosis; it is being stripped of its real global character and transformed into "U.S. politics." Western support for the state of Israel along with complicity by the Left are, to say the least, *influenced by the way in which the state of Israel presents itself.*

Israel has succeeded in representing itself not only as a democratic state but as a nation. The state of Israel is also the Jewish state or the state of the Jewish people. This presentation is particularly significant because of the mutuality or sameness assumed between nation (Jews) and the zionist state. Here, the interests of the "nation" (the Jewish people) are deemed by the state to be similar to if not the same as the interest of the state and vice versa. The interest of the state is carried out in the name of the Jewish people — without having to consult them.

It is exactly these arbitrary equations and assumptions made by Israel which feminists fail to understand. It is the inability of Western feminists, and Western Jewish feminists in particular, to differentiate between what is state policy and what is in a people's interest. *It is feminist to support the struggles of Sephardic Jews — the majority of the Jews in Israel — to live as equals in Israel and not to be robbed of their culture and identity. It is also feminist to struggle for and support the plea of Ethiopian Jews who were brought by force to Israel, who had to undergo conversion (to become "really" Jews) and were left to live in utter poverty and humiliation. But it is anti-feminist to continue to support that state in such treatment and most importantly, it is anti-feminist to support that state in its genocidal policies against the indigenous Palestinians. It is also anti-feminist to insist on presenting Israel — the victimizer — everytime a Palestinian voice is allowed to be heard.*

Finally, there is another factor that needs to be addressed here: anti-semitism. It is ironic that anti-semitism, a form of racism that has had a genocidal impact on European Jews, has been misappropriated by the Israeli state and misplaced by the latter's proponents. Arabs, like Jews, are by definition semitic peoples and under no circumstances can they be associated with this phenomenon, which is characteristically Aryan-European. Yet, Israel's successful appropriation of the Holocaust and the subsequent guilt it nourished among Europeans and North Americans has further complicated the political scene and particularly Jewish progressive struggles.

For the majority of Jewish feminists, Israel is a metaphor for survival. This metaphor has a silencing effect, precluding any possibility of debate or of change. Jewish feminists have invested heavily in this metaphor, a metaphor which makes possible the denial of the realities of the Occupation and allows such statements as "There are no Palestinians" or "They are all terrorists" or "Palestinians are grasshoppers or cockroaches." It ultimately requires that the "Occupied" be seen, when they are seen at all, in terms less than human — as murderers, terrorists, parts of a mass, never as persons. Marta Romer, an Australian Jewish feminist and member of Jewish Women in Black says:

> It can be tempting to distance myself from the conflicts of Palestinian Arabs and Israeli Jews, enacted far away in a land I've never seen. But as a Jew I do have, for more than historical reasons, a relationship to Israel and an investment in the ideologies that shape that nation. This

is so because Israel claims the right to speak for all Jews, worldwide — more than this, Israel justifies its actions in the name of our survival as a people...If I am silent, I am in tacit agreement, complicit...If I speak critically, I'm told my voice has no legitimacy — I'm not Israeli, how can I understand?...Or-I'm called a traitor, because to question Israeli policy and action is, I'm told, to endanger not only the survival of the state of Israel, but the very existence of Jews, and to betray our history of suffering, and the lessons learned...This position, widely, sincerely and passionately held, grieves and frightens me.

By Way of Conclusion: What Is To Be Done?

The many forms of silencing and of "Othering" faced by Arab/Muslim feminists in general and Palestinian feminists in particular are not immutable. Increasingly, the forces of oppression and silencing are being challenged, especially from within feminism. Since the Palestinian intifada of 1987 it has become clear that Palestinian women, through their unrelenting struggles, have begun to make a dent — small but effective — in the Western feminist movement. In the past two years Palestinian women have carved out spaces that were previously denied to them in the feminist movement.

The unifying banner for the more than three thousand women who marched on International Women's Day in Toronto in 1991 read: "Make the Links: From Oka to the Gulf — Self-Determination for Native Peoples, Self-Determination for the Palestinian People and Fight Racism." For Palestinian self-determination to be adopted as a goal by this body is no small achievement. A path-breaking event also occurred in January 1992 when the National Organization of Women (NOW) in the U.S. for the first time in its history made the Middle East a major concern, invited Arab women from various countries to address American women and gave a Palestinian activist, Hanan Ashrawi, a space at its opening plenary. Finally, in the March-April 1992 issue, *Ms.* magazine's feature article was "The Feminist Behind the Spokeswoman: A Candid Talk with Hanan Ashrawi."[32]

None of these events, I must add, could have happened before the intifada. More importantly, none of these changes could have happened had it not been for the arduous work of Palestinian women, work strongly supported by anti-zionist Jewish feminists. The dilemma of Marta Romer is not confined to Jewish feminists in Australia. Romer's decision to unlink herself from zionism as an oppressive state ideology and to take up the struggle for democracy and freedom is being adopted by an increasing number of Jewish feminists throughout the West, in North America in particular. Women in Black, albeit small and faced with many difficulties, is nonetheless becoming increasingly vocal.

This article did not set out to break new ground in feminist theory. Nor did it set out to discover a new feminist strategy. I am not sure if there will ever be international feminist unity, nor do I believe there will be a consensus about what feminist culture means. What I wanted to do, instead, is open up taboos in feminist theory and practice. I wanted to shatter the artificial boundaries of inclusion-exclusion erected by feminists, consciously or unconsciously, with their consent, through their complicity or because of their ignorance.

Notes

1. *The Ottawa Citizen,* September 15, 1992, p. A10.
2. E. San Juan, Jr. *Racial Formations/Critical Transformations: Articulations of Power in Ethnic and Racial Studies in the United States* (London and New Jersey: Humanities Press, 1992).
3. *The Ottawa Citizen,* September 4, 1992, p. A1.
4. San Juan. *Op. cit.*
5. Edward Said. *Orientalism* (New York: Vintage Books, 1979).
6. Malek Alloula. *The Colonial Harem* (Minneapolis: University of Minnesota Press, 1986).
7. Rana Kabbani. *Europe's Myth of of the Orient* (Bloomington: Indaina University Press, 1986).
8. Leila Ahmad in "Western Ethnocentrism and Perceptions of the Harem" in *Feminist Studies*, Vol. 8, No. 3, Fall 1982, pp. 520-534 and in "Feminism and Feminist Movements in the Middle East in Aziza al-Hibri, ed. *Women and Islam* (London: Pergamon, 1982).
9. Edward Said in "Representing the Colonized: Anthropology's Interlocutors" in Critical Inquiry, Nos. 19-20, Fall 1989.
10. *Ibid.* p. 47.

11. Martin Bernal. *Black Athena: The Afroasiatic Roots of Classical Civiliza-tion. Vol. 1: The Fabrication of Ancient Greece 1785-1985* (London: Free Association Books, 1987).

12. For more about the zionist social, economic, cultural and physical oblitera-tion of Palestine and Palestinians, see Nahla Abdo in "Colonial Capitalism and Rural Class Formation," a University of Toronto Ph.D. dissertation, 1989, and in "Racism, Zionism and the Palestinian Working Class, 1920-1947" in *Studies in Political Economy*, No. 37, Spring 1992, pp. 19-34, and Sheila Ryan in "The Israeli Economic Policy in the Occupied Areas: Foun-dations of a New Imperialism" in *Middle East Report*, No. 24, 1974.

13. Said. "Representing the Colonized."

14. Bryan Turner. "From Orientalism to Global Sociology" in *Sociology*, Vol. 4, No. 23, 1989, p. 632.

15. Ella Shohat in "Sepahardim in Israel: Zionism from the Standpoint of its Jewish Victims" in *Social Text*, Nos. 19-20, Fall 1988.

16. Alloula. *Op. cit.*

17. Kabbani. *Op. cit.*

18. Marnia Lazreg in "Feminism and Difference: the Perils of Writing as a Woman on Women in Algeria" in *Feminist Studies*, Vol. 14, No. 1, Spring 1988, pp. 81-107.

19. Abdo. "Colonial Capitalism and Rural Class Formation."

20. Lasreg. *Op. cit.*, p. 88.

21. *Ibid.*

22. Nadia Hijab. *Women's Power: the Arab Debate on Women at Work* (Lon-don: Cambridge University Press, 1988), p. 13. Emphasis added.

23. *Ibid.*

24. Valerie Amos and Pratiba Parmar in "Challenging Imperial Feminism" in *Feminist Review*, No. 17, 1984, pp. 3-18.

25. Reza Hammami and Martina Rieker in "Feminist Orientalism or Oriental-ist Marxism" in *New Left Review*, No. 120, 1988.

26. Mai Ghossoub in "A Reply to Hammami and Rieker" in *New Left Review*, No. 120, 1988.

27. Michell Barrett and Mary McIntosh in "Ethnocentrism in Socialist Feminist Theory" in *Feminist Review*, No. 20, 1985, pp. 23-48. For Amina Mama's response to Barrett and McIntosh, see *Feminist Review*, Nos. 17 and 20, 1984 and 1985 respectively.

28. See Reza Hammami in "Women, the Hijab and the Intifada" in *Middle East Report,* Nos. 164-165, May-August 1990, pp. 93-106; Fatima Mernissi in "Muslim Women and Fundamentalism" in *Middle East Report,* July-August 1988, pp. 8-11, and in *Beyond the Veil: Male-Female Dynamics in Modern Muslim Society* (London: al-Saqi, 1985) and *The Veil and the Male Elite* (Reading, Massachusetts: Addison-Wesley Publishing Company, 1992); Nawal Saadai. *Women at Point Zero* (London: Zed Press, 1983); Nahla Abdo in "Women of the Intifada: gender, class and national liberation" in *Race and Class,* Vol. 32, No. 4, 1991, pp. 19-34; Farzaneh Milani. *Veils and Words: the Emerging Voices of Iranian Women Writers* (Syracuse: Syracuse University Press, 1992); Chandra Talpade Mohanty in "Under Western Eyes: Feminist Scholarship and Colonialist Discourses" in Chandra Talpade Mohanty *et. al.,* eds. *Third World Women and the Politics of Feminism* (Bloomington: Indiana University Press, 1991).

29. For work on the racist ideology of the Israeli state, see Nira Yuval-Davis in "Front and Rear: Sexual Division of Labour in the Israeli Military" in H. Afshar, ed., *Women, State and Ideology* (London: Macmillan, 1986), pp. 185-203 and in *The Veil and the Male Elite.* For an analysis of zionist racism from the viewpoint of its Jewish victims, particularly from that of Arab-Jewish women, see Ella Shohat in "Sepahardim in Israel" and in "Gender in Hollywood's Orient" in *Middle East Report,* No. 162, January-February, 1990, pp. 40-42. For an historical analysis of the zionist colonial-settler movement and its impact on indigenous Palestinians, see Nahla Abdo in "Colonial Capitalism" and in "Racism, Zionism and the Palestinian Working Class." The works cited cover many aspects of the Israeli-Palestinian conflict but fall short of the impact of the conflict on Western feminimism and do not address the effect of zionism on Western feminism.

30. Sherry Gorelick in "The Changer and the Changed: Methological Reflections on Studying Jewist Feminists" in Alison M. Jaggar and Susan R. Bordo, eds. *Gender/Body/Knowledge* (New Brunswick: Rutgers University Press, 1989) pp. 336-358.

31. Ellen Cantarow in "Zionism, Anti-Semitism and Jewish Identity in the Women's Movement" in *Middle East Report,* September-October 1988, pp. 39 and 41.

32. *Ms.,* Vol. II, No. 5, March-April 1992.

II
POLITICIZING SEX
AND SEXUALITY

WHO GETS TO BE FAMILY

Some Thoughts on the Lesbian

and Gay Fight for Equality

Carol Allen

The struggle for equal rights has acted as a mobilizing force for those of us who experience discrimination because we are lesbians or gay men. In Canada, many barriers have been broken during the past twenty-five years, and in 1993 we live in a society where lesbians and gay men are protected from discrimination by eight provincial human rights codes and by the federal code.[1] The equality provisions of the Canadian Charter of Rights and Freedoms[2] have been interpreted by the courts to include sexual orientation as an protected analogous ground.[3] In light of such substantial legal change, it is time to examine the effects on the lives of lesbians and gay men and to consider where we go from here. What have we learned so far in the struggle for equality and how will these lessons help us in the future? Unfortunately, this type of evaluation and inquiry is not taking place to the extent that it should.

Many lesbians and gay men seem content to accept the idea that protection on the basis of sexual orientation is the linchpin that will secure equal treatment in law and ultimately in society. Few realize that sexual orientation is a neutral term that also protects heterosexuals and that in the hands of a homophobic legal system it may be used to further discriminate against lesbians and gay men. Even more frightening is that this is just *one* problem with the term that we are betting our collective futures on. Although we may know who the term "sexual orientation" was meant to protect, its neutrality leaves it open to judicial interpretation. This should give us cause for concern. The numerous problems with continuing to use the term "sexual orientation" are not what I want to discuss here. Rather, I want to move on to another controversial issue, the fight for family and spousal status.

It is too simplistic to say that lesbians and gays are entitled to family benefits. Few of us would disagree, however, that careful thought and reflection is required before we voice our wholehearted agreement. We must consider what "family" means in the context of our particular social and legal structure and what it means from a historical and cultural standpoint. At the very least, we must reflect on the particular meaning "family" has for us individually, for our own culture and for the broader society.

We all know that from a social and legal standpoint the "family" is considered to be a natural entity, the bedrock of our society. Marriage between two adults of the opposite sex is society's binding and unifying force. Sexuality is thought to be best confined within the boundaries of monogamous heterosexual marriage. As such, the "family" and the institution of marriage act to regulate and repress all but one expression of sexuality. This, as we all know, is heterosexuality.

Today's "family" is privatized and nuclear and held out as the model for social and economic stability. Its roots are patriarchal and oppressive to women and children and to anyone who challenges this idealized lie. Given its context, "family" has more frequently than not had an instinctual definition for most of us, one that is unfortunately based more on stereotyped assumptions rather than on reflections of *our* experiences. If we do not take the time to separate truth from fiction, the implications are serious for lesbians and gay men.

Unfortunately, we need only look at the types of arguments being made before the courts by lesbians and gay men seeking equality and specifically at the arguments for family benefits and spousal status to realize that many are not yet separating truth from fiction. Consequently, lesbians and gays have gone into court and painted a picture of their lives that is as close to an idealized heterosexual life as possible so as to demonstrate that there is but a minimal difference between lesbian and gay couples and heterosexual couples.

There may be strategic reasons for doing this, but the effect of but-for-the-sex-of-our-partners-we-are-just-like-you is the same. Had they been successful, and to the extent that they have been, we are left to wonder how many lesbians and gays are really able to take advantage of the victory. Certainly, those whose conceptions and experiences of family are different could not. Our unsuccessful court appearances may have been a victory in disguise. As unbelievable as it may seem, the homophobic attitudes of judges have given us something precious: time. Time to reconsider what we mean by equality, so when we re-enter the courtroom, we will be less preoccupied with sameness and more concerned with presenting arguments that challenge the institutions that penalize us because of our difference.

Let me be clear. We want equality. We demand it. But not at the cost of buying into social and legal institutions which will accept our membership only on their terms. Simply because definitions of spouse include lesbians and gays, simply because we have access to family benefits, does not mean that we have brought about a necessary and long overdue social awakening. We do not change the institutions of marriage or family simply by our inclusion. These institutions are flawed at their very core.   Lesbians and gays who are considering litigation need to take a look at who they are and to acknowledge their true interests. Race and class determine interest and access to the legal system. We must stop making legal arguments which, if successful, will only help other professional, white, middle-class, able-bodied lesbians and gays, whose family form looks very much like the traditional heterosexual ideal.

If we want benefits, the approach we take to getting them must take the bigger social and economic picture into consideration. We cannot fool ourselves into believing that these issues are only ours. Changes in our society's definition of "family" or "spouse" have far-ranging effects on the entire social, political and economic system. This will necessarily change the basis of entitlement to social benefits and how legal rights and responsibilities are imposed. Such change affects everyone.

We need to be sure that our arguments include rather than exclude those of us whose family structures are different. Some of us live in collective houses with people we consider our family. Some of us are non-monogamous, others are monogamous and don't live together, still others have relationships which don't look like anything mentioned here. If this is the reality for some, why should we promote legal strategies aimed at securing benefits that will only apply to some lesbians and gay men? The legal arguments used to date indicate that a choice has been made about who gets the status and the resultant benefits and responsibilities.

Part of that bigger picture means looking outside our needs as lesbians or gay men for a moment and considering what a particular benefit plan was meant to achieve. Such consideration might have prevented one argument made before the Ontario Court (General Division) in *Haig and Birch*.[4] Section 3(1) of the *Canadian Human Rights Act* (*CHRA*) sets out the grounds upon which discrimination is prohibited. It states, "For all purposes of this Act, race, national or ethnic origin, colour, religion, age, sex, marital status, disability, and conviction for which a pardon has been granted are prohibited grounds of discrimination."

While grounds such as race and sex are "neutral," I am sure we can all recognize that in the area of race and sex discrimination, it is women and people of Colour who most need this protection in our society, not men or white people. In *Haig and Birch* complainants argued that Section 3 of the *CHRA* was unconstitutional because it did not list sexual orientation as a protected ground and that this under-inclusiveness ran contrary to the equality provision in Section 15(1) of the Canadian Charter of Rights and Freedoms. In this case, a strategic choice was made to ask the court either to declare Section 3 unconstitutional or read in protection for lesbians and gays. The court found the section unconstitutional and gave the government six months to either amend the Act or appeal the decision. If not, Section 3 of the *CHRA* would be invalid.

The litigants were prepared to risk losing protection for all those for whom the Act provided protection against discrimination. This was a callous and shortsighted strategy, one which exemplifies the blinkers currently worn by some lesbian but mostly by gay litigants. How dare they take such a risk without consulting with the people who would have seen their rights under the *Canadian Human Rights Act* eroded? Remember who Section 3 protected. It protected among others disabled people, people of Colour, women, religious minorities. I am not in any way saying that lesbians and gay men should not be similarly protected from discrimination. What I am saying is that we need to be very careful in choosing our legal strategies. We cannot act so as to roll back the small gains that have been made by other disadvantaged and disempowered groups.

Let me give you another example. Poor lesbians on social assistance will likely suffer economically when the definition of spouse changes in the applicable Acts. Today, for example, if a lesbian couple lives together and one is on social assistance and the other is not, the government does not consider them spouses and therefore does not assume that a relationship of dependency exists.[5] For many years, if a woman on social assistance lived with a man she was deemed to be his dependent. This was the infamous "spouse in the house" policy of the Ontario government. Many women's organizations fought against this discriminatory policy and it is no longer in force. There is no reason to believe that this policy will not be reactivated, especially in light of government initiatives to cut back on social service benefits. It is more likely that if and when the definition of spouse is broadened, poor lesbians will be one group that is hit where it can least afford it. Aside from the fact that the relationship of economic dependency that is automatically assumed to exist when one is female and considered a spouse may not in reality exist, there are numerous problems with broadening the definition of spouse.

Even where one woman is working, statistics show that women earn much less than men and are likely to be in jobs which have little or no benefits. Women of Colour and disabled women earn even less and have fewer opportunities because of their race and disability. Therefore, if the social assistance received by one lesbian is reduced or eliminated, the result is that these two women are placed in a more economically vulnerable position than they would have been had the definition of spouse not been changed. It is imperative that we think through carefully the ramifications of the arguments that we make to the courts. We must consider both the positive and negative aspects of every argument we make, the ramifications of its success and failure, and we must do this with more than ourselves in mind.

An immediate problem facing all women is how to achieve sex equality. Women must battle the social, political and economic effects of a society structured upon sex inequality. Lesbians as women *and* as lesbians face particular discrimination because we are lesbians *and* because we are women. Furthermore, Black lesbians face discrimination *because we are Black, because we are women and because we are lesbians.* In this context, white gay men have advantages over lesbians because they are men and therefore do not experience sex and race discrimination. They are advantaged because they earn more, have more opportunities and have more social and political power because they are white and because they are men. That they are gay does not, cannot, neutralize this power. Our fight for equality, whether on the legal or political front, must not lose sight of the fact that some of us are doubly or more disadvantaged. It is time to recognize on more than a superficial level that discrimination against sexual orientation has a gender and race cut to it.[6]

Does this mean we should not be entitled to benefits that flow from family and spousal status? No. If these public and private benefits are going to be provided on the basis of whether a particular collection of individuals is a family or whether a particular relationship is spousal, then the basis of entitlement should not be discriminatory. However, we owe it to ourselves to argue for broad definitions of both spouse and family and to ensure that in any legal argument claiming entitlement to family or spousal benefits we seriously consider the purpose of the particular benefit scheme. Again, we do not want to put ourselves in a situation where the legal arguments we develop have the potential to roll back gains made by other disadvantaged groups.

The task we have before us is monumental. We need to remember that as lesbians we challenge gender stereotypes inside the family and in society generally. We challenge the presumption of male access to our bodies and in defining our sexuality. We cannot risk inclusion into a system which has historically oppressed lesbians and gays and subjugated women. We must argue for fundamental changes in determining benefit entitlement so it is not exclusively linked to marriage, monogamy or kinship. We risk too much if we do any less.

Notes

1. The Federal government has recently introduced an amendment to include sexual orientation as a protected ground under the *Canadian Human Rights Act.* This new amendment comes after years of struggle to protect

lesbians and gay men over whom the Federal government may have jurisdiction.

2. Section 15(1) of the Charter reads, "Every individual is equal before and under the law and has the right to the equal protection and benefit of the law without discrimination and, in particular, without discrimination based on race, national, or ethnic origin, colour, religion, sex, age or mental or physical disability."

3. In *Veysey v. Correctional Services Canada*, the Federal government acknowledged that sexual orientation is analogous to the protected grounds listed in Section 15 of the Charter.

4. Fortunately, these problems were resolved by the Ontario Court of Appeal which held that sexual orientation should be *read into* Section 3 of the *Canadian Human Rights Act.*

5. For years, feminists have fought with governments over what have become known as "spouse in the house" policies. Under these policies, if a woman on social assistance lived with a man he was deemed to be her spouse and she was considered dependent on him. Social services often resorted to incredibly intrusive measures to determine whether a man was residing with a female recipient of social assistance. For example, it was not uncommon to check closets, the number of tooth brushes, look under beds for men's shoes, etc. In Ontario, this policy is apparently no longer in force. However, there is no reason to expect that it could not be used in situations where lesbians are living together. Rather that waiting for this type of policy to further disadvantage lesbians we should consider how we want economic dependency to be defined in relation to our lives.

6. When we talk about sexual orientation we do so as though its inclusion will protect us all equally. It is assumed that discrimination is the same for all lesbians and gay men. This is not true. Sexual orientation will protect white gay males the most and does little to alleviate the multiple oppression faced by lesbians and lesbians and gays of Colour.

TALKIN' BOUT A REVELATION

Feminist Popular Discourse

on Sexual Abuse

Debi Brock

Whostandard{W}hen I first wrote about the sexual abuse[1] of children and young
people in 1984 my purpose was to offer a critique of the then
recently released Federal government sponsored *Report of the Committee on Sexual Offences Against Children and Youths* (known as the
Badgley Report, after its chairperson).[2] I was initially interested in how
issues that feminists make visible get taken up by the state after pressure
from feminists only to become legal, medical and administrative categories or problems which may bear little relation to our original demands or intents.[3] Capitalist and patriarchal relations are deeply
embedded in our state institutions and practices and state responses to
our demands often do little in the way of practically addressing the
oppression of women, children and adolescents. State responses may
ultimately result in our losing control over how social problems like
sexual abuse are thought about and addressed. In doing this work, I
became increasingly uncomfortable with how feminists put the issue
forward, with what we might refer to as "popular feminist discourse on
sexual abuse." I offer a number of cautions about the approaches that
have general currency among feminists. This is not intended as a comprehensive critique but merely to draw attention to a number of areas
where it is necessary to challenge prevailing assumptions. Nor is this a
critique of the burgeoning literature which, though much more complex
than what boils down in popular discourse, also poses these same
problems.

While children and young people (primarily female) are the targets of sexual abuse, its existence and extent is, as MacLeod and Saranga assert, a "problem of masculinity," of how masculinity is socially constructed so men can sexually abuse children and young people.[4] To begin by addressing sexual abuse as a problem of masculinity is to question from the outset the "cycle of abuse" theory which has gained general acceptance — some feminist acceptance included. This theory, that those who have been sexually abused become abusers of their own children, has been accepted rather uncritically. How can this make sense, when most who are abused are female and the vast majority of abusers are male? Women rarely sexually abuse their children, whether they themselves have been sexually abused or not.[5] The perspective appears to be derived from the more orthodox literature on sexual abuse which categorizes women as colluders in the sexual abuse of their children by men, assigning to women responsibility for somehow allowing it to happen. "Blaming mother" is generally rejected by feminists, as it shifts attention away from the real male perpetrator. But nevertheless, the notion of a "cycle of abuse" lingers on.[6]

The call to action against sexual abuse is supported by horrifying stories of the coercion and trauma inflicted upon the victim/survivor. While this certainly speaks to the reality of a great number of women's and girls' lives, it is not the entire story. How, then, do women who have experienced sexual abuse in a non-coercive context locate and make sense of their experiences? What about those who participated not because they were violently coerced but because they "didn't know that it was wrong"? What about those who found the experience pleasurable (and later felt ashamed about that)? Or those for whom molestation was such a part of the fabric of their everyday lives that it was "just the way that it was"? Without presenting a wide range of stories conveying how sexual abuse occurs, we do not get a picture of how normalized (and therefore all the more insidious) sexual abuse can be in the lives of women and girls. It is difficult for those who have had these other abusive experiences to connect their abuse with the sensational stories that have so much currency in feminist discussion, media reports and in the first-person accounts of traumatic abuse now part of the dramatic "true story" genre of mass market paperbacks.[7]

Of course, the ability of children and young people to give *informed* consent to sexual activity with an older male is rightly questioned. Any form of sexual contact constitutes an abuse of power on the part of the perpetrator and the absence of physical or psychological force does not justify the act.[8] But knowing this does not address the issue at hand.

I suspect that the conflation of sexual abuse and "sexual violence" adds to the obfuscation. This conflation identifies all sexual abuse as inherently violent towards women; it does so to identify and to convey women's social powerlessness and to link a range of practices inflicted upon women as a result of this lack of social power. Use of the term "sexual violence" obscures the different ways that sexual abuse occurs. It would be less analytically fuzzy to map out patterns of "sexual exploitation," a term that identifies the operative power relations without conjuring up images of beatings and other forms of physical force which may not have been part of the sexual abuse. Liz Kelly also raises the point that we need to account for the "range and complexity" in how women define their abuse, develop terms for those and locate them on a "continuum" of sexual violence.[9] While such accounting is essential, Kelly's approach does not address the problems of using the term "sexual violence" as the description, which can actually work against her intentions. Nor is the continuum a very useful model, as it can be used as a linear model, with an implicit hierarchy of experience, from the mild (i.e., inappropriate touching) to the horrific. To think about sexual exploitation through a *mapping* of experiences allows us to understand better the complexities of women's experiences and permits the inclusion of other, non-sexual experiences (for example, beatings, racism, poverty) which are part of oppression and exploitation. Then we might get a more integrated picture of women's lives and the place of sexual abuse in them, a picture obscured by the use of a continuum model. This leads to a further concern.

All too often, analyses and discussion of the dimensions and impact of sexual abuse are separate from consideration of other abuses of power which women experience, particularly physical violence. Where physical violence is recognized as contributing to the victim's trauma (for example, when it accompanies sexual abuse), it appears to be subordinated to the impact of the sexual acts. Physical violence may also be occurring apart from sexual abuse and may have a far more traumatic impact than the sexual abuse. For example, young women and girls may be subject to frequent beatings at different times and in different contexts than the sexual abuse (and the beatings may also be inflicted by a person other than the one responsible for the sexual abuse). In Canada, at least, this subordination of physical violence to sexual abuse has had an impact on government policy. When the Badgley Committee was mandated to investigate the sexual abuse of children and youth in Canada, following demands by feminists that the state take action, it did so by addressing sexual abuse as a discrete phenomenon. The findings and recommendations of the Badgley Committee have substantively shaped changes to legal and social policy since their report's release; for example, through the passage of Bill C-15 which introduced numerous revisions to sex-related legislation in the Criminal Code. While studies undertaken by the Committee found that the rate of physical violence was higher than that of sexual abuse (which was itself alarmingly high), the studies failed to address the significance of physical violence, as it was beyond their mandate.

Finally, emotional trauma need not be the direct result of physical and sexual abuse or even of the abuse of male power. Everyday conditions like poverty, racism, or neglect, or traumatic events like the early death of a parent also shape who we are. These cannot be simply dismissed as separate issues. Any of these factors may do more to shape our identity (and our pain) than the experience sexual abuse. We need to be more aware of how all of our experiences intersect and merge. Sexual abuse cannot be considered in isolation.

An example of how sexual abuse becomes interpreted as key to shaping who we are is revealed in the belief that it can "cause" women and girls to become prostitutes. At least one study of prostitutes has found a high incidence of sexual abuse in the backgrounds of female prostitutes.[10] If there really is a direct causal relationship, a great many more women and girls would work in prostitution than currently do. I suspect that a high incidence of sexual abuse among prostitutes indicates just how common sexual abuse is generally, particularly if a broad definition is used in the data collection. And if one is looking for evidence of problem sexual histories to attempt to prove a point, studying a group of prostitutes is often assumed to be a good place to start, given the sex-related character of their work. Prostitutes have been scrutinized more frequently than almost any group one can imagine.

A commonly-held perspective is that women become prostitutes because they learn through the experience of sexual abuse that they are valued most as sexual objects. That women are paid more for prostitution than almost any other form of female labour might appear to confirm this logic. However, many women who have been sexually abused also become feminists who *oppose* prostitution on the grounds that it objectifies women. Does the experience of sexual abuse cause some women to become prostitutes and some feminists? To pose a causal link is reductionist and simplistic. We need to account for other factors — like economic need — which come into play in determining who finds work in prostitution.[11]

In feminist discourse, abuse becomes constitutive of the identity of women who have been sexually abused. Other experiences are subordinated to the power of the narrative of the victim/survivor. Women who reveal themselves to have been sexually abused when young risk having this fact become seen as the crux of their identity and *the* formative experience of their life. Other events in or conditions of their lives appear to take on lesser importance. Their actions are perceived always as related to their status as victims/survivors, making the abuse the root of personality and the source of troubles. While we want women to break the silence that has surrounded sexual abuse by telling their stories, this prescriptivism can mean that to reveal having been sexually abused as a child is to lose further control over others' perceptions of yourself. How then can women take control of their lives by speaking about their sexual abuse?

In feminist analysis, "sexual abuse" has become a monolithic category, a totalizing discourse that blurs women's experiences while it seeks to uncover them. This is accomplished, in part, through originating analysis in a unitary category, "women."[12] It is a basic truism of feminism that the way sexuality is gendered is the cornerstone for the oppression of women; through the use or threat of sexual abuse and rape our sexual capacities are always available to men without our consent. It is a form of oppression which all women are subject to, which we all experience simply in being women and knows no boundaries of race, class, age or sexual orientation. But emphasizing what unites us so powerfully also blurs differences in how women experience abuse. We need to know how abuse is experienced differently *by women* and how to devise strategies for addressing it which do not focus *solely on gender*. Some feminist therapists encourage women to re-think their lives to fit the narrative of the victim\survivor into the context of patriarchal social relations. But the "victim of patriarchy" only makes partial sense of the experiences of a young Black female who is sexually abused by an older white male or of the experiences of the girl from an impoverished family who must share a room with an older, abusive brother. When devising strategies for addressing sexual abuse, we need also to account for the diversity of conditions which women face in, for example, reporting the abuse of their children to social service agencies or to police. The Brixton Black Women's Centre points out that Black women who report abuse then have to face the racism of the police and the courts toward themselves, their children and the perpetrator of the abuse. The manner of redress is likely to be shaped more by racism than be a response to the abuse.[13]

Perhaps once we show how oppression like sexual abuse reveals a "collection of experiences,"[14] entailing both similarities and differences, the term "women" will develop a more fluid, open interpretation and will become easier for us to use in this context. Knowing women's different experiences of subordination is essential for understanding women's lives, making connections and forging a strategy for political action. The personal is as ever political. However, the current thinking on sexual abuse may be leading us away from rather than toward clarifying the dimensions of sexual abuse and what we need to do to stop it. Feminist analysis must be a tool to help us to understand and to act to change our lives and the social relations which have made them as they are.

Notes

1. Here I use the term "sexual abuse" to include both incestuous and non-incestuous relations, since this term is adequate for the points I want to raise. I want to note, however, that there is no single agreed-upon definition of sexual abuse. The main points of contention are over the range

of sex-related acts to be considered sexual abuse (for example, whether verbal comments or limited but inappropriate touching should count as sexual abuse) and over the appropriate age boundaries for defining child sexual abuse. The latter is important in determining when a young person can give informed consent to non-coercive, non-incestuous sexual activities.

2. The Badgley Committee carried out a comprehensive study of the incidence and prevalence of sexual abuse in Canada and made recommendations for changes to legal and social policy. See the Committee on Sexual Offences Against Children and Youth. *Sexual Offences Against Children* (Ottawa: Department of Supply and Services, 1984). For critiques of the report, see John Lowman *et. al.*, eds. *Regulating Sex* (Burnaby: Simon Fraser University School of Criminology, 1986).

3. See Deborah Brock and Gary Kinsman in "Patriarchal Relations Ignored: An Analysis and Critique of the Badgley Report on Sexual Offences Against Children and Youths" in Lowman, *op. cit.* Thanks to Gary for the many fruitful discussions about sex, the state in general and sexual abuse in particular

4. Mary MacLeod and Esther Saraga in "Challenging the Orthodoxy: Towards and Feminist Theory and Practice" in *Feminist Review*, No. 28, January 1988, p. 43.

5. Louise Brown also raises this point in her very useful (and brave) critique of recent literature on sexual abuse. See "The Personal is Apolitical" in *Women's Review of Books*, Vol. VII, No. 6, March 1990, p. 1.

6. For a more comprehensive critique of the notion of colluding mothers, see MacLeod and Saraga, *op. cit.*

7. Linda Gordon also notes in her study of family violence that the media pick up on the sensational, dramatic cases of violence and abuse in families, thereby missing the everyday character of violence and how it occurs. See *Heroes of Their Own Lives* (New York: Viking, 1988).

8. Again, however, the matter is not so cut and dried as we would hope, given the problems of age and consent noted earlier. The most disputed point involves same-sex sexual activity between older men and young men or boys, where there is no imbalance in gender power relations (unlike in cases involving older men and young women or girls), but unequal power relations based on age remain. Many gay men have asserted that their

initial sexual experiences when young were with older men and recall these experiences as positive and pleasurable (which is not to say that all do, as testimonies at the 1991 inquiry into the wide-spread sexual abuse of young people at the Mount Cassel orphanage makes clear.) For more discussion of same-sex cross-generational sex, see the debate in the pages of *The Body Politic,* a now defunct Toronto-based lesbian and gay liberation newspaper in the late 1970s. The debate, which followed the publication of the pro cross-generational sex article, "Men Loving Boys Loving Men," has been reprinted. See Ed Jackson and Stan Persky, eds. *Flaunting It!* (Toronto: Pink Triangle Press, 1982). I maintain that sexual activity between an older man and a boy is an abuse of power by the older male (although I admit that I am not fully sure of what age limits are appropriate in determining when the impermissible becomes permissable), even though the sexual activity may not be abusive in its effects but a welcome experience for the younger male. To dismiss unequal power relations in instances where the sexual encounters were pleasurable for the younger male is to leave the problem of masculinity unchallenged.

9. Liz Kelly in "What's in a Name? Defining Child Sexual Abuse" in *Feminist Review, op. cit.,* pp. 65-73. See also Liz Kelly. *Surviving Sexual Violence* (Minneapolis: University of Minneapolis Press, 1988).

10. For example, see Florence Rush. *The Best Kept Secret* (New Jersey: Prentice Hall, 1980).

11. As some activist prostitutes and former prostitutes have asserted, it is also the case that being a feminist and being a prostitute are not mutually exclusive. They state that participation in prostitution reveals sexual autonomy rather than sexual objectification.

12. On the problems of using the unitary category "women," see Denise Riley. *Am I That Name?* (Minneapolis: University of Minnesota Press, 1988).

13. Marlene T. Bogle in "Brixton Black Women's Centre Organizing on Child Sexual Abuse" *in Feminist Review, op. cit.*

14. For more on this emphasis, see Carla Freccero in "Notes of a Post-Sex Wars Theorizer" in Marianne Hirsch and Evelyn Fox Keller, eds. *Conflicts in Feminism* (New York: Routledge, 1990).

DIFFERENT PLACES WE ARE BUILDING

Lesbians Discuss Politics and Organizing

This discussion was facilitated by Sheila Block and edited by Ann Decter.

T he last decade has seen profound changes in lesbian and gay men's visibility, organizing and lives. Ten years ago, white lesbians and lesbians of Colour were criticizing mainstream feminism for ignoring lesbian issues; the lesbian AI baby boom was but a gleam in a maternal dyke's eye. AIDS was just beginning its deadly path through Canada; Toronto was still shaking from the bath house raids; there were no publicly-elected "out" officials in Canada. The ground on which changes have taken place has been created by the organizing work of lesbians on our own, in conjunction with gay men and occasionally with non-lesbian feminists. Lesbian publishing has seen periodicals like *The Body Politic*, *Broadside* and *Rites* come and go, *Fireweed*'s *Lesbiantics* issues, groundbreaking books such as *Dyke Versions*, *Lesbians in Canada* and most recently, Sister Vision's release of the first lesbian of Colour anthology, *Piece of My Heart*. Lesbians have founded key community-based organizations such as Asian Lesbians of Toronto (ALOT) and worked in conjunction with gay men on the 1988 International Lesbian and Gay People of Colour Conference in Toronto, the 1990 Gay Games in Vancouver, in Two-Spirited Peoples of the First Nations, Desh Pardesh and a in wealth of agencies fighting the AIDS epidemic. Lesbians have joined with straight and bisexual women to defeat the criminal law on abortion and prevent another being adopted. It has been a decade of building in the face great opposition, but deep in the chill of continental conservatism and state censorship lesbian visibility has continued to rise, lesbian organizing has continued to grow, and lesbians themselves have continued to provide feminism with an informed perspective on

117

sexism and heterosexism, as well as massive organizing energy. It has long been recognized but rarely been said that lesbians are hugely over-represented — relative to the percentage of lesbians in the general female population — in the forefront and in the grassroots of feminist organizing. Quite simply, lesbians have provided a commitment to feminism that has, throughout the second wave, been essential to the existence of the movement.

On a cold Saturday in February 1993, nine lesbians came together to discuss issues in organizing, current issues and those of the past decade. They were Beth Brant, a writer whose primary activist work is within the Native community, where she conducts workshops with Native women, encouraging the spoken and written telling of their stories; Carol Camper, a writer/visual artist who works at Hassle Free Women's Clinic and is active in the Black Coalition for AIDS Prevention (Black CAP) and came out politically and as a lesbian in 1988; Sharon Fernandez, a visual artist working in the Toronto community since 1984, primarily with women of Colour, who was the first woman of Colour on the collective at the Toronto Women's Bookstore; Connie Fife, a Cree writer from Saskatchewan who works on HIV and AIDS in her community as a PHA supporting parole worker; Amy Gottlieb, an artist and teacher and activist in the Jewish Women's Committee to End the Occupation of the West Bank and the Gaza and in Lesbians Making History, an oral history group exploring the lives of women who loved women in the 1940s, 1950s and 1960s in Toronto; Sandra Haar, a writer/artist who works at the Toronto Women's Bookstore and with *Fireweed: A Feminist Quarterly*; Mona Oikawa, a *sansei* — third-generation Japanese Canadian — writer, student and editor who helped found Asian Lesbians of Toronto (ALOT) with Sharon Fernandez, Tamai Kobayashi and Pui Ming Lee; Natasha Singh, a South Asian lesbian, born in Jasper, Alberta, who currently studies English and history at Concordia University; Kristyn Wong, a student and community activist who helped start the Lesbian Youth Peer Support (LYPS) in Toronto and is involved with The National Forum on East Asian Youth and Alienation.

Homophobia

CAROL: I work in a setting that is not very high up on the homophobia scale. It's a pretty good place to work if you're gay or lesbian. But it comes up sometimes. I remember one of my co-workers — who's also a long-term friend — said something one day referring somebody to speak to me because I was "more firmly entrenched in the lifestyle." I laughed at her and said, "Your homophobia is showing, using words like 'entrenched.' That's not a very positive word." She laughed and admitted it. Sometimes you confront like that. That everyday homophobia is always there. I'm a board member at a place where a lot of the people are gay and lesbian, but some aren't. I don't think there's a lot of dialogue about sexuality. A lot of the people who are straight, who are perhaps there on a volunteer basis, I don't know that they really want to talk about it. They're just committed to the cause, so to speak, to be there, work there, do their best not to be offensive. But it's not like they really want to know what I do when I go to bed. That's homophobia too, because it's fear. You're not sharing all of yourself and you have this feeling that they don't want to know.

CONNIE: Interesting. I work specifically now with other two-spirited people. But it's the first time in my community that I have chosen to work specifically with others like me. Up until now I've always been within the mainstream Native women's community. I think I know that homophobia exists in our community. We've been as colonized as the next person. But I've also been fortunate that I've been around a lot of very strong straight Native women who have a very clear understanding of who I am, who they are and what our responsibilities are. The one time that the homophobia was really evident was when I was on a board and there were three or four other lesbians on that board. They tried to get rid of the board because of the lesbian content. And the community just re-elected us. Nobody wanted us to leave. It's there. I don't feel like our community has dealt with homophobia. I don't think it's even begun to, just in the same way that we haven't dealt with sexism or internalized racism. I feel very strongly about that.

BETH: It seems like part of the question has to do with, "How do you come out in a group that's not all lesbian or gay?" I think about this every time I go into a setting where I know I may be the only one. Like you use terms like "my partner, she…" SHE, did you all get that? I never really quite know what it is I'm going to say. But inevitably I know that I have to say it, I want to say it, of course. One time, a long time ago, the early 1970s, I was working at organizing some conference. There was a woman from the Revolutionary Communist Party. I used the word homophobia and she didn't even know what that meant. I said, "This is what I'm talking about, that you don't even know what this word means, so how can you even begin to think about the rest of our lives?" To me that's the first step — how does one come out in a group, and do we want to? I always want to, I don't want to deny any part of myself.

CAROL: I've really been tokenized as a lesbian. I've been tokenized as everything. In one of the jobs that I had a few years ago — I'd been there for years, my husband worked at the same place and in front of the world we split up and I came out — they always knew I was Black so they could tokenize me for that reason right away. Then later I came out as an incest survivor, so I was immediately tokenized. I worked in a shelter for street kids. Once I was out as an incest survivor then, immediately, any opinion I had about sexual abuse, its after effects, causes, settings, anything, was suspect. I was no longer objective. Then, when I came out as a lesbian I was actually told by my boss, "Don't flaunt it." It's hard to come out, I want to be out. I don't hide my sexuality (except from my ex-in-laws, although my ex-husband probably told them). Those are some of the consequences of being out. They're maybe not as harsh as some, but you still can get tokenized.

BETH: You can also get very hurt. You could have people get up and walk out on you — your own people — and that hurts a great deal. But it also enrages, which is another form of energy. Although it can work the opposite way on bad days.

CAROL: People hide behind their ignorance too. As if they are ignorant of things like people who are of another colour, or like people who are of another anything, then they hide behind their ignorance, as if that were not a part of homophobia or not a part of racism.

SANDRA: This is the sort of stage I'm at with dealing with the Jewish community. It's amazing for me to hear about people going into their "own communities" and being out. I have a real terror about it. It seems like an impossible thing, like addressing homophobia in the community is a huge, daunting task. But I feel that within the feminist community, grassroots feminism, there is a lot of acknowledgement of lesbian participation.

But sexuality really isn't discussed. Straight women are like, "Yeah I realize that there are a lot of lesbians here and homophobia is an issue." It's always "We'll leave it to the lesbians to discuss it." If there is anything to do with sexuality or homophobia, the lesbians will take care of it. We will accept what they say, because we can't understand it or something. I find that particularly frustrating because for me the issue has to belong to everyone. I don't see that happening.

AMY: I was thinking about my relationship to the Jewish community, more specifically about the progressive Jewish community, mixed organizations that have been around for a number of years. A group of us from the Jewish Women's Committee to End the Occupation of the West Bank and Gaza (JWCEO) go to the Passover seders that are held at the United Jewish People's Order. Most of us are lesbians, a few are bisexual or straight. We are there because we want to be at this progressive seder, a place for our feminist voice, our voice that speaks strongly against the Occupation, a voice that is clearly about women being together at a progressive seder, celebrating the struggle of Jews against persecution and the struggle of all people against oppression and persecution. There have been varying levels of comfort in that situation, but one thing that we've always felt comfortable about is the fact that we go en masse, we have our own table. Several years ago at the seder, we were singing that Holly Near song, "We are a gentle, angry people." There's a verse that says we are gay and lesbian people — that was left off the song sheet. When the singing stopped we sang it. And other people sang it too. But what I remember is our clear women's voices asserting our identity from one part of the room. This year's seder mentioned homophobia as one of the many oppressions we must all struggle against.

CAROL: It's hard to be the only anything. It's hard to be the only lesbian. I've been in work situations where I was the only person of Colour.

The weird thing is straight women really bristling when you call them straight and really just not wanting to own up to that. I would say, "since you're straight" in conversation and they just didn't like it. They wanted to be the same as me, for some political reason. They would murmur something about maybe being with a woman one day and then talk about men. I don't know what they're doing. They have the best stuff in terms of status. They have the whiteness, they have the straightness. You come in and they want your sexuality, they want your colour. It becomes something good to acquire somebody else's oppression, provided you can take it off when you go home at night or something.

MONA: I work in the Japanese Canadian community. My school work is very much connected to my work in that community. It's a really complex situation for me because those people represent my history in a real way. I don't find that in other places in this country. Yet I think there's a tendency too to look at peoples of Colour as not as aware as perhaps other communities or white people are. And it's really difficult to describe my work in the Japanese Canadian community, I do find it painful. I don't feel that I leave my lesbian part of myself behind when I do that work, but I think what's difficult for me is when I am assumed to be straight. I'm out to people, individuals, in that community. I think I've taken a lot of risk in doing that, but it is painful for me at times. I also see how women in that community have had to really struggle against sexism. It is a community that has lost a lot and is really trying to at this point to heal a lot of the losses. What I like to do now is to see the kinds of things we do to resist and to educate in our communities. I went to a conference in Vancouver in the fall of 1992, and there were 700 people, most of whom were Japanese Canadians and most of whom had been interned during the Second World War. I learned a lot from those people who shared their stories with me. And I was sad because as a lesbian, I didn't talk about that. Yet a group of us organized and met as lesbians at that conference — I think there were about six or seven of us meeting — and I feel this was an act of resistance. I take a lot of strength from the work that I see, especially by women of Colour, lesbians of Colour who I know are resisting and being all of who they are in the work that they do. It's really important for me to see that.

Divisions

BETH: What divides us? Class and race.

KRISTYN: Age.

AMY: Culture. Disability.

SANDRA: Politics.

KRISTYN: Preference for bars.

BETH: But often some of those things can be worked around whereas racism and class biases are extremely difficult for some people to get around to. You haven't found that to be so?

KRISTYN: There are different dividing factors among the lesbians and the bisexuals in this community. I can't say which one is the biggest wall to overcome or to knock down. As someone who is twenty-one — I came out five years ago — age is still a big thing within the women's community. My most recent experience was going to the March 8th Coalition and International Women's Day (IWD) for 1993 and running into huge walls where women who have been in the movement for fifteen or sixteen years are so used to doing things one way. We have a lot of energy. We may not have a lot of experience, but we're willing to take on work that needs to be done. We're finding a lot of resistance to letting go of the knowledge, the contacts and where to find the resources. That knowledge is a lot of power. And when we get into a relationship with someone who is older, who has a degree already and who has a career and all of that, age plays a big part to us.

CONNIE: I guess for me very much it has to do with race and class. In the sense that after all this time of so-called feminism there is still no place for me in the white middle-class women's movement and it's not necessarily that I want to fit in, because I'm not the same. I don't want to be like them. I don't have any desire to be like them, but there is no place. Actually we were talking about this around the March 8th Coalition again. This year, what are they doing about Native women? It's the year of Indigenous People, but we aren't being used as resources. You know, it's one year, but not much has changed. When I helped organize IWD in 1986, when the theme was No to Racism from Toronto to South Africa, all the workshop spaces went to women of Colour. There was one workshop put aside for white women to deal with racism, to sit down and dialogue with themselves on racism, but the only person that showed up at that workshop was the facilitator. That tells me a lot.

KRISTYN: But it's not just IWD.

CONNIE: No. No. No. It's the whole movement that claims to represent me as a woman, as a lesbian.

CAROL: For me the race and class thing within the lesbian community hit me a little while after I came out. I was raised and lived my life in quite a lot of isolation from other Black people, so when I was leaving my marriage I was coming out and I was seeking Black community. I connected with the Black Women's Collective, became a member, met a whole bunch of Black women and women of Colour. A lot of my organizing and activity was centred on that. In some ways I was very supported and protected and provided with the companionship of a lot of women like me. Then when I branched out further I ran into a completely different group of people, in bars, at Michigan, and I just couldn't relate. What would have happened to me if I'd had come out into that group? Never seeing anybody who looked like me or who had my experience or who could relate to me? I just feel so lucky that that is not the way I came out. I feel very alienated in some of those big spaces where the people who — this is sort of generalizing — but the sort of typical Michigan-goer, or whatever you want to call them, age forty, has more than one degree, came from a "good" class and wears expensive clothing that just looks poor.

SANDRA: Except the Birkenstocks.

CAROL: That's expensive, but they look poor. At one time, when I didn't know myself very well, I could relate — no problem. Now I find there's a big difference. If you just went by numbers and visibility, you would really think that that was the whole lesbian community world-wide. Often I'm counselling women who are on the way out and I really make sure that they can try to connect with their own community, not just the lesbian community but the lesbian community within their own community in terms of culture or race. I talk about class too. Because you can just feel like you don't fit, like you'll never find anybody, because they all want the rich, educated women or whatever.

SHARON: That's one side of it. Back to homophobia — a lot of discussion now has been about the communities that we face, the standard in the institutions and in our work places. But I think for me now, having been in the grassroots for a long, long time and working with women of Colour a lot, I find that when I'm going into women of Colour spaces there's a hell of a lot of alienation and there's a hell of a lot of homophobia even from lesbians who are South Asian. That's a very interesting thing that I would like us to talk about in terms of our own communities. It's very hard to know how we as women — because this is our space within our own communities — how we deal with all those internalized things like class and race. What strategies can we use to break that down, to build communities again, especially also inter-generationally, for the young people coming out? No work has been done. For those of us who have been organizing for a long time, there hasn't been a link of bringing forth, of communicating the history, facilitating continuity and sharing experience.

When I came into the scene in the lesbian community here I was the only South Asian lesbian. Now, if you come into the scene there may be twenty South Asian lesbians, so you have much more choice. And what goes along with that choice is sometimes not a recognition of the history. It's very important for us as women who have been a part of that work to make those links so those things are not forgotten or taken for granted. We're going into women of Colour spaces, or we're going into all South Asian spaces and the divisions are just phenomenal and very, very hard to break down. We're isolated within isolation. It would be interesting to talk about how we can find a way of moving through our own internalized stuff because I think we all understand the structures and the powers-that-be and how they are going to intimidate us. Sometimes it's easier to deal with because it is so clear. It is not so subtle. We can react. But when we're dealing with someone who is a lesbian, or if you're dealing with a bisexual woman who feels more comfortable dealing with a gay man than dealing with you as a lesbian sister, you're dealing with a very, very deep and difficult area too. The gay man is dealing with you in a certain way because of sexism. The bisexual woman may find it easier to deal with a gay man because of heterosexism. There's many complexities going on. How do you deal with all that?

SANDRA: My feeling is that sometimes we want to get into smaller and smaller groups with feminists or with lesbians. I was doing a project with women who were primarily Jewish lesbians. We disagreed wildly on just about everything. A lot of it could have been, "Oh well, we couldn't deal with each other for all kinds of reasons — internalized anti-semitism or internalized homophobia, etc." But I feel that sometimes we just don't recognize that we might be coming from different political positions. There are certain things I believe in that are widely different than what most members of the Jewish community believe and it's not because I'm a lesbian. It might have some bearing. I have a different viewpoint.

SHARON: That's what it's about. You may have a different viewpoint, but you've always got to put it in the context of power. If you are the only lesbian in the room with ten other people who have a different viewpoint from yours, it becomes a whole different thing. It's not just about a different viewpoint, it's about power and how you are respectful around dealing with power between ourselves as women, especially as women of Colour and women with a lot of differences. There are many issues, it's complex.

SANDRA: It's not always reduced to power. I don't think it always is. I think power always has to be in the foreground, but there is still a lot of difference in terms of opinions.

SHARON: And differences are fine. There's nothing wrong with having differences; differences lend a lot and enrich a discussion and bring a lot of strength to something. It only becomes difficult when you are not recognizing someone's difference, when you are not being sensitive to their history or where they are coming from, when you don't make the analogy between your particular oppressions and someone else's when it's a different oppression. Then it becomes an issue.

AMY: We have a difficult time recognizing and acknowledging difference. I was thinking back to some of the earlier organizing that I've done, when the Lesbian Organization of Toronto was around. This was back in the late 1970s, and I think about some of the discussions that we had, the ways we set ourselves apart, without recognizing what our power was. It was primarily an organization of white lesbians. What differences there were among those women never got talked about. Class rarely got talked about in a political sense. It didn't get talked about as a political issue within our community. And certainly race was never addressed whatsoever. Nor was disability. It feels now that organizations are just starting to deal with race, class, homophobia, disability and their impact on political analysis and direction. We have a debt to women who have raised issues of difference in terms of our identities and are questioning power and privilege within our movements. I still feel like it becomes explosive because women still have a difficult time acknowledging difference — particularly where we have privilege — and then coming together on the basis of a common cause. It feels like what you were saying about coming together in these smaller groupings, whether it's Jewish lesbians or lesbians of Colour or younger lesbians — whatever those groupings are, all the contradictions and the differences are there. I have certainly found it difficult among Jewish feminists or Jewish lesbians to feel that there's a common political goal. That brings us to the limitations of identity-based politics. On the one hand, we find strength in our identities and understand the basis of our oppression(s) and where we have power and privilege. For me as a white-skinned woman, I recognize that as a place of power in the world, but I also recognize that as a lesbian and Jew I do have places of pain and oppression in my life. But I don't want to become so self-absorbed in those oppressions that I can't figure out a way to be an ally with someone else whose oppression operates in a very different way and with whom I may have differences in power. We need to create solidarity between our different communities. How do we that and how do we have a sense of community? It is an uphill battle in this society where our sense of location is so disrupted. We need to feel and to understand our location *and* to enable ourselves to work and act together. Those are really central to our survival as communities and as political movements making radical change for all of us, not just for some of us. The differences among us get harder. My hope, at some point, was that they might get easier the more that we acknowledged them. But the more we acknowledge them, the more we need to be able to figure out how to deal with having those differences and how we can create alliances from those understandings.

Coalitions

CAROL: I have a lot of unanswered questions about coalitions. I can see the benefits of coalition work. But what I've been hearing about coalition-building lately, the last couple of years or so, has made me suspicious. All right, I come from a place where a lot of suspiciousness is very necessary. It has caused me to question what are the good things about coalitions. Why should I want a coalition? I haven't answered those questions. There's some basic, obvious answers, like sheer numbers will get things done perhaps better than small isolated groups, and we do want certain changes. But there have been times when I've heard people ask for coalition when what they wanted really was for the women of Colour to shut up. That has made me very suspicious. I almost only ever hear white women asking for coalition. That's just what my experience has been, I don't know if that's the norm. That's what made me suspicious because I feel like are white women sort of angry at being shut out of something — situations like, say IWD in previous years, where it was really clear that they wanted to know what those women of Colour were up to. I get defensive. I feel like, "Get out of my stuff, okay. Let me do my whatever and leave me alone." But because of that I get pushed back into separateness again, not having the numbers that you need and not doing anything about some of the healing in the larger sense. I'm not in a hurry to find solutions for coalition, to be quite honest. A lot of work needs to be done on an individual basis. I've tried to look at some situations where mixed groups seem to work and what was the common denominator. One of the things was a basic respect for one another, not always putting your own thing forth and obstructing. Sometimes just having a focused task — do that and not worry about other stuff. You go into groups, there is a power structure and people participating in keeping it going. That's a real problem. You can't even get far enough to get people looking at that power. It gets very blocked and that's when I leave.

MONA: I have a problem with this whole notion of accommodation around difference. I don't want to be accommodated. You have to look at who's doing the accommodating. What I want is for people to understand how those differences get made, how they're taken up and how we live and to listen to what the differences are. Around racism, I have been thinking a lot about when I go some place and I'm the only woman of Colour or lesbian of Colour. Somehow I'm the one who's expected to talk about race, like racism is *my* issue. I'm telling white people to examine what their "whiteness" has to do with racism, rather than always asking people of Colour to describe their experience. The way that these issues get taken up in various groups is through accommodation, rather than through political connections. It's analysed as somehow *you're* different and that's your thing. I'd like us to be able to work together and see how all of these things affect all of us...differently.

BETH: The last successful coalition I worked with was an anti-Columbus demonstration. Natives and African Americans and Sephardic Jews and Arabic-speaking people, primarily Lebanese and Palestinian, and that was extremely successful because the focus was this march. Did we ever get together afterwards? No. I think it's important for political work that we all would have kept up the political camaraderie we had preparing for this demonstration. Sometimes I remember the old consciousness-raising. Are there consciousness-raising groups anymore? There wasn't anything wrong with them. I can remember some way back in 1971 or 1972, when you'd stand up complaining. What are we doing for the younger generation coming into our movements and who are helping to make new movements? And isn't a consciousness-raising group a valuable tool? Or has it just gone over the hill?

NATASHA: Perhaps if there was more honesty among us and less fear…people don't seem to want to do that — to be so vulnerable.

BETH: So why did we want to do it twenty years ago and not do it now? What has happened in between?

AMY: Maybe we had a more unifying understanding of ourselves. Now we're trying to get back to that point but from a completely different place, travelling on a completely different road to understanding how we can be together.

KRISTYN: We can't take breaks for twenty years and think, "Oh god, we have to get it going again." It has to be continuous.

BETH: But hasn't it just under another name or another…?

KRISTYN: There's a young women's feminist movement that's popping up all over the place. It's very multicultural. Working within my small circle, we have been able to bridge the gaps, but when we look at the older women's movement I see it as almost like there are two movements. I would like to see it converge. The only times we get together are for the pro-choice rallies and IWD. We party, it's all separate, and when we go and do work it's all separate again. We come together a couple times a year for specific events. We need to do this work continually.

BETH: I just get very distressed that there's so much that isn't being spoken anymore, of those who went before us. That distresses me a great deal. There were so many elders, elder women who did things that we couldn't have imagined doing, and we don't know their names anymore. This is very sad. How can you have a future if you don't have a history? On the other hand, I have seen this ageism at work with women my age who completely dismiss women your age. This is another thing that's so distressing. Why don't we ask more: why are you here, what is it you want to say? Why don't we listen more?

KRISTYN: We hear about Stonewall, we hear about the drag queens rising up, but when ALOT was formed that was history — Lesbian Organization of Toronto, that's history. And yet you are absolutely right; we don't know about it. It's not documented. We don't know where to find it. Groups come and go so quickly. We're trying to document it. One of the main questions is, "where do I come from?" Like lesbians and gays have no history, no idea where we come from, immigrants to this country. What about Chinese queer history? We don't know it and our own community contributes to that. If there is anything we can walk out of this room with, it is to write it all down, and I think this is great — the fact that we have come together and talked about it. Writing and reading is not always so accessible.

AMY: It is really important to have a sense of that continuity. I've been doing some oral history with some older lesbians. One of the things that has motivated me to do that is to find out more about what it was like for women who had relationships with other women prior to the latest wave of the women's movement. At the same time, I had to come to terms with the fact that I couldn't fall into the trap of romanticizing. The race and class differences we have among us now operated in different ways and in similar ways in that period. What it meant to identify as a gay woman was different than it is now. But overall, the sense of continuity is really powerful. It allows all of us to have an opportunity to tell our stories, something we rarely have the space to do and be listened to, just like Beth was saying.

CAROL: One of the ways difference is minimized is by the use of the word "tolerance." You say that you don't want to be accommodated. I don't want to be tolerated. There has to be something more than that. And sometimes even acceptance doesn't seem the right attitude. It's implying something that I don't feel right about.

AMY: The question I would add is, how do we talk about our differences across our communities? That's where we get into discussions around political solidarity — having political differences with women who are identified as part of our communities. We may have a more similar view with other women from other communities. How do we come together even around this table and talk about differences within our own communities?

Working Together

SHARON: We have bridged differences within the women of Colour communities, where we have gotten really close in working on something that related all our issues. At the end, you did not go away with a sense that it was over. We came through with a kind of a bond that stands today, even if we don't see those same people we worked with. Something was built in that time. We don't seem to work together anymore in this women of Colour community. And I am talking specifically women of Colour. We don't seem to work together. We don't seem to come together. Everybody is sort of retreating and going into smaller and smaller areas. I'm finding that I am coming more out of the women of Colour community, into the mainstream community and hooking up with people who can relate to me, whatever community, all across communities now. In my own community I'm not finding that I'm getting the kind of openness to listen, to hear, to be heard. There is a lot of fear. One of the strongest things that helped me to bridge some of the differences was working together.

CONNIE: I agree, but also I'm not sure — and I hate the terms lesbians of Colour, women of Colour — that we've begun to deal with racism among our communities. We have always come together in solidarity against racism, against class bias. Yet I'm not sure if we have done a lot of the work, the dialogue, that we need to do also.

BETH: But are some of those differences cultural differences? I mean you and I come from closed communities in a sense, for obvious reasons.

CONNIE: A lot of why we don't work together — not why we don't work together but rather that it didn't happen often — is that we're all trying to survive.

SHARON: But it's all about survival isn't it? Every point, every time, even back then we were trying to survive. Isn't it because we are working in our own communities now?

CONNIE: I think that has a lot to do with it. A lot of our energies have been a lot more focused on our own communities. For me too, I don't spend a lot of time or energy outside of my community or outside the people of Colour community because I don't see that things have changed that much. There is no place for me outside that.

SHARON: If you could envision that and how that change would be, what would you do? You say that things haven't changed that much. What is the vision then? The change? How would you envision working or something different that would allow us to move? It's one thing to look at a community, how do we move?

CAROL: I think one thing missing is the courage to take some of those really difficult steps, say, for instance, around racism. It's really, really tough to look at your own racism and really work to eliminate that. And other isms. Racism is what really comes to my mind at this point. In the struggle to deal with it, especially in the one-to-one struggle or in the struggle from one small group to another small group, there could be a lot of side-stepping. You just don't get anywhere. Instead of looking at racism and the fact that it's systemic, that it oppresses everyone in different ways, there are feminists who are still looking at racism as if it were an isolated aberration and only something common to bad people. Because they are insisting on doing that they are constantly engaged in this side-stepping, "I am not racist." Wasting a lot of time and energy doing this little dance instead of standing still and admitting that you are racist. Looking at it. Being up to the challenge. Being up to the scrutiny. People are so afraid, especially people in progressive movements, that somebody is finally going to hunt them down and expose them for the racists they really are. I had a conversation with a white feminist woman friend of mine — we've had our things in the past around her racism. I knew she was racist. In many cases you know that everybody is racist, yet you don't always observe it happening. I had come across it with her. Then years later we had a discussion about it. She is being constantly challenged by clients and co-workers and she is backed into a corner. What I said was, "You are really afraid that somebody is going to point the finger one day and you'll be found out. All the racism will be right there for all to see." Like moving a rock and the thing squirms out and whatever. She said, "Yeah, that's it." And I think that's terrifying because then you see yourself as such a bad person. You don't want to give up your image as an okay person.

SANDRA: It's the dirty secret of liberalism.

CAROL: Yes. Absolutely. I like that.

AMY: The fear behind that is the fear of having to give up power.

CAROL: That's a big part of it.

AMY: First, it is the fear of being a bad person, but maybe some people will still talk to you. But then, if you have to give up power — that is central. Moving aside.

CAROL: That's another big thing to all this coalition thing or unity or just getting along. People don't want to look at the things that keep their power in place — part of an abusive destructive system — and get out of it.

AMY: What I often see is a lot of white women who have learned to use language in a particular way that covers up. The language of the dominant white women's movement has changed to include race and class. It's just taken for granted. It's like the stuff we were talking about earlier.

Do you tell somebody you are a lesbian and they just look right through you? It's a similar experience. The "politically correct" words on race and class don't always affect what is going on — it's a good line. We come across it a lot. Recently I was interviewing women for a job. I felt much more open to a woman who was struggling with these issues and didn't have the "right line," than with the women who came in and said, "Oh yes, I work with immigrant women, refugee women, and I deal with this and that and women of Colour this..." and it sounded like a line. That's disturbing.

CAROL: When you have that much power you have access to everything, you have access to the language to cover things up and to manipulate situations. Stepping smoothly into some position where you have the perfect résumé, the perfect proof that you are not a racist. Right there, without ever having done the work.

KRISTYN: I think you were right when you were talking about the language. What I find annoying is when people start talking about difference or diversity or inclusiveness. I like those words because I always actually wonder what they mean behind them. Do they mean to say, "and Black people, too, or Asian women, too"? It's very cosmetic. They have almost learned to absorb our issues. They have absorbed them into the whole framework of what they are talking about. But they absorb them cosmetically. There is nothing behind it, beyond these wonderful words that they know how to use and manipulate.

NATASHA: What I find really interesting in the dialogue about differences is our ability to become so easily side-tracked as we focus on white women and how they oppress us. This sole focus facilitates a unification on our part, yet this focus on unification allows for a focus away from how our own language oppresses and how we silence one another. Addressing the differences between us is challenging and can be quite painful, but I think we need to talk about that. Just as women cried sisterhood in order to present a united front against sexism, we as women of Colour are also crying sisterhood in the face of racism in the women's movement. Yet just as white women did not acknowledge the differences among women, we too are not acknowledging that there are varied voices among us. We must learn from the mistakes made before us — and the mistakes being made around us. We must learn to value the differences in our voices. We need to envision a space where there can be honesty among ourselves, honesty without fear, where there is a desire to listen and speak across our differences.

BETH: What about the secrets that our various communities don't want to see exposed? Like Davis Inlet made a nice little media splash for a couple of weeks. There is a part of me that doesn't want anyone to know about that except my own community because it's going to be used against us in some way. So how can we speak the truth, be honest and yet want to protect these occurrences, these secrets within our own community? How can we even talk about being truthful and honest with each other when there are things we don't want anyone to know? On the other hand, how do we get together to work on issues that are of importance to all of us, if we're not telling the truth?

CONNIE: That process has to, somewhere along the line, become a collective process, not just personal.

Visions

SANDRA: I want to add the question, what are people and what are communities prepared to do? I was speaking to a friend of mine, a Jewish woman, and she was really up on coalition work, "This is a thing we must be doing." We were talking about organizing against racism. She said, "I'm right into this," and I said, "Well, think about it. Would you sit down with a group of Anglo white women and coalesce on racism?" There was a big hesitation and she said, "Yeah, sure I would." I said, "Wait a minute, why were you hesitating, what was that problem there?" I have had to talk about anti-semitism in my workplace and I don't think I could do it in the same way if I was dealing with a group of people who were predominantly white. I couldn't do it with the same sort of assumption that people would understand when I said racial stereotype and talked about it. I couldn't assume that. It's very different in terms of who you are dealing with and also in terms of what you are willing to risk. I don't think it's just about the truth of your community but what you're willing to expose. If I stand in front of a group of people and say this is a stereotype of Jews, to people who don't already consciously know it, there is a risk that I might be putting this idea into their heads.

CAROL: It's very hard to admit things that you don't like that were done by people in your group because people are just so ready to say, "Oh yeah, you know that fits, they are like that," instead of looking at the factors that make everyone do bad things sometimes. Getting back to this white thing, how nobody ever says when some horrible crime is done, "It's those white people." I get into arguments with my family because they are very anti-Caribbean. They discuss the behavior of Caribbean youth on the subways and whatever. I say, "If a bunch of white hoods got on the subway and did the same thing you'd say, 'Look at those hoods'. You wouldn't say, 'Look at those white boys.'" But it is painful to look at all this stuff. People go right to the stereotype. It's not surprising that we want to keep quiet. Then we lose because we don't work through that stuff for ourselves and get any healing. We just cover it up. The price of openness is so great.

KRISTYN: I have a little mini-vision because it is only an individual vision. I can only work within my own community. I would never give up on East Asian youth. No matter how Westernized we seem, it's because of where we live. What are we doing here? It's our location. I know no matter how Westernized we are, eventually we will come back. And the last thing I want to do is give up and walk away. My vision is to work within my community, which is divided because there is China, Hong Kong, Taiwan, Chinese from the U.K., Chinese from Jamaica, Chinese from Trinidad. And people who are of Chinese descent have different issues, depending on where they are coming from, what they are involved in, what class they are from, their educational background. My vision is focusing on that first. As a young Asian dyke, I guess that's what I need to work on. That's my vision.

MONA: The reason I use the term lesbian of Colour, including myself in it, is because it makes us seem like more. In my case, being a Japanese Canadian lesbian and having been one of the only ones out and visible in this city for awhile, it's very isolating. I use it as a political term, I try to select it as such. I want to show that I have sisters who are struggling in similar ways, as I am. I've noticed too how we have chosen to do our anti-racist work or our historical recovery work in our own groups. They seem to be more and more separate from each other. I recognize how we're trying to create safety in a really unsafe world for us. I reminisce, too, about how we did work together. I don't know whether at that time there just weren't a lot of us so we really appreciated being with other lesbians and gay men of Colour. I find myself working more in alliance with a lot of different women now, trying to share my political vision at the same time as I am trying to develop it and be challenged by their visions. But I worry too because of the rise of the Right and how they are funded and what we're going to do about it and what I'm going to do about it. Those are really important questions.

AMY: I think about that a lot, too. Survival and our vision of working together has a lot to do with countering the rise of the Right. I don't only mean the rise of neo-Nazi groups. It's a climate. It has to do with the corporate world, it has to do with the Tory government, it has to do with the North American Free Trade Deal, it has to do with the whole structuring of our lives and what's imposed and how to resist that. All of us sitting around this table and all the people that we are a part of are attacked in different ways. I feel a heightened fear and the sense of being under attack, personally and in terms of communities of people. Recently I compared it to my parents, who were both in the Communist Party living through the American anti-communist hysteria of the 1950s. In some ways I do have hope that we can come together, but when I look around I feel that we are very separate. Can we bridge the differences, while also recognizing that we may hurt each other in that process? Do we have the generosity, with an understanding of the power differences, that we can somehow push through it? Maybe part of the answer is in the process itself, or in pushing it, because of the great fear that we are all facing, because of the attack that we are all facing. We are talking about our differences; what is it that we can make common cause around? One of those is around the attack that we are facing. There are more positive things that come out of working together.

BETH: Sometimes I don't know if I even allow myself to have a vision. There are moments when I have in my mind how it could be, but then quickly I pull it back because I see it as an impossibility. I have been in many groups for over twenty years. And for the past five or six years, I am working primarily with Native women, primarily having to do with speaking and writing. More so speaking, because that comes first. The writing is important but also my people, fifty percent of us are illiterate. So just the act of speaking becomes incredibly powerful. This spring and fall I will be working with Native women in prison, in Kingston, on a weekly basis. I guess that would be where my vision is mainly. Native women. Speaking. Telling our stories. Somehow being able to collect all that for others to see, to be moved by. I can't see myself moving too much out of that in the near future. I just feel that it is the path that I am on at this moment. That is a vision of some kind. But we need to find a deeper sense of strength and self-love, I think, before it is even possible to coalesce or even meet people half way.

SHARON: It's really personal. When you say, how much are we willing to participate? How much am I willing to do myself? That's the question I ask myself. How much am I willing to change? Because as I change, things around me are going to change. Because I'm going to fight back and I'm going to resist. Vision, for me, is very similar to Beth's. It's about communication. When you are talking about Native women and speaking and being heard it's about communication. When we as different women communicate openly from our hearts something happens, something changes. It is not something we can define. That is my vision. We can have serious discussions that contain the awareness that good will is not enough, where there is a realization of the complexity of experience and the emotional costs of working across differences, and yet being open to making the connections and seeing things in new contexts.

AMY: I have been teaching a photography course this year, focused on recovering family and community history, family not necessarily in a traditional sense. The most profound experience I have had in doing this work is that it is so important for us to be able to tell our stories and be heard. Even doing that in the class — people go away having learned together, there is a trust that has been built because we have spoken and we have listened. We are hearing people's stories that have never been heard, let alone acknowledged or recognized as valuable. That alone is such a profound experience.

KRISTYN: It is really frustrating that since we are constantly under attack we have to keep this solid front like "solidarity forever." We have so many differences, yet we're not allowed to be open about it. We have to be closed about it. When we come together we have to be closed because there is a bigger picture involved, and then within our smaller picture there is another bigger picture involved. It's frustrating and energy-draining. I don't even know what to do with it. Seeing all those cops come down on my peers, all I could think for the next two weeks was, "I'm going to carry around a baseball bat. I'm just going to do it." This was after being so passive for so many years — peace and love and harmony and joy. For someone to evolve that way over five years and to say, "Fuck it, I'm just going to blow away everybody and vandalize everything," yet this is the way we are evolving. I am not alone in this feeling. And it's just really frustrating to have to keep up a united front when we are not united all the time and it is only under attack that we become united. Protecting who we are in our communities, making sure we don't air our dirty laundry because it can be used against us, it's this vicious cycle that continues and continues. You want to put your foot down and say, "I can't deal with this anymore." But, at the same time, it just adds to the vicious cycle. It's hard to come to a solution. That's why I say I can only work within myself before I do anything else. I see a world of colour. I don't see the vision that everyone sees, and because there are so many different visions we have to come together and make a collage of visions together. At the age of twenty-one I feel like I'm already burned out.

NATASHA: It's true. It is sometimes difficult to feel safe with women from different cultural backgrounds when we don't feel safe within our own cultural spaces. It is difficult to develop trust with one another when we have not yet developed trust among ourselves. And although I think it is important to recognize the realism of this process of developing trust and the reality of our fears, I think it is also important to envision a place where we can address these realities and the reality of our differences.

SANDRA: I'm twenty-six and I started doing feminist stuff about five years ago. I look at an organization like NAC or like LEAF and they seem like outer space. They seem completely irrelevant.

BETH: Gee, I wonder why you say that.

SANDRA: The first feminist conference I went to, Buseje Bailey was on the stage talking about racism in the arts community. So, to me, that's feminism. I do think there are differences when we talk about how we define feminism or the lesbian community. There are really definitely different areas. My experience has been very tied into one area. More mainstream, older feminist organizations are sort of like the Tory government: they sit there and they do their thing.

KRISTYN: I really resent the fact that they think they represent us. I really hate that. Everytime Judy Rebick gets on I think, "Who are you? Who the fuck are you?" Those organizations, the top two, they do no consultation with us whatsoever. They have an institution and an office and they have a budget and they are totally out of touch with reality now. Everytime they open their mouths they piss me off. Is that going to be published?

AMY: There is an acknowledgement among us that we need to find sources of strength and deal with differences within our own communities. But I am also interested in discussing and taking action against racism, against anti-semitism, against homophobia beyond my own community. I don't just want to talk with Jewish women about anti-semitism. I do want to be able to have that discussion with non-Jewish women of Colour, Native women, etc. I know that they are not easy discussions and that there are tears involved and pain involved and a sense of conflicting interests. I want to feel that I can deal with it within my own community, and I want to be able to figure out a way that I can do that with women from other communities. That's what I want to be able to envision.

SHARON: That's about the different places we are building. We're all coming from different places. What you're ready to do and what somebody else may be ready to do, we don't all need each other to be at the same place, because we are not.

AMY: No.

SHARON: I think what was asked to be acknowledged is that we are not at the same place in our communities, especially in some of the communities of Colour.

AMY: Yes. It's good to state it that way.

SHARON: I think that there has to be a real recognition of patriarchy in all of this, because when you talk about systems and nothing changes... There has to be a real recognition outside of the word *vision*, but we as women have to acknowledge that we can change things. We have a sense of being that is different. There is a patriarchy out there that has a system in place that absorbs things, the same system with different faces. There has to be a real consciousness around that system because nothing is going to change unless we come up with a way of being that is different. Being attached to our communities is very integral to that kind of change. It's ourselves and others that should be informing how things should be. It's our needs and experiences, as individuals and diverse communities, that should begin to be addressed and validated. There has to be a different way of being that allows everybody to have voice.

Women's Press apologizes for the ableism in the organization of this discussion group, which excluded lesbians with disabilities from participating. Since this discussion, Women's Press has made a commitment to identify and remove barriers to the participation of women with disabilities in Women's Press.

III
RECOVERING
WOMEN'S HISTORY

THE HOUR-A-DAY STUDY CLUB

Peggy Bristow

Rooted in Courage

In addressing the Fourth National Congress of Black Women, held in Windsor, Ontario in 1977, Cleata Morris, president of the Hour-A-Day Study Club in Windsor, reminded her sisters, "With our roots set firmly in the ground we must exert our attributes of courage to sustain our growth..."[1]

Her words resonate with those of Harriet Tubman, a Black female activist of an earlier century: "We're rooted here," said Tubman, "and they can't pull us up."[2] Morris' comments also reflect two recurring themes in the history of Black women (and Black men) in Canada: first, Morris notes the connections between and the continuity underlying Black women's lives and Black women's struggles; second, she underscores the point that Black women (and Black men) have always had to legitimize their presence on Canadian soil.

This article looks at those links and that continuity through some specific moments in the work of the Hour-A-Day Study Club in Windsor, Ontario, an organization that typifies the range of political organizing by Black women past and present.[3]

Although Bonnie Thornton Dill was not writing about the Club, her words aptly describe it: "While [the] political identities of Black women have largely been formed around issues of race, Black women's organizations were and still are feminist in the values expressed in their literature and in many of the concerns which they addressed, yet they also always focused upon issues which resulted from the racial oppression affecting all black people."[4]

Speaking to the same point in 1973, Rosemary Brown, then a Member of British Columbia's Legislative Assembly, told the National Congress of Black Women, "Because we are Black and because we are female, this conference has given us the opportunity to explore the two liberation struggles which we are sitting astride at this moment...'"[5] And in keeping with a tradition of recognizing foremothers, Brown went on to acknowledge the Black women who came before her: "I could speak of women who fought for liberation — I could speak of Louise Stark, who came as a young woman to B.C. to escape the *Fugitive Slave Act* in the U.S., who died in 1944 at age 106 after a life of struggle — and whose legacy to us was the history of her family's life in B.C., written in the most beautiful free verse...I could tell of the stories of the life of the early Black settlers in B.C. and in Ontario and in Nova Scotia, and of the strength and stamina of those women."[6]

Black women's activism has taken many forms, individually and collectively. They have not only asserted their womanhood by initiating activities in their own community but have seen themselves as an active part of a larger citizenry. As Nellie Y. McKay reminds us, for Black women "group identification also denotes a self that transcends socially imposed limits of race, class, and gender."[7]

Black women's political organizing, then, can best be understood from a perspective that includes an understanding of race, class and sex. As Thornton Dill asks, "Where does [sic] Black women fit into the current analytical frameworks for race and class and gender and class? How might these frameworks be revised if they took full accounting of Black women's position in the home, family, and marketplace at various historical moments? This must begin with an analysis of the ways in which Black people have been used in the process of capital accumulation."[8]

A full account of Black woman's political organizing is beyond the scope of this article. It is crucial to remember, however, that in Canada, as elsewhere in the Americas, a Black woman's chance for education remains largely tied to her class, and her options in the workforce remain confined by racism, a bind that weakens the benefits of education. [9]

In his study on Blacks in Canada James Walker points out, "in 1941, 80% of Black adult females in Montreal were employed as domestic servants."[10] There is every reason to believe that this proportion held true for Black women in other Canadian cities. Indeed, Verda Cook tells us that in the 1920s and 1930s the only work Black women could get in Toronto was as cleaners.[11] Esther Hayes remembers, "We all worked domestic work, in service."[12] And as Eleanor Hayes, Esther's sister adds, "When I was in high school the girls who wanted to take commercial courses or secretarial courses...weren't encouraged to do so. We were told, 'Well, who would want to hire you?'"[13] Darlene Hine Clarke reminds us that Black women entered domestic service because private household work is women's work. It is also a working-class occupation, has low social status, brings low pay and few if any guaranteed fringe benefits. It is within these terms that Black women, as individuals and as a group, have defined their strategies for fighting racial and sexual oppression.

It is, of course, also true that white immigrant women from Britain and Europe were actively encouraged to settle in Canada as domestics.[14] But while Black women remained, as Dionne Brand points out, "a permanent service caste in nineteenth and twentieth century Canada," white women from various ethnic groups who worked in service saw it (with varying degrees of success) as a steppingstone to other working-class occupations or as a way station before marriage.

In contrast, Black women in Canada have, as a group, been excluded from all aspects of what is conventionally recognized as the building of Canada. "Free" Black people were never encouraged to settle in Canada. On the contrary, one historian notes, "The most important legal protection given to slavery by Britain for the northern provinces was contained in an Imperial act of 1790 to encourage immigration into British North America."[15] This Act permitted the importation of all "Negroes, household furniture, utensils of husbandry or clothing."[16] Furthermore, "free" Blacks were "not encouraged to come to Canada."[17] As Linda Carty points out, Black women's relationship to the Canadian state has been purely in terms of their labour.[18]

Indeed, a look at official correspondence reveals that any growth in the number of Black people in Canada has always been looked at askance by officials. During the mid-nineteenth century one colonial governor recommended that Black people be encouraged to settle in the West Indies. The trick, he thought, was to offer them free passage there and land grants. But, he warned, such grants "must be no more than a mere garden or they would rely on it for subsistence instead of depending on their work for wages, and would sink into the normal condition of the emancipated slaves already there."[19] By the turn of the century Canada's immigration officials did not encourage Black people to settle here. As another historian relates, "While the Immigration Branch of the Department of the Interior maintained an active network of immigration agencies in the United States, the American Blacks were covertly excluded from promotional work."[20] At the same time no chance was missed to remind Black people living in Canada that they were subordinate. As another historian reports, when the president of the Canadian Imperial Bank of Commerce addressed a group of Black leaders in 1915 he "indulged in ritual condemnations of slavery, praise for the Underground Railroad and the fugitive slaves and urgings of race pride. However, he told his audience that Negroes should not hope to jump to the front in one or two or three generations, since they were the closest of all people to aboriginal man. The white man's scale is immeasurably greater than the black man's. That is a thing that the colored race should remember with pride."[21] Thus in 1918, when the Canadian parliamentary under-Secretary for external affairs, Francis Keeper, "reminded the Prime Minister Robert Borden of the possibility of uniting with the British West Indies" Borden found that the disadvantages of "having members of a backward race" become part of Canada, far outweighed the advantages of territorial gains.[22] Fifty years earlier, when the Canadian Parliament debated the retention of capital punishment for rape, Canada's first Prime Minister, John A. Macdonald, wrote: "We still have retained the punishment of death for rape ... We have thought it well ... to continue it on account of the frequency of rape committed by negroes, of whom we have too many in Upper Canada. They are very prone to felonious assaults on white women ..."[23]

Nor would the first wave of feminism prove more hospitable to Black women. At the turn of the twentieth century, the emphasis on "maternal feminism" and the drive to create a white and Protestant nation, raised questions about the proper type of immigrants. White Anglo-Saxon women activists in the Canada of the time argued for political and "social rights as a matter of equal justice...[and] also used utilitarian and organicist arguments that grounded women's cause in an affirmation of their role in biological and social reproduction."[24] In other words, white women "did not merely have just enough babies or too much sex: through their childbearing they either helped or hindered the forward march of (Anglo-Saxon) civilization."[25] This principle underpinned much of the debate around contraception during the period.[26] Black women found themselves excluded from the debate by virtue of their race and class.

It is not surprising, then, that political organizing has been a necessary part of the lives of Black women in Canada. Without it, Black women could not — indeed, still cannot — survive. Certainly, it is as necessary in today's hobbled economy as it was in the depression of the 1930s, or when Blacks fled to Canada to escape slavery in the U.S., or when "freed" Blacks left the houses of their masters after Emancipation was declared in 1833.

Racism denied Black women access to factory jobs until World War II, when the demands of the war effort meant accepting all hands. But as Ruth Roach Pierson points out, "Canada's war effort, rather than any consideration of women's right to work, determined the recruitment of women into the labour force."[27] Some Black women, however, had to fight to gain entry into factory work. Although Winks reports that the National Selective Service accepted racial restrictions from employers until 1942,[28] a year later, the Amherstburg Community Club was still demanding equal treatment for Black women applying for such jobs. In responding to this demand, government official H.E. Stratton had no qualms about admitting discrimination. "It is," he replied, "sometimes difficult for us to place certain types by virtue of the fact that we are governed by the orders we receive from the different employers ... In other words, they place an order in this office for their help requirements and specify age, weight, height sometimes religion, race..."[29]

Similarly, racism meant that nursing, teaching and other professions open to white women remained closed to Black women. As Gwen Johnson would remember, "Young Black women could not get into a hospital to train as a nurse."[30] Grace Fowler also remembers that Black women were excluded from nursing.[31] Esther Hayes poignantly reveals "Every mother hopes her daughter would be a nurse."[32] Ironically, Eleanor Hayes tells us, "Those who wanted to be a nurse had to go to the States — you couldn't train here."[33] However, as Esther says, "We [also] had Black Cross nurses with Garvey's group. We used to take first aid — the St. John's Ambulance course — and home nursing."[34] Bee Allen "wanted to be a teacher but when she was young there weren't that many Blacks teaching in Toronto. I knew of one, Mr. Jones."[35] Hine Clark makes the point that for U.S. Blacks:

[A] devastating combination of poverty and the marginal and seasonal jobs available to most black men dictated that black women work both inside and outside the home. Whether she was wife, daughter, or sister, the black woman's income was critical to family survival, so much so that she never enjoyed the option of retreating into the so-called private sphere. White women, but not black women, found employment in an expanding number of sex role-stereotype jobs in department stores, factories and offices. The social construction of gender roles within the black community could not afford to confine black women to as narrow a band of occupations and jobs as was the case in the larger white society. The larger reality of race and class oppression confined and restricted them more.[36]

This holds true in large part for Blacks in Canada as well.[37]

Study Club scholarships helped young Black women break through the barrier. In 1947 Cecile Wright, a graduate of a vocational secondary school in Windsor, won a fifty-dollar Study Club scholarship to help pay for her nurse's training.[38] That year the University of Toronto had decided to consider accepting Black women as nursing students. The Study Club wrote to the provincial minister of health and to the University of Toronto to press the case for admission.[39]

Earlier Organizing

Fifteen Black church mothers in Windsor, Ontario, set up the Hour-A-Day Study Club during the depression of the 1930s. The work of the Windsor Study Club reveals some of the many ways that Black women have rejected the wider society's notions about Black womanhood. Study Club members were not the first Black women, however, to define Black womanhood on their own terms nor the first to act outside what some would have argued was their proper sphere.

Nearly a century before the club's founding, Black women had come together with Black men to organize the True Band Society. Active in the mid-nineteenth century, the True Band Society set about bettering Black schools, encouraging increased school attendance, arbitrating disputes between members of the community, giving assistance to those in need and resisting racism. Created in Amherstburg in 1854, the Society spread quickly, and by 1856 there were thirteen True Band Societies in southwestern Ontario.[40]

Early Black women's organizations took many forms. There were church-related gatherings organized by women. Church women taught Sunday school and set up young women's organizations. Black women did missionary work. In 1882 Black women established the Women's Home Missionary Society, and Elizabeth Shadd Shreve, who became the Society's first president, "travelled about, on horseback, through the bush, and over roads almost impassable at time, ministering to the sick, collecting and delivering food and clothing for the needy, and, preaching the Gospel ..."[41] Late-nineteenth-century clubs like the Busy Gleaners Club and the Frederick Douglass Club, both formed in Amherstburg, are examples of organizations started by church women for young single Black women. Another early women's organization was the Ladies' Union Aid Society which was formed in 1878 by a group of women in Chatham.

Black women set up self-help societies to help the many Black people in need. Other self-help societies helped many Black people in settling. In Chatham Black women who formed the Victoria Benevolent Society during the mid-nineteenth century saw themselves engaged in a "profession, trade or occupation." Accordingly they set up a fund to help those among them and others who fell ill and could not work.[42] Individual Black women like Mary Bibb in Windsor and Amelia Freeman Shadd in Chatham started literary clubs in their mid-nineteenth-century communities. In Montreal the Colored Women's Club was started in 1902, and the Phillis Wheatley Club was later established. In 1910 a group of church women in Toronto formed the Eureka Club. The British Methodist Episcopal Church women in Buxton formed the Sunshine Club in 1916, and in 1924, these women organized their first annual homecoming. Most Black women's organizations were local ones until the Canadian Negro Women's Club was started in 1951 in Toronto.[43] It sponsored the Congress of Black Women, with chapters all over Canada. The national focus on organizing had already started with the Universal Negro Improvement Association (UNIA) which had chapters not only in various cities and towns in Canada but in the United States and the Caribbean.

Though not a women's organization, Black women within the UNIA played a significant role. In Vancouver, for example, Black women in the UNIA organized a branch of the Universal Black Cross Nurses. [44] In the early twentieth century, Black women also played significant roles in the organizing of the Brotherhood of Sleeping Car Porters. As Dionne Brand reminds us, "They organized Negro History Weeks and raised money for educational scholarship well into the late 1950s."[45]

In Nova Scotia, Black women's organization evolved in much the same way as they did in Ontario.[46]

More Than a Cup of Tea on Offer

Ardella Jacobs opened her home at 1130 Lillian Street, on the border of Windsor's "Black Belt," one cold wintry evening in February 1934. For Jacobs and for the other fourteen mothers, the occasion meant much more than an evening cup of tea. Jacobs, Rachael Harding, Vivian Nall, Elizabeth Washington, Verna Stewart, Hilda Watkins, Gladys Browning and the others had come together to plan collectively how they could be most effective in moulding the character of their children to make them "the best possible citizens."[47] Having defined a community need, they moved into action.[48]

The Mothers' Club, as it was initially called, opened its doors to all mothers in the Black community. (Most Study Club members were married mothers. However, I came across three single women, Beatrice Castleman, who died in November 1950, Cleata Morris and Naomi Edmonds.) These were hard times. In describing the devastating impact of the 1930s on most Canadians, Michael S. Cross and George S. Kealey write about the men and the "long, deep scars left by the depression and war" as "tens of thousands of young men rode the rails from place to place searching for somewhere that economic conditions were better."[49]

Organizing in Hard Times

The Crash of 1929 and its aftermath hit the Black population hard. Young Black men could not move around the country in search of work. Nor had industrialization benefitted Black women wage earners. The only work to be had for most in the best of times was as a hired hand or a household servant. Food and lodging were hard to come by and some towns had "sundown laws" that ordered Blacks out of town before nightfall.[50] For the women, "the scarcity of work and wage made them reach ever deeper for ways of stretching their limited resources."[51]

The need to organize was as pressing as it was difficult. A letter sent by the Amherstburg Community Centre to the National Association for the Advancement of Colored People in June 1943 reads in part:

> The racial problem of today is indeed becoming a matter of national interest and our organization has for the past eight years tried to cope with the situation in every way but to no avail. For owing to the few in number among our group we are handicapped, but, nevertheless the community is fully conscious of the great need for building a strong movement among people who are seriously concerned about the great issues of freedom and democracy... Our organization has just proposed a "Bill of Rights" to our Dominion government regarding the abolition of discriminatory and segregational practices against men and women regardless of race, color or creed, religion or national origin.[52]

Up river in Windsor it was no easier to escape racism. Often denied certain jobs because of their race, Black people were also refused admittance to many public spaces. Carol Talbot describes life for her father in the Windsor of the 1920s. If, for example, her father and his Black friends "went to the movies, they were permitted to sit only in the first rows of one theatre in Windsor, the back of the balcony in another, and not at all in Walkerville, an east-end suburb of Windsor. Dad and his young friends also knew why they could only swim, on those hot, humid, summer days of southwestern Ontario, at certain beaches....Such signs as 'Whites Only,' 'White Gentiles Only,' were not uncommon sights."[53]

What happened to Talbot's father when he graduated from high school faced many young Black men his age. "Dad completed Grade 13 in the early thirties, but he could not get a job at the time at the Ford Motor Company, although white classmates of his did get hired. Instead, he found himself working as a bellhop at the Prince Edward Hotel."[54]

Against this backdrop the Central Citizens' Association formed in Windsor to press for access to jobs and accommodation and access to public space.[55] In 1950, Association member Hilda Watkins, also a founding member of the Mothers' Club, was still at work, this time distributing leaflets for the Central Citizens' Association calling for the advancement of coloured people in Windsor, Ontario.

As hard as times were for Black men in the 1930s, the situation for women was worse. Talbot's mother's experience is no doubt representative of that of most Black women of the time:

> She quit school after Grade 11 with fine grades, but with no incentive at home, school, or in the work world to continue. After all, a girl doesn't need a fancy education to be a housewife, or failing that, to be a menial worker in the business world or a domestic...Accordingly, her first jobs were babysitting and housekeeping jobs and then she did marry and become a full-time housewife. When I was about 12 years old, Mom went to work again, this time as an elevator operator in a large department store....Later she received a "promotion," working the basement marking prices on clothes, with more pay but less visibility....She always wanted to be a teacher, but never made it, except in Sunday school and for junior piano pupils."[56]

The Mothers' Club

It was in this climate that the Mothers' Club set out to mobilize. Talbot details what it was like to grow up as a Black child in Windsor. "To be a black child in Canadian society, even in my generation, was a painful experience. The positive vibrations and the wholesome warmth of family and church could not counter-balance the forces of the dominant white world. I saw my mother and my aunts [working] as white people's servants and elevator operators...I saw poorly paid preachers and well-spoken deacons who were garbage collectors 'out there.' The dignity achieved in our small community could not erase the scars of humiliation imposed on the battleground of the larger Canadian society."57

Talbot's Windsor experiences were somewhat similar to those of

Viola Berry Aylestock who lived in Toronto. "It was hard being a Black person: the fact that you had the education and you still couldn't get the jobs really that you were fitted for — it was frustrating and that's why so many Blacks left. I can remember my mother saying that in the early 1900s some friends of our family left, and they went and settled in Cincinnati." [58]

Club mothers were troubled about Black students leaving school early. "The black boys seemed discouraged early, and success in sports was not enough to sustain them. By the age of sixteen, I saw very few black boys, or girls for that matter [in school]."[59] During Talbot's entire schooling in Windsor she had no Black teachers: "I've never had the opportunity of having a black teacher in any public education institution in my life, that is, one public school and two high schools, in historically high-density black settlements, and two universities, and I have been the only black teacher in the six schools I have taught in."[60]

The Mothers looked for strategies to encourage Black students to stay in school. Some of the Mothers had attended Mercer Street Public School, in the centre of the "Black Belt" in Windsor. Carol Talbot reports that in 1925, when her father was a student at Mercer Street, a significant percentage of the students were Black. The school was:

> one of the oldest buildings in the city, but it had no gym, auditorium, or extracurricular facilities. The play area was a cinder-covered yard not even large enough for a full-scale softball game. This was not an unusual school when it was built, as far as facilities were concerned, but it stayed open long after similar schools had been closed. The situation in other southwestern Ontario communities where blacks lived were [sic] similar. The poorest facilities were for blacks, except that places like Buxton, Harrow, and Shrewsbury had black teachers who took an interest in the children.[61]

In 1934, when the Mothers' Club formed, Mercer Street School, unlike most other Windsor schools, had no Home and School Association. Already hard-pressed by other urgent needs in the community, Black parents had little time to spare. By 1934, however, the social, political and economic conditions of Blacks had not improved. Members of the Mothers' Club knew they had to act.

They acted on what they knew: neither the curriculum nor the teaching practices offered much to Black children. Making the most of their limited resources, the Mothers decided first to host a graduation celebration for students who graduated from Mercer Street. These students would have been getting ready for the entrance examinations for secondary school. The Mothers recognized the tedium of preparing for those exams and sought to boost the morale of the new primary school graduates. (At the time, Black children were leaving school early and in disproportionate numbers. In addition, when Black children attended secondary school they tended not to be in academic programs.) Cleata Morris' narration captures the tension between Black parents–Black teachers and the school system. In sharing some moments of her teaching experiences in Windsor, Morris says:

> One year, the principal came in and said, "Is your report ready? "I said, "It will be ready, o.k.?" and I stalled for time, really stalled. He came back, and he said, "Look, is it ready?" I said I was working on it. And he said, "I've got to go to a meeting and these things have got to be in." So he started through and he put a checkmark beside the Black names. The principal put an X besides all Blacks. And I've filled these things out for umpteen years! What could it mean when they put it like that, except they're starting to label these kids.
>
> They wanted to keep track of every student in Windsor, and what he or she was capable of doing, and who they were going to shove into the remedial classes…. I would go to the parents, and I would say, "Get behind those teachers. Raise more fuss. Go to school boards. Make yourselves heard. This is what is happening — don't let them put your kids there.
>
> I initiated some sort of campaign among the parents of these students. I was able to talk with parents when we had parent-teacher interviews. I would call parents in. I can remember on one occasion they had a feeling that Morris is down there talking, and the principal would like of duck in for something….
>
> …Even some of the poor white children, they were discriminated against as well. As far as I am concerned, it is still a major problem, and

I don't think that it's going to get any better. It will if we have Black teachers who will stand up — and I mean stand![62]

There was still no formal Home and School Association, but the Mothers unofficially monitored student progress. In the meantime, they had begun the annual graduation celebrations.

The Hour-A-Day Study Club

By 1935 the Mothers' Club had changed its name to the Hour-A-Day Study Club, to reflect more adequately its purpose. The Study Club's activities were wide-ranging. Child-rearing practices were a key item on the agenda. In addition to what members already knew about and expected from the school system, they were worried too about the mental development of young children. Study Club members therefore pledged themselves to set aside at least "one hour each day" for the growth and development of the mind. Study Club members also wanted to understand how young children grow emotionally. They had confidence in their children, but the children needed teachers and other adults who believed they could and would excel. Not limited to any one topic, the Study Club dealt with a wide range of issues which affected the Black community.

By 1936 the Black community's Dr. H.D. Taylor had won representation on the Windsor Board of Education. Study Club members invited him to speak at a meeting to discuss schooling. This was a landmark meeting, open to all parents and students, and addressed by an individual who would speak directly to the needs of Black children with the authority of personal experience.

In 1946 Mercer Street School finally got its Home and School Association, with Mrs. C. Laqnson Van Dyke becoming the first Black woman in Canada to head a Home and School Association. Three years later, in 1949, Mrs. Raymond F. Watkins would win the presidency of the Western Home and School Association in Sandwich. She would be the first Black woman to be a delegate at the Ontario Educational Association's annual convention in Toronto. In another three years the local government would condemn the Mercer building.

If Black children were to go on to further study, Study Club members knew that graduates of both the academic and the vocational schools would have to get active and practical encouragement. Stalwart Study Club member Hilda V. Watkins noted, in April 1946, the need for a scholarship program: "[I]t is my feeling that we [should] launch upon a scholarship aid program. The program should make available at least $50 each year to be given to the outstanding senior matriculation colored student of Windsor and $50 each year to the outstanding Windsor colored graduate of the W.D. Lowe Vocational School who intends to further his or her education."[63]

The announcement that the "notice of scholarship aid is to be posted on bulletin boards in churches during months of May, June, July and August" and be "read from pulpits each Sunday" underscores the strong links between the Black church and the Black community.[64] The sense of possibilities would spread: by December 1947 the first Students' Rally, held at the Masonic Temple on Mercer Street, would replace the Graduates' Party that the Study Club held each June.[65]

During the Study Club's first ten years members concentrated on the rearing and schooling of Black children. Despite busy schedules, members met twice a month to set strategy and to plan Study Club activities. The agenda of all regular meetings was divided into a study period and a business section.

Correct child-rearing practices were seen as crucial to the proper upbringing of future citizens. Study Club members viewed *Parents' Magazine*, which included such topics as "Parents are an asset" and "Learning to be socially acceptable," as a vehicle for promoting the kinds of ideals they associated with good citizenry. Accordingly, Club members subscribed to this publication and distributed it to mothers in their community.

When the Study Club formed in the midst of the depression of the 1930s, its members agreed that members would not be obliged to contribute to its day-to-day functioning, although donations were occasionally received. Several members attended a three-month course on child psychology, conducted by a Miss Lewis, a teacher of child psychology at the University of Western Ontario. The course took place at the Windsor YMCA in 1937.

Organizing support for progressive movements was also important to the group. Accordingly, the Study Club dispatched a representative to the Marcus Garvey meeting, held at the British Methodist Episcopal Church (the B.M.E.) in Windsor on September 17, 1937.

In 1938 Prince Edward School's Home and School Association held a "Progressive Education Association Conference." The Study Club sent a representative to the Conference. Study Club founding member Ardella Jacobs also belonged to that Association. Ardella Jacobs was an extremely busy woman. She was also a member of the Sara Simons Child Study Club, the organization which sponsored a lecture at the Windsor YMCA in May 1938, where Dr. Edith Hale Swift from Wayne State University in Detroit spoke on "The Needs of Present Day Youth." Many Study Club members attended.

Hard times did not keep Study Club members from raising the money they needed to do their work. In October 1938 the Study Club held a Contribution Tea at Ardella Jacobs' home.

The Study Club started off its 1939 program with a lecture on child psychology. At the beginning of the event, the mistress of ceremonies introduced the guest speaker by pointing out that the topic of child psychology was not new. Even Plato, Locke and Rousseau, she said, were interested in it. The guest speaker, Rev. C.L. Wells, the pastor of the First Baptist Church in Windsor, chose as his topic "Training Children to Meet the Social Needs of Society."

Members recognized early on the importance of recording the history of the Study Club. Hilda Watkins, the historian, prepared the first history in 1939, five years after the Study Club formed. The importance of recording and passing on the history was such that the historian read it aloud each year at the Annual Graduates' Party.

By 1940 the Study Club had decided to hold an Annual Parents' Dinner each February. Goldie Robbins opened her home for a Contribution Tea in 1940. By that year Study Club members had also begun to celebrate Mothers' Day by attending church together. In 1940 they attended the B.M.E. Church; the 1941 Mothers' Day service was held at the First Baptist Church. Club members also turned out in full force in April 1940, to a lecture and movie sponsored by the Maternal Health League in Patterson Collegiate's auditorium.

During the Study Club's first eight years members normally met at Ardella Jacobs' house. They might meet elsewhere, however; in October

1940, for example, the Study Club held its regular meeting in Willistead Library in the Parent-Teacher Room, where members devoted their time to consulting books and other works on child psychology and related topics.

In 1941 Study Club members decided that members of the executive should take turns hosting a meeting, starting in September, and that lunch should be served at each meeting. Previously, "except on special occasions, no lunch had been served."

Study Club members actively recruited new mothers to join. They had to keep in close touch with the Windsor community to keep track of new mothers and formed a committee to do this. How successful these membership drives were is not clear, but committee members visited new mothers, presented them with a small gift (and, by 1952, had begun to give them a copy of *Parents' Magazine*) and invited them to join. Usually, the gifts were garments, but by 1947 the Study Club decided to give baby books.[66]

When finances did not permit all Study Club members to take part in activities of interest to the group, the Club sent a few members who then passed on what they had learned. Thus in 1942 two members attended classes at the Handicraft Guild and then taught other Study Club members.

By October 1942 Ardella Jacobs had become honourary president, after having served as president during the Study Club's first eight years. It would not be until 1943 that the group wrote its by-laws. Elizabeth Washington, who was now president, appointed a committee to work on the matter. By 1944, the study liaison convener, Mrs. Leon DeShield, had announced that the Study Club could get free films, both educational and entertaining, from the National Film Board.

Child development, however, would remain the foremost activity. Book discussions and book reviews figured strongly in Study Club meetings. In October 1944 the Study Club held a round table discussion during "Better Parenthood Week," with doctors, dentists and church people participating. The Study Club also kept close links with the Current Topic Study Club of Detroit. In 1944 Study Club members turned out for a meeting of that club in Detroit. When the Study Club held its Annual Parents' Dinner in 1945, the Detroit Current Topic Study Club came.

The war ended, but Study Club fund-raising continued. Elizabeth Washington and the Finance Committee held a successful Penny-A-Meal Campaign in 1947 and continued to send Club members for training. That year the group sent Naomi Edmonds to a leadership training course in London, Ontario, and paid most of her expenses. And Study Club members Mrs. Charles Butler and Mrs. James Stewart took a ten-week leadership training course at Assumption College in 1956.

Other Study Club fund-raising activities included a Contribution Tea held in September 1951 to raise money to help Martha Elliot further her musical education. In 1952 Study Club members read and discussed the Massey Report. Club members enjoyed the successes of such students as Charlene Stewart, whom the group congratulated for winning a prize at Victoria School for Music Studies.

By 1952 the Study Club had taken on a more formal structure, with executive now holding regular monthly meetings. The executive prepared an outline of study for the year and appointed a Program Committee to arrange entertainment for each regular meeting. Two years later, in 1954, the Study Club marked its twentieth anniversary with the theme Negro History.

Former member Ada E. Whitney (and daughter of Club member Elizabeth Christian Kelly) had moved to New York. Whitney came back to give the keynote address at the anniversary celebrations. In describing the work of Study Club members she reminded them, "You were born in the adversity of the depression. You have worked together, laughed, played and wept, but here you are now a full-fledged grown-up.... You have made the community aware of your purposes, because you have put words and dreams into action. You have given your children encouragement in school. You have helped them financially through your scholarships. You have inspired them to achieve further than you could achieve. You have helped other parents...given them courage."[67]

Whitney remembered an earlier time: "Many years ago, when a student at the old WCI, I must have been something of an introvert and always had a sense of not 'belonging' to the group. I had a feeling that I was not wanted.... When I returned to Windsor to teach, I found many children of the friends of my parents in High School, but frustrated and frequently discouraged to the point of wanting to drop out of school. I, along with a few others, brought them together into the organization known as the Windsor Educational Association." Whitney went on to remind her Study Club sisters that the Windsor Educational Association was a forerunner of the Hour-A-Day Study Club. In her speech, "The Community and World Events" Whitney articulated the Study Club's emphasis on global analysis in looking at issues.[68]

What influence did the Study Club have on new mothers? We know that through the distribution of *Parents' Magazine* members sought to influence new mothers in child-rearing. How effective this magazine proved is not certain. The Study Club did not confine its work to infants and young children, however, but made adolescents the prime target. The Child Study Discussion Groups, organized by Hilda Dungy and Verna Stewart in October 1952, focused on "What Recreational and Social Activities Are Available for our Adolescents and Juniors?" Even so, Study Club members were troubled by young children's behaviour, as reflected in the topic chosen by Althea DeShield: "They Have Such Awful Manners," a group discussion held in October 1952.

Both the Study Club's lectures and its discussion series centred on its Child Study Program, a program shaped according to age groupings. Typical topics on adolescence, for example, were "Helping Teenagers Solve Their Problems" and "Accident Prevention." The mothers of pre-schoolers discussed such topics as "Preparing the Child for School."

In September 1953 The Study Club gave money to two nursing students, Teresa Patterson and Helen Turner, and presented Eleanor Vincent with a scholarship. In 1955 Carol Vincent won a Study Club scholarship for one hundred dollars.

Study Club members also worked in other organizations. In 1956 Mrs. Elizabeth Kelly represented the Study Club at the Educational Council's meeting on "Television and the Part it is Playing Today." By 1956 Study Club members like Luella White and Vivian Nall were also going to the meetings of the Windsor Board of Education.

By 1956 Black women like Teresa Patterson, Helen Turner and Eleanor Vincent were graduating from the Hotel Dieu Hospital nursing school. Study Club representative Mrs. W.C. Kelly attended their graduation at the Capital Theatre in Windsor. Eleanor Vincent received a Study

Club citation for "leadership and personality." In September 1956 Sharon Coates won a Study Club scholarship.

The Study Club helped young women like Delina Nolan with one hundred dollars to help her prepare for a position as a court clerk in Toronto in 1956. In 1957 Marilyn Talbot won the Study Club scholarship and in 1959 Carol Dungy won it. Study Club members attended the openings of Assumption University Library and of the new addition for exceptional children at Glengarda School. In 1958 a missionary woman, Ethel Alexander of Amherstburg, addressed the Study Club. In 1959 the Students' Rally held a "A Career Forum," with panellists discussing law, social work, teaching, medicine, business administration. Eighty-two students turned out.

In 1960 past-president Louise Rock and Vivian Nall responded to a call from a Mr. McIssac of Maryvale, who wanted the Study Club to help two Negro girls adjust to the program at Maryvale, a place for "delinquent" girls. In 1961 Sharon Browning, Patricia Kelly and Charlene Stewart won scholarships. The Study Club had limited means, but in 1961 it formed a Loan Fund Committee, made up of Miss V. Ladd, Mrs. L. Lucas, Louise Rock, Gladys VanDyke and Hilda Watkins.

In the meantime, the group gave several students small donations to encourage them to go on with their studies or to recognize their accomplishments. In 1962 it gave Burnetta Day a ten-dollar donation for her accomplishments in music. In 1963 Mrs. Rose Ann White received a donation of fifty dollars to further her education. By 1967 the scholarship fund had grown to two hundred dollars and was to be awarded to a "Grade 13 Senior Matriculant" from a Windsor secondary school. That year, Ann Marie Haynes won the award. The 1968 scholarships went to Beth Ann Allen, Hilda Watkins, Wanda Scott and Cynthia Dungy.

By 1966 the Study Club had started to recruit younger women, with Sharron Freeman responsible for this activity. I do not know what success the group had, but there is evidence that younger women like Hilda Watkins, a granddaughter of a Study Club founder, participated in Study Club activities. She spoke to the group on her experiences on a youth travel project in 1967.

By October 1970 the Study Club had set up a committee to register the scholarship trust fund as a charitable organization with the Department of National Revenue. Janice Steele and Josephine Starks won Study Club scholarships, with the money coming from fund-raising activities like the group's annual cultural program. That program was now being reviewed.

Affiliations

From its beginnings, the Hour-A-Day Study Club took on more than child development and throughout its work has had strong links with the Black community in Detroit. This connection would prove crucial. And while it was not always practical for all Study Club members to attend every Detroit event, those who could went to the conference on "Interracial Problems of Today" held at the Central Detroit YMCA in 1937.

A year after the Hour-A-Day Study Club formed it affiliated with the Windsor's Local Council of Women, a chapter of the National Council of Women. During 1946, Study Club members actively participated on the Citizenship Committee of the Local Council. In the 1947 election they were actively engaged in getting women out to vote. In the 1960s Verna Chatters was elected president of the Council.

During World War II a War Committee of six members formed, with Elizabeth Washington as the general convener. Study Club members knitted and sewed for the war effort. They also distributed wool, taught other women how to knit and sew, collected the finished garments and worked with the Red Cross and Salvage Office. Study Club members made quilts in whatever spare time they had, with Elizabeth Washington opening her house in May 1941 for a quilt drawing and tea. Members made and donated a quilt in celebration of Canada's 100th birthday. The Study Club hired a lawyer to defend Howard Berry Jr. who had accused the Windsor police of brutality. Vivian Nall and Hilda Walkins attended the court case. Study Club members participated in planning the Emancipation Day Celebrations held in Windsor. In 1954 Mary McLeod Bethune and Eleanor Roosevelt were part of the Emancipation festivities. During the 1960s the Study Club returned to a focus on Negro History. Hilda Dungy reviewed the life of Malcolm X; Hilda Watkins spoke on the history of the Study Club and members reviewed books by Negro authors and viewed a film on Martin Luther King, Jr.

At its regular meeting in November 1972 members discussed the liberation of women. In February 1974 Hilda Dungy gave a lecture on Karl Marx and Dr. Algra Harrison spoke on the liberation of women, particularly about Black women having to establish their own identities, and about their educational attainments and their high self-esteem.

In 1977 the Study Club made "Working Together for Community Betterment" its motto. That August it hosted the Fourth National Congress of Black Women, held at the Holiday Inn in Windsor, under the theme "Impetus — Black Women." A important event in the history of the Study Club is its annual spring musical in Windsor. Besides being a fund-raising event, it provides a cultural space for Black women and men in the arts.

The Hour-A-Day Study Club continues to make a strong contribution to the lives of Black women. In 1984 Shirley Chisholm, a former member of the United States House of Representatives, was the keynote speaker at the Study Club's fiftieth anniversary celebration. In all areas of education, but particularly in nursing, it has encouraged and supported many young women. More importantly, the women who have come together in the Study Club give hope to youngsters as they carve out spaces for themselves, as they define Black womanhood.

Black women's long history of organizing in Canada has many strands, but most of these efforts are little known outside the community. (Among the many groups whose stories have yet to be told is the Black Education Project, a highly effective group of women and men who organized to combat racism in the schools and among the police in Toronto, between 1969 and about 1980.)

Nearly six decades after the founding of Windsor's Hour-A-Day Study Club, the Black Women's Collective, too, organizes its work around the continuity underlying Black women's lives and Black women's struggles.

Conclusion

The Black women who formed the Hour-A-Day Study Club drew strength from each other as they developed a distinctive female culture rooted in a strong sense of themselves.[69] While their community remained besieged, Study Club women resisted at every turn. (Anti-discrimination legislation passed in the 1940s by the Drew government in Ontario acted principally as a pacifier and did not fundamentally address the issue of racism.[70])

They also raised children, mended socks, cooked and fed families, planted flowers and vegetables, sang in church choirs, did missionary work, took care of the sick, taught school, did volunteer and paid work. They did all those things and more. Most of the women who started the Study Club were in their thirties. Adella Jacobs' only child, Ken, was a teenager at the time. Louise Rock, the president from 1945-1948 and again from 1952-1955, not only played the organ at church services but pioneered a program to bring musical activity to developmentally disabled children in Windsor.[71] These women defined their commitment to Study Club activities not only in terms of their commitment to their families but to a wider citizenry. The Hour-A-Day-Study-Club membership grew steadily over the years. By 1945 two-thirds of the founding members were still members and the Club had by that time almost tripled its numbers.

In recalling the organizing of a group of Black women in Windsor, we need to remember that Black women's tradition of struggle reaches back to our earliest foremothers across the Americas and their fights against racial, class and gender oppression. Mary Ann Shadd, the nineteenth-century newspaper editor, pointed out that her gender stirred objections within her community to her as spokesperson.[72] But as Evelyn Brooks-Higginbotham writes, "If the overwhelming reality of racism has tended to obscure the class differences in the black community, it has obscured the system of gender relations even more."[73]

In organizing specifically around schooling, the Windsor mothers continued the work the Black women and men who organized the True Band Society in the 1840s and the Black women who established and ran schools, taught in them in the mid-nineteenth century (Mary Ann Shadd, Mary Bibb, Amelia Freeman and others).

Black women's political work was all-encompassing; they did not confine themselves to narrow definitions of women's sphere. Indeed, by virtue of their race and class, Black women were excluded from the Victorian concept of "womanhood."

One may argue that the role these mothers played in the Study Club was traditional, since child-rearing has traditionally been the province of women. The Hour-A-Day-Study Club women, however, were (and are) engaged in resistance; they challenged the very structure of society, reminding women "factors of class and race make any generalization of womanhood's common oppression impossible.[74] Moreover, only "by addressing the problem of race, women's history will more clearly see how race and class give meaning to gender."[75]

Notes

I would like to express my thanks to the staff of the North American Black Historical Museum in Amherstburg, Ontario. I am specially indebted to the curator, Elise Davis, who facilitated my research. My thanks also to Anthony Bristow whose encouragement and support has sustained me during this reclamation.

1. Cleata Morris' address to the Fourth National Congress of Black Women of Canada. *Impetus — The Black Woman*, Proceedings of the National Congress of Black Women of Canada, Windsor, 1977.

2. Earle Conrad. *Harriet Tubman: Negro Soldier and Abolitionist* (New York: International Publishers, 1942).

3. Black women in the Americas have a long history of organizing against racist oppression and in so doing they have necessarily forged links with their sisters throughout the region.

4. Bonnie Thornton Dill in "Race, Class and Gender: Prospects for an All-Inclusive Sisterhood" in Mary Jo Deegan and Michael Hill, eds. *Women and Symbolic Interaction* (Boston: Allen & Unwin Inc. 1987), p. 162.

5. Rosemary Brown. Keynote speech to the National Congress of Black Women, April 1973, in the Daniel Hill Papers, National Archives of Canada, Ottawa.

6. *Ibid.*

7. Nellie Y. McKay in "Race, Gender and Cultural Context in Zora Neale Hurston's Dust Tracks on a Road" in Bella Brokzki and Celeste Schenck, eds. *Life/Lines: Theorizing Women's Autobiography* (Ithaca: Cornell University Press, 1988), pp. 175-176.

8. Bonnie Thornton Dill. *Op. cit.,* p. 164.

9. *Ibid.*

10. James W. St. G. Walker. *A History of Blacks in Canada* (Hull: Minister of Supply and Service, 1980).

11. Verda Cooke in an interview in *The Toronto Star*, Sunday, August 5, 1990, p. D1.

12. Esther Hayes in an interview. Dionne Brand. *No Burden to Carry: Narratives of Black Working Women in Ontario 1920s to 1950s* (Toronto: Women's Press, 1991), p. 206.

13. *Ibid.*, p. 207.

14. See Barbara Roberts in "'A Work of Empire': Canada Reformers and British Female Immigration" in Linda Kealy, ed. *A Not Unreasonable Claim: Women and Reform in Canada: 1880s-1920s* (Toronto: Women's Press, 1979); Genevieve Leslie in "Domestic Service in Canada, 1880-1920" in Janice Acton *et. al.*, eds. *Women at Work: Ontario, 1850-1950* (Toronto: Canadian Women's Educational Press, 1974); Sheelagh Conway. *The Faraway Hills Are Green: Voices of Irish Women in Canada* (Toronto: Women's Press, 1992). Conway reminds us that "British" is a misnomer: Irish (and Scots) women who came to Canada to work as domestics were grouped with English women. Because of the conflating of the three nationalities, the record remains unclear. For a discussion on the relationship between Black women and the Canadian state, see Linda Carty in "African Canadian Women and the State: Labour Only Please" in *We Are Rooted Here, And They Can't Pull Us Up: Essays in African Canadian Women's History* (Toronto: University of Toronto Press, Forthcoming Spring 1994).

15. Robin Winks. *The Blacks in Canada* (New Haven: Yale University Press, 1971), p. 26.

16. *Ibid.*

17. *Ibid.*

18. Carty. *Op. cit.*

19. Edmund Head to Lord Grey. CO42/167, PRO, London. See also Ged Martin in "British Officials and Their Attitudes to the Negro Community in Canada, 1833-1861" in *Ontario History,* Vol. LXVI, No. 2, June 1974.

20. Harold Martin Troper in "The Creek-Negro of Oklahoma and Canadian Immigration, 1909-11" in the *Canadian Historical Review*, Vol. 53, 1972, p. 272.

21. Winks. *Op. cit.* p. 316.

22. *Ibid.*, p. 320.

23. Constance Backhouse. *Petticoats & Prejudice: Women and Law in Nine-teenth-Century Canada* (Toronto: Women's Press, 1991), p. 98.

24. Mariana Valverde in "When the Mother of the Race is Free: Race, Repro-duction, and Sexuality in First-Wave Feminism" in Franca Iacovetta and Mariana Valverde, eds. *Gender Conflicts: New Essays in Women's History* (Toronto: University of Toronto Press, 1992), pp. 4-5.

25. *Ibid.,* p. 5.

26. Angus McLaren and Arlene Tigar McLaren. *The Bedroom and the State: The Changing Practices and Politics of Contraception and Abortion in Canada, 1880-1980* (Toronto: McClelland and Stewart, 1986), p. 17.

27. Ruth Roach Pierson. *"They're Still Women After All": The Second World War and Canadian Womanhood* (Toronto: McClelland and Stewart, 1986), p. 22.

28. *Ibid.*

29. H.E. Stratton to the Amherstburg Community Club. Alvin D. McCurdy Papers, Reference F 2076, Ontario Provincial Archives.

30. Gwen Johnson in Brand, *op.cit.,* p. 184. Bernice Redmon, who trained as a nurse in Virginia, became the first Canadian-born Black registered nurse to be employed, in 1944, in public health in Ontario. See Enid F. D'Oyle and Rella Braithwaite. *Women of Our Times* (Toronto: self-published, 1977). Ruth Bailey, having been denied admission to several Ontario hospital nursing schools, graduated as a registered nurse in Halifax, Nova Scotia, in October 1948.

31. Brand. *Op. cit.,* p. 184. As well, in most sections of Ontario during the nineteenth century, Black children were excluded from attending the com-mon schools with white children. See documents in Alison L. Prentice and Susan E. Houston, eds. *Family, School and Society in Nineteenth-Century Canada* (Toronto: Oxford University Press, 1973), pp. 233-346.

32. *Ibid.,* p. 206.

33. *Ibid.*

34. *Ibid.,* p. 204.

35. *Ibid.,* p. 535.

36. Darlene Hine Clark. *Black Women in White: Racial Conflict and Coopera-tion in the Nursing Profession 1890-1950* (Bloomington: Indiana University Press, 1989). See also Angela Davis. *Women, Race and Class* (New York: Vintage Books, 1981); Paula Giddings. *When and Where I Enter: The Impact*

of *Black Women on Race and Sex in America* (New York: William Morrow & Company, 1984); Jacqueline Jones. *Labor of Love, Labor of Sorrow: Black Women, Work and the Family from Slavery to the Present* (New York: Basic Books, 1985).

37. As Dionne Brand comments, "Black women's work is historically rooted in slavery in the Americas. As a consequence, it is hidden, devalued, and marked by gender." See *Fireweed: A Feminist Quarterly*, No. 26, 1988. p. 87. See also Agnes Calliste in "Canada's Immigration Policy and Domestics from the Caribbean: The Second Domestic Scheme" in Jesse Vorst, ed. *Race, Class, Gender: Bonds and Barriers* (Toronto: Between the Lines, 1989); Makeda Silvera. *Silenced* (Toronto: Williams-Wallace, 1983); Linda Carty in *We Are Rooted Here*. See in *Legacy to Buxton* (North Buxton: Arlie C. Robbins, 1983) p. 168.

38. Unpublished history of the Hour-A-Day Study Club. The North American Black Historical Museum Papers, Amherstburg, Ontario.

39. *Ibid.*

40. Gwendolyn Robinson and John W. Robinson. *Seek the Truth: A Story of Chatham's Black Community* (Canada: Self-Published, 1989); Daniel G. Hill. *The Freedom-Seekers: Blacks in Early Canada* (Agincourt: The Book Society of Canada Ltd., 1981).

41. Dorothy Shadd Shreve. *The AfriCanadian Church: A Stabilizer.* Ontario: Paideia Press, 1983), pp. 52-53; C. Peter Ripley, ed. *The Black Abolitionist Papers, Vol. II* (Chapel Hill and London: University of North Carolina Press, 1985), p. 306. Black women, of course, worked in the anti-slavery societies in various parts of Canada. See Ripley, *ibid.*, p. 222.

42. *Provincial Freeman*, 1855, Ontario Provincial Archives. See also Daniel Hill, *op. cit.*, p. 179. Hill mentions the Queen Victoria Benevolent Society, led by Ellen Abbott. See also Adrienne Shadd, "300 Years of Black Women in Canadian History: Circa 1700-1980" in *Tiger Lily*, Vol. 1, Issue 2, 1987.

43. Brand. *Op. cit.*

44. Winks. *Op. cit.*, p. 319.

45. Brand. *Op. cit.*, p. 17.

46. Sylvia Hamilton in "Naming Names, Naming Ourselves" in *We Are Rooted Here*.

47. Unpublished history of the Hour-A-Day Study Club.

48. Stephanie Shaw, in the *Journal of Women's History*, suggests that club

women's work is "another step in an internal historical process of encouraging and supporting self-determination, self-improvement and community.

49. Michael S. Cross and George S. Kealey. *Readings in Canadian Social History, Vol. 5: Modern Canada 1930-1980s* (Toronto: McClelland and Stewart, 1984).

50. Carol Talbot. *Growing Up Black in Canada* (Toronto: Williams Wallace, 1984), pp. 20-21. Talbot notes

   ...blacks were not allowed to own property in the towns of Essex, Kingsville, Leamington and Tilbury in southwestern Ontario. It was even said that blacks were not allowed to stay after sundown in some of those towns. Working in those towns was out of the question for blacks, except as hired hands and domestics....Dad says that, as a young man travelling with his father to the rural Baptist parishes of North Buxton, Dresden and Chatham Township, there were few places that would serve them meals and even fewer where blacks could spend a night. In other communities...London, Brantford, Hamilton, Niagara Falls and St. Catharines, there was essentially the same situation. The blacks remained in small clusters in and around the cities, living on the fringes of the mainstream society.

51. Brand. *Op. cit.*, p. 15.

52. Letter written by Alvin McCurdy on behalf of the Amherstburg Community Club to the NAACP in Detroit, June 1934. Alvin McCurdy Papers.

53. Talbot. *Op.cit.*, p. 69.

54. *Ibid.*, p. 74.

55. Alvin McCurdy Papers.

56. Talbot. *Op. cit.*, pp. 74-75.

57. *Ibid.*, p. 80.

58. Brand. *Op. cit.*, p. 101.

59. *Ibid.*

60. Talbot. *Op. cit.*, p. 79. In 1855 Emaline Shadd earned a teaching certificate from the Toronto Normal School. It is not known whether this was standard practice at the time. Eunice Hyatt Kersey taught in the Windsor public schools in the first quarter of the twentieth century. See Rella Braithwaite and Tessa Benn-Ireland. *Some Black Women* (Toronto: Sister Vision Press, 1993), p. 51. Mary Bibb ran a school in Windsor during the mid-nineteenth century. See Afua Cooper "The Search for Mary Bibb, Black Woman Teacher

in Nineteenth-Century Canada West" in *Ontario History*, Vol. LXXXIII, No. 1, March 1991.

61. Talbot. *Op. cit.*, pp. 79-80.

62. Brand. *Op. cit.*, pp. 259-260.

63. Unpublished history of the Hour-A-Day Study Club.

64. *Ibid.*

65. *Ibid.*

66. *Ibid.*

67. *Ibid.*

68. *Ibid.*

69. Higginbotham argues that "the club movement among black women [in the U.S.] owed its very existence to the groundwork of organizational skill and leadership training gained through women's church societies." See Evelyn Brooks Higginbotham *Righteous Discontent: The Women's Movement in the Black Baptist Church, 1880-1920* (Cambridge: Harvard University Press, 1993), p. 17. The same can be argued for Canada as well.

70. Winks. *Op. cit.*, p. 427.

71. *Ibid.* See also *Commemorative Booklet* (Amherstburg: The North American Black Historical Museum, 1984).

72. Dorothy Sterling. *We Are Your Sisters* (New York: W.W. Norton & Company, 1984), p. 172. Mary Ann Shadd told her male critics "...it is fit that you should deport your ugliest to a woman," as she handed over the *Provincial Freeman* to Newman, the new editor. Newman acknowledged that Shadd was slighted because "she wore the petticoat instead of the breechers." See Ripley, *op. cit.*, *Provincial Freeman*, 1855.

73. Evelyn Brooks-Higginbottam in "The Problem of Race in Women's History" in Elizabeth Weed, ed., *Coming to Terms: Feminism, Theory, Politics* (New York: Routledge, 1989), p. 131.

74. *Ibid.* p. 133.

75. *Ibid.* p. 132.

DISCOVERING DISABLED WOMEN'S HISTORY

Diane Driedger

Women with disabilities have a past, a history yet to be discovered. The history of the post-World War II years worldwide has been one of oppressed people discovering their own histories and challenging their oppression through social movements. It has been important for marginalized, oppressed and colonized peoples to confront their histories of oppression, to throw off society's view of them as *different* and society's tendency to decide *for* them. This can only happen through people learning to *name* their oppression. As Paolo Freire states, "Those who have been denied their primordial right to speak their word must first retain this right and prevent the continuation of this dehumanizing oppression."[1]

Through "conscientization" — the awareness of the past and of what needs to be changed — disabled women will better be able to demand changes in their lives, to rename the world according to their experiences. Women with disabilities are doubly oppressed — they are disabled and they are women. This article looks at the history of disabled women's organizing in Canada and worldwide since 1945 and at ways to research the history of women with disabilities.

The Roots of the Disabled People's Movement

Disabled people have been oppressed through the centuries, shut away in asylums and family attics, regarded as possessed by spirits and shut out of the mainstream of life the world over. But, after World War II, life began to change for people with disabilities. Improved rehabilitation techniques had been developed for war-injured veterans. People with spinal cord injuries began to live longer. The polio epidemics of the 1950s produced survivors with a range of disabilities, many of whom were kept alive by iron lungs. Vietnam war veterans also joined the ranks of young disabled people in the 1960s and 1970s. In all, many more disabled young people were alive. Improved technical aids such as portable respirators and electric wheelchairs meant that disabled people were much more mobile and could live independently in the community.[2]

The post-World War II and post-Vietnam War eras also saw the rise of the rehabilitation professions — doctors, physiotherapists, nurses and social workers who became trained in how to deal with the lives of disabled persons. This led to many more rehabilitated people, but it also medicalised *all* aspects of life for disabled persons by classifying them as sick. As society generally excuses sick people from participating in everyday life, this became an excuse to exclude people with disabilities and to deny them responsibility for their lives. As Jim Derksen, a Canadian disabled activist says:

> The disabled person is allowed less self-determination than would normally be available to adults in his/her society...he/she is made to feel lacking or defeated as he/she is most often unable to meet the chief responsibility given him/her of becoming well or able-bodied since most disabilities are permanent in nature.[3]

Meanwhile, in the 1960s and 1970s, liberation movements swept the developing world and countries emerged from colonialism in Africa, Asia and the Caribbean. Liberation became a word in popular vocabularies. Many people became disabled as a result of liberation wars in the developing countries.

In North America, anti-Vietnam war protesters, Ralph Nader's consumer Raiders and Blacks organized in the 1950s and 1960s. Women again began to organize against their oppression in the 1960s and 1970s. All this set the stage for the rise of the disabled people's movement all over the world.

Canada

In the early 1970s people with disabilities began to organize for their rights in the U.S. Canadian disabled people organized soon after, starting provincial groups in Alberta, Saskatchewan and Manitoba from 1972-1974.[4] These were "cross-disability," groups, that is, they were

open to people with various physical disabilities, founded on the premise that people with various disabilities had a stronger voice united than
each group speaking out on its own. The western provinces struck a
national organization in 1976 — the Coalition of Provincial Organizations of the Handicapped (COPOH) — and other provinces across
Canada became affiliates soon after.

Unlike other national groups at the time, COPOH was made up
entirely of disabled people speaking for the rights of disabled people.
Previously, rehabilitation organizations and professionals had spoken
on behalf of disabled people. Over the years, COPOH was to successfully lobby government and to influence legislation on protecting the
rights of disabled persons in the Charter of Rights and Freedoms and in
the *Canadian Human Rights Act,* winning these victories for all disabled
persons, as these measures potentially protected the rights of every
disabled person. But in the early 1980s the concerns of women with
disabilities were not an issue for COPOH. It did not represent the
concerns of all disabled persons.

Disabled Women's Issues Excluded in Canada

Women with disabilities were included in the memberships and held
some positions in organizations of disabled persons in the 1970s. However, their involvement tended to be in supporting roles. Women were
committee members and sometimes members of the governing councils
of disabled people's provincial organizations. Yet in these roles they
often were the carriers of coffee or the workhorses that got committee
work done.[5]

In the early years of these organizations women with disabilities
generally saw themselves as disabled first, women second. As Pat
Danforth related, "Disability issues were so horrendous in those years."[6]
Indeed, if a woman could not even get affordable transportation to
public events or shopping places then how could she *not* join disabled
people's groups to lobby for those things?

In addition, some of the few women with disabilities who were
involved felt tokenized. Yvonne Peters who was involved in the *Human
Rights Act* lobbying efforts in Ottawa on behalf of COPOH, felt that she
was the token woman.[7]

While the women felt they were token women at times, they also believed that they were taken seriously in discussions on issues. But that depended on the issues. As long as a woman acted like "one of the boys" she was accepted. Women's issues were not regarded as "serious" issues by disabled men in the 1970s and early 1980s. As long as women brought up "important" issues such as transportation, accessibility or housing they were listened to. When disabled feminists Peters and Pat Israel sat on the national council of COPOH and brought up women's issues, they were brushed off. The women wanted the word "chairperson" to be used instead of "chairman." Men changed the subject every time the women raised it. Peters and Israel also wanted the number of women in leadership to increase.

Women with disabilities were few and far between on the COPOH Council, which had about fifteen representatives. There were usually two or three women on the Council, but in the late 1970s there was usually only one woman who was a feminist. Speaking out on women's issues only began when Yvonne Peters and Pat Danforth, then in Saskatchewan, sat on the COPOH Council in 1979. They then felt that they had the support to begin to speak out on women's issues.

Even so, they often felt patronized and laughed at. Women with disabilities began to see that their concerns were not going to be addressed by the "greater" disabled person's community. There had been a workshop that discussed "minority representation" in COPOH at the 1981 national conference in Quebec City. Women were included there. And a resolution had passed calling for equal representation for women and men in leadership positions in COPOH and for affirmative action policies to make this happen. A resolution calling for the study of women's issues had passed at the National Conference in Edmonton in 1983, but was not followed up until 1987, when COPOH published a discussion paper on disabled women.[8]

Women with disabilities did not perceive COPOH as being very serious about their issues. At the same time, women with disabilities also did not feel an affinity with the greater women's movement.

The Canadian Women's Movement and Disabled Women

While women with disabilities were active in disabled persons' organizations, women's groups did not see them as part of their constituency. Disabled women did not feel welcome in the women's movement — which did not really see them as "women" only as "different" and "disabled." The women's movement tended to define disabled women as the rest of society did and disabled women were not encouraged to join women's groups. In general, many women with disabilities did not even identify themselves as "women" because of society's and the women's movement's attitudes about them.

According to Paula Keirstead, a disabled feminist from Manitoba,

> From a very early age when a woman has a disability as a child, the whole concept of sexuality is very much in question. When you look at how society...places emphasis on appearance, your conscious feeling of being a true woman is in question if you buy that stuff. And many of us do...So for even your own self-image of saying and declaring proudly, "I am a woman with difference," for many women had not worked it's way through at all, especially if you have a husband leave you, if your doctor says get sterilized, you shouldn't have kids. So just even admitting to being happy about being a woman is often a big issue for women with a disability. Therefore, attaching themselves to a movement of creatures they are not sure they are a part of, women, would be the last thing on their minds.[9]

In addition, many women with disabilities were isolated, with no access to information about women's issues. Even if they did, they did not have accessible transportation, or could not get into a women's centre because of stairs, or could not participate in meetings because there was no sign interpretation.

Feminists with disabilities were not encouraged to join the women's movement. In 1984 Pat Israel and Yvonne Peters of COPOH attended the National Action Committee on the Status of Women's (NAC) conference in Ottawa. They talked with one of the leaders of NAC about women with disabilities and their concerns. Her reply was "Our agenda is so packed with so many issues we can't take on another one."[11] Peters felt that at the very least the response should have been "Let's talk about the issues." But, the worst of it was that Pat Israel had to enter the meeting in demeaning circumstances: "...When I attended a national women's conference I had to use a dirty, foul-smelling freight elevator to get to the workshops. There was garbage on the floor and walls. I felt degraded and dirty every time I had to use it."[11] When Israel raised her concerns with conference organizers, their response was that they had to pick between money and accessibility and they could not afford to hold it in an accessible place. But the meeting was held at the Holiday Inn, not exactly an inexpensive place![12]

Even before being rebuffed at the national meeting, Israel had attempted to become involved in the women's movement in Toronto. When she called and asked about accessibility because she was a wheelchair-user, the answer was "We have stairs" and that was the end of it. Not only are the offices of women's organizations inaccessible, so are many women's events, women's shelters and hotlines (which lack TDDs for hearing impaired women).[13] Thus not only were disabled men saying disabled women's concerns were not valid, so were non-disabled women. Women with disabilities, confronted by barriers, decided to organize on their own.

Canadian Women with Disabilities Organize

Like the disabled people's movement ten years before it, the disabled women's movement also had its birth in Western Canada, where disabled women first began to organize in Saskatchewan and Manitoba. Women with disabilities met in 1984 in Regina, Saskatchewan, and decided to hold a one-day conference of disabled women. These women saw that the Saskatchewan Voice of the Handicapped had few women leaders, even though there were many disabled women in the membership who were active as the grassroots workers for the movement.

The women raised the $600 budget for the conference by writing to women's groups and unions for donations. The conference was held in 1984 and a few women from outside Regina also attended. There was difficulty in raising enough travel money for women from all over the province to attend. A six-member steering committee came out of the conference and this was the beginning of the DisAbled Women's Network in Saskatchewan.[14]

Around the same time, in Manitoba, a small group of disabled and non-disabled feminists started to meet around the concerns of women with disabilities. The Manitoba Action Committee on the Status of Women's coordinator, Charlynn Toews, was one of the two women who spearheaded the group; Elizabeth Semkiw, a long-time activist and leader in the Manitoba League of the Physically Handicapped, was the other. At this meeting of the women's and disabled people's movements in Manitoba a core group of disabled and non-disabled women initially formed to deal with the abuse of a woman with a disability in Winnipeg. Ultimately, the group began talking about other issues facing women with disabilities and saw that more research and public awareness needed to be done. The Consulting Committee on the Status of Women with Disabilities (CCSWD) was born in 1984.[15]

Nineteen eighty-five was an important year in disabled women's organizing. That year women in COPOH began to discuss women's issues and COPOH hosted a National Conference in Montreal in March where several informal women's meetings were held. Resolutions from these meetings called for a workshop on women's issues at the next conference and for "an investigation of women's participation within the COPOH structure."[16]

And in early 1985 a small group of women with disabilities met with representatives of the Department of Secretary of State in Ottawa. These meetings led to a "Women with Disabilities Networking Meeting" in June 1985, in Ottawa. Two disabled women from each province and from the North West Territories came to that four-day meeting. DisAbled Women's Network Canada formed a committee to coordinate national expansion and the founding of DAWN Canada. All delegates agreed to return to their provinces and, where none existed, to start groups of disabled women.

That year groups were founded in Toronto, Montreal, Ottawa, PEI and Halifax. British Columbia founded its group in 1986.[17] In March 1987 the founding National Meeting of DAWN was held in Winnipeg. [18]

Since the founding meeting, DAWN has been researching issues of concern to disabled women. Four position papers were published in February 1989, on self-image, employment, parenting and violence.[19] These are issues — especially violence against women with disabilities — that neither the women's nor the disabled persons' movements were addressing.

In recent years, though, DAWN has been working with both the women's movement and the disabled people's movement. After Pat Israel's initial demeaning elevator ride at the National Action Committee on the Status of Women's national meeting, she talked to organizers about choosing accessible sites. In subsequent years NAC's meetings have been held in locations accessible through the front door. Also, Israel was elected a board member of NAC in 1986 and served for a year. That year NAC passed a resolution to ensure accessibility to NAC meetings and offices. A resolution also passed which urged NAC members across Canada to "contact DAWN and/or other disabled women in their communities and determine how they can best lend support to their disabled sisters." [20]

DAWN has also joined COPOH as an associate member, to work with it on issues of concern to women with disabilities. The first woman chairperson of COPOH, Irene Feika, was elected in 1986 and served until 1990. During that period, at least half the members of the COPOH executive were women. Currently, COPOH again has a woman chairperson, Francine Arsenault, elected in 1992. And DAWN has also worked with a group of disabled persons, the Canadian Disability Rights Council (CDRC), on challenges under the Charter of Rights and Freedoms, to ensure the rights of disabled Canadians. DAWN and CDRC published a series of papers in 1990 on the implications of new reproductive technologies for women and disabled persons.[21] However, both the women's and the disabled persons' communities need to do more work to recognize disabled women's issues as important.

Disabled Women Worldwide

Women with disabilities have been organizing to have their voices heard in other countries and at international forums. Their stories are similar to those of Canadian disabled women. While organizations of disabled persons sprang up in over 100 countries after 1945, women have either been not well-represented or not represented at all in decision-making positions. As in Canada, women's issues have not been seen as important by the greater disabled persons' movement, or by the greater women's movement.

Representation in the Disabled People's Movement

Within the worldwide disabled people's movement, there are two ways that women are demanding their rights. First, women with disabilities have risen up within Disabled Peoples' International (DPI), an organization formed in 1981, and have pointed out that very few women are leaders in local, national or international organizations. This call for change began in 1983, with a resolution calling for more representation, but it was not acted upon. In 1984 women with disabilities met separately at a DPI symposium on development in Jamaica and again asked for equal representation. Again, nothing was done.

As in Canada, 1985 became a watershed year for women with disabilities; they attended the DPI World Congress in the Bahamas and demanded that women make up fifty percent of the leadership in DPI member organizations at all levels. Crucial to the women's organizing were the women of DAWN Canada and the women from Australia who called women together in three separate meetings where women cited their lack of participation in leadership and drafted a resolution requiring fifty percent representation. Dr. Fatima Shah of Pakistan warned that disabled women would separate and form their own organization if DPI did not include women. The resolution passed.[22]

In the years since the 1985 resolution, the representation of women in DPI has increased at all levels but not significantly. Of twenty-eight World Council members, only seven are women. In 1985 there were two women on the World Council. At the same time, DPI has also held leadership training seminars for disabled women in different parts of the world. This has increased the skills of women, especially in Africa, Asia, the Caribbean and Latin America, where it is difficult for a woman with a disability to get even a basic education. Indeed, in many countries the limited educational opportunities for disabled children are usually given to boys.

DPI has also created a Deputy Chair position on its executive, which will look at the inclusion of underrepresented groups in DPI, including women, deaf persons and developmentally disabled people. Zohra Rajah of Mauritius was elected to this new position in 1990. Overall there are a few more women on the governing bodies of disabled persons' organizations, but even when women are on the executive they are almost always the secretary, a traditional female role.

Disabled women's second solution to under-representation in the disabled persons' movement has been to form their own caucuses within those organizations. The caucus solution has the potential for only limited impact, especially in countries in the developing world where women's issues and participation is not really seen as important, due to traditional views of women. Nevertheless, disabled women do at least have an opportunity to formulate their own ideas and present those to the greater membership for action. There are women's caucuses in organizations in Zimbabwe, New Zealand, Jamaica, Thailand, Mauritania, South Korea, Dominica and Trinidad and Tobago.

Disabled Women's Organizations

Several international disabled women's organizations have formed in the last few years. In 1985, as women were challenging DPI to include disabled women, women with disabilities had already organized Disabled Women's International. At the World Conference to Review the Achievements of the United Nations Decade for Women, July 15-26, in Nairobi, Kenya, disabled women decided to form their own organization, but few of the disabled women in Nairobi would attend the DPI World Congress in Bahamas later in the year.

In Nairobi the lack of accessibility to the women's movement again left disabled women no option but to organize: "No sign language interpreters were provided, none of the meeting schedules were in Braille or recorded on cassette, and access to most workshops was blocked by at least one flight of stairs in each building."[23]

There was, however, a workshop about barriers to women with disabilities. The thirty-five women with disabilities who attended discussed barriers to education, jobs, attitudes towards disabled women, health, family and marriage. The workshop presented recommendations to the conference; these included a call for the United Nations to ensure the accessibility of all future major conferences. The final report of the Women's Decade Conference called on governments to provide opportunities for disabled women to participate in all aspects of life.

Women had come from fourteen countries, both from the developed and developing worlds, but they saw that they had one thing in common. "We are women, we happen to have a disability and we are determined to cope with that problem."[24] Disabled Women's International (DWI) was born out of the workshop. It was a loose network and women returned home to encourage others to join. DWI has published one information-sharing newsletter a year since 1986, but lack of funding has meant that DWI has done little else.

DWI has been slow to organize. In August 1990, partially as a result of this inaction, the World Coalition of Women with Disabilities was founded. At the United Nations Meeting of Disabled Women in Vienna, women with disabilities noted that both the women's movement and the disabled persons' movement remain slow to recognize and include the concerns of disabled women. Women with disabilities may live different lives from country to country, but all experience oppression as women with disabilities. The women attending realized that they needed a world organization to tackle the barriers.[25] Members of the organization met again in Vancouver in 1992, at Independence '92, an international conference of disabled persons.

At the national level, very few separate disabled women's organizations exist worldwide. Women have formed their own groups in Australia, Uganda, the United States and Canada. In Australia, the Women with Disabilities Feminist Collective demonstrates against beauty pageants, a protest that is particularly relevant to disabled women because not only do beauty pageants promote perfect bodies, they raise funds for disabled persons' charities in Australia. The WDFC has also published its own anthology of disabled women's writing, *Women and Disability: An Issue.*[26]

In the United States, Handicapped Organized Women (HOW) has a different view on beauty pageants. While the Australian women deplore that society measures women by perfect bodies (disabled women cannot fulfill this requirement), HOW was founded by women who had won wheelchair beauty pageants. HOW's philosophy is that disabled women can do anything they set their minds to. HOW provides peer counselling — women helping women — but it does not appear that HOW has been connected with other disabled people's rights groups over the years.

The Uganda Disabled Women's Association, formed around 1986, is also involved in self-help. Its goal is to "uplift the well-being of disabled women in Uganda."[27] The group makes handicrafts such as mats, baskets, trays, shopping bags and bed linens when it meets once a month. Its members sell these crafts on behalf of the Association, give one quarter of the sales to the group and keep the rest. The group's development worker travels in the more rural areas to mobilize women with disabilities to join the Association. The group states, "Not only do we see ourselves as disabled, we are women. And thus, on March 8, 1988, the International Women's Day, we participated in marching through the city roads...Our speed was slow, but we enjoyed ourselves."[28] The group continues to fight for the rights of women with disabilities.

Writing Disabled Women's History

Since there is a tendency for academics and writers to write *about* people without consulting them, it is important to work *with* the people one is researching. For too long, people with disabilities have had others — medical professionals and social workers — do things to them or write about them. This, of course, includes women with disabilities, probably to an even greater degree. Since disabled women are women, they have tended to be more silent, in keeping with to society's prescription for women. Writers researching the history of women with disabilities should rely heavily on writings by, not about, disabled women, or, at the very least, look at writings where the authors have consulted with women with disabilities.

Until just ten years ago, very few women with disabilities were writing about their situations, their histories or their philosophies of liberation. This has begun to change through books such as *Voices From the Shadows* in Canada *Visions of Flight* (1991) and *With the Power of Each Breath: An Anthology by Women with Disabilities* in the U.S. There have also been anthologies published in Australia, Norway and Sweden. An international anthology, *Imprinting Our Image* was published in 1992.[29] These books provide examples of women's everyday experiences and some theories about their lives.

And *Women with Disabilities: Essays in Psychiatry, Culture and Politics* and *Living Inside Outside,* both by women with disabilities, look at barriers and how they came to be.[30] In the area of historical research, though, there is very little written by women with disabilities or by others.

In the face of the dearth of published information, one needs to turn to primary sources in archives and rehabilitation centres, to look for evidence about disabled women's lives. For history since 1945, interviews with disabled women are an invaluable source. Portions of this article rely heavily on interviews. While the history of all disabled persons has been largely buried or ignored, men, particularly disabled war vets, still have more of a presence than women. There is little mention in any country of the women civilians disabled in war.

The ignorance of the lives of women with disabilities in written history can be corrected through further research. In doing this research, however, one should consult the women themselves about philosophical frameworks and research directions as well as for the documentation of events. After all, twenty years ago, who thought women's history was important or that women should be consulted about their lives? Indeed, the history of women with disabilities is a vast frontier waiting to be discovered.

Notes

1. Paolo Freire. *Pedagogy of the Oppressed* (New York: Seabury Press, 1970), pp. 76-77.
2. Diane Driedger. *The Last Civil Rights Movement: Disabled Peoples' International* (London and New York: Hurst & Co. and St. Martin's Press), pp. 7-8.
3. Jim Derksen. *The Disabled Consumer Movement: Implications for Rehabilitation Service Provision* (Winnipeg: COPOH, 1980), p. 5.
4. Diane Driedger in "Speaking for Ourselves: A History of COPOH on its 10th Anniversary" in *Caliper*, Vol. XLI, December 1986, pp. 8-13.
5. Interviews with Paula Keirstead, of the Consulting Committee on the Status of Women with Disabilities, in Winnipeg, Manitoba, September 20, 1990, and with Pat Danforth, of DAWN Saskatchewan, in Winnipeg, Manitoba, October 4, 1990.
6. Danforth interview.
7. Interview with Yvonne Peters, Former COPOH council member, in Winnipeg, Manitoba, September 20, 1990.

8. Peters interview; see also the *Conference Report* from COPOH's Fifth National Forum, Edmonton, Alberta, 1983 (Winnipeg: COPOH, 1984), p. 14.

9. Keirstead interview.

10. Peters interview.

11. Pat Israel in "Editorial" in *Resources for Feminist Research: Women and Disability Issue*, No. 14, 1985, p. 2.

12. Israel interview.

13. Israel and Danforth interviews; interview with Maria Barile, of Action des Femmes Handicapees Mtl., in Winnipeg, Manitoba, September 24, 1990.

14. Danforth interview.

15. Telephone interview with Charlynn Toews, the former coordinator of the Manitoba Action Committee on the Status of Women, October 16, 1990; Keirstead interview.

16. April D'Aubin. *Disabled Women's Issues: A COPOH Discussion Paper* (Winnipeg: COPOH, 1986), p. 1.

17. Sharon D. Stone and Joanne Doucette in "Organizing the Marginalized: The DisAbled Women's Network" in Frank Cunningham et al. eds. *Social Movements/Social Change* (Toronto: Between the Lines, 1988), pp. 82-83; Barile interview.

18. DisAbled Women's Network. *National Organizing Meeting of the DisAbled Women's Network Report* (Vancouver: DAWN Canada, 1987).

19. See four position papers by Jillian Ridington: "Beating the 'Odds': Violence and Women with Disabilities," Position Paper 2, "Different Therefore Unequal: Employment and Women with Disabilities," Position Paper 4, "The Only Parent in the Neighborhood: Mothering and Women with Disabilities, Position Paper 3, and "Who Do We Think We Are: Self-Image and Women with Disabilities," Position Paper 1 (Vancouver: DisAbled Women's Network Canada, 1989).

20. NAC Resolution, cited by Joan Meister in "DisAbled Women Win NAC Support" in *Kinesis*, July-August 1986, p. 7.

21. Canadian Disability Rights Council and DisAbled Women's Network Canada (DAWN). *Four Discussion Papers on New Reproductive Technologies* (Winnipeg: CDRC and DAWN, 1990).

22. Diane Driedger. *The Last Civil Rights Movement*, pp. 86-89.

23. Michele Magar in "Disabled Women Organize" in *Ms.* magazine, January 1986.
24. Nina Ellinger in "Forum 1985 in Retrospect" in *Disabled Women's International Newsletter*, No. 1, June 1986, p. 10.
25. Israel interview.
26. Women with Disabilities Feminist Collective. *Women and Disability: An Issue* (Melbourne: Women with Disabilities Feminist Collective, 1987).
27. Rosallie B. Bukumunhe in "I Will Definitely Go" in Diane Driedger and Susan Gray, eds. *Imprinting Our Image: An International Anthology by Women with Disabilities* (Charlottetown: gynergy books, 1992), p. 78.
28. *Ibid.*, p. 79.
29. Gwyneth Ferguson Matthews. *Voices From the Shadows: Women with Disabilities Speak Out* (Toronto: Women's Press, 1983); Kelly Wheeler and Gem Wirszilas, eds. *Visions of Flight: A journey of positive thought by and about women with disabilities* (Surrey: self-published, 1991); Susan E. Browne, Debra Connors and Nanci Stern, eds. *With the Power of Each Breath: A Disabled Women's Anthology* (Pittsburgh: Cleis Press, 1986); Diane Driedger and Susan Gray, eds. *Imprinting Our Image.*
30. Michelle Fine and Adrienne Asch, eds. *Women with Disabilities: Essays in Psychiatry, Culture and Politics* (Philadelphia: Temple University Press, 1988); Susan Hannaford. *Living Outside Inside: A Disabled Woman's Experience. Towards a Social and Political Perspective* (Berkeley: Canterbury Press, 1985).

THE WOMEN AT THE WELL

African Baptist Women Organize

Sylvia Hamilton

African Canadian Women — An Unexplored Activist Tradition

In addressing the question of women organizing in Canada, we most often think of the period of the 1960s, when the women's movement, benefitting from the ground-breaking organizing and struggles of the civil rights and Black liberation movements, began to blossom. Or we think of a predecessor, the women's suffrage movement. For Canadian women, the Person's Case of 1929 has become a landmark in the struggle for women's equality. The case heralded the Privy Council decision which gave women the right to sit in the Senate.[1]

At the same time that the famous five women from Alberta were fighting for the legal right to be recognized as persons, African Canadian women citizens were facing widespread discrimination and exclusion in all aspects of their lives, not only because of their gender. For them, race also sharply etched the parameters of their place in Canadian society.

Historian James Walker notes, "white Canadians have had an image of Blacks which has generally been translated into a 'place' for Blacks in Canadian society." He further suggests that the "place" and "image" that have defined Black people as a primary source of cheap labour are rooted in Black slavery in Canada.[2]

During the 1920s, the Ku Klux Klan opened chapters in British Columbia, Saskatchewan and Ontario. Racist attitudes were evident at the most senior levels of the state and society. One former headmaster of a prominent Canadian college remarked that one advantage of Canada's cold climate was that it kept Black people out of the country.[3]

Clearly this individual either had no knowledge of the longstanding settlements of Black people in Canada dating back to the late 1700s or saw it in his interest and in that of those who shared his views to continue to ignore their presence. As late as 1947, then-Prime Minister Mackenzie King, speaking about Canadian immigration policy, stated that Canadians did not want to alter fundamentally the "character" of the population.[4]

Not surprisingly, the colour line, discrimination in and denial of basic services and employment, and legally segregated schools in Ontario and Nova Scotia were among the visible legacies of slavery. Combined with historically segregated settlement patterns, these factors served to locate African Canadians at the extreme margins of Canadian society.

While the Person's Case may have signalled the potential for gender equality for some women through the parliamentary system, for African Canadian women there were still formidable obstacles to overcome before they could win participation in the "official" political process.

Feminist theorist Patricia Hill Collins comments on the conundrum for African American women: "The external constraints of racism, sexism and poverty have been so severe that ... the majority of African American women have found it difficult to participate in organized political activities .... Possessing neither the opportunity nor the resources to confront oppressive institutions directly, the majority of Black women have engaged in the struggle for group survival."[5]

This is not to suggest that women of African descent have not been activists. Collins advances a framework for examining what she defines as a "Black women's activist tradition" of individual and group actions designed to bring about social change at two levels: the struggle for group survival and the struggle for institutional transformation."[6]

For more than seventy-five years African Baptist women in Nova Scotia have been activists and organizers in their communities. In 1920, nine years before the Person's Case, African Nova Scotian women organized the first-ever convention of "coloured" women in Canada to address a range of community, educational and spiritual concerns. This convention had its root in the women of the African Baptist Churches, which in 1917 began to organize themselves, and subsequently, all sectors of their communities.

This article is a preliminary examination of the development and role of Black women's organizations within the African United Baptist Association (AUBA) and, by extension, within Black communities in Nova Scotia. Preliminary research supports three essential arguments: first, that the women's organizations that developed in the African United Baptist Churches became a major part of what we call the "social service safety net" that provided a range of services within Black communities and the women themselves became key community educators and activists; second, that the importance of and need for these organizations were a direct result of the lack of state-provided services for Black communities, because of the systemic racism extant within Nova Scotian and Canadian society; and third, that physically and structurally, since Black communities were cut off from access to many services, Black women both individually and collectively developed a tradition and a spirit of self-reliance and self-help which have greatly contributed to the survival of African people in Nova Scotia.

Historical Context

Nova Scotia is home to the oldest population of African people in Canada, with the first recorded person of African descent listed in 1604. The earliest period of colonization included the importation of enslaved Africans. The late 1700s and 1800s saw major migrations of former slaves — Black Loyalists and Black Refugees from the American colonies and a group of Maroons, former slaves who had liberated themselves from the Jamaican colony.

Most women who became involved in the African United Baptist Church were the direct descendants of approximately two thousand refugee Blacks, also known as the Chesapeake Blacks, who arrived in Nova Scotia from the United States nearly two hundred years ago, following the War of 1812.[7]

Overall economic conditions in Nova Scotia from 1812 onward were bleak. Epidemics, poor agricultural land, extreme weather conditions and white racial attitudes dealt the refugees a difficult life. Inspite of these conditions, the women worked to cull from the land whatever they could to ensure the survival of their families.

While domestic work on a daily basis and living "in service" in white homes became the main work for Black women, census records for the late 1800s reveal the variety of other work the women found. They are listed as female labourers, farmers, washerwomen, teachers, shopkeepers and dressmakers, among other occupations. What is also clear is they worked until the later years of their lives. For example, Mary Ann Carvery of Preston was listed as sixty-one years, a female farmer with two children. Women gathered wood to turn into baskets and kindling; mayflowers, pussywillows and other wildflowers and evergreen boughs were harvested for wreaths which they sold door to door in white neighbourhoods and at local markets.

They were resourceful and hardworking, two characteristics which would later be recognized by the male leadership of the African Baptist Association in its decision that an organization be established to handle the "women's work of the Association."

African Baptist origins in Nova Scotia are traced to 1782, with the arrival of David George, a former slave and Baptist preacher from Virginia. George, his wife Phillis and their children came to Nova Scotia in 1783 as Loyalists at the end of the American Revolution. When Black Loyalists left Nova Scotia for Sierra Leone, West Africa, in 1792, the George family and the vast majority of Baptists were part of that migration.

A revival of the Baptists occurred when John Burton, a white minister from England, set up a congregation which was racially mixed. One member was Richard Preston, a former slave who came to Nova Scotia with the Black Refugees. In 1831 he travelled to England to study for and then receive official credentials to preach and establish a church.[9]

An abolitionist, Preston lectured widely against slavery in Nova Scotia and England. He was the principal organizer of the African Abolition Society which operated in the 1840s.[10] "Father Preston," as he was known (the term "father" was used for African/Black ministers at that time), organized an African Baptist Church at Cornwallis Street, in Halifax, on April 14, 1832. While all the officers listed were male, women were listed in the founding membership. In 1854, at Granville Mountain, Nova Scotia, Preston organized the twelve African Baptist churches he had established throughout Nova Scotia into an association. It would be another thirty-seven years before a woman was listed as a delegate at the Association's annual convention.

Traditional models of analysis would argue that the women in the churches were and are simply compliant followers of male dictates. However, Collins, in exploring the role of women in African American churches across denominations, uncovers evidence that suggests that while "men dominate positions of formal authority in church hierarchies, women make up a large percentage of the congregations, hold positions of authority and generally exert a powerful influence on African American church communities." She suggests that men and women exert different types of leadership within Black church communities.[11] Women in the African Baptist churches have held and continue to hold significant positions of authority and to exert strong influence in these churches. It should be remembered, moreover, that slavery was not abolished in the British colonies until 1834. For the most part Black people were still considered to be property and were not accorded the same rights, services and resources offered their white neighbours at the time.

The African Baptist church, then, not only served the "spiritual" needs of its congregation but out of necessity became an institution to serve the social, economic and educational needs of its members and of the broader communities where Black churches were located. As Walker points out, "The single most important institution in the preservation and transmission of a black culture has been the church."[12]

An 1891 statement by a prominent Nova Scotian leader, a former lieutenant governor, indicates the prevailing attitudes toward Black people and demonstrates just how vital it was for the community to attend to its own needs: "A negro with plenty to eat and drink, with clothing and shelter has little care for anything. He has no ambition. To him labour is only a last resort."[13]

Walker notes, "The historical experience reveals that blacks were rejected by white churches and white society before distinctive black churches developed."[14] In contrast, African Baptist records reveal that these churches were open to white members and white ministers such as the John Burton mentioned earlier and James Thomas, a Welsh Baptist.

African Baptist churches were located in rural, isolated Black communities on the outskirts of major towns in Nova Scotia. Cut off from access to the main centres of commerce and social, economic and political resources, the communities coalesced around their churches. Churches became the single most important institution within the community, a sphere of independence for Black people where they controlled what happened. They were welcome havens from the daily indignities suffered by their members. Church leaders were also community leaders who championed the struggle for equality for the entire community. The African Education Committee (c. 1880), which petitioned the provincial legislature to eliminate racially segregated schools, had key African Baptist church officials at its core.[16]

The Women at the Well

Women were active in most early African Baptist churches. They taught in Sabbath schools and in day schools that were usually located next to the churches. Churches such as Campbell Road (1849), near Halifax, Dartmouth Lake (1844) and Falmouth (1876) among others, listed women on the membership rolls. Commenting on the work of women in the early churches such as Falmouth, Peter E. McKerrow, African Baptist Association clerk, said in 1895, "Sisters Gray and Fletcher are most earnest workers. [They] manifest a lively interest in the cause of Christ and deserve to be encouraged. ... Rev John A. Smith has laboured with them, and found them earnest Christians contending for the 'faith.' The women here, as in most of the churches take the lead. Good women are like precious stones." McKerrow's early comments coincide with feminist critic bell hooks, who points out that even with the faults of the traditional Black church, it has always been " a place where Black women have dignity and respect."[18]

Women delegates began attending annual sessions of the African Baptist Association in 1891. Over the next few years they made their presence known, speaking about education, mission work and temperance. Some organizing work also took place in individual churches after

1891. Church historian Pearleen Oliver, a central figure in the African Baptist women's movement, documents the first organized women's work as the establishment of a Pastor's Aid Society in Halifax in 1895.[19]

In 1908 women were the first to offer financial pledges for the development of a Normal and Industrial Institute to train and educate young people. By 1913 each member church in the Association had a women's missionary society. Three years later, all churches were mandated to send at least one woman to the annual session in 1917, where a province-wide organization would be established.

That historic meeting, held on September 3, 1917, in East Preston, Halifax County, became known as "The Women at the Well" because the women met outside of the church around a well. The goal was to organize women and to promote women's activities and their participation in the work of the African Baptist Association. As recorded in the Association's minutes, a ladies' auxiliary would be established for the "stimulation of the spiritual, moral, social, educational, charitable and financial work of all the local churches of the African Baptist Association."[20]

Given the centrality of the African Baptist Church to the Black community, this mandate demonstrates the scope of the so-called women's work of the churches. Analyses advanced by Collins and others contend, "Black women's activities in the Black church have been profoundly influenced by the vision of Black women as educators of African American families and communities and Black churches have been central in supporting a variety of social, economic, political and ethical actions essential to Black community development."[21]

Maude Sparks became the first president, and Bessie Wyse the official organizer. There were three other executive positions. The official organizer would become responsible for organizing auxiliaries in member churches. One year later, in 1918, recognizing that the work of women was crucial to the development of the Association and thus to the Black community, a resolution was passed at the 65th Session that every local church should organize a Ladies' Auxiliary. [22] In 1919, just two years after the first meeting, Maggie M. Upshaw, then the official organizer of the Auxiliary, was given a permanent position and made responsible for "women's work."

The executive committee of the Association, predominantly male at the time, proudly reported on the position in the Minutes of 1920: "It has proved to be one of the most successful things that has been done by your Board. Sister Upshaw has been instant in season and out of season, absolutely tireless, and her accomplishment well merits the thanks of this Convention. She has not only stimulated the work, but has collected a large portion of the allotments, raised money by concerts, collected hundreds for the Coloured Home and General Association, and on the minimum of expense."[23] There is no reference to a salary for Mrs Upshaw in the minutes, though she may have received one.

The Home referred to is the Nova Scotia Home for Coloured Children, established in 1917 by organizations in the Black community to house destitute and orphaned Black children who were refused entry into other institutions for "orphans." The 1920 Minutes went on to praise women and to identify concrete results from their work, noting: "We have accomplished more during the past year for the uplift of the race than can be shown by the record of any other one year." The amount of money raised was listed in several places, for example: "The Ladies' Auxiliaries of the African United Baptist Association have done splendidly, and we believe their accomplishments will be quite surprising. In 1917, they raised $170, 1918 they raised $368, 1919-20, they raised over $1100 for the Association and the Home.[24]

It should be remembered that this activity was taking place during the post-war period, when segregation was legal and blatant, and when the vast majority of Black people were prevented from ever reaching junior or senior high school.

Continuing the move forward, Maude Sparks, Maggie Upshaw, Muriel States, Bessie Wyse and other women leaders organized the first Convention of Coloured Women in Canada on May 27, 1920, in Halifax. The Convention attracted an unusual level of press coverage for the time, as seen in the headline for the *Sunday Leader* of June 13, 1920: "African United Baptist Association, An Organization Nova Scotia Should be Proud of: The First Congress of Colored Women to Be Held In All Canada Assembles in Halifax — The Aims and Ambitions of This Special Band of Women Representing Nearly 40,000 Colored People in Nova Scotia." [25]

Writer Mrs. Donald Shaw, who covered the event and whose article was accompanied by photographs, was generous in her assessment of the event and its organizers, "… The promoters of the movement have every reason to be proud and gratified with the result of their initial effort to organize the women of their race as a great Auxiliary force to work for their Church in Canada and also of the sincerity and earnestness and intelligence with which the whole affair was carried out from start to finish."[26]

The Convention, which drew fifty delegates, included business sessions, prayer services and discussions and special papers on such topics as "A Call to Baptist Womanhood," "The Past and the Future," "Women and Missions," "Education, Christian Womanhood, Domestic Girls' Needs, Social Service, and Organization." Music formed an integral part of the Convention with selections from soloists and choirs.

During this early period there were no comparable men's groups within the African Baptist churches. Men would only become organized in 1929 and they would be organized by a woman, Muriel States, a founding member of the Auxiliary, one of the "Women at the Well" and the official organizer of the Ladies' Auxiliary.[27] In October 1929 (the year of the Person's Case), Muriel States organized the Men's Progressive Club at Hammond's Plains Church, in Halifax County. While Muriel States' organizing of a men's group may appear to fall beyond "feminist" tradition, it nonetheless fits squarely within what Collins identifies as the "Afrocentric feminist political activism essential to the struggle for group survival."[28] At its Convention in 1930, the African Baptist Association outlined a Five-Year Program, with a plan to raise no less than $2,500 annually.

The Program also contained the following resolutions: "that social service and child welfare investigations be made; that the Association have a permanent organizer in connection with ladies auxiliaries, Social and Welfare Work; that men's organizations be formed in each church to assist the work in all its varied phases."[29]

Between 1939-1945, the work begun by Muriel States to organize the men was continued in all of the local churches. A formal Laymen's Council was held in 1945, 28 years after the Ladies' Auxiliary formed.

By 1956, all member churches had a Ladies' Auxiliary, and some churches had organized other women's groups, including the Helping Hand Society and the Women's Missionary Society.

The women now decided that a formal governing body responsible for all women's work in the AUBA was needed. Official organizer Muriel States told the one hundred delegates who came together to establish the Women's Institute of the African United Baptist Association, "Today, we women of the African Baptist Association have taken another step which will go down in history as the first Women's Institute held this day at this church. We feel that we as women have accomplished much and are aiming to do great things in the future. We are already reaping the reward of untiring and united effort in all that tends to the promotion of the church and community welfare."[30]

The women met at Cornwallis Street Baptist Church, known as the Mother Church of the Association, on Thursday October 18, 1956 at 9:30 a.m. Their theme, "Building Better Communities," demonstrates that "women's work" encompasses the overall moral, social, spiritual, educational and financial sectors of the Black community. Topics under discussion included "Improving Our Health Standards Within Our Community," "Raising Our Educational Standards Within Our Community," and "Strengthening Our Family Relations."

Dr. Pearleen Oliver, who would become chair of the social services committee, presented the film *Out Beyond Town* to delegates, which was followed by a discussion focusing on what women could do to promote better health habits around the farm and in the home.

These women were continuing the activist tradition established in 1917 at the founding of the Auxiliary and reaffirmed in 1920 at the first Convention of Colored Women. Collins contends, "By placing family, children, education and community at the centre of our political activism, African-American women draw on Afrocentric conceptualizations of mothering, family, community and empowerment."[31] The work of these women represents a profound challenge to the belief cited earlier that the "negro" lacked ambition and that labour was a last resort.

Since 1956 the Women's Institute of the AUBA has met annually, on the third Saturday in October. Sessions rotate among the member groups, which take on the responsibility of organizing and hosting the sessions in their home churches. As many as two hundred women participate in the meetings. The Institute continues to be responsive to community needs; some members regularly visit those in hospital and the elderly; others are involved in providing assistance to families in need.

Over the years, Institute organizers have worked with young people to develop their skills in public speaking and leadership. A preliminary survey of Institute themes since 1956 reveals the continuing but contemporary focus on elements first articulated in 1917. In addition to its annual sessions, the Institute organizes a range of social action and community projects, including workshops on media and race relations, on women and the law, on family violence and on leadership and financial development.

An educational thrust remains central to the work of the Institute. The Gertrude E. Smith Scholarship, named in memory of one of the leaders of the Women's Institute, was initiated in 1981 by Dr. Pearleen Oliver, to support students pursuing studies beyond high school.

Dr. Oliver herself has been instrumental in the work of the Institute, having served as its official organizer and as the first woman moderator of the AUBA. Recognizing an absence of people of African descent in the media, and following the media workshop mentioned earlier, the Institute recently worked with a broadcast agency to establish a Radio Apprentice Program for indigenous Black students of Nova Scotia. The Program provides summer employment, tuition fees at college, bursaries and employment beyond graduation.

Many women in the current and past leadership of the Ladies' Auxiliary and the Women's Institute also held key positions in other community organizations devoted to Black community development and human rights. Joyce Ross, a day care Director in East Preston, Nova Scotia, has also served as the president of the Women's Institute of the AUBA and is active in a range of community organizations.

In the 1940s Dr. Carrie Best established *The Clarion*, a newspaper published in the interests of Black Nova Scotians. She uncovered and reported on discrimination and racism and wrote about community events. Dr. Best, a former broadcaster and a poet, has also been an active member of Second Baptist Church in New Glasgow.

In her autobiography she reflects on her involvement in International Women's Year activities and the role of Black women: "Long before there was a Women's Liberation Movement as such, the Black female was involved in a death struggle for [the] physical and mental survival both for herself and her family. Her strength has been the Black church and the strength of the Black church has always been the Black woman. From this checkpoint she and her children took their first feeble hounded steps to freedom. Men write history; Women are history."[32]

That many African Baptist women were also teachers (formally and informally) reminds us of Collins' point that the "meaning of education in what was formally called race uplift but what is now called Black community development."[33]

Women in the African Baptist Church, as in many churches, work within church doctrines and structures. In this context Black women used their skills and acquired additional ones not available to them elsewhere because of gender and racial discrimination. For example, every women's group provided opportunities for women to gain experience in leadership, financial management, negotiation, public speaking, conflict resolution and fund-raising.

bell hooks acknowledges the role of the Black church in her personal development: "... When I'm called to talk about the roots of my own critical consciousness, I invariably go back to the black church."[34] At the same time that Women's Institute members are involved in activist work, they remain firmly rooted in their spiritual connections to other members of the community, as demonstrated by the officially designated position of hospital visitor, whose responsibility it is to coordinate visits to those who are ill. In 1985, then hospital visitor, Bessie Sparks reported 380 visits to people at home, in hospitals and in nursing homes.

Every annual Women's Institute session also has a Praise Service, affording a time for testimonies, prayers and spirituals. Acknowledging the importance of every member of the Women's Institute, a memorial service is held to remember members who died during the year. The service held in 1985 is of particular note. Lead by Sister (Dr.) Pearleen Oliver, it made special mention of the death of Sister Edith Samuels Sparks, the last of "The Women at the Well." These activities of the Women's Institute connect contemporary members to their traditions and history and to the daily lives of members of their communities.

The words of Sojourner Truth have for many feminists become essential to their understanding of the struggle for women's equality. bell hooks reminds us of the origins of Sojourner Truth's philosophy, one not unlike that of "The Women at the Well." hooks says, "... When feminists, white feminists, appropriated the words of Sojourner Truth, they conveniently ignored the fact that her emancipatory politics emerged from her religious faith. People need to remember that the name Isabel Humphrey took, Sojourner Truth, arose from her religious faith.... [in] choosing God, she was choosing to serve in the emancipation struggle of Black people. She was also the first Black woman to publicly link the struggle against racism with gender liberation."[35]

Women within the African Baptist Church have laboured for many years within their churches and communities to build a place of equality not only for themselves but for their children and their partners. Their spiritual beliefs guide them and provide the strength and support they need continually to carry their struggle forward in the activist tradition that provides the framework necessary for social and institutional change.

Notes

1. On October 18, 1929, women in Canada and the British Empire won the legal right to be recognized as persons, thus giving women the right to become senators. The victory resulted from a petition filed by five Alberta women who had taken the case to the courts seeking an amendment to the *British North America Act,* which would grant women "persons" status. See Status of Women Canada, Call for Nominations for Person's Award, 1984.

2. James W. St. G. Walker. *A History of Blacks in Canada: A Study Guide for Teachers and Students* (Hull: Minister of Supply and Services Canada, 1980), p. 77.

3. *Ibid.,* p. 80

4. *Ibid.,* p. 94.

5. Patricia Hill Collins. *Black Feminist Thought* (New York and London: Routledge, 1990), p. 145.

6. *Ibid.,* p. 141.

7. For a detailed discussion of the settlement of Black refugees, see John N.

Grant. *The Immigration and Settlement of the Black Refugees of the War of 1812 in Nova Scotia and New Brunswick* (Hansport: Lancelot Press Ltd., 1990).

8. For an examination and analysis of Black Loyalist history, see James W. St.G. Walker. *The Black Loyalists: The Search for a Promised Land in Nova Scotia and Sierra Leone 1783-1870* (New York and Halifax: Africana Pub. Co. and Dalhousie University Press, 1976/Toronto: University of Toronto Press, 1993).

9. Savanah Williams in "The Role of the African United Baptist Association in the Development of Indigenous Afro-Canadians in Nova Scotia, 1782-1978, " p. 5. Reprinted from Barry Moody, ed., *Repent and Believe: The Baptist Experience in Maritime Canada* (Hansport: Lancelot Press Ltd. for Acadia Divinity College, 1980).

10. See Frank Stanley Boyd, ed., for P.E. McKerrow's 1895 work, *A Brief History of the Coloured Baptists of Nova Scotia and Their First Organization as Churches A.D. 1832* (Halifax: Department of Education, 1975), p. 22.

11. Collins. *Op. cit.,* p. 152.

12. Walker. *A History of Blacks*, p. 135.

13. Walker. *Black Loyalists*, p. 41.

14. Walker. *A History of Blacks*, p. 135.

15. McKerrow. *Op. cit.,* p. 30.

16. *Ibid.,* pp. 35-36.

17. *Ibid.,* pp. 55.

18. bell hooks and Cornel West. *Breaking Bread: Insurgent Black Intellectual Life* (Toronto: Between the Lines, 1991), p. 79.

19. Pearleen Oliver. *A Brief History of the Colored Baptists of Nova Scotia, 1782-1953* (Halifax: N.p., 1953), p. 39.

20. Minutes of the African United Baptist Association of Nova Scotia, 1917. Maritime Baptist Historical Collection, Acadia University, Wolfville, Nova Scotia.

21. Collins. *Op cit.,* p. 151.

22. Bridglal Pachai. *Beneath the Clouds of the Promised Land: The Survival of Nova Scotia's Blacks, Vol. 2: 1800-1989* (Halifax: Lancelot Press Ltd., 1990), p. 142.

23. African United Baptist Association (AUBA) Minutes, 1920.

24. *Ibid.*

25. The Halifax *Sunday Leader*, June 13, 1920, p. 17.

26. *Ibid.*

27. Pachai. *Op. cit.*, p. 148.

28. Collins. *Op. cit.*, p. 151.

29. AUBA Minutes, *op. cit.*

30. See Sylvia Hamilton in "Our Mothers Grand and Great: Black Women of Nova Scotia" in *Canadian Woman Studies,* Vol. 4. No. 2, 1982, p. 36.

31. Collins. *Op. cit.*, p. 151.

32. Carrie M. Best. *That Lonesome Road: The Autobiography of Carrie M. Best* (New Glasgow: The Clarion Publishing Company Ltd., 1977), p. 172.

33. Collins. *Op. cit.*, p. 150.

34. hooks and West. *Op. cit.*, p. 5

35. *Ibid.*, pp. 51-52.

IV

THE STATE, WOMEN'S LABOUR AND FEMINIST STRUGGLES

PROBLEMATIZING PRIVILEGE

Another Look at the Representation

of "Women" in Feminist Practice

Sue Findlay

The past decade of feminist organizing in Canada began with significant challenges to white women's domination of feminist organizations by women of Colour. Responding to these challenges, some white feminists and women of Colour who have led the challenges have begun building anti-racist practices to undo the privileges of white women and to increase the representation of women of Colour in Canadian feminism. However, in spite of these initiatives, the privileges of white women still shape many feminist organizations. Racism is still alive and well in the feminism of the 1990s.

Some of the limits of anti-racist practices must be attributed to the resistance of white women, individually and organizationally, to the loss of privileges related to race. However, the implementation of anti-racist practices is also systematically and systemically limited by everyday practices in feminist organizations, practices that organize and reproduce a hierarchy of relations among women, a hierarchy that has historically privileged white women. These practices have been formed over the last two and a half decades by feminists representing the interests of women in the policy-making of the state and other institutions in civil society. They are a fundamental part of the reorganization of the representation of "women" that has taken place in Canadian society since the Royal Commission on the Status of Women and the more general reorganization of the relationship between state and civil society that followed challenges to the political system in the 1960s. To challenge privilege is also to challenge the way the state organizes representation into a set of practices that feminists now use to represent women.[1]

A Look at Anti-Racist Practices in Feminist Organizations

Issues of representation are not new to feminist organizations. Differences — political, sexual orientation, class and race — soon became points of conflict for the new organizations that emerged in Canada in the 1970s. Speaking for "women" was almost as impossible in the early women's centres as it was in the single-issue coalitions that emerged in the 1980s. Feminist quickly learned that "sisterhood" was something that must be organized. Caucuses organized to give voice to differences among women were standard practice in many feminist organizations in the early 1980s.

Many factors made racism a particular issue for feminism in Toronto in the mid-1980s. By the beginning of the 1980s, the demographics of Toronto had changed significantly. Toronto became increasingly multiracial and racism was a feature of life in Toronto.[2] Organizations from racial minority communities put racism on the agendas of governments and social movements.[3] The Coalition of Visible Minority Women formed in October 1983, following "The Visible Minority Woman: A Conference on Racism, Sexism and Work."[4]

In 1986, in Toronto, "IWD (International Women's Day) was the centrepiece in a confrontation between feminist women of colour and white women about racism in the women's movement."[5] In a statement to the IWD Coalition, members of the Black Women's Collective commended their white sisters for the courage to make "Women Say No to Racism from Toronto to South Africa" the theme for that year. But they also asserted the need to struggle for a new kind of sisterhood within feminist organizations: "We feel that the contradictions raised at this year's Coalition were/are necessary steps in building that base of sisterhood. There was no going around it, no shilly-shallying about it. It had to be lived in order to be analysed and understood. In other words, sisterhood must be struggled for." [6] The struggles within the Coalition were echoed in other feminist organizations in Toronto, including Women's Press,[7] and the Toronto Rape Crisis Centre.

Out of the struggles of these and others groups grew a more systematic anti-racist practice, focused on increasing the representation of women of Colour in feminist organizations to make women of Colour part of feminism in Canada. Reliance on increases in the representation of women of Colour in feminist organizations, as a strategy to undo the privilege of white women, is not surprising. It fits with the commitments to sisterhood and the building of mass movements that have characterized the women's movement since the 1970s. But there is another reason — one that links the structures of representation to the "relations of ruling."[8]

Representative structures are central to the workings of liberal democracies as mechanisms that link the voices of the "people" to the decision-making of the state. Demands for participation in these structures mark the history of liberal democracies. We are most familiar with representation in the electoral process, but representation has become an issue for state administrations and for community-based organizations formed to lobby the government since the 1960s. Social movements of the 1960s attacked the elitism of representative democracy and argued for a more participatory form of government and for community organizing. In the last three decades, however, representation has been asserted by most of the players in the political system as *the* strategy to get "designated groups" a voice in existing policy-making bodies of the state in Canada. Since the mid-1980s, commitments to outreach and diversification have become priorities for white-dominated organizations responding to racism at the levels of the state and civil society.

By the 1990s such major feminist organizations as the National Action Committee on the Status of Women (NAC) and the Legal Education and Action Fund (LEAF) had committed themselves to the reorganization of the representation of "women" in the organizations' decision-making and in the work they do. Politically, the strength of these organizations depends on their ability to represent the diversity of women and to hold this diversity together with a common agenda. Many of them have embraced an anti-racist practice with a commitment that goes beyond an increase in the number of women of Colour to extensive outreach programs.

Anti-racist practices have also focused on the representation of women of Colour by white women in feminist writings. Women of

Colour have argued — and still do — that this representation has ignored and misrepresented the realities of the lives of women of Colour and hence distorted feminist history and the definition of feminist issues. In 1988, the Toronto-based Women's Press launched "Anti-racist Guidelines for Submissions" as a step towards making the Press "a racially integrated publishing house which is anti-racist in all aspects of its work." Part of a larger critique of writings that appropriate the voices of women of Colour, the guidelines hit the heart of the publishing network in Canada. Although the network responded at the time by condemning the guidelines as an attack on freedom of expression, today they are accepted as common practice by many of their former critics. Anti-racist practices such as these and the shift in the priorities of other white-dominated feminist publishing houses and periodicals to include writings by women of Colour are examples of attempts by white feminists to make the resources of feminism accessible to women of Colour.

The representation of women of Colour has become a political issue for the state as well as for feminist organizations. Special attention to women of Colour has been added to state initiatives that had been limited to gender. For example, the grants program of the Ontario Women's Directorate has placed a priority on projects organized by and for women of Colour. In a more *ad hoc* way, women of Colour have been drawn into the Ontario New Democratic government as advisors at the political level or as administrators within the bureaucracy.

Speaking of the way that racism is still treated as an "issue" rather than as a "fundamental form of social organization" that has shaped the Canadian nation, Himani Bannerji has this to say about relations between white academic feminists and women of Colour in the academic world: "Not even feminist theorists of the left seem to know how to build this "issue" as an integral aspect of their theoretical/analytical enterprise....We continue to work in separate streams, white women and us engaged in producing different kinds of knowledges."[9]

Looking more specifically at the development of Women's Studies curricula, Linda Carty argues, "There is a great deal in this seemingly progressive action ('anti-racist pedagogy') which is evidently racist."[10] Both women question the willingness of white academic feminists to engage in questions about the reproduction of racism.

Some of the limits of anti-racist practices are undoubtedly related to resistance by white feminists to loss of their privileges. These privileges are deeply rooted. White feminists must continue to focus on understanding how everyday practices as white feminists reproduce our privileges.[11] But we must also understand how privilege is organized by practices that put us — according to our class, race, gender, ability, education, skills, age and so on — into the particular hierarchy of relations that shapes our lives and work in specific moments. The undoing of racism cannot be limited to feminism.

The privileges of white feminists are systemic and systematic — and deeply embedded in the practices used by feminists to represent "women" in policy-making since the 1960s. These practices are fundamental to the organization of the representation of women by the state. They have worked to the advantage of white women who have the skills and political connections deemed appropriate for participation in the political system and they create a hierarchy among women. Privilege, then, is reproduced by practices now used by feminists in community-based organizations and institutions and by femocrats inside state administrations to represent the interests of "women."

Representing "Women" at the City of Toronto: A Lesson in the Reproduction of Privilege[12]

In August 1991 I was given a contract by the City of Toronto's Women and Work Institute to look at how representation worked for "women with special needs" — immigrant and visible minority women, Native women and women with disabilities. The City had, over the past decade, introduced a number of initiatives to increase the representation of its "designated groups" — women, racial minorities, Native people and people with disabilities — in the city's policy-making process and in its workforce. The Women and Work Institute wanted to know how immigrant and visible minority women, Native women and women with disabilities fit into these initiatives.

Initiatives to reorganize representation at the City began at the political level, with the appointment by a reform council of the Task Force on the Status of Women in 1974. In 1981, in response to pressure from racial minority groups, the mayor established a Committee on Community and Race Relations, to look at racism in Toronto. Ten years later, City Council created a Council Committee on the Status of Women to provide an ongoing forum on women's issues in Toronto.

On the basis of many of the recommendations made by these committees and task forces, City Council extended the representation of the designated groups into the administration by creating the Multicultural Access Program (MAP) and the Inter-Departmental Action Committee for Disabled People. Council also established an Equal Opportunity Program, to increase the representation of the four "designated groups" in the City's workforce. The Equal Opportunity Program is administered by the Equal Opportunity Division which, in the 1980s, informally played the role of advocate for women's issues at City Hall.

In these initiatives, immigrant and visible minority women, Native women and women with disabilities — whose lives are shaped by the intersection of race, class, gender and differing abilities — have apparently fallen between the cracks in programs that separate gender from race from disability. Although these women were not necessarily excluded, their inclusion depended on the interests of those who organized and administered the work of the committees or the Equal Opportunity Program.

In practice, the Mayor's Committee on Community and Race Relations did not find "gender" an issue; nor was it an issue for the Inter-Departmental Action Committee on People with Disabilities. For departmental managers responsible for the implementation of the goals and timetables of the Equal Opportunity Program, gender should have been an issue — "women" are a "designated group." But managers have the authority to determine who they hire as representatives from the broadly defined categories of the designated groups and for what jobs. This practice allows them to exercise preferences about the race or gender of people with disabilities, about the gender and abilities of racial minorities, and about the race and abilities of women in either categories. The number of women employed by the City of Toronto increased by 36.6 percent between 1985 and 1990; however women still represent only 29 percent of the civic workforce.[14] Twenty percent of the women employed by the City of Toronto are from racial minority groups, 1.3

percent are Native women, and 2.6 percent are women with disabilities.[15]

What is apparent is the very limited capacity of the new forms of representation at the City of Toronto to democratize either policy-making process or the workforce of the City. There is meagre evidence of substantive changes in City policies or of the organization of a more representative workforce. Yet the "public face" of the City has changed. When you enter the rotunda of Toronto's City Hall, or when you approach the Personnel Department of the City of Toronto, there is a good chance that you will be greeted by a "representative" of one of the "designated groups." There has been a change in who is "visible" to the public.

But the effect of MAP and the Inter-Departmental Action Committee for Disabled People on the main business of the City — development and property management — has been minimal. As the report on "Gender and Housing in Toronto" illustrates, gender is still not an issue in the City's housing policy.[16] Although advocates for the "designated groups" have managed to establish their presence at City Hall, they have not been successful at integrating the issues facing these groups into mainline departments such as finance, planning and development, public works and the environment, and housing. Programs such as MAP are clearly only regarded as "special" measures rather than permanent measures to integrate the "designated groups" into City priorities and ways of operating.

Similarly, the limits of the Equal Opportunity Program as a strategy for creating a representative workforce are beginning to emerge. Although representatives of "designated groups" are more visible in the provision of City services, this visibility should not be mistaken for an integration of these groups throughout the civic workforce. Because of the nature of the program — a model which was honed over the 1980s to maximize managers' "flexibility" in implementing employment equity at the expense of the more radical demands for quotas — and the relatively powerless position of the Equal Opportunity Division in relation to departmental managers, the negotiation of the implementation of the Program has worked to the advantage of the status quo. Most of the positions targeted by departmental managers for the program —

in negotiations with the Equal Opportunity Division to establish goals and timetables — are entry-level positions, temporary or casual positions. Few of those hired under the Equal Opportunity Program have been hired into permanent jobs.[17] Even in the Equal Opportunity Division, most of the work done as advocates for women's interests is done by temporary contract staff. While numbers may have increased, the impact of the Equal Opportunity Program on the historically white, male, able-bodied, workforce is minimal.

What these limits reflect is a system of government that — despite common beliefs that municipal government is more open, responsive and democratic than the federal or provincial governments — is firmly guided by the interests of business and developers. These limits are not a simple reflection of the domination of the political system by the business elite. They are also a reflection of the relationships between elected politicians and City administrators, and between the City and the community, that have been organized historically to promote development and business interests. These relations are now held in place by administrative practices that include new forms of representation, such as employment equity policies.

City politicians who attempt to respond to community demands for a more democratic system are faced with the power of City administrators. Without the agenda or the discipline that membership in political parties can offer, municipal officials in Toronto are often left to their individual efforts and rather reactive positions in the face of the hegemony of business interests. In these struggles, they often lack knowledge and expertise about issues and administrative procedures. This puts them at a distinct disadvantage in relation to the gate-keepers of policy — the departmental managers.

City departmental managers are reluctant to incorporate new priorities, identified by City Council, into their ongoing work. This reluctance is rooted, in part, in the failure of City Council to provide the necessary leadership in the development of City's administration over the years. Without this leadership, the work of City departments is dominated by networks and practices that have been forged historically. These reflect the long-term interests of the business community rather than the shifting priorities of elected politicians. Managers of these departments work relatively independently from City politicians and are accustomed to exercising their expertise and power. New political priorities can easily be seen as intrusions in practices that managers believe make sense for the City. Their advice to politicians is more likely to suggest the need to contain new initiatives than to engage in full-scale reform of institutional practices where it is required. Efforts by politicians to democratize City Hall, then, are often restricted to relatively powerless committees that may offer a forum for consultation and advocacy on behalf of community groups to other levels of government but have little effect on shifting the traditional priorities of the City.

Advocates of "designated groups" within the City's administration can do little to support a reform program. They, like elected politicians at the City, are also relatively powerless in relation to departmental managers. Departmental managers — the Committee of Heads — call the shots in the development and implementation of policy within the City's administration. Their authority rests on tradition and on control of resources, and on rules and regulations established over decades. Advocates appointed to represent community interests are subordinate to this authority in an unequal structure of representation. Although policy-making ostensibly rests on negotiation — and is characterized by struggles within the state — the outcome, predictably, favours the interests represented by managers of the mainstream departments over the advocates of the "designated groups."

Community activists now have little influence at City Hall. The representation of "designated groups" is the business of the advocates and advisors within the administration, who run the equal opportunity/employment equity programs and City committees. With these advocates in place, the argument for more direct participation by the community has lost much of its political force. It has fallen into the realm of principles and can easily be overlooked by state administrators in the chaos of making policy. The relation between the community and City politicians is mediated by City advocates who organize consultations with community activists and provide expertise to the mayoral and Council committees and by City administrators who organize the more formal deputations to City Council on policy proposals. Community activists are expected to speak for their respective communities in consultation with City politicians rather than to participate in the formulation of policies.

The new forms of representation the City of Toronto has introduced to integrate "designated groups" into its policy-making and workforce are unique. They bear the stamp of the mandate and functions of the City that derive from its relationship, as a municipality, to the provincial and federal governments. In the larger sense, however, these forms reflect a model established by the federal government in the 1970s and early 1980s. This model was established to reassert control over the political system by the powerful economic and social interests it reflects. These forms have since that time become part of the political commitments and everyday practices of provincial governments and of such major institutions in civil society such as school boards, unions, universities and so on.

State administrations, vulnerable to charges of under-representation, can point to the new forms of representation — equal opportunity programs, City committees for women, racial minorities and people with disabilities, provincial and federal directorates for women — to display their commitment to inclusiveness and representation. And, for the most part, these new forms of representation work for state administrators as a way to regulate the participation of "designated groups" in the public service, even though they might not want to bother with them.

As the City of Toronto study shows, however, these forms of representation have been significant in increasing the representation of "women" in state administrations in a way that favours white women. As these forms "travelled," they have also had a significant impact on the representation of "women" in the other sectors of the state and civil society where feminists have taken up the representation of "women."

Reproducing Privilege: How it Works in Feminist Organizations

Community leaders are well-versed in the limits of the policies produced for the "designated groups." However, they are reluctant to challenge the new forms of representation, and "experts" on race relations, who speak on their behalf, legitimate their usefulness as strategies to contain racism.[18] Members of the Women and Work Institute were quite resistant to my suggestion that representation might be more of a problem than a solution. By now, representation is quite clearly tied to ideas about democratization in their minds and in the minds of many community activists. It is tied to democratization not simply because it is "natural" but because it is the work of a multitude who are engaged in representing particular groups.

Inherent in this representation by community groups is the same categorization of the "designated groups" and their separation from each other that defines the representation of these groups in state administrations. This categorization began with the development of "communities" forged by state practices and policies in the making of Canadian nation.[19] It has continued in a process that has translated our lived realities into categories that separate race, gender and class. These categories make sense to the community. It is this categorization that encodes privileges in both state administrations and the policies they produce and in the work of community organizations. Today, these categories link the work of community groups and their advocates within state administrations and make opposition to forms of representation difficult in spite of evidence of their limits.

What contains opposition to these obviously limited policies for increasing the participation of "designated groups" in civic government is the capacity of the state to categorize our lived realities and embed them in forms of representation like equal opportunity programs that "make sense" to us. These policies work for us because they offer us what has become *the* way to have our interests — as reflected in these categories — represented in the policy-making of state administrations. Even though their effect is limited, it is the only game in town and it has worked for some white women.

The categorization of "women" as the subjects of the political process and as the objects of public policy, began with the Royal Commission on the Status of Women in 1967. The effect was to shape the representation of "women" by feminist groups in a way that fit with existing hierarchies of class, gender and race that define our system of governing and maintain the interests of the dominant groups in society. This fit is regulated by the everyday practices used by feminists to represent "women" in state administrations and in community-based feminist organizations.

As an issue, the status of women in Canada was a very "white" issue, as were the groups that organized to speak about it. The public face of the women's movement, organized in the 1970s to speak for women's issues in the political process, for the most part adopted a set of administrative and political practices (granting, consulting, contracts, lobbying) that require, support and reproduce particular ways of working, speaking, writing, organizing. The representation of "women" in feminist organizations has privileged the participation of white women who are articulate and well-educated, middle-class, able-bodied and most often heterosexual.[20] These are the women who had access to the Commission in 1967 and who shaped the face of Canadian feminism through the 1970s. While these practices shaped the work of feminist organizations, they also organized relations among white women within feminist organizations, relations that mirrored the relations of ruling. These practices — evolving as they did from the relation between white feminists and the state in the course of defining government responsibilities for the status of women, through participation in the Royal Commission and in lobbying the government to implement the report — played and still do play a major role in linking the work of feminist organizations to the ruling practices of the white world and in reproducing these practices. [21]

Since these early years feminists have taken the struggle for women's equality beyond the formal corridors of state power. Those engaged in anti-racism face limitations derived from those practices. It has been very difficult for feminists to see the way their practices reproduce a representation of "women" that works on the basis of privilege, a representation in conflict with genuine efforts to develop a more inclusive form of representation.

For example, trade union feminists and feminist lawyers in the Equal Pay Coalition — yielding to pressures to take advantage of a minority government situation — found themselves supporting a model of pay equity for Ontario in 1987 that privileged unionized women in the Ontario Public Service and in other large organizations in the broader public sector over women in non-unionized, small social service organizations without male comparators. A high percentage of the women in these small service organizations were women of Colour. Although the problem was recognized, it was defined by the feminists as a problem related to unionization.[22] How the pay equity legislation privileged white women was rarely noted; when it was, it was not connected to the fact that the majority of feminists in the Equal Pay Coalition were white.

In the 1990s some the key feminist organizations like NAC are more openly critical of the representation of women in their own organizations and state mechanisms (e.g., opposition to the Canadian Panel on Violence Against Women, to the Royal Commission on New Reproductive Technologies and to proposals for parity in an elected Senate), but the problem is usually defined as one of exclusion and the privilege inherent in it. The solution, determined by the formulation of the problem, is inclusion: "more and better representation." How our organizational practices shape representation — how these have been formed historically to determine which feminists speak for women in the political process, how they regulate feminist participation in policy-making and in our negotiations with state policy-makers, how they limit opposition to or the continuing evaluation of feminist strategies and proposals — is rarely addressed. Some feminists quite correctly emphasize the work feminist organizations have done to develop new models of working that are inclusive and non-hierarchical.[23] But without a critique of our practices, explanations for the limits of the very considerable efforts of feminists to build more inclusive organizations are reduced to the resistance of white feminists.

Beyond Representation

What I am arguing for, then, is an anti-racist practice that sees the privilege of white feminists in its full complexity — as something reproduced by the everyday practices of feminists and by their relationship to a set of practices inside the state and inside the major institutions in Canada that have been organized in the past three decades to represent "women." With this definition, anti-racist strategies must look at "representation" — within state administrations and within feminist organizations — as a part of the problem rather than as one of the solutions. The challenge to racism (and to sexism and other forms of exploitation and discrimination) must rest on challenges to all of the forms of representation in which hierarchies of race, gender and class are now embedded. This means that feminists must seek a vision of society in which our demands for "voice" (i.e., participation that includes power) will not be captured in the forms of "representation" offered to groups today as *the* way to exercise power in liberal democracies.

Once we understand the connections between privilege and the practice of representation, it is clear that challenges to the privilege of individuals or groups of women must be carried out in the context of a larger commitment to the democratization of state practices, major community-based organizations, institutions and feminist organizations. A tall order. Even though liberal democracies are dominated economically by the interests of a male-dominated capitalist-imperialist class and politically by their representatives in state administrations, those of us who have moved into state administrations have learned that the relationship between state and society and between "women" and the "state" is never fixed. Challenges from women of Colour have forced many feminist organizations to question the way they represent "women." In the apparently never-ending consultations with community representatives about policies[24] and about the way representation works, there are also spaces where groups can challenge the way the state represents "women's" interests in its policy-making and challenge the requirements this imposes on the way feminists in the community represent the interests of women in the political process.[25] As NAC discovered when it decided to oppose the Panel on Violence and the Royal Commission on Reproductive Technology on the grounds that neither represented Native women nor women of Colour, it is possible to say No to the forms the state organizes to represent the interests of women. What is important now is to question representation itself, to question a set of practices that feminists use to represent "women," practices that hold a hierarchy of privilege in place, rather than to ask for more and better representation in them.

Notes

1. I am using the term "representation" to refer to a set of political and administrative practices that shape the way our interests as citizens are represented by those we elect as leaders of social movements and political parties, by those we elect to the federal parliament, to provincial legislatures or to municipal councils, and by those who are appointed to represent our interests in state administrations. The particular way this representation has been organized since the 1960s determines the relationship between state and civil society and the influence that groups in civil society have on the development of state policies. It also has profoundly affected the way that groups have organized to represent the interests of their members in the policy process.

2. See Linda Carty in "Women's Studies in Canada: A Discourse and Praxis of Exclusion" in *RFR/DRF,* Vol. 20, Nos. 3-4, p. 14, for her comments on the changing racial composition of Canada and the need for feminist scholars to account for it in their work.

3. Daiva Stasiulis describes some of the issues these groups addressed in the 1980s in Toronto in "The Politics of Minority Resistance Against Racism in the Local State" in Roxanna Ng, Gillian Walker and Jacob Mueller, eds. *Community Organization and the Canadian State* (Toronto: University of Toronto Press, 1990).

4. See Carmencita Hernandez in "The Coalition of Visible Minority Women" for an account of the development of the Coalition in Frank Cunningham *et. al.,* eds. *Social Movements/Social Change* (Toronto:Between the Lines, 1988).

5. "Cayenne Takes Up the Debate" in *Cayenne,* Vol. 2, No. 2-3, June-July 1986, p. 25. See also Carolyn Egan *et. al.* in "The Politics of Transformation" in Cunningham, *op. cit.,* for the way this worked in the organization of Toronto's International Women's Day Committee.

6. *Statement of the Black Women's Collective to the International Women's Day Coalition, February 5, 1986.* Reprinted in *Our Lives,* Vol. 1, No. 1, March 1986. The statement came from the Black Women's Collective; the women do, however, refer in the statement to the leadership given by both the Collective and the Native Women's Resource Centre to the organization of the 1986 event.

7. See Gabriel and Scott elsewhere in this anthology for an analysis of the struggles against racism at Women's Press in this period.

8. By "relations of ruling" I mean the term Dorothy Smith uses to describe the hierarchy of relations of class, race and gender that shape the process of governing in liberal democracies. See *The Everyday World as Problematic* (Toronto: University of Toronto Press, 1988).

9. Himani Bannerji in "Re:Turning the Gaze" in *RFR/DRF,* Vol. 20, Nos. 3-4, p. 9.

10. Carty. *Op. cit.,* p. 14.

11. See Peggy MacIntosh in "White Privilege and Male Privilege: A Personal Account of Coming to See Correspondence Through Work in Women's Studies." *Working Paper No. 189* (Wellesley: Wellesley College Centre for Research on Women, 1988). In the paper, MacIntosh identifies forty-six examples of her privileges as a white woman, privileges that she argues work in the everyday lives of white women.

12. This articles draws substantially on my article "Democratizing the Local State: Issues for Feminist Practice and the Representation of 'Women' " in Greg Albo *et. al.,* eds. *A Different Kind of State* (Toronto: Oxford University Press, 1993).

13. "Women with special needs" was the term used by the Women and Work Institute to refer to immigrant and visible minority women, Native women and women with disabilities in their call for research proposals. In spite of the convenience of this clustering, it does encourage us to lose sight of the differences among these groups of women. For this reason, I use more specific labels (with an understanding of their limits as well).

14. "Equal Opportunity Corporate Review 1986-1990." (Toronto: City of Toronto, 1991), p. 83.

15. *Ibid.,* p. 84.

16. Gerda Werkerle and Sylvia Novac in "Gender and Housing in Toronto," a report prepared for the Women and Work Institute for the City of Toronto, June 1991.

17. City of Toronto. *Op. cit.*

18. As temporary adviser on race relations to Ontario Premier Bob Rae, Stephen Lewis called on the New Democratic government to introduce employment equity legislation by December 1992. He noted the sentiment in the racial minority community that "there may be no other explicit

legislative initiative which will mean so much to establishing a positive climate of race relations in the minds of every single minority grouping..." Reported in "Blacks Are 'Focus' of Racism" in the *Globe and Mail*, June 10, 1992, p. A11.

19. See Roxana Ng in "Sexism, Racism and Canadian Nationalism" in *Socialist Studies*, No. 5, 1990.

20. See Becki Ross's account of the privileging of heterosexual feminists by the Women's Program. The criteria for grants in the late 1980s explicitly forbade the Program to recommend grants for projects that had anything to do with lesbianism. "Heterosexuals Only Need Apply: The Secretary of State's Regulation of Lesbian Existence" in the *RFR/DRF* special issue, "Feminist Perspectives on the Canadian State," Vol. 17, No. 3, September 1988.

21. See "The Feminist Manifesto" (Vancouver: Working Group on Sexual Violence, 1985). The manifesto was prepared for a National Action Committee on the Status of Women (NAC) annual meeting to argue for a return to a feminism that worked from and supported grassroots, community-based activity rather than one that was organized to lobby the government. See also Drucilla Cornell. *Beyond Accommodation: Ethical Feminism, Deconstruction and the Law* (New York: Routledge, 1991).

22. Sue Findlay in "Making Sense of Pay Equity: Issues for Feminist Political Practice" in Judy Fudge and Patricia McDermott, eds. *Just Wages* (Toronto: University of Toronto Press, 1991).

23. In a talk to a workshop on the "Canadian Political Economy in Hard Times," sponsored by *Studies in Political Economy* in Toronto in January 1993, Meg Luxton argued that socialist men had a lot to learn from organizations like NAC about ways to build more inclusive and more effective political organizations.

24. See Susan Phillips' description of the community's dissatisfaction with consultations on environmental plans and on constitutional changes in "How Ottawa Blends: Shifting Government Relationships with Interest Groups" in Frances Abele, ed. *How Ottawa Spends: The Politics of Fragmentation, 1991-92* (Ottawa: Carleton University Press, 1991).

25. Roxana Ng makes this argument quite forcefully in her analysis of how state practices disorganized and depoliticized the work of an agency organized to support immigrant women. See *The Politics of Community Services*

(Toronto: Garamond Press, 1988). See also her piece on "State Funding to a Community Employment Centre: Implications for Working with Immigrant Women" in Ng, *op. cit.*

"UNDER MILITARY OCCUPATION"

Indigenous Women, State Violence

and Community Resistance

Donna Kahenrakwas Goodleaf

T he Oka Crisis of 1990 is a recent case in which the Kanienkehaka (Mohawk) Nation was forced to take up arms in self-defence against colonial police and military force. Kanienkehaka women continue their tradition as leading activists in political resistance. Kanienkehaka women's powerful leadership strengthened and sustained the nation's resistance against colonial forces once again.

In March 1990, the Kanienkehaka people of Kanehsatake (also known as Oka) discovered that the mayor of Oka, Jean Ouellette, along with his councillors had hired a developer to construct an additional nine-hole golf course and some condominiums to increase the community's tax revenues. The construction would result in the deliberate destruction and desecration of the ancient sacred burial grounds of Kanehsatake and the destruction of the pine trees. In response to several demands from the Kanienkehaka people of Kanehsatake that federal government officials meet with them on a nation-to-nation basis to resolve conflict, once again the state sent in the cavalry (the Sureté du Quebec) to wage a massive paramilitary attack against defenceless Kanienkehaka women and children.

Historical Context of the Struggle

Since the colonial invasions of Turtle Island — also known as North America — Indigenous nations, specifically the Haudenosaunee Six Nations Iroquois Confederacy (also known as the Longhouse People) have been under a state of siege. Euro-American and Canadian state regimes have methodically employed racist and genocidal policies and practices to obliterate whole Indigenous societies and cultures. The Kanienkehaka Nation, a member of the Haudenosaunee Six Nations Iroquois Confederacy, has been and continues to be the target of Euro-American and Canadian racist and genocidal policies and practices today.

Early colonial U.S. policy was based on extermination campaigns by the military, campaigns which, in addition to the spread of European diseases, led to the annihilation of whole Indigenous societies and cultures. Shifting from extermination campaigns to legislation, major racist and genocidal policies — the 1830 *Indian Removal Act,* the 1887 *Dawes Severalty Act,* the 1924 *Indian Citizenship Act,* the 1934 *Indian Reorganization Act,* the *Termination Act* of the 50s and 60s — were enacted to destabilize Indigenous communities and speed up their assimilation into Euro-American society.[1] The implementation of the 1887 *Dawes Severalty Act* broke up the communal landbase and introduced oppressive Euro-patriarchal notions of private property and individual nuclear households by dividing Haudenosaunee lands into family plots of 160 acres per family. Equally significant is that this law severed the spiritual and economic ties of Indigenous peoples to the land, which in turn profaned the sacred relationship of women with the earth, viewed as our mother in Haudenosaunee society.

The establishment of colonial institutions such as elected band councils during the 1800s also destabilized and depoliticized the traditional political systems of the Haudenosaunee Confederacy. The Euro-Canadian government's apartheid system, known as the 1876 *Indian Act* (the model for the apartheid regime later imposed by the colonizers in South Africa) was part of the colonizer's broader scheme to intensify political cleavage within Haudenosaunee territories. The *Indian Act* legally sanctioned the imposition of Euro-patriarchal "elected band council systems" set up deliberately to undermine traditional government systems, based on the Kaianerakowa or Great Law of Peace, and to deny the political power of such traditional systems, power rooted the collective decision-making of the Clan systems. The Kaianerakowa is the Haudenosaunee Confederacy's ancient constitution. It predates European colonialism.[2]

The forced imposition of such Euro-patriarchal political institutions undermined the powerful political, economic and social role of women within Haudenosaunee society, which is matrilineal. Land was and is invested in the power of the women. In accordance with the political principles set forth in the Kaianerakowa, "The lineal descent of the people of the Five Nations shall run in the female line. Women shall be considered the progenitors of the Nation. They shall own the land and the soil. Men and Women shall follow the status of their mother."[3] Since Haudenosaunee women owned the land, to dispossess and expropriate Haudenosaunee lands, the colonizers had to eradicate the political power of the women. From the colonizer's perspective, undermining the political power of the women would then lead to the destabilization of the Clan systems and therefore of the government within Haudenosaunee communities. Thus in 1924 the Euro-Canadian regime sent in the Royal Canadian Mounted Police and occupied the Kanienkehaka national territories of Grand River known as Six Nations and Akwesasne and forcibly imposed the Euro-patriarchal political structures the form of "elective band council systems."[4]

Church and colonial educational institutions also destabilized and then destroyed the socio-economic, cultural and spiritual aspects of Haudenosaunee society. To break the spiritual base of Haudenosaunee people, the colonizers' ambassadors — the missionaries, in particular, the Jesuits — became destructive agents, who despiritualized and destroyed Indigenous communities. The missionaries "[split] off individuals from families, families from villages, villages from nations, one by one ... They specifically attacked the spiritual ceremonies as 'pagan,' and thereby sought to end the practice of giveaways and public feasts. In addition, they sought to break the power of the clans by causing division which would split the people into nuclear households."[5]

Controlled and operated by the missionaries, colonial educational institutions such as residential schools were another weapon in the destruction of traditional extended Indigenous families and Clan systems, the expropriation of Indigenous lands and in the dissolution of the political/cultural identity of Indigenous nations. The primary objectives of such colonial institutions were and are to serve the economic and political interests of the colonizers — to pacify and "bring in indigenous peoples into the imperial/colonial structures."[6] Such institutions were laboratories for indoctrination; colonial schools functioned primarily to speed up the assimilation of Indigenous peoples into mainstream society while simultaneously inflicting cultural genocide. The Haudenosaunee Confederacy has always defiantly resisted against such colonial, racist and genocidal policies and practices.

Kanienkehaka women today, as in the past, continue to be in the forefront, actively protecting and defending our people, land and culture against the racist and genocidal policies of the state and of multi-national corporations. They continue to serve as the political ambassadors of our nation. They are teachers, mothers, grandmothers, sisters, environmental activists, spiritual leaders, lawyers, nurses, all working collectively in rebuilding our communities. Kanienkehaka women continue to confront "the issues and are leading the resistance — not by hosting tea parties or seeking federal funding, but by openly confronting the oppressor."[7]

Kanienkehaka Resist SQ Paramilitary Assault — Oka, July 11, 1990

On the morning of July 11, 1990, the mayor of Oka sent in over one hundred heavily armed tactical police squads — the Sureté du Quebec (SQ) — to conduct a massive paramilitary assault upon defenceless women and children during a tobacco burning ceremony. One Kanienkehaka woman, Debbie Etienne, reports what she witnessed from behind the barricades:

> The actual attack started during the tobacco burning. We were up early, just about the whole village was there. At sunrise we were thanking the Great Creator for the sun and a new day. That's when the first shots and tear gas came in. The women went out to talk to them (SQ). They wanted to talk to our leader. We told them the truth— that we had no leader — it was the people together that spoke. The officer couldn't grasp this and kept insisting that he talk to our leader. We went back and asked Johnny Cree to talk to them. He is our faith keeper...He [the SQ officer] told Johnny they had orders to open fire if we all didn't leave the area so they could take down the barrier. Johnny said he would talk

to us and when he came back he told us he thought it was more than just arrests they wanted. But we told him to tell them we were staying. Johnny went back and told them and asked that at least they give us time to finish our prayers so we would be prepared to meet our Creator. The SQ leader said we had five minutes then they were coming in...All this time the women were making breakfast...There were a lot of kids around and we just sort of did it to keep the kids happy and our minds occupied. When Johnny came back he almost pleaded with us to leave because he felt blood would be shed. Again, we said, "No" and asked Johnny to offer up a prayer...Denise asked them, "Why do you want to kill me? Why do you want to kill my children?" That trooper slowly lowered his gun until his leader signalled him to reload and keep his weapon up. The girls spread out in a line. They [SQ] yelled "Time is up. Are you going to leave?" We said, "You know what our answer is. We cannot leave." Then the concussion grenades and tear gas started. Soon after bullets. The women started to run back. Our men were back in the bush behind the lacrosse rink. None of them had fired up to then because no order had been given. Around then there was a war cry given up to bring the Great Creator's attention to what was happening to us. When our men saw they [SQ] were firing with women and children up front, the command to fire was given and they opened fire too. The youngest of the children was two and he was on a tricycle on the road. His little feet were peddling like heck. Bullets were kicking up dirt next to him. One of the men went out and grabbed him and pulled him behind a big pine. A woman was terrified and she fell. A warrior ran out and covered her with his body so he would take the bullets. The exchange lasted maybe five minutes but it seemed forever. Then I heard someone say, "look they are running" and the firing stopped.[8]

Ellen Gabriel and Denise David-Tolly were among the dozen women of Kanehsatake who decided to confront the SQ. Respected elder from Kahnawake, Eba Beauvais, a grandmother, Clan Mother of the Turtle Clan, was one of the dozen women who walked arm-in-arm with her sisters up to the SQ, demanding them to leave Kanehsatake territory. Laura Norton, Lorna Delormier, Shirly Scott, and Kahentiiosta were among the many women from Kahnawake who had gone to Kanehsa-take to help protect and defend our people and our land.

Immediately after the firing stopped, women began to organize themselves by establishing food banks, a make-shift first-aid centre and designating women to be spokespersons. Others were selected by consensus to sit on the negotiating team of both women and men from Kanienkehaka communities of Kahnawake, Kanehsatake and Akwe-sasne.

In Kahnawake, to survive future paramilitary SQ assaults on our sisters and brothers in Kanehsatake, my community took up arms in self-defence, sealing off two major highways leading to and from Kahnawake and connecting to Montreal. In response to the blockade of the Mercier Bridge, the SQ sealed off the entire territories of Kahnawake and Kanehsatake and denied delivery of food and medical supplies to both communities, now under siege. Kanienkehaka women of Kahnawake immediately organized themselves accordingly. They met in the cookhouse located next to the Longhouse to assign various tasks to individuals who had the skills or knowledge needed in the areas of food supply, politics, medicine, and public relations. The women organized food banks and community kitchens to ration food to families. One elderly Kanienkehaka woman, Rita McComber, describes the establishment of food banks:

> We wanted to open up the food bank in the Kateri Hall [a community centre]. I called around and got the "OK" to start up a food bank there.— We were getting short on food. It reached a point where people could not go over [to Montreal or Chateauguay] to get food....The Quebec Native Women's Association and other groups who were helpful in getting food over to us used boats to cross the river. We had some men come through the fields smuggling food in...The food bank gave our people the security of knowing that they were not going to starve, that there was a place they could come to...A few of the older people would come every day to sort out, so they had some place to go, they felt secure, they felt safe....[9]

Kanienkehaka women working in the food banks organized themselves to work on a 24-hour schedule, divided into three eight-hour shifts. During the day one would see groups of youth, women and men delivering food to the men staffing the barricades. At night groups of women would gather in trucks or cars and visit the men at the barricades. When a nation of people is at war with the state, "kitchen duties" are political acts. Women's responsibility for establishing food banks and distributing food ensured that a community of over 6,000 people would not starve and was crucial to the survival of a people living under military occupation — especially when the state had imposed food and medical embargoes against the community.

In addition to organizing food banks and participating in the daily resistance to police and military occupation, women also had to feed their own children, families and relatives. Clanmothers and other women also provided political leadership, as they served on the negotiating team throughout the Oka crisis.

In understanding the Euro-sexist imperialist attitudes white males have towards women, Kanienkehaka women found themselves constantly challenging governmental and military officials who would not look at the women sitting across the table when political discussions were taking place. As one Kanienkehaka woman told to me, "Government and military officials consistently looked to our men for final decisions or a response to their questions. Instead of responding immediately, our men would consult with our women and then organize in our traditional clan system to discuss issues raised during negotiation talks. Not only did this irritate government and military officials, they also found themselves answering questions by our women concerning the daily human rights violations conducted by the SQ and the military."

On the international level, Clanmothers also served as ambassadors, representing the Kanienkehaka Nation at the United Nations in Geneva, speaking out against the daily human rights violations and other forms of political violence committed by the Euro-Canadian and Quebec regimes against our nation. Their presence countered any lies the Canadian ambassador to the UN may have been spreading about how well the Euro-Canadian government treats "its" Aboriginal people.

Kanienkehaka Women Resist Military Invasions

On August 27, the Quebec Premier Robert Bourassa announced that all negotiations with the Kanienkehaka nation had been called off and stated it was time to use military force to dismantle the barricades in both besieged communities. At that point, all negotiations shifted from the political to the military front. When the Kahnawakeronon (people of Kahnawake) heard this news, they prepared for warfare. The Kateri Hospital in Kahnawake had bodybags and stretchers taken to the barricades. Medical units were on standby.

On a political level, women and men working in the Kanienkehaka Nation Office immediately faxed notices to local, national and international communities, church groups and political organizations, requesting their intervention to pressure the Euro-Canadian government to withdraw its military troops immediately.

Kanienkehaka women organized a mass demonstration, sending a message to the world and specifically to the Rotiskenrahkete (those who carry the burden of protecting the origins, the Carriers of Peace), expressing their enduring love and reaffirming their support for the men who were putting their lives on the line. This message deserves to be quoted at length:

> Our people of Kanehsatake and Kahnawake have been acting in good faith. Our people have given and are still giving the governments of Canada and Quebec every opportunity to avoid a violent confrontation and find a peaceful resolution to the situation we have been in resulting from the armed attack by the Sureté du Quebec police on Mohawk men, women, and children in Kanehsatake. We have come together today to show our support for the men — Rotiskenrahkete, The Carriers of Peace — who through their dedication to the Mohawk Nation have put their life on the line. It is always for the same reason — to protect and defend our Territories, our land, the women and children, the nation. As women, we stand [with] our men who are carrying out their duties and responsibilities. We also wish to show our support for those negotiators who have been acting in good faith in meeting all the terms of the governments in order to sit down at the table.
>
> The world must see that we stand together as the Mohawk Nation and will not fall under the iron fist of the oppressive police state and military aggression which Premier Bourassa and Prime Minister Mulroney initiated. We the Mohawk women have our duties and respon-

sibilities as mothers and keepers of the land and stand alongside our men (Rotiskenrahkete) in this time of defending the nation.[10]

Then, on September 3rd, under the direct orders of the state, my people were the targets of a massive military invasion. When the people heard that the army was going to conduct a military operation, specifically on the Longhouse in search of weapons, the women immediately began to mobilize at the Longhouse, a place where we gather to conduct all spiritual and socio-political affairs.

Backed up by ten to fifteen SQ vehicles, the military sent in over forty armored personnel carriers (APCs) to attack the Longhouse. A Kanienkehaka woman, Margaret Horn, who witnessed this event at the Longhouse, remembers:

> ... At 2:00 p.m. while sitting at the Longhouse in Kahnawake with ten to fifteen other women, one of the men announced that there were about 40 Canadian Army A.P.C.s coming into Kahnawake. The women rushed out to the road [Highway 207] and stopped the line of tanks by standing across the road. Some of the women laid down in front of the first tank. The officer in charge ordered the men out of the tanks and stood face to face in front of the Mohawk women. The Mohawk women demanded that the army leave our territory. The soldiers were prepared with their guns on their back as the women were unarmed. Eventually approximately 75 to 100 Mohawk women had arrived. There was a couple of hundred soldiers present. The first tank was beginning to roll forward even though there were women in front of the tank. The commanding officer ordered the tank to stop until he received further orders. The soldiers were then ordered to remove the women. The women stood their ground with their arms locked together and refused to move. The soldiers began to push and grab women. The soldiers threw some of the women in the ditches on the side of the road. This series of events took approximately one to two hours. The soldiers and some of the tanks then went onto the Longhouse grounds. The Mohawk women continued to attempt to block their way onto the Longhouse grounds. I saw two women [get] hit with rifle butts in the head, and one that was hit in the rib cage. Two of the women had to be taken to the hospital for medical treatment. The

> soldiers always had their guns ready to open fire and were pushing the women.[11]

Although many of the women were seriously injured, the women defiantly stood their ground. There were also instances in which some of the women managed to pin down several soldiers or keep them bay.

September 18

Women, children and men were subject to another and more massive military invasion in Kahnawake. This was another joint SQ-military operation. On the afternoon of September 18th, I was working at the Kanienkehaka Mohawk Nation Office when we were informed of a military build-up. Three Chinook and several Bell UH-1 helicopters landed on Tekwawitha Island with over four hundred military troops clad in riot gear, while four Huey gunboats surrounded the island.

People immediately rushed out of the office and headed to the island to see what was happening. Margaret Horn and I were both working in the office. We dashed out the door, jumped into her car and drove to the tip of the island.

As we approached the marina at the tip of the island, we saw a couple of huge green Chinook helicopters land on the ground. Seconds later, out of the bushes swarmed hundreds of soldiers, charging with their guns pointed directly at us. Margaret floored her car and sped down the road, heading back to the bridge that connects the island to the community. By this time, the community siren was sounding and over 1,000 Kahnawakeronon rushed to the island.

At the sound of approaching helicopters, many elders, men, women and children stood on the bridge which connects the island to the community. To prevent further military advances, the people began to form a human wall on the bridge. As tensions mounted, people began to shove and shout at the soldiers. Elderly women standing face-to-face with the soldiers demanded that they leave our territory.

Positioned in front of the bridge, I saw women rip away with their hands the razor-wire that separated us from the army and physically confront the soldiers. Kahnawakeronon held their position, then surged forward to force the army troops to back off. Fights broke out. Troops aimed their rifles at the people and used their rifle butts in their attack against women and men. The army shot volleys of tear gas at the people. Panic set in. This forced people to jump off the bridge or retreat. With my people on the bridge and tear-gassed, I suddenly started to black out from the tear gas. I was clinging to the fence of the bridge, watching people screaming, choking and running desperately for their lives. Many people were forced to jump off the bridge. Fifty to seventy-five women, men and children were hospitalized for tear gas exposure. In spite of the tear gas attacks, Kahnawakeronon, more angry and defiant than ever, returned in full force, pelting soldiers with sticks and rocks. This forced the army to retreat several hundred yards from the bridge.

The following testimony is signed by five witnesses, two of whom are ministers:

> ...Elderly women were yelling at the troops to leave the Island. Tensions were very high; highest rate at the razor-wire; people were shouting...pushing at the soldiers across the razor-wire...soldiers began assembling a machine gun...women walked down from the bridge onto the south shore...troops moved to the shore and near the bridge to prevent other people from joining those women...on north shore, by water, people punching and kicking at soldiers...soldiers retreat several metres; confused; apparently lacking order...soldier advanced and began hitting all people within reach with the butt of his rifle...people regrouping, women gathering rocks on mainland end of bridge, piling them up beside bridge to make them accessible. People throwing rocks at army, army retreats approximately 7 metres. Second tear gas canister fired.... throughout the event, several military helicopters hovered low above the area, adding to the confusion...[12]

The army seemed unprepared for the strong resistance they encountered from the community. We demonstrated such collective defiance and resistance against military power that the army was forced to retreat, unable to complete its mission. Instead of the military paralyzing the people with fear, it angered us all the more and strengthened our determination to resist. Women continued to confront the military, sustaining our collective resistance as a nation in defending and protecting our people against military invasions.

Responses by Indigenous Nations

As news reached the Kanienkehaka Mohawk Nation Office in Kahnawake about the SQ's massive paramilitary invasion in Kanehsatake on July 11th, the people in the office immediately faxed communiques and press releases to the media, Indigenous communities, church groups and political organizations, informing them of the violent assault.

On the west coast, the Lilooet Nation of Seton Portage in British Columbia blockaded the B.C. rail line and set up a roadblock on Highway 12, approximately 180 kilometres northeast of Vancouver. The Okanangan Nation of Pentiction, B.C. also constructed roadblocks to protest of the state's use of police and its military assaults against the Kanienkehaka Nation. In northern Ontario, the Long Lake Nation blocked off the main line of the Crown-owned railway just north of Lake Superior, approximately 300 kilometres northeast of Thunder Bay. The Canadian Pacific (CP) railway was also blocked by Indigenous people of Mobert Territory, approximately 200 kilometres north of Sault Ste. Marie.

On August 28th, on nationwide television, military officials held a press conference describing various kinds of military equipment and detailing military operations they said were necessary to dismantle the barricades in Kahnawake and Kanehsatake. They displayed photographs and diagrams that revealed. the defensive positions of Kahnawake and Kanehsatake. A video display was included to inform the Kanienkehaka people of the lethal weapons — including APCs and C-7 and C-9 machine guns — the military possessed and would use against them. Klare and Kornbluh write about such psychological warfare:

> Psychological operations (PSYOP), like civic action, is intended to enhance the popular image of the government and to isolate and discredit the insurgent movement. According to the Army, PSYOP entails the utilization of multiple communications channels — in order to create attitudes and behaviour favourable to the achievement of political and military objectives. Such activities are considered to play an especially vital role in counterinsurgency, where the struggle over public attitudes is so critical. Typically, such efforts include the dissemi-

nation of audio, visual, and printed materials designed to portray the government in the best possible light while characterizing the insurgents as...terrorists. PSYOP can also entail the dissemination of faked enemy documents designed to discredit the insurgents or to stir up divisions within their ranks.[13]

The live broadcast of military operations and the show of force was classic psychological warfare, meant to terrify the Kanienkehaka people and to justify the state's intended armed assault against my people.

In response to the military's announcement that it would use force to dismantle the barricades, Indigenous Nations across the continent immediately began to mobilize their communities to take action on all levels, from mounting massive demonstrations and increasing the number of blockades to other political tactics.

In Winnipeg, an emergency meeting was called in which leaders from Indigenous Nations across the land gathered to discuss various plans in response to the bloodbath that seemed imminent. From Indigenous peoples' perspective, the state had declared war not only upon the Kanienkehaka Nation but on all Indigenous Nations. As Chief Gary Potts of the Teme-Augama Anishnabe Nation of North Bay stated to the press, "The government of Canada has declared war on all natives...There will be a coordinated effort across the country to prepare to meet the army...it's a war situation now...each nation will be taking their own actions..."[14]

As Indigenous leaders met to strategize against the military's operations, the news created a shock wave. Demonstrations erupted across the country. The Union of B.C. Chiefs called upon First Nations citizens throughout British Columbia to organize and take immediate action to "make themselves visible at roadsides and bridges in their territories as well as in the streets of cities, towns and villages."[15] Demonstrators were arrested in Toronto for occupying the Conservative Party's office to protest the army's decision. In Fredericton, New Brunswick, approximately fifty people demonstrated in front of the Conservative Party's office. In the meantime, well over three hundred Maliseet and Miq'Mac people organized a convoy of cars and buses to act as a buffer between the military and the Rotiskenrahkete staffing the barricades. No doubt, sisters and brothers from other Indigenous Nations clearly understood that placing themselves between the military and my people might mean they would have to sacrifice their lives to ensure there would be no bloodshed against the Kanienkehaka people.

Further west, Indigenous Nations mounted new waves of mass demonstrations and set up fortified barricades to protest the military's plans. While Indigenous sisters and brothers in British Columbia repeatedly disrupted traffic and rail lines by putting up new barricades, the Heron Bay-Pic people in Ontario threatened to blockade the CP rail line passing through their territory if Canadian National (CN) and Via decided to use it as an alternative route. The continued demonstrations and blockades by Indigenous Nations cost the state very heavily. *Maclean's* reported, "One five-day blockade of a B.C. Rail line at Seton Portage in the Fraser Valley...cost the railway between $500,000 and $750,000 per day in lost revenues, according to the company...rail blockades may prove even higher for CP rail...barricades disrupted its main transcontinental line in Northern Ontario. Said CP rail official John Cox: 'Virtually all our transcontinental traffic has been disrupted. We are at the mercy of individual bands and whatever decisions they make.'"[16]

During the first week of August, the Okanangan Nation of British Columbia sponsored a nationwide Peace Run to Oka, with more than thirty women and men, including four women from Kahnawake and sisters and brothers from the Cree and Anishnabe Nations. The significance of this spiritual run was two-fold. First, it symbolized the spiritual and political unity between two sovereign confederated nations from the west and the east coasts. Second, the run carried a message of peace and justice for all Indigenous Nations across the country and helped awaken the public to continued aggression by the SQ and the military in Kanienkehaka territory. The establishment of the Oka Peace Camp at Paul Sauvé Provincial park in Kanehsatake was an activity collectively organized by Indigenous and non-Indigenous people. Buses and carloads of people came from all over the country to show support for the Kanienkehaka people and to monitor the police and the military. Well over seven hundred people came to camp out in the park.

The Grandmothers' Walk

Another event that caught the nation's eye was the Grandmothers' Walk in Solidarity with Mohawk Clan Mothers, a journey across the country by Indigenous grandmothers representing the Métis, the Plains Cree and the Cree-Ojibway women. One non-Indigenous woman took part. On the forth day of their journey, a press release from Saskatoon, Saskatchewan, was faxed to the Kanienkehaka Mohawk Nation Office, Kahnawake:

> To the Mohawk Clan Mothers, grandmothers and women we say: Our prayers are with you. With each mile we cover, tobacco sends our prayers for your safety and a fair and just resolution of your crisis. You are not alone.... We love our lands and our children as you do and if either were threatened, we would do no different. We will not stop our trek until we reach Mohawk country, or until Ellen Gabriel [one of the Kanienkehaka Mohawk] spokeswoman behind the barricades in Oka publicly states that your crisis is over...To the Canadian and provincial governments we say:...the Mohawk, like all Indian nations in the Americas, never gave up their right to self-determination and sovereignty; our land is sacred and we will not stop until our claims are justly dealt with...We support the actions of our young people who defend our lands and rights to self-determination. We say further that if Mohawk blood is shed, you had better be prepared to shed the blood of aboriginal grandmothers, women, and children because, A NATION IS NOT BROKEN UNTIL ITS WOMEN ARE DOWN.[17]

Our grandmothers too continue to be on the frontlines, providing active political leadership in the protection and defence of our people. The protection and the survival of our people, land and culture continue to be the spiritual and political underlying principles of Indigenous women's resistance today.

A Call To Consciousness

As Indigenous women, we continue the tradition of providing powerful leadership to a nation collectively resisting five hundred years of colonial domination. Current struggles by Indigenous peoples are not only against the state and multinationals, but, as Winona LaDuke states, against a state of mind based on conquest, that believes the land and all peoples are expendable in the name of "progress" and "Western civilization."

To non-Indigenous peoples of the Western hemisphere: ask yourself what is your relationship to the land and to the liberation struggles of Indigenous peoples nationally and internationally? What are your responsibilities in the healing of the earth and in the survival of the next seven generations? What is the position of the white feminist movement on the liberation struggle of Indigenous peoples? As an Indigenous woman, I have studied the deep contradictions, elitism and white supremacy in the mainstream, primarily middle-class, feminist movement. Feminist theory and practice that focus only on male supremacy, without analyzing the impact of colonialism, race and class, reveal the narrow-minded thinking of white, middle-class women who make sexual politics the top priority. This creates a "politics" that is Euro-supremacist and exclusionary. I have yet to encounter any white feminist theory that provides an in-depth analysis of the historical construction of the nation-state and its racist and genocidal policies against Indigenous peoples and peoples of Colour. As Oneida scholar Pam Colorado notes, "It seems to me the feminist agenda is basically one of rearranging social relations within a society which is occupying our land and utilizing our resources for its own benefit. Nothing I've encountered in feminist theory addresses the fact of our colonization, or the wrongness of white women's stake in it...Instead, feminists appear to share a presumption in common with the patriarchs they oppose, that they have some sort of inalienable right to simply go on occupying our land and exploiting our resources for as long as they like."[18]

As an Indigenous woman, I can only conclude that the mainstream feminist movement is only interested in maintaining the hierarchial power relations of an industrial-militaristic, racist, sexist and homophobic society. Ask yourself: How does the white feminist movement participate in and benefit from the continuous exploitation of Indigenous peoples and the colonization of our homelands and natural resources? Is white feminism *perpetuating* or *challenging* a state of mind based on conquest? Does your vision of liberation include the liberation of Indigenous peoples, the land, the waters, the air, the four-legged...?

A CALL TO CONSCIOUSNESS IS IN ORDER for "left wing" or "radical" social movements. All peoples must broaden their narrow concept of liberation and go beyond the human to a vision rooted in a spiritually- and politically-based worldview of Indigenous peoples that encompasses the four-legged, the waters, the air, the earth — all things which support the sacred web of life. As Anishnabe scholar and activist Winona La Duke succinctly points out, "As the land suffers, so suffer the people.... No movement or group of related movements can succeed in offsetting present circumstances merely through a shared rejection. Not only must they struggle against something, but they must also struggle toward something. Action alone can never provide the required answers. Only a unifying theory, a unifying vision of the alternatives can fulfill this task. Only such a vision can bind together the fragmentary streams of action and resistance currently at large in America into a single multi-facet[ed] whole capable of transforming the synthetic reality of a death culture into the natural reality of a culture of life."[19]

Our strategies for and visions of liberation must include a worldview that challenges the colonial ideology of the earth as a commodity to be exploited and must also "develop in people a consciousness that all life on the earth is sacred and that the sacredness of life is the key to human freedom and survival...that it is the renewable quality of earth's ecosystems which makes life possible for human beings on the planet..."[20]

▼▼▼

Portions of this article are taken from the author's 1992 dissertation, *Kanienkehaka (Mohawk) Nation, State Policies, and Community Resistance: A Pedagogical Tool.*

Notes

1. Rebecca Robins in "Self-Determination and Subordination in The Past, Present, and Future of American Indian Governance" in M. Annette Jaimes, ed. The State of Native America. Genocide, Colonization and Resistance (Boston: South End Press, 1992).
2. "Basic Call to Consciousness" in *Akwesasne Notes* (via Rooseveltown, New York: the Mohawk Nation, 1986).

3. See "Wampum 44" in Arthur C. Parker. *The Constitution of The Five Nations or The Iroquois Book of The Great Law* (Albany: New York State Museum Bulletin, 1916), p. 42.

4. "Basic Call."

5. *Ibid.*, p. 65.

6. Martin Carnoy. *Education As Cultural Imperialism* (New York: David McKay Company, Inc., 1974), p. 16.

7. Carol Cornelius Mohawk in "Native Women: Working For The Survival of Our People" in *Akwesasne Notes,* Late Fall, 1982, p. 4.

8. Interview with Debbie Etienne in Craig Maclaine and Michael Baxendale. *This Land Is Ours: The Mohawk Revolt At Oka* (Toronto: Optimum Publishers International Inc., 1990), pp. 30-31.

9. Kanienkehaka Solidarity Group. *Bridges & Barricades: In Defense of Mohawk Land* (Montreal: McGill University, 1991), p. 29.

10. Mohawk Women of Kahnawake. Press Release, August 31, 1990.

11. Testimony by Margaret Horn, taken at Kahnawake on September 3, 1990.

12. Testimony of events at Tekawitha Island Bridge, taken at Kahnawake on September 18, 1990, pp. 1-2.

13. Michael T. Klare and Peter Kornbluh. *Low Intensity Warfare: Counterinsurgency, Proinsurgency and Anti-Terrorism in the Eighties* (New York: Pantheon Books, York, 1988), p. 60.

14. Told to Canadian Press and printed in *The Montreal Gazette*, August 29, 1990, pp. A1-A2.

15. B.C. Union of Chiefs. Press Release. "B.C. Chiefs Call For Immediate Action in B.C. to Save Lives and Protect Rights at Oka," September 3, 1990.

16. Chris Wood *et. al.* in "Sending in The Troops" in *Maclean's*, September 3, 1990, p. 17.

17. Grandmothers in Solidarity with Mohawk Clan Mothers. Press Release, September 2, 1990, pp. 1-2.

18. Annette M. Jaimes and Theresa Halsey in "American Indian Women: At the Centre of Indigenous Resistance in Contemporary North America" in Jaimes. *Op. Cit* p. 332.

19. Winona LaDuke in "Natural to Synthetic And Back Again" in Ward Churchill, ed. *Marxism and Native Americans* (Boston: South End Press, 1982), pp. iv-vi.

20. "Basic Call," p. 77.

THE TROUBLE WITH DEMOCRACY

Child Care Reform in Ontario and

the Politics of Participation[1]

Lois Harder

In the spring of 1992 I found myself in a stuffy conference room in an Etobicoke hotel "participating" in one of a series of public consultations on the reform of child care in Ontario. This meeting was part of a process set up in the NDP government's public consultation paper, "Setting the Stage." I was attending this meeting in the interest of researching this article and I knew that as a white, educated, appropriately-dressed, middle-class woman I would seamlessly meld into the crowd. Unsurprisingly, my privilege was reinforced even in a meeting that was supposed to be about "public" participation. Who exactly did the organizers of this meeting think would appear on a weekday afternoon? Clearly, it was not going to be child care or domestic workers. Perhaps the organizers thought these women would come for the evening session, but as there was no child care available at the meeting and as there was limited access to the hotel by public transit (at least for this consultation) the possibility of their participation was unlikely. (Other barriers to participation such as the formality of the process and the expectation of a certain level of "cultural capital" will be considered later.)

Then there was the organization of the meeting itself. The speakers' list spanned seven hours and only allotted fifty minutes for comments from the floor. Only four of the seventeen presenters were apparently unaffiliated with either the non-profit or the commercial child care lobbies: two male citizens and two female parents. As the meeting progressed, the tension created by the animosity between the two child care lobbies meant that only the bravest and most self-confident members of the "public" would dare to make use of the already limited time allotted to us.

This brief experience with the practice of state-sponsored participatory democracy points to three areas in which the notion of democratic participation needs to be questioned. First, we must consider participation as it relates to the organization and provision of child care itself. Second, we need to analyze the implications of co-operation between progressive advocacy groups and a social democratic, *capitalist* state. And finally, we must consider the limitations on participation within the existing structures of "public" consultation. The NDP's public consultation paper on child care reform and the consultation itself served as the vehicle for this analysis.

"Setting the Stage" necessarily draws on current practices in the organization of the provision of child care as the starting point for reform. For the purposes of this discussion, I draw on the document's assertions of a need to move towards a universal child care system, its desire to foster a variety of child care services and parental involvement in child care centres as these relate to the government's goal of a community-based service.

Child care has been a social policy issue in Canada for more than 150 years. However, the welfare versus universal service debate confronted in the Ontario NDP government's child care consultation document is largely the product of the post-war welfare state. Unlike the pillars of Canada's welfare state — health care, social security and education — all viewed as necessary services available to all comers — child care has until very recently been viewed as aid to the poor. This class aspect of the provision of child care has done much to stigmatize those who avail themselves of child care services and to limit their participation in determining the form and content of child care provision.

At present, the state's role in supporting child care is primarily fiscal: offering subsidized daycare spaces and child tax credits. Underscoring this role is the notion that by subsidizing the costs of child care, Canadian parents "participate" in child care as consumers. The market provides the range of services available for those seeking child care; parents exercise their "democratic choice" by selecting from the various options available to them. If a particular service is not to their liking, consumers express their displeasure by seeking an alternate child care centre or mode of care.

There are considerable limitations in this view of participation. It assumes that all "consumers" are on a level playing field because subsidized spaces in child care centres can be had by those who cannot afford to pay the full cost of child care and because income tax deductions are available to all Canadian tax payers. The reality of the child care "marketplace" is somewhat different.

In the case of state-sponsored child care subsidies, the state has attempted to reduce the "welfare" role of public child care and to encourage a more market-oriented approach by providing child care subsidies to parents themselves. At the same time, a certain number of subsidized spaces are allotted to most child care centres, both profit and non-profit. While these subsidies appears to enhance options for consumers on the lower end of the income scale the restricted availability of child care subsidies may prevent these people from entering the market of regulated child care in the first place.

Similarly, the opportunity to avail oneself of child tax credits is considerably less equitable than it appears. Eligibility for these deductions is dependent on the taxpayer's ability to provide receipts for the purchase of child care services. Families who cannot afford to place their children in a licensed child care facility (because they are ineligible for a child care subsidy, or because a subsidized space is unavailable or simply because they choose not to) must rely on child care from private individuals. These individuals are primarily women and are available for this kind of work because they are elderly, are recent immigrants or are not employed in more structured settings for a variety of reasons. Often these unlicensed caregivers are reluctant to claim income garnered from child care since they, like many of the people who use their services, are living at the margin. As a result, neither the receipts for this form of unregulated care nor the tax credits to which these people are entitled are forthcoming.

The real world functioning of both the child care subsidy system and the *Income Tax Act* reflect the class, gender and racial oppressions at work within the flawed notion of consumerism as free choice. When subsidies in regulated child care facilities are in short supply and hiring a nanny is beyond one's financial capacities free choice in the market place is severely attenuated. Because most Canadian women continue to carry responsibility for arranging their children's care, the retention of the notion of child care as a marketplace rather than as an imperative for women's emancipation is a direct expression of the state's ambivalence towards the participation of women in the public realm of work. Finally, the fact that Black, Asian, Latina and Native women are over-represented in the ranks of the poor means that these women are most susceptible to having their choice in the marketplace restricted.

In the NDP's current child care reform proposal there is clearly a commitment to move towards a system of universal care. Nonetheless, without the support of the federal government this goal cannot be realized. Access to affordable child care will continue to be limited. The question becomes how to minimize the effects of this limitation.

The Ontario NDP has committed itself to increasing parent participation in child care services. Given this, the Ontario government's proposal has focused on increasing the availability of non-profit child care services while simultaneously advocating for community-based child care resource centres. These resource centres would provide support for child care workers, toy swaps and emergency support. Here "choice" refers to the increased likelihood of subsidized positions in non-profit child care and to an increase in unregulated care.

Policy proposals designed to encourage the participation of the community in the operation of child care services necessarily require a structure for child care that is open to public involvement. In choosing non-profit child care as the means to this goal, the NDP has become the opponent of enraged commercial child care operators. The commercial child care lobby continues to cling to the notion of participation as consumption and argues that increasing the availability of child care should not erode the opportunity to place one's child in a for-profit child care centre.

There are many issues involved in this debate, but for the moment it will suffice to point out that the threat to child care reform posed by the commercial child care lobby is a serious one. The commercial lobby represents the market-oriented, conservative value system that is hegemonic in Western society. In contrast, the NDP government of Ontario is attempting to mediate the workings of this value system by increasing the role of the community in decisions about how child care is to be produced. As a result, debates surrounding participation are largely circumscribed by a hegemonic worldview that sees the facilitation of capital accumulation as the primary function of the state.

How is it that the Ontario government seeks to overcome the dominant view of market primacy through a view that posits participation as primary? The child care reform document proposes that parents participate in the organization of regulated child care. This involvement may happen on a number of levels. "The Parents Newspaper" that was circulated as a means of informing parents about the reform initiative, advises parents to:

- stay informed about your child's program: have regular conversations with your child's caregiver.
- learn about early childhood development — and how to spot high quality in a child care setting.
- call your local child/family resource program to find out more about child care in your community.
- try volunteering in your child care centre for a few hours a month.
- ask to attend a meeting of the board of directors for your community child care program.[2]

Clearly there are some serious oversights on the part of the government in proposing these forms of participation. While it may be a relatively simple matter to speak with your child's caregiver, the rest of this list makes assumptions about access to physical and financial resources, time, energy and skill levels that, depending on the parent, may be largely unfounded.

In the case of volunteering, one of the background papers to the consultation document does express "...a concern that for some families, especially those with few financial resources and limited free time, this role [as volunteer] may be stressful."[3] The government might have replaced "stressful" with "impossible." For many parents, the possibility of taking time off from paid employment to volunteer in a child care centre for a few hours a month simply does not exist. The expectation also falls largely on the shoulders of mothers, as most employers are unwilling to provide their male employees with time off for "parental" duties.

Educating oneself about early childhood development is a similarly empty suggestion. It implies that resources will be available. While this might be true for urban centres, it may not be the case in less populated areas. The suggestion also implies that parents have achieved the level of English fluency that permits the comprehension of abstract concepts related to childhood development. It is unlikely, especially in this era of education cutbacks, that most resource centres would provide these resources in a variety of languages. There is also the matter of when this education would occur. Once again, it is women who would be responsible for informing themselves about the development of their children. Presumably this would happen after a long day of paid employment and often several hours of unpaid domestic labour. One could hardly blame "parents" for their inability to avail themselves of this kind of information.

The limitations of participation implicit in the suggestion of attending a board meeting will be considered more fully when the child care consultation is discussed. Here, one might simply point to the limitations of time and question the expectation that parents will necessarily feel competent to assert their views on the management of a child care facility.

This cursory look at of some of the factors that might prevent parental participation in child care demonstrates that government suggestions on how to be more involved will not lead to more participation. The government's background paper, "Parents' Roles in Child Care," states, "although providing opportunities for parents to participate can be mandated, it is still up to each individual parent to choose whether to become involved."[4] This assertion reveals no understanding of what it means to provide opportunities to participate and no understanding of the material conditions that must be met if one is really to be in a position to "choose" to become involved.

If parents could participate in the ways the government suggests, the reform proposal would be a far more radical document. It would entail an increase in access to resources, information on how to achieve that access and how to get the tools to decipher the information made available. Providing parents with opportunities to volunteer at their children's child care centre would mean a progressive labour policy, one that legislated time off for such activity. And if the government was seriously interested in encouraging participation, fathers, too, would be explicitly expected to meet "parental" responsibilities. It would truly be a revolutionary undertaking.

The election of a nominally social democratic government in Ontario was met with cautious optimism from the province's progressive advocacy organizations. It seemed that the NDP government might be willing to consider some of their recommendations as it began to formulate its policy initiatives. This was the case for progressive child care lobbyists, who found their long standing critiques of the existing child care domain wholly absorbed in the NDP government's public consultation paper. Rather than responding to this co-optation by radicalizing their demands, the progressive child care lobby drafted a response to the public consultation document that was largely supportive of the government's initiatives.

The result has been the absence of the Left from the child care reform debate. Although the non-profit advocates are not *wholly* in agreement with the state, their differences of opinion are rather inconsequential compared to the opposition raised by the commercial child care lobby. As a consequence, debates surrounding the quality, affordability, accessibility and community management of child care (the four pillars of the reform proposal), not to mention the reform process itself, are obscured. Instead, the child care reform debate has been reframed in the terms of the commercial child care lobby versus the state. By taking up the position of the Left, the state has compromised the democratic process. Rather than fostering political debate among the people, even as narrowly constituted as profit versus non-profit child care operators, the state has succeeded in undermining a potentially lively discussion. Ultimately, the state's co-optation of progressive child care advocacy groups has shifted political debate to the Right and has played a significant role in closing off the possibility for a radical critique from the Left.

The Ontario government's child care consultation was organized around the circulation of its reform proposals, a series of public meetings held between April and June 1992, round tables centring on questions of local management, and "invitation only" focus groups designed to explore quality of care, human resources, regulated home based care, informal care, care for special needs children, the multicultural aspects of care, the particularities of care in rural and remote areas, base funding, the role of municipal organizations and the concerns of parents.[5]

A first impression of this elaborate process might lead to the conclusion that public consultations would indeed address a wide variety of concerns and would generate participation from those people directly affected by child care and from the community at large. Again, unsurprisingly, the situation was not as it appeared. A look at a public meeting and at the impressions of advocates and government workers reveals the internal machinations of the process.

The public meeting I attended in Etobicoke was structured around seventeen presentations by interested parties who had managed to secure positions on the speakers' list. These people presented their briefs to a government panel of four people and then returned to "the audience." In effect, their participation was primarily as performers. Members of the government panel asked only questions of clarification. Just as in a concert, the only interaction between the presenters and their "public" observers was applause, silence or boos. Substantive matters of quality and accessibility could not be discussed in any depth because the speakers' list was almost exclusively inhabited by government supporters (progressive child care advocates) or by government opponents (commercial child care operators). The consultation's structure further reinforced the state versus the Right debate and made the absence of critiques from the Left all the more acute.

A recounting of a presentation from the commercial child care lobby illustrates the flavour of the for-profit versus the state debate. A representative of the Association of Day Care Operators (ADCO) began her oral submission with the charge that Ontario premier Bob Rae was guilty of dishonourable conduct in claiming to support small business while at the same time subverting commercial child care through the government's commitment to a non-profit child care system. She questioned the honour of initiating such a reform since it would obviously mean an increased financial burden on tax payers already reeling from the recession. Maintaining personal wealth or reducing individual tax burdens was considered a greater social good than the provision of adequate child care. Having found her stride, and with encouragement from a like-minded audience, we learned of the lurking dangers of the government's child care reform proposal, an initiative that for her was reminiscent of the collectivization of Soviet farms during the 1930s.

The substantive issues of the ADCO representative's position revolved around the need for more subsidies, directly conflicting with the position that public funds should not be put toward private profits and conflicting with the presenter's own concern for the people's tax burden. The ADCO representative also argued that adequate monitoring and strict fines would ensure the meeting of provincial standards for quality care. Finally, the familiar argument about choice in the marketplace was trotted out and decorated by colourfully derisive comments about monopolies and the creation of a socialist utopia.

A further and more complex revelation of the ideology underscoring the commercial child care lobby came in its supporters' reaction to a statement made by a young mother during the time allotted for comments from the floor. This woman posited that the Ontario government should not be discussing the reform of regulated child care but rather should be providing funding to parents to remain at home with their children. Strangely, this comment met with loud applause from the commercial child care lobby, which presumably would have much to lose by such a reform. This reaction provides an insight into the conservative world view that informs the commercial lobby and shows it to be wholly subversive of progressive politics.

From the perspective of the commercial lobby, child care is a necessary evil. Starting from this premise, it follows that regulated child care is simply a stop-gap measure for children until they can be at home with their parents, where their real development takes place. When one considers that many children spend more of their waking hours under the supervision of child care workers than with their parents, the dangers of such an outlook should be readily apparent.[6]

In the reduction of the child care reform debate to that of profit versus non-profit service, the subversive character of the commercial lobby is never revealed. Instead, their conservatism hides behind the rhetoric of consumerism and the free market — obvious goods in a political environment currently steeped in the ideology of the Right. By using already established criticisms of the Ontario government, commercial operators further remove the government's and progressive child care advocates' substantive concerns about child care reform from the scope of public debate. Witness the following quote taken from the April 28, 1992 edition of the *Toronto Globe and Mail*: "Ms. Preston of the Day Care Operators saw another reason behind the government's determination to promote the non-profit system. 'One of the main reasons of trying to have a government-funded universal system that is centrally controlled is that it would be unionized. We see that as a method that the NDP has in order to pay back the unions for their support....'" On the one hand, such a comment seems outrageously silly; at the same time, it has proven to be more newsworthy than any issues of concern to the progressive child care lobby.

In the face of such tactics the absence of the organized women's movement, anti-poverty groups and anti-racism organizations from the child care reform debate must be viewed as extremely unfortunate. The lack of a gender-based critique of the commercial lobby further perpetuates the exclusion of women from the child care debate, while insidiously reinforcing the view that women should be confined to hearth and home. The absence of class and race critiques allows the commercial child care lobby and its like-minded colleagues in the broader business community to position themselves as the defenders of freedom against an ever-encroaching state. The public is not made aware of the extent to which the commercial lobby contributes to the ghettoization of child care workers through low wages and hence perpetuates the feminization of poverty.

What accounts for the absence of these groups on the Left? To consider this question is to embark on an exploration of the organizational issues that surround the child care reform consultations. This exploration reveals the extent to which various civil servants and advocates disagreed about the "reality" in which the process was being administered.

From the perspective of one government employee, the absence of representatives of immigrant women and the absence of representatives from the anti-poverty and battered women's shelter movements was largely unexplainable. This government worker observed that notice of the public consultations on child care had been more widely dispersed than in other consultations and argued that information was certainly accessible to anyone wishing to seek it out. Personal experience of unreturned phone calls and circuitous responses to simple queries about the dates for the public meetings, ending eventually in the revelation of a 1-800 number providing all the relevant information, suggests a certain lack of organization on the part of government bureaucrats, despite the good intentions of the political staff.

According to one child care advocate, this lack of organization plagued the consultation. Her observation is that the government rushed into the public meetings without adequate planning. Many of the bureaucrats relied upon to organize the meetings had never been involved in this sort of activity. The government had recently implemented a child care wage enhancement program, the administration of which was already consuming the working hours of the Child Care Policy Branch. In the midst of this, workers were being asked to familiarize themselves with the various interests in the child care reform debate and to ensure that these interests would be duly represented at the various consultations. Given the already strained bureaucratic resources, this advocate argued, it was not surprising that people already engaged in advocacy would monopolize the proceedings. Effectively, this meant that contestations over the process would be easily narrowed to a debate between the government and the non-profit child care advocates versus the commercial child care operators.[7]

It should be stressed that the absence of a well-rounded debate is not necessarily the result of malicious intent on the part of bureaucrats. In conversation with an employee of the Child Care Policy Branch, her concern about the lack of parental involvement in the public meetings was very apparent. While she acknowledged that parents had been informed of the consultation rather late in the game, she was puzzled by their hesitancy in participating in the open sections of the public meetings.

There are a number of possible explanations for this "reluctance" to participate. The inability to find a babysitter in order to attend the evening meeting is one likely explanation. (As stated earlier, attendance at the afternoon session would likely be out of the question for wage workers.) The presumption that a public meeting with the government would not allow for a full airing of views — a presumption rooted in a long-held public mistrust of the government — may also have dampened enthusiasm for the public meetings. For parents who did choose to attend, the extremely intimidating environment fostered not only by business-suited officials but by a booing, hissing and alternately cheering commercial lobby did not create an atmosphere particularly conducive to the airing of the perspective of someone unaffiliated with either lobby. Finally, the well-rehearsed arguments of the opposing sides, laden with statistics and research, may have created the impression that a single mother's observations on the care of her child were not particularly relevant. As should be clear by now, her lack of relevance in the process is evident in the very structure of the public consultation itself.

The government's failure to make the child care consultation truly participatory is the product of unwitting oversights by well-meaning bureaucrats and politicians and the product of the structure of the capitalist state itself. In absorbing the position of progressive child care advocates, the NDP government limited the scope of public debate and consequently found its progressive initiatives easily reframed by an increasingly ascendent conservatism within the hegemonic class. Clearly, progressive child care advocates must bear some of the responsibility for refusing to challenge the state from the Left, but one can certainly understand how, after so many years of fighting for reform, left-wing advocacy groups could be seduced into relinquishing their independent struggle for a powerful alliance with the state.

Another example of the government's dis-organization of participation is found in the language of the child care consultation document. The words "parents" and "child care workers" mask the centrality of women to the issue. Clearly, the intention was to demonstrate that "child care is a benefit for all"[8] and to broaden the base of support for child care reform. The consequences of this decision, however, are very serious. First, it casts the organized women's movement out of the debate. Second, it obscures the reality of women's everyday existence. Child care continues to be a women's issue because the care of children continues

to be women's responsibility. It is *because* of the unquestioned association of women with child care and *because* of a feminist desire to
redefine the care of children as everyone's responsibility, that struggles
over child care reform must continue to be fought within the context of
women's broader struggles for emancipation.

As shown by the child care consultation, attempts to bring about
more popular participation in the formation of the policies of the capitalist state ultimately leads to challenges to the foundations of that state.
If the interests of capital are threatened, participation is likely to meet
serious challenges. Interestingly, however, it is far from clear that child
care reform in Ontario and the proposed non-profit system would
threaten capital accumulation, whatever the rhetoric of the commercial
child care lobby. By partially freeing women who are not child care
workers from the responsibilities associated with their children, capital
would increase both its labour supply and the productivity of that labour
supply. This may be the reason that the commercial lobby has not been
graced by much public support from its fellow capitalists. Were the NDP
to produce a more radical reform document, one that called upon capital
to limit its accumulation in the interests of allowing citizens more time
to participate in the governance of or to volunteer their time in their
children's child care centre once a month, the commercial child care
lobby might find itself with powerful allies indeed.

To the extent that the state is viewed as patriarchal, attempts to
formulate a process that allows people who have been marginalized by
the aggressive, competitive structure of interactions with institutions to
participate might be similarly challenged. Some of this challenge will
happen because the organizers of consultations have never been forced
to think critically about the implications of certain structures through
which they participate and, ironically, are threatened by more congenial
methods of interaction. The most significant threat, however, is that the
hegemonic power of affluent, white men would be reorganized.

The Ontario government's insufficient realization of a participatory
consultation not only harms the broad democratic process, it also serves
to create an extremely awkward position for the NDP, a political party
committed to democratic principles. Given that the debate on child care
reform was posed as profit versus non-profit child care and that the

consultations were laden with presentations from commercial operators, how will the government interpret the outcome? On the one hand, the government has committed itself to a non-profit child care system, to the realization of the objectives set out in the public consultation document. On the other hand, the point of public meetings is to allow the people some say in how they are governed. If the argument that commercial operators should maintain a position in the child care system prevails, ignoring that message demonstrates a rather cynical commitment to participatory democracy. Arguing that disorganization led to a skewed result, however, creates the impression of incompetence.

At this writing, the outcome has yet to be determined. However, some indication of the direction in which the government is moving is provided in the *Summary Document of the Consultation on Child Care Reform*, released in the autumn of 1992. This document recounts the positions of groups ranging from parents to Francophones and First Nations People, with a large interspersal of "expert" opinion. Interestingly, the position of organized labour manages to capture three pages of text while the business community, for all its representations, only manages a single page and women's groups receive no text at all, again underscoring the limitations of this consultation. If the summary document provides any indication of the direction in which the government is moving, it would seem that it is maintaining its commitment to child care reform through a non-profit system. While I would certainly support this effort, I have very strong reservations about presenting this reformed child care policy as the product of an equitable, participatory and democratic process.[9]

I have argued that a truly participatory practice requires a thoroughgoing commitment to exposing the sexism and racism that supports the capitalist state. When openings for resistance occur, such as the child care consultations, it is incumbent upon us to reveal the internal contradictions of that process. Such a strategy will bring confrontation from powerful forces, attempts to erase the legitimacy of our claims and misrepresentation of our motives. It may also bring us closer to realizing a more participatory, more equitable and hence a very different form of state.

Notes

1. I would like to express my thanks to Isa Bakker and Linda Carty for their comments on previous drafts of this article. I am also indebted to Susan Prentice for her knowledge, inspiration and insight.

   In preparing this article, I had telephone interviews with John Argue of the Ministry of Community and Social Services (Toronto, April 22, 1992), Patricia Baynham of the Ministry's Child Care Policy Branch (Toronto, April 24, 1992), Martha Friendly of the Child Care Resource and Research Unit (Toronto, April 14, 1992), Sara Kramer of the Ministry's Child Care Policy Branch (Toronto, April 21, 1992) and Evelyn Napier of the Metro Coalition for Better Child Care (Toronto, April 21, 1992).

2. "The Parents' Newspaper." (Toronto: Ministry of Community and Social Services, March-June 1992,) p. 4.

3. *Background Paper #4 Parents Roles in Child Care* (Toronto: Ministry of Community and Social Services, February 1992).

4. *Ibid.*

5. Conversation with Sara Kramer of the Child Care Policy Branch on April 21, 1992.

6. My thanks to Susan Prentice for helping me to decode this seemingly paradoxical event.

7. Conversation with Evelyn Napier of the Metro Coalition for Better Child Care on April 21, 1992.

8. Ontario Ministry of Community and Social Services. "Setting the Stage, A Public Consultation Paper" (Toronto: Ministry of Community and Social Services, 19), p. 6.

9. This line of argument is not to be interpreted as latent sympathy with the commercial child care lobby. While ADCO and its supporters may share my displeasure with the consultation as carried out by Ontario's NDP government, we do so, as should be clear by now, for very different reasons.

PAY EQUITY FOR NON-UNIONIZED WOMEN

A Case Study

Jennifer Keck and Daina Green

In the winter of 1990 a group of fifty administrative, office and clerical workers from Sudbury launched one of the first group complaints under the Ontario *Pay Equity Act.* Their complaint challenged the pay equity plan posted by their employer, Inco, formerly the International Nickel Company Limited, a large multinational mining company. In laying the complaint the women took on the community's largest employer without the protection of a union. They also won a precedent-setting order from the Pay Equity Commission, requiring their employer to release confidential information related to compensation and job comparison practices. Within several months of launching their complaint, several of the women went on to active roles in a successful union organizing drive with the United Steelworkers of America (USWA). The organizing which led to the group complaint was an important factor in determining the success of the subsequent union organizing drive.

The process of organizing a pay equity complaint and a union drive was politicizing for the women involved. The women had a connection dating back more than two generations to the working class community of Sudbury. Most were over the age of thirty, white and Anglophone. They worked at jobs ranging from clerical and secretarial positions to accounting and administration. The women had long years of service with Inco, ranging from ten to twenty-three years. This was the first time any of the women had been part of a collective action to challenge their employer or their working conditions.

Both authors worked in supportive and organizing roles throughout the complaint and the union drive. Jennifer Keck was initially invited to work with the group as a member of the local Women's Centre who had organizing experience and some understanding of the *Pay Equity Act.* Later, the group hired Daina Green as a consultant, to help prepare and present their case to the provincial Pay Equity Commission.

As feminists and organizers, we were committed to stretching the limits of the legislation and building on its relative strengths. We wanted to demystify the technical aspects of pay equity and to ensure the women had the resources necessary to lead their own struggle. The courage and resolve of the women involved, supported by this analysis and approach, helped transform this struggle from a dispute under the *Pay Equity Act* to a political challenge of their employer's right to determine their wages and working conditions. While this is in many ways a "success" story, as a case study it also serves to illustrate the potential strengths and limitations of pay equity legislation as a strategy to deal with the problem of low pay for non-unionized women workers.

Pay Equity: Victory and Contradiction

Activists in the labour and women's movements have been struggling for equal pay for work of equal value since the early seventies. Interest in the concept developed out of frustrations with the minimal gains women workers could achieve under existing equal pay laws. These laws prohibited lower pay for women who performed work that was the *same* as (or substantially similar to) that of men. Since men and women tend to perform *different* jobs, feminists and trade unionists advocated legislation that would allow value comparisons of dissimilar male and female jobs. The alternative strategy of moving large groups of women workers to male fields of work to achieve higher incomes was neither practical nor desirable. Pay equity legislation became part of a broad strategy for women's economic equality, a strategy that involved training, better childcare, parental rights, reproductive rights and employment equity legislation.

The principle of equal pay for work of equal value addresses the fact that women's work is paid less because it is women's work. Comparisons of dissimilar jobs are based on a composite of four factors, including skill, effort, working conditions and the responsibility required. The problem with this concept is the assumption that men's wages are fair or that they are set in accordance with the four factors in pay equity laws. This ignores the power relations central to wage determination. Male unions have historically used their power to negotiate wages directly, without job evaluation. Unionization is still the best indicator of higher wages and a reduced wage gap between male and female workers.[1]

In 1987 the Ontario government introduced the *Pay Equity Act*, based on the principle of equal pay for work of equal value. The bill was a condition of NDP support for the Liberal-NDP Accord that had helped defeat the Tories two years earlier. The legislation marks an important precedent in the development of pay equity legislation. Ontario is the first jurisdiction to introduce pro-active legislation covering unionized and non-unionized workers in the private and public sectors. The legislation acknowledges the systemic nature of gender-based wage discrimination and allows for comparisons between dissimilar male and female jobs. A separate Pay Equity Commission and a Tribunal are responsible for monitoring and administering the legislation. The *Act* obliges employers with more than ten employees to develop pay equity plans based on a "gender-neutral" method of job comparison.

The strength of Ontario's legislation reflects the lobbying efforts of the Equal Pay Coalition, an alliance of women's groups and trade unions. However, for women workers in the province, the impact of the *Pay Equity Act* has been uneven and inconsistent. Concessions made to business regarding the implementation of the legislation seriously limit its impact. Large groups of women workers have been excluded. At least fifty percent of the women in workplaces covered by the *Act* cannot claim pay equity adjustments under it.[2] This includes women who work in predominantly female jobs (such as child care workers, health care and social service workers) who do not have a male comparator in their workplace.[3] The *Act* also excludes women who work in establishments with fewer than ten employees. The legal and technical aspects of the legislation restrict the scope of who is covered and the dollar amounts of wage increases applied to female jobs.

Overall, there is little evidence that the legislation will make more than a slight dent in the wage gap between male and female workers, especially among non-unionized workers.[4] Without the resources, protection or bargaining power of a union, most workers face terrible odds in taking advantage of the legislation. They are not likely to have access to the training needed to criticize complex job evaluation schemes.

Pay equity has resulted in a windfall for management consultants selling their job evaluation tools as "objective," "scientific" and "gender-neutral" for assessing and comparing jobs. The *Act* specifies that the pay equity plan developed by an employer must be "gender-neutral," but it does not specify what constitutes a "gender-neutral" plan. The technical aspects of most job evaluation schemes can conceal what is essentially a *political* decision about how "skill" and "value" are determined and how jobs are evaluated.[5]

Non-unionized workers are also unlikely to have access to information about their employer's wage compensation practices. Maintaining secrecy about earnings is usually an important rule in non-unionized establishments. (Wages of unionized workers are usually published in the collective agreement.) Under the Ontario legislation, unionized workers won the right to negotiate a pay equity settlement directly with their employers. Non-unionized employees can launch individual or group complaints with the Pay Equity Commission only after a pay equity plan has been prepared and posted by their employer.

The limited impact of the Ontario *Pay Equity Act* has renewed feminist debate about the relative merits of equal value legislation as a strategy to address the problem of women's low pay.[6] This debate is rooted in broader questions about the role of the state and the nature of social reform. Pay equity is on the policy agenda in Ontario and other jurisdictions as a result of pressure from trade unionists and feminists. Once taken up by the state, however, pay equity has been institutionalized in a manner that considerably distances it from the principle of equal value envisioned by feminist and trade union activists.[7]

Proponents argue that pay equity legislation represents an important challenge to the ideology of a "neutral" market by acknowledging the systemic nature of discrimination and its impact on women's wages. Others contend that the legislation represents an attempt by the state to co-opt the feminist agenda and further divide women on race, class and ethnic lines.[8]

It is not our intention to enter into this debate directly. We do contend, however, that pay equity legislation does not lead inevitably in one direction.[9] "Contradiction" refers to the fact that state action can and often does improve social conditions *at the same time as* it represses or limits the potential for transformation. We need to look at the relative strengths, weaknesses and contradictions in the *Pay Equity Act*, to assess its value as a political tool to empower particular groups of women workers and to push the limits of the legislation. We also need to examine the concrete ways women covered by the *Act* can get the most out of it in higher wages and a political awareness of the value and conditions of women's work.

Our experience working with the women in Sudbury illustrates some of the strengths, weaknesses and contradictions in the Ontario legislation. There were aspects of the legislation that provided opportunity and "space" to help organize the women and to politicize the pay equity process.

Pay Equity at Inco

Sudbury is a community with a population of approximately 90,000, located in northeastern Ontario. Historically a mining town, Sudbury has seen a significant expansion of its public and service sectors and an increase in the labour force participation of women since the mid-seventies. It is primarily a working-class community, with a strong tradition of union militancy and an active women's movement. Inco is Sudbury's largest employer and one of two multinational mining corporations located there. In 1990 the company employed approximately 9,000 workers. Seventy-two hundred were hourly-rated workers represented by the United Steelworkers of America (USWA) Local 6500, all but a few of whom are male. Another 1,600 were non-unionized administrative and clerical workers, also mainly male. At the time of the group complaint, 239 women worked in the administrative and clerical unit. Another twenty-eight women were employed in unionized production jobs.

In February of 1990 Inco posted a pay equity plan at its Sudbury operations, as required under the provincial *Pay Equity Act*, although two months late. All the comparisons between male- and female-dominated jobs were made within the non-unionized administrative and clerical unit. Jobs in the production unit were not affected by the legislation because these job classes were at least seventy percent male. Two months after the plan was posted, fifty of the 239 women affected by the plan launched one of the first group complaints under the legislation. In doing so, the women organized, hired their own pay equity consultant and took on the community's largest employer without the protection of a union. A few months later they joined a union organizing drive and within a year they became members of Local 6600 of the USWA. Organizing became a politicizing experience for all the women involved in the pay equity complaint and the union drive.

A number of factors helped set the stage for this struggle. First, the Sudbury Women's Centre had been part of a local coalition lobbying for equal value legislation since the early eighties. It was one of the few members of the provincial Equal Pay Coalition located outside of Toronto. The Centre's involvement with the Coalition meant that there were feminists in the community with some knowledge and a critical analysis of the legislation. Second, media coverage of the legislation was quite extensive by 1990. A number of the women affected by Inco's pay equity plan were aware that the company was obliged to post a plan and they expected salary increases for the female job classifications.

One woman in particular had followed announcements of the legislation with great anticipation. In January of 1990 she and a friend organized an educational workshop at the local Women's Centre, with representatives from the Pay Equity Commission, to discuss the impact of the pay equity law on the private sector. More than forty women attended that workshop, ten from Inco. By the time the company posted its plan, the Pay Equity Commission had already received a number of calls from women at Inco inquiring about the legislation and their employer's obligations.

Getting Organized

There was interest in launching a complaint against Inco's pay equity plan immediately upon the posting of the plan. Adjustments in the plan fell far short of the expectations of many of the women workers affected: most women received no increases, and other women's wages had been frozen, which is illegal under the *Act*. Annual salary increases and a new performance evaluation (merit) system were applied at the time the plan was posted, adding to the confusion about how to interpret the plan. Nonetheless, a large number of women felt cheated.

A week after the plan was posted, two women organized a well-attended open meeting at the Women's Centre, for women affected by the Inco plan. They invited Jennifer Keck to facilitate and explain the legislation. Keck teaches at the local university and had been active at the Women's Centre and in the provincial Equal Pay Coalition. At the meeting, many women objected that unskilled male jobs were used as comparator for skilled clerical positions. In one example, clerks were compared to a groundskeeper. Others had complaints about pay and working conditions that were unrelated to pay equity.

The strongest indignation was directed at the company's refusal to provide more information or answer questions about the plan. Instead, management denied any obligation to explain the plan or divulge information about compensation practices or the basis for the job comparisons.

It did not take long for members of Inco management to hear about the meeting at the Women's Centre. Within days they called a meeting to discuss the plan with employees. At the meeting, attended by over one hundred women, management explained that the pay equity plan was based on a job evaluation conducted in the plant during the previous year. It agreed to meet with the women individually to explain how their jobs had been assessed, compared and evaluated. It maintained, however, that the job evaluation system used was "too technical" for most of the women to understand.

The condescending attitude of management at this meeting only reinforced the resolve of the women to pursue the matter further. At their next meeting the women decided to seek legal advice. A lawyer they contacted advised that there were probable grounds for lodging a complaint under the *Act* and that they should consider launching a group complaint. At the same time, she cautioned that they would probably need to hire a consultant to help build their case and prepare a strategy for their complaint.

There was considerable risk involved in carrying out this plan. Many of the women had families to support and were only too aware of the risks involved in challenging a powerful employer. At the first meeting only a few women had been willing to give more than their first name or say where they worked. These fears eased as the women continued to meet and discovered that they shared common concerns; the pay equity plan had failed to raise their wages and management was dodging requests to discuss how the plan had been developed. The more the women learned about the legislation, the more convinced they were that they could build an effective case to challenge Inco's pay equity plan and win better adjustments.

Pay Equity as a Political Process

The decision to hire an outside consultant marked an important turning point for the group. There was consensus that the women needed a better understanding of pay equity and job evaluation to draw up their complaint. Some members of the group favoured getting free advice from the Pay Equity Commission and believed the Commission would advocate for them. Others thought that the group should turn to a local management consulting firm with expertise in job evaluation to help them prepare their complaint. Still others, influenced by Keck and the advice of the Equal Pay Coalition, thought the group needed more than technical advice. They needed to hire someone with a critical understanding of the legislation who would be able to help them organize and develop a political strategy for their complaint.

As a compromise, the group agreed to sponsor a day-long workshop with Daina Green and Jennifer Keck. Green had been recommended to the group by members of the Equal Pay Coalition in Toronto. She had experience as a labour organizer and pay equity advocate. To cover her fee and transportation, the women agreed to charge a fee of twenty dollars for each woman attending the workshop.

The workshop provided an overview of the legislation and then focused on helping the women strategize around how they would launch the complaint. As workshop leaders, both authors, were committed to ensuring that the women had a critical understanding of pay equity and the legislation as well as the political nature of job comparison and job evaluation.

A significant part of the day was dedicated to identifying the problems with the employer's pay equity plan and the limitations of conventional job evaluation methodology. Green pointed out that Inco's plan was based on a job evaluation scheme developed and implemented by Hay Management Consultants, a giant management firm, the year before the *Pay Equity Act* came into effect. It had been represented as a straightforward job evaluation effort. The employees in the administrative and clerical unit had been asked to rewrite their job descriptions. The workers had not been told that this was related to pay equity. Green discussed the fact that workers had not been given any direction about ways to counteract the tendency to under-represent the hidden aspects of women's work. Quite the opposite, the women were told to be as brief as possible in describing their work on the forms, which the women had the opportunity to review in the workshop. Green further criticized the fact that the job descriptions had to be approved by immediate supervisors.

Based on documents the women shared with her, Green explained how the company had used a market survey provided by Hay to help Inco adjust wages to those paid for comparable jobs in the regional labour market. The comparisons did not reflect "post-pay equity" salaries; instead, they reinforced the status quo. The women began to see contradictions: pay equity was supposed to *challenge* the use of the market as the sole determinant of women's wages.[10]

The women spent most of the day in a hands-on review of the job descriptions. Working in groups, they started to write composite descriptions for their jobs. This activity helped illustrate how gender-bias affects the assessment of skill, effort, responsibility and working conditions. Alternative job descriptors would more closely reflect what the women actually did and the skill required to perform their work. Clerical workers, for example, were encouraged to look at overlooked aspects of their work: multiple simultaneous tasks and deadlines, composing and correcting correspondence, the interpersonal skills needed to gather information and communicate it throughout the establishment, the use of complex computer programs and the in-depth knowledge they needed of both mining and refining processes and of the workings of the company. Many of these aspects of their jobs were omitted in the job description forms and were therefore not reported on the job evaluation questionnaires.

By the end of the day, the problems with the employer's plan and the factors that would form the basis of their complaint were beginning to become clear. Looking at the way factors related to skill, effort, working conditions and responsibility had been assessed showed the women how the evaluation shaped the plan. This was an important part of building their case.

The women also began to see the legislation's strengths and weaknesses. Our critique of the legislation included a discussion of the role of unions and collective bargaining in determining wages. This made some of the women uneasy. Others were interested in the relationship between pay equity and collective bargaining. The workshop also provided an opportunity for the women to discuss a range of shared concerns related to the workplace and to develop a sense of group trust and solidarity.

When the session ended, women agreed to form a group to launch group complaint to the Pay Equity Commission. There was a careful discussion of the risks involved, but only two women declined to sign the complaint for fear of management reprisal. The women agreed on a loose structure with two chairpersons and a treasurer. They also agreed to hire Green to help prepare their case. They set up a system to collect dues of forty dollars a month to help finance her expenses.

The Group Complaint

In 1990 the *Pay Equity Act* was still relatively new. There were virtually no precedents on pay equity in non-unionized settings or in the private sector. Although the legislation contained provisions for group complaints, there were no guidelines advising how to launch one. In contrast to almost every other aspect of the legislation, the Pay Equity Commission had no educational materials prepared on the subject for workers or employers.

With the consultant's assistance, the women agreed that their joint complaint would address the job information and how it was gathered, the gender-neutrality of the job comparison system, the inappropriateness of certain male comparators and the effect of a performance review system that had been set in place at the same time. Members of the group would file individual complaints to address more specific concerns.

The group complaint was filed with the Commission in April 1990. In her first meeting with the group in June, the Review Officer assigned to the case explained that her role was not that of an advocate for the women. Her role was to help the parties arrive at a resolution of their dispute and to enforce the law "neutrally." If the issue could not be resolved by the parties, she would write an order. This would involve certain constraints because as non-unionized workers the women did not have the right to negotiate pay equity. The Review Officer also expressed her concerns about who would be authorized to respond to a proposal for settlement of the group complaint.

At its next regular meeting, the group named seven women who would act as signatories for the group to obtain required information from the employer, including confidential data which would not be shared in a detailed way with the entire group, and formed a committee to recommend a settlement for the entire group. This committee would remain accountable to the group of signatories to the complaint.

The lodging of the group complaint and the more formalized committee structure were signs of increased commitment and reflected a higher level of risk-taking for the group. By now management was clearly aware that the group was continuing to meet. Rumours abounded. After much debate, the women decided to take the situation head on and requested a face-to-face meeting between their representatives, the employer and the Review Officer, to discuss their complaint and to pressure a settlement. This represented exposure for the women, for whom time off to attend the meeting was requested by the Review Officer. However, the company refused to meet directly with the women or to acknowledge the committee's authority to negotiate a settlement on behalf of the others.

Progress on the complaint was very slow. The Review Officer often mentioned settlement to the group, although she did not lead the women to believe that a settlement would provide a significant salary increase. She relied on the consultant for the women to provide an analysis of the facts from the women's point of view and to propose a basis for a settlement.

From the outset, the negotiating committee maintained that it could not proceed without basic information about the employer's plan, its method of comparison and its compensation practices. The employer resisted, arguing it was not obliged to release this information to non-unionized workers. When Inco ignored the Review Officer's request to disclose information, the women were surprised and disappointed to see the roundabout response of the Review Officer. Her response was to exhaust other ways of obtaining information before resorting to an order.

It later emerged that the request for disclosure of such information to workers without a union had never been the subject of an order. In fact, the interpretation of that section of the *Pay Equity Act* was in dispute within the Commission. Apparently, the Review Officer met resistance at the Commission before finally getting a go-ahead in October 1990 to issue a precedent-setting order obliging Inco to release compensation information to the group.

As part of the order, the Review Officer also required the company to provide the long-awaited opportunity for the women to challenge management directly on its job evaluation system. At the meeting, the women floored management representatives by asking penetrating questions of the consultant brought in from Hay to explain the system to the women. The women were prepared, on the basis of several study sessions, to enter into debate with the consultant over the gender-neutrality of the company's job evaluation package. The women left the meeting confident that they had shown their employer that they were a force to be reckoned with and that real changes would have to be made to the plan in order to settle the complaint.

There were several more meetings with the Review Officer and the women's representatives, who, in turn, maintained contact with the whole group. The main tasks were to develop alternative job descriptions for each of the most common jobs done by the women as a basis for re-evaluation and to keep up their fighting spirit. The group continued to focus on presenting a proposal to the Review Officer which could form the basis for a written order. This project was put on hold at the point when it seemed likely that the campaign to certify a bargaining unit would provide a more powerful tool for developing a suitable pay equity plan for most of the women. The women involved in the complaint who were excluded from the new bargaining unit because of their confidential or managerial duties later settled their cases individually and privately through the Review Officer.

Organizing a Union

By mid-October of 1990 there were signs that the group was becoming increasingly disillusioned with the legislation and the complaint process. The women had been meeting on a weekly then monthly basis for approximately seven months. The complaint process had yet to yield any significant results and the outcome appeared uncertain. Management remained intransigent on every point. Many of the women were puzzled at this response. They had worked hard to understand the legislation and build their case. From the beginning they had been willing to sit down and discuss their concerns with management. Unfortunately, management was not obliged to sit down with them.

The women were aware that they would have had considerably more power to influence Inco's pay equity plan if they had been represented by a union. The authors had emphasized the separate-and-not-equal implementation processes for unionized and non-unionized workers. We shared our view that the group's best chance for success in pay equity, job security and other grievances with the company lay in joining a union. As management continued to stonewall on the group's demands, the women's disadvantage in terms of labour rights became increasingly apparent.

While the complaint process had started to weigh them down, as a group the women had developed confidence in their ability to launch a collective action and stand up for what they considered to be important. Building their complaint had provided them with information about Inco's compensation practices and the arbitrariness of the system. It was not until the pay equity complaint started to bog down, however, that the women began to seriously discuss joining a union organizing drive. Some of the women were concerned that pay equity would become less of a priority if they joined forces with the men in the unit around a union organizing drive. Others were convinced that by playing an active role in the organizing drive itself the women could ensure that their concerns about pay and working conditions would be dealt with by the union.

The potential for organizing was not lost on staff members of the

Steelworkers. An attempt to organize the administrative and clerical workers at Inco in the early seventies had been unsuccessful. The presence now of a group of workers with considerable energy and a demonstrated willingness to organize and challenge the company was a hopeful sign to the union.

The consultant was in a position to act as a bridge between the Steelworkers union and the women. Prior to meeting the Sudbury women, Green had already contracted with USWA District 6 to develop a leadership training course for union women. As the pay equity case dragged on, it was clear that the women would not be able to pay for Green's services without outside support. She approached the union to see if the leadership would be willing to provide assistance to the women with pay equity, either through its own staff or through her. The union agreed to pay her fees, with no strings attached.

Green then told the women of the union's offer, emphasizing that it was not conditional on them becoming involved in a union drive. The women agreed to the funding arrangement. They also expressed interest in an information meeting with a Steelworker representative. The meeting was well-attended. Later, the women's representatives for the pay equity complaint were invited to a two-day seminar held by the union to discuss the possible drive, a seminar that other members of office and technical staff unit also attended.

A full-scale union drive began soon after. Women from the pay equity struggle played key roles on the inside committee. The unit was certified on April 24, 1991, as Local 6600 of USWA. The first union elections saw one of the co-chairs of the pay equity group voted into the executive position of guard and as a member of the negotiating committee. Another female activist was acclaimed as treasurer. A third woman, not directly involved with the pay equity process, was acclaimed as recording secretary. With women holding three key positions (out of eleven on the local's executive), the place of women is already well-established.

Most of the women who were involved in the group complaint are now members of a bargaining unit. The unit has recently served notice to bargain a pay equity plan with Inco and the Review Officer will meet with the group again, now under the rules that apply to certified bargaining units. This time they will have the right to sit down with the employer to resolve the dispute.

Lessons

The experience of the office workers at Inco raises a number of issues about the strengths and weaknesses of pay equity legislation and the factors that can affect the outcome of organizing efforts. The clearest lesson is that a non-unionized worker needs extraordinary resources to gain access to the *Pay Equity Act.* The technical and legal aspects of the legislation can be intimidating, employers will try to use complex job evaluation schemes to minimize payments and maintain the status quo and there is only limited protection against harassment for workers who lodge a complaint with the Commission.

For the Sudbury women, access to resources sprang from the community context of a city with a strong trade union culture and an active women's network, including the Sudbury Women's Centre. Making contact with the Centre gave the women access to a place to hold their first meetings. It also helped them to find someone local with knowledge of pay equity and organizing experience, free legal advice, access to an advocate and consultant and eventually financial and moral backing from a strong union committed to pay equity. These resources would not be available in most communities in the province, nor would most small groups be likely to seek them out and pursue them.

A second set of resources came from the women themselves. One group member in particular proved to be a special asset to the group. She was off work due to disability and spent long hours researching pay equity and finding community contacts to help get the project off the ground. Without her commitment and tenacious energy, much of the organizing involved with the complaint might not have taken place. The leaders who emerged in this struggle were quickly able to grasp the nature of the law and soon came to understand some of its limitations. They are mature women with long years of experience with the company. Their jobs as clerical workers gave them access to workers throughout the company's Sudbury operations. Collectively, they also knew a great deal about the functioning of the employer from their work in jobs ranging from Payroll to Personnel.

At the same time, aspects of the *Pay Equity Act* provided the opportunity or space for the women to organize. The Commission's publicity about the bill, for example, helped raise expectations that "something" would happen to address the problem of women's low pay. When the company's plan proved to have little impact on their salaries, the women understood that they had been cheated. The group complaint involved potential risks, but it also provided the women with the opportunity to meet on a regular basis, discuss common concerns and develop a sense of solidarity. The Review Officer's order regarding disclosure of compensation information meant that the women had access to critical information that was previously withheld by the company.

Ironically, it was disillusionment with the complaint process and the recalcitrance of management that helped persuade the women to organize the union drive. The separate-but-not-equal provisions of the legislation dealing with unionized and non-unionized workers provided important insights on the role of unions and the benefits of collective bargaining rights. This political learning was an important step towards "radicalizing" the women to take steps on their own behalf. Organizing a collective action meant challenging a very powerful employer. For many of the women, this action also meant raising conflict in their own homes, since many of their partners also work at Inco, some in management roles and some of whom were satisfied with the employer's actions and uneasy about "rocking the boat."

While the legislation provided the opportunity, this struggle was shaped by an analysis and an approach to organizing that ensured that the women retained "ownership" of their fight. As organizers, we wanted to put resources in their hands directly and collectively, making sure that they were the ones involved in drawing up composite job descriptions and in the search for useful information within the company. This helped to demystify the complex and confusing pay equity law as well as to highlight the many contradictions. The women were the experts about their jobs and their complaint. They learned to fight the tendency to become divided over the inequities in salary and treatment by focusing on the joint goals of the struggle. When the law gave us lemons, we made lemonade.

The work of the women in the subsequent union drive helped to ensure their continued role within the bargaining unit. Even before the unit was certified, a number of the women announced their intention to seek office on the new executive. They were determined not to be left out of positions of power in the bargaining unit, despite their small numbers. By immediately running for election, activist women now hold approximately one-third of the positions of the Local 6600 executive, though only one-quarter of the members are female.

A negotiated pay equity plan, combined with collective bargaining on wages, holds the best chance of yielding significant pay equity adjustment for this group. It is almost a certainty that, campaign without a union would not produce such positive results. Even if the Review Officer had issued an order imposing a more favourable system, one requiring direct comparisons between male and female jobs, this employer, like any other would be free to appeal the order to the Pay Equity Tribunal. A number of employers faced with a large potential liability on pay equity adjustments have upped the ante on dissatisfied workers, by appealing the Review Officer's Order to the Tribunal, a lengthy, costly and highly "worker-unfriendly" process.

Epilogue

As this article goes to press, plans for a negotiated pay equity settlement at Inco have been upstaged by the company's plans to restructure and downsize its Sudbury operations. In December 1992 Inco announced that eighty-six office workers were being given the choice between layoff or going underground to work as miners at their Sudbury operations. This decision is part of the company's overall strategy to reduce the number of workers in the office and technical unit. Fifty-eight of the affected workers are members of the recently organized Local 6600 of the Steelworkers and thirty-nine of them are women. Many of these workers were active in the pay equity complaint and the union organizing drive.

It would be difficult not to make the connection between the pay equity complaint, the union organizing drive and these latest announcements. The announcement of the transfer offers came the day after the company posted a settlement of the pay equity complaint for the period leading up to certification. The notice was given on the last day of work prior to a three-week shutdown that would cover the Christmas period. There was no prior consultation with the workers or the union. The message was clear: accept the offer to work underground or lose your job. The impact was devastating for many of the workers (men and women) involved and their families. The affected members of Local 6600 have up to seventeen years experience with the company.

The reaction of the union was swift. Within days the story of the women at Local 6600 had achieved national prominence in the news media. In January 1993 the company responded to this pressure by agreeing to meet with the workers and the union to discuss plans for the restructuring and the transfer notices. A management-union committee was established to review the transfer process. Affected workers received counselling support and training. The union has successfully bargained a reduction in the number of affected workers and a significant improvement in the transfer criteria. The number of affected workers has been reduced to about thirty-eight in total. Fewer than five women have been transferred to underground jobs and another ten to fifteen work in other parts of plant operations.[11]

The women involved in the pay equity complaint at Inco have learned a great deal over the last three years about corporate strategies to minimize the value of their work and hold down wages. They have a keen sense of who has power and who does not. Now some of them are facing a fundamental occupational shift. Without the protection of a union, many of these workers, women and men, could be facing no job at all. The so-called choice between transferring to production jobs or being laid-off is no choice at all. They will be going to production jobs. They have families to support, rent to pay and college tuition to provide for their daughters and sons. These women are not quitters. As production workers, they will be moving to Local 6500 of the USWA. And they will still be willing to fight.

Notes

We would like to acknowledge the helpful comments of Pat Armstrong, Mary Powell, Marge Reitsma-Street and Laurell Ritchie in the development of this article. This article would also not have been possible without the dedication and insight of Sidnie Lawton, Judy Gilbert and the other members of the pay equity group at Inco.

1. J. White. *Mail and Female* (Toronto: Thompson Press, 1990) and *Sisters and Solidarity: Women and Unions in Canada* (Toronto: Thompson Educational Press, 1993); P. Phillips and E. Phillips. *Women and Work: Inequality in the Labour Market* (Toronto: James Lorimer and Co., 1983); I. Bakker in "Women's Employment in Comparative Perspective" in J. Jenson, *et. al.,* eds. *Feminization of the Labor Force* (Toronto: Oxford University Press, 1988).

2. S. Findlay in "Making Sense of Pay Equity: Issues for a Feminist Political Practice" in J. Fudge and P. McDermott, eds. *Just Wages: A Feminist Assessment of Pay Equity* (Toronto: University of Toronto Press, 1991).

3. In July 1993 the NDP government in Ontario passed legislation to amend the *Pay Equity Act* to allow workers whose jobs found no direct comparators to compare proportionately to higher paying male jobs. The law also allows all-female public sector workplaces to find pay equity comparators in other establishments.

4. P. McDermott in "Pay Equity in Canada: Assessing the Commitment to Reducing the Wage Gap" in Fudge and McDermott, *op. cit.*

5. J. Acker in "Sex Bias in Job Evaluation: A Comparable Worth Issue" in C.Bose and G. Spitze, eds. *Ingredients for Women's Employment Policy* (Albany: State University of New York, 1987); P. Armstrong and H. Armstrong in "Lessons from Pay Equity" in *Studies in Political Economy,* No. 32, Summer 1990; M. Cassin in "Women, Work, Jobs and Value: The Routine Production of InequalityA Report with Special Reference to Consumer's Gas." Unpublished Paper, Dalhousie University, 1990.

6. D. Lewis *et. al. Just Give Us the Money: A Discussion of Wage Discrimination in Canada* (Toronto: McGraw-Hill Ryerson Limited, Toronto, 1988); D. Lewis with J. Barnsley. Strategies for Change (Vancouver: Women's Research Centre, 1990); P. Armstrong and H. Armstrong H. in "Limited Possibilities and Possible Limits for Pay Equity: Within and Beyond the

Ontario Legislation" in Fudge and McDermott, *op. cit.*; C. Cuneo. *Pay Equity: The Labour-Feminist Challenge* (Toronto: Oxford University Press, 1990) and in "Class Through Political Parties in Ontario" in Fudge and McDermott, *op. cit.*; R. Warskett in "Wage Solidarity and Equal Value" in *Studies in Political Economy, op. cit.*

7. L. Briskin in "Feminist Practice: A New Approach to Evaluating Feminist Strategy" in *Women and Social Change: Feminist Activism in Canada* (Toronto: James Lorimer and Company, 1991).

8. Lewis. *Op. cit.*; Cuneo. *Op. cit.*

9. Armstrong and Armstrong in Fudge and McDermott, *op. cit.*

10. P. Mc Dermott. *Op. cit.*

11. Interview with executive member of Local 6600 USWA, August 25, 1993.

"THE BEAUTIFUL STRENGTH OF MY ANGER PUT TO USE"*

Women Against Poverty in Canada

Naomi Binder Wall

Poverty, Politics and Power

In April, 1991, a charity event called the Taste of Nations raised $70,000 to buy a refrigerated truck to take leftovers from the tables of the rich and deliver them to the poor. How many events like this would it take just to replace the amount taken from poor people with incomes under $15,000 a year by government UI cuts? If they were all on the same huge scale as the Taste of Nations event in Vancouver, it would be about 8,349 — or 24 fund-raisers every day for a year. Charity cannot hope to fill the need created by government's poverty-creation policies.

> *"The Waste of a Nation: Poor Speak Out About Charity,"*
> *End Legislated Poverty, Vancouver, B.C., August, 1992*

Sometimes when women organizing against poverty in Canada get together to form ad hoc committees around one or another poverty-related issue they toy with the idea of calling themselves, "Women Against Wealth." I had a friend who took her own placard to demonstrations. It didn't matter what the demo was for or against, she'd bring the same placard. "Eat the Rich," it proclaimed. "Get rid of the rich exploiters and we get rid of all the world's ills," she'd say.

Anti-poverty activists know full-well that it is essential to understand the dynamics of capital and its accumulation if we are to achieve even minimal reforms. Across the country, women organizing against

---

* From Tema Nason. *Ethel* (Glasgow: William Collins, 1990).

279

poverty are combining their knowledge of local, national and international restructuring with their experience of the links between this economic agenda and the political and social realities confronting poor people in Canada. This information is being parleyed into dynamic, effective action in base communities throughout the country. Poor women — Native, Black, immigrant, women with disabilities, white-skinned, lesbian — while continuing to organize within their own communities have begun a tentative networking. Non-poor community workers and activists, with some history of working within the anti-poverty movement, are increasingly having to give up control of organizing and agenda setting. Poor women are preparing to drive the anti-poverty movement in Canada.

My link to anti-poverty organizing dates from the early 1980s. I am a white-skinned, middle-class Jewish lesbian. In the late 1960s, I left my marriage and became a single mother. Prior to the divorce, I enjoyed the relative material security and privilege in which I had been raised. My family, though not wealthy, had been successfully upwardly mobile. I was college-educated, with an accumulation of skills well-suited to women's work. I had gone without question into marriage from my childhood home. My dependency on white male privilege and power was complete. Then, after the divorce, I was catapulted into a spiraling downward mobility offset by my being a white woman from a middle-class background, holding inherent relative power vis-à-vis other groups of women.

All women are vulnerable to economic violence and the myriad manifestations of misogyny in this society. Once we grasp this, the link between gender and class is more easily understood.

As a lesbian, I experience the systemic interplay of misogyny and lesbophobia. I experience anti-semitism because I'm Jewish. And as a Jewish woman I confront the perpetration of race and class oppression being waged in my name by the state of Israel. At the same time, as a white woman, I hold relative power in relation to communities of Colour, including Jews of Colour. And because I am middle-class, I hold a position of relative power vis-à-vis my white sisters who are forced to live in poverty.

Noting these realities of my own life aids my understanding of the interplay between gender, class, race and sexual identity. Any of us will be able to see that interplay when we have identified where we are located in this society and what our relative position is vis-à-vis control over our lives, based in our background and cumulative experience.

White-skinned middle-class women have to acknowledge the relationship between the relative power we hold and the oppression of women who are poor. Being white gives us an ethnicity of our own, a *colour* of our own. Being middle-class gives us relative protection from poverty. These identifications have shaped our perceptions, our attitudes, and have defined our position in relation to the way power is distributed in this society. Feminists have to attack race and class oppression at the same time as we struggle against misogyny. These are not parallel. They are intersecting and inextricable.

Some Impacts of Race and Class Bias

Legislative changes are blurring the lines between UIC — considered a more respectable form of social assistance as it is based in earnings — and welfare. Many more people will go into welfare-type programs as they are displaced out of unskilled, low-paid work...and women will feel it the worst. Thousands more children will be raised in poverty. Particularly among white feminists who are in positions of relative power, the educated, have not been addressing issues of poverty, putting these issues front and centre.

Sandra Capponi,
Quebec Anti-poverty Activist

That federal and provincial government policies entrench a system that forces thousands of people into unemployment and hunger, uses racism to maintain institutions rooted in colonialism and wages war on women is of no consequence to the powers-that-be. At the same time, telling-it-like-it-is doesn't get anti-poverty activists anywhere with the liberal politicians, social service agencies and professionals we depend on to lobby governments for changes in their poverty-creation policies. But in the harsh light of the brutal impact of these policies, women organizing against poverty in Canada *do* expect active support and solidarity from people who identify themselves as staunch critics of governments and their corporate partners.

Unfortunately, women who are poor and anti-poverty activists continue to struggle in isolation from other progressive organizations. While struggles against racism, misogyny and homophobia have achieved a dynamic status within some diverse communities of activist women, anti-poverty activists often face opposition from feminists when they try to place their issues front and centre. The majority of Native women, women with disabilities and women of Colour are living on insufficient incomes, their place in the spectrum of poverty determined by gender, race and class. And women of Colour, white women, lesbians, Native women, women with disabilities, older women and young women are all found in low-income communities. Yet only Native women, women with disabilities, and anti-poverty activists *ground* their fight for social justice in the specific and brutal realities that poverty engenders. I do not mean that middle-class feminists do not *raise* poverty-related issues. I mean that the specific realities endured by women who are poor do not constitute a *focus* of their attention.

It is also true that progressive "think-tank" groups of political economists and social analysts — mostly white, middle-class males — even with the best of intentions, obscure the functions of capital, its accumulation and expansion in unclear, pedantic language. This academic language distorts realities, perpetuates untruths about people living in poverty and denies crucial information to the people who need it most. It maintains the power imbalances rooted in class, race and gender. Women who are poor are becoming increasingly adept at interpreting this information and putting it forward in clear and effective language. But the information gap works both ways. The hard facts anti-poverty activists need to understand the forces driving the corporate agenda may be obscured by inaccessible language. But is equally true that activists working outside the anti-poverty movement are not getting the information they need about the particular impact of the corporate agenda on people who are poor. Without knowing the specific ways that the corporate agenda and global restructuring affect people living in poverty in Canada, activists outside the anti-poverty movement can not fully comprehend how these policies work against all of us.

Many inner-city teachers...routinely deal with the welfare poor...the problem is not really poverty but more a lack of social skills, expectations and models for healthy childrearing.

Globe & Mail,
September 1992

Professional and community workers apply for government grants to make new and improved poor people...and if you are chosen, you get to take a course to improve your self-image and take lessons in how to be a new and acceptable poor person.

From a speech by Pat Chauncey,
taken from Flawline, *the newsletter of*
End Legislated Poverty, Vancouver, B.C.

The stereotypes we may hold about poor women are rooted in the dominant white, middle-class culture, language and institutions. Among the most prevalent of these notions are the "standards" regulating what good parenting is. According to the prevailing mythology, poor women live off the system, lack self-esteem and need instruction in all aspects of their lives.

There are countless courses funded by different levels of government offered across the country to women who are poor to help them improve their self-esteem. They are told they need to learn to parent better, to make themselves more acceptable to potential employers, to learn to cook and clean their apartments properly and to improve their self-images. It is the woman who is attacked — not the inadequate, dangerous housing she is forced to live in or the inadequacy of her income.

The brutal reality is brought home in Kings County, Nova Scotia, where single mothers on welfare get less than five hundred dollars a month for themselves and two children. Recently, in rural Nova Scotia a single mother became anorexic because she stopped eating so her children would have more food. Her doctor was alarmed by the deterioration in her health and wrote a letter to the welfare office, asking that she be given a supplementary payment for a special diet to build up her strength. It took three months before she received any extra money. In the meantime, she continued to give her portions of food to her children and ended up in the hospital.

> The bottom line is death. Poor women are killed more often and poor women's children are more likely to die due to poverty-related health problems.

> *Pam Fleming, "Gender Bias & the Law,"*
> Canadian Woman Studies/les cahiers de la femme,
> *Summer 1992*

Our beliefs about who is violent and where violence occurs are part of the racist and anti-working class attitudes we hold which help perpetuate those oppressions. One bias held by some community and social agencies is that violence is a way of life among some immigrant groups, that it is condoned in some developing countries and that immigrant women and their men have to learn that here in Canada we don't tolerate that sort of thing. It is a feeling among some white community and social workers, for example, that one of the reasons it's so hard to get immigrant women from developing countries to report abuse is because in their countries it's allowed. This is patently false. It's not that it is allowed, but that the way of confronting it and stopping it may be more rooted in community sanctions than in state law. The fact that here in Canada we have some laws that are supposed to protect women from violence and sexual assault has not stopped or prevented the abuse. On the contrary, violence and sexual abuse against women is systemic in this society, and for women of Colour and Native women, the entire policing apparatus designed to deal with it is rife with racism and danger.

The particular circumstances of being poor are rarely cited as reasons for violence in poor communities. Instead, middle-class mythology maintains that the violence is part and parcel of the "makeup" of people who are poor and is therefore to be expected. In addition, the manifestation of violence in low-income communities is highly visible. The media is filled with it. The ministries of corrections and of social services document the incidence of violence in low-income communities and publicize it through their networks and grapevines. The information ends up in the school records of children from poor families and in their medical records. When a woman who is identified as living on social assistance brings her child to a hospital emergency service, it is often assumed the child is being abused.

There is considerable violence against and sexual abuse of women among the middle and upper classes. But the circumstances surrounding this are not the same as they are for women who are poor. That violence against women cuts across class lines does not mean we can ignore the brutal realities of economic violence as a cause of other forms of violence in poor communities.

Making the links between poverty and violence is highly political. By looking at violence in low-income communities politically, rather than individualizing the problem, women who are poor act in their own interest. They do the educating and "empower" themselves, the current catch-phrase among community workers. They focus on the hazardous environment that poverty produces. They keep front and centre the fact that poverty is a factor in a parent's behaviour. A welfare mother with children cannot easily pay for a babysitter every time she has to leave the house. If she leaves her children alone, she's gambling with their safety. If she stays with them, it may mean being unable to provide food or other immediate necessities. She may not have all the carfare she needs to take them all out. Mothers subsisting on insufficient incomes are caught up in difficult and potentially dangerous situations that have nothing to do with their adequacy as parents and everything to do with the brutal material circumstances of their lives. Poverty is dangerous for children. It is itself violence against women and children. It is in itself abuse.

Members of the white middle class are beyond suspicion and scrutiny in this society, their private lives protected from the prying eyes of the schools, the courts, the teaching, legal and medical professions, from public administrators and the media. A woman who is Black, whatever her class, is never beyond suspicion and scrutiny. A poor woman isn't either, whatever her colour. Like racism and misogyny, class oppression is in the marrow of this society.

Below the Poverty Line

> They're trashing the country from sea-to-sea...What we're seeing is a concentrated attack on all of the institutions of caring in Canada.
>
> *Jean Swansen,*
> *End Legislated Poverty*

Since 1984 the Tories have implemented poverty-creation policies, deliberately designed to wipe out our social safety net and to put us on par with the United States. These include deficit reduction, privatization, deregulation, trade liberalization, deindustrialization and cutbacks in social services.

More specifically, they placed a cap on the Canada Assistance Plan, making it impossible for provincial governments to bring welfare rates even up to the poverty line, slashed the UI program, causing increased poverty for hundreds of thousands of people and their families who are already poor, signed the Free Trade Deal, which has helped destroy over half a million jobs and pushed wages down, used the GST to shift $4 billion in taxes from corporations to individuals and eliminated the universality of the family allowance.[1]

In addition, corporations have been allowed to defer $40 billion in taxes — taxes that will never be collected. In 1987 a third of the major corporations, earning a total of $25 billion in profit, paid no tax at all. By 1988 taxes from individuals accounted for 55.5 percent of federal revenues, while direct corporate taxation amounted to only 10.5 percent. The banks made profits over $7.64 billion between 1980 and 1987 and paid less than 2.5 percent in federal income tax. To top it off, out of twenty-four industrialized countries Canada has the lowest rate of taxation on wealth. This helps to enshrine the stark contrast between the rich and the poor. The wealthiest ten percent of Canadians hold 51.3 percent of the wealth, while the poorest twenty percent have minus .3 percent.

From Coast to Coast

Many women imprisoned in Canada today are there for having committed offenses which can best be described as crimes of poverty.

Everywoman's Almanac 1991
Women's Press, Toronto

Recent statistics and studies distributed by anti-poverty activists expose
the depth of the current poverty crisis in Canada. More than seventy
percent of Native households live below the poverty line. Nearly forty
percent of all Native households are single-parent families headed by
women. Unemployment estimates for Native women and men range
from fifty percent to ninety percent across Canada.

Eighteen percent of all women are disabled. Seventy-four percent of
women with disabilities are unemployed and sixty-five percent live
below the poverty line. Women with disabilities face a greater risk of
sexual or violent assault.

There were nearly three million people on either municipal or provincial welfare in Canada by the winter of 1993. Across the country,
welfare recipients face a maze of local and provincial assistance schemes,
varying from province to province and even from municipality to municipality within the same province. Nova Scotia has a two-tiered system
for determining its assistance rates. In Halifax a single mother can get as
little as $486 a month for herself and two children. In Cape Breton, where
unemployment is over twenty-seven percent, single mothers can expect
the lowest welfare rates in Canada — as little as $120 a month.

Over one-third of the people in Quebec are living on fixed incomes.
Unemployment in Montreal is reported to be at twenty-five percent. In
1990 the Quebec legislature passed Bill 37, a punitive provincial welfare
law that created 144 different pay scales for welfare recipients. The law
forces people on assistance into minimum wage jobs disguised as training programs where employers receive government funding and are
exempt from legal employment standards; it penalizes recipients who
share housing and gives sweeping powers to welfare investigators. The
so-called training programs in Quebec, which finance employers to hire

welfare recipients at minimum wage, are on the cutting edge of forced employment programs.

In 1991 the poverty line in Ontario was estimated at $30,000 for a family of four. Women earning the minimum wage, even in Ontario where the bottom line is higher than elsewhere in Canada, live on yearly incomes at least $3,000 below the poverty line. If they are on municipal or provincial government assistance their incomes can be as low as twenty-five to forty percent below the poverty line. More than thirteen percent of people in Metro Toronto are on municipal or provincial government assistance. At last count, thirty percent of food bank users in Metro were working at low-wage and minimum wage jobs. In 1991 Metro Toronto Council cut $20 million from its welfare budget, including non-emergency dental services, beds, bedding and last month's rent.

More than twenty-six percent of welfare recipients in Canada are people with disabilities. In Saskatchewan a pensioner with a disability might get a monthly shelter allowance of $110, a basic allowance of $225, $35 for utilities, and $20 for transportation. All this in a province that hadn't seen a rise in welfare rates in more than nine years! The NDP took power in 1991; after ten months in office they raised the child payments by five dollars a month per child. A family of five lives on a welfare check that is fifty percent below the poverty line. Any money earned is docked dollar for dollar.

In Alberta, four percent of the population is Native; thirty percent of the people in prison are Native. Nationally, twenty percent of children in the care of children's aid agencies are Native, yet only two percent of the whole population of children are Native. Less than fifty percent of Native houses have sewer and water connections. Almost forty percent of the homes on reserves have no central heating.

In downtown eastside Vancouver the average household income in 1986 was $8,594. In greater Vancouver it was $30,009. The average incidence of tuberculosis was two-and-a-half times greater in the downtown eastside than the rest of Vancouver and seven times higher than the British Columbia rate. Children from the downtown eastside were placed in foster or agency care twice as often as children living in greater Vancouver. Referrals for mental health were almost six times higher than the rest of Vancouver. Women who were twenty to forty-five years old had a risk of death that was ten to twenty times higher in the downtown eastside than women in greater Vancouver.

Maddening Contradictions

> The lower on the economic scale you are, the less choice you have. I was forced to put my daughters into foster care at a crucial time in their lives. The foster parent was given more by the state to care for my kids than I got on welfare. If I had received the same money, I could definitely have cared for them. But my emotional state was involved as well. Poverty…grinds you down. People become unable to cope.
>
> *Sandra Capponi,*
> *Anti-Poverty Activist, Quebec*

There are additional pressures on the incomes of poor women. Maintenance payments from ex-partners are deducted from welfare and provincial assistance. The ex-partner can then deduct any payments from his income tax. In the meantime, the woman gets less money from welfare. Often a payment will be deducted from a woman's welfare cheque before she receives any support payment. It can take weeks to retrieve this money from the government. In some provinces she will never get the money back from welfare. The assumption is that at some point her partner will come through with the support money. In the meantime, a cheque that is woefully inadequate becomes even more so. Earned income is also deducted from government assistance cheques. In some provinces it is deducted dollar for dollar. In Ontario, women can earn between $150 and $175 over their fixed income. After that, the money is deducted from their welfare cheque.

Public housing policies also abuse poor families, most often headed by single mothers. When children become eighteen, if they aren't in school they're no longer eligible for rent-geared-to-income housing. They have to move out and their families have to move to smaller units. Eventually the mother ends up in a one-bedroom. She may have lived in the same apartment for more than twenty years, but because she is poor she is forced to leave the home she has made for herself and her family.

Sexism and Paternalism: The Issue of Control

Single mothers on welfare are controlled by a system that is meant to help them, controlled through the sexist and paternalistic attitudes and practices of social service agencies and case workers. These practices reflect the same patterns of control and power that are often characteristic of relationships between men and women, and between parents and children.

The lives of women on government assistance can be scrutinized on a daily basis by one or another social service worker or agency. A woman can have as many as four social workers in her life at one time, each of them mandated by the social service system to monitor a specific aspect of her life. This might include her parenting, her housekeeping skills or how she uses her leisure time. School systems employ social workers and psychologists who work cooperatively with child service agencies and welfare administrators to identify children with "special needs." The vast majority of these children are poor and their mothers are expected to account for every aspect of their behavior.

A friend of mine in Toronto receives just over $850 a month from Family Benefits (provincial welfare) to support herself and two small children. She lives in public housing. Her rent is geared to her income, so she pays twenty-five percent of her monthly cheque for housing. That leaves her $637.50 a month for other expenses.

In April 1992 she cashed her cheque. On her way home she lost the money. She reported the loss to social services and asked for a replacement cheque. She was told there was no emergency money. "Can you give me a couple of hundred to tide me over?" she asked. Their answer? "Use the food bank."

After a few days my friend became terribly worried and demoralized. Knowing that the Children's Aid Society has a policy of relieving mothers under stress by taking their children into care on a short-term basis, she asked for their help. She explained that she didn't have the money to feed the children and didn't want to go to the food bank for the rest of the month. She made it clear that if they'd just replace her cheque she'd be able to manage. Rather than give her the money, the agency took her kids, put them in a foster home — and gave the foster parents more money for the children than she had lost, including the baby bonuses she usually receives for each child. In addition, the Metro Toronto Housing Authority (public housing) took her name off their waiting list for a larger apartment because she no longer had her children with her.

She was allowed to visit with her children on the weekend. One weekend she was extremely distressed and she took her children to a friend's place in a nearby town. She had reason to believe that they were being spanked by the foster mother and was not satisfied with the social worker's assurances to the contrary.

A warrant was issued for her arrest. She was charged with abducting her children. She was finally apprehended in her own apartment when the police broke into her home, and — with her children present — body-searched her, handcuffed her and put her in a police car. Her children were returned to the foster home. It has been almost a year since her children were placed in foster care. She is now in litigation to get them back.

Food Banks

Charity is nice, but power is better.

"The Waste of a Nation: Poor People Speak Out About Charity,"
End Legislated Poverty, Vancouver, August 1992

There are twice as many food bank outlets in Canada as there are McDonald's franchises. The first food bank opened in Edmonton in 1981 and others spread quickly across the country. Now there are more than 345 food banks serving over a thousand community food depots.

If a woman goes to a welfare office at the end of the month for financial help because her government cheque doesn't cover the cost of feeding herself and her children, she's usually told to go to the local food bank. Some welfare agencies make it a practice to give women lists of food banks with monthly welfare cheques because agency workers themselves know that the assistance payments are ridiculously low.

Food banks are inherently political. From the corporate point of view, food banks function as controls on poor people. In addition to the considerable tax write-offs allowable for donating damaged canned goods that would otherwise be discarded, corporations are always pleased when public protests against poverty and hunger are under-mined by charity drives. They recognize the potential power of masses of poor people in Canada organizing to eliminate hunger.

The Fraser Institute, a right-wing think-tank has stated, "There is no problem, of course, with private charity to the unemployed, or to the poor, at whatever level...for private charity, by its very nature, is far more flexible than the public version. First of all, since it is voluntary, it can be cut off if contributors feel it is doing more harm than good."

Organizing: The Strength of Our Anger

> We can see a future where many, many more people will be living on way below the cost of living and will be expected to work for practically nothing in terrible conditions — back to workhouse conditions and the "lash" of necessity. Our goal is to fight and to win the battle against poverty.
>
> *Saskatchewan Anti-Poverty Legal Rights Committee,*
> Everywoman's Almanac 1991

The Tory economic, political and social agenda deliberately structures poverty-creation policies and their implementation into legislation, and into bilateral and international trade arrangements. More and more women organizing against poverty are recognizing the need to learn about the impact of the corporate agenda on poor communities. This growing practice of study and analysis has led to the increasing partici-pation of poor women in workshops designed to bring information into communities most severely affected by governments' brutal economic and political partnership with big business. There is — across the coun-try — a growing number of women who are combining the fight for needed reforms with the broader, long-term struggle for an equitable distribution of the wealth of the country and the creation of policies compatible with that goal.

Global restructuring and economic integration in this hemisphere are escalating government and corporate moves to reduce minimum wages across the country and to restrict worker's rights. Increasingly, when women organizing against poverty develop educational materials or workshop formats in poor communities, they make links between poverty and the broader spectrum of issues like the relation between forced employment programs at minimum wage, the Free Trade Deal and global restructuring.

In the summer of 1990, anti-poverty activists in Quebec protested Bill 37. Quebec anti-poverty activists and welfare advocates know that forcing welfare recipients into minimum wage jobs advances the corporate and government goal of increasing the pool of cheap labour. They know that the so-called training programs in Bill 37 are a door to forced employment initiatives and part and parcel of federal and provincial government plans to entrench brutally low employment standards in Quebec. They incorporate this information and analysis into educational materials and forums, thereby broadening the base of poor women who have the analytical tools to confront the injustices being brought about by global restructuring.

In Nova Scotia anti-poverty activists and welfare advocates are waging a campaign to get the province's social assistance standardized and to provide information about the discrimination and humiliation women on welfare face. The Women's Action Coalition supported the research and distribution of a report by Barbara Blouin, "Women and Children Last: Single Mothers on Welfare in Nova Scotia." The report is based on interviews with thirty single mothers throughout the province and over fifty social assistance workers and administrators, child protection workers, legal aid lawyers and transition house workers. It cites examples of the power and control the social service delivery system maintains over women on welfare:

> I called my worker to ask for some money for moving expenses. "Do you have a man?" he asked me. "Yeah," I said, "I do." And he said, "If you have a man and you have five kids, get your man to move you. Don't you believe in birth control pills, or getting your tubes tied?
>
> *Barbara Blouin,*
> *"Welfare Workers and Clients:*
> *Problems of Sexism and Paternalism"*

The report also describes the serious information gap created when social workers fail to give women on assistance information about their rights. It documents evidence of powerful workers who control their clients through mistrust, fear and humiliation. Providing women on welfare with this kind of information and analysis can help them deconstruct the ways they internalize patterns of power and powerlessness.

In 1991 social service cutbacks brought in by Metro Toronto Council catalyzed a massive protest spearheaded by women organizing against poverty and by welfare advocates. Called Fightback Metro, the struggle attracted people throughout the city and broadened the base of poor women in the anti-poverty movement. Though most of the cutbacks originally proposed by Council went through, Fightback Metro stopped several budget cuts in services for people with disabilities. As part of their campaign, activists produced print and visual materials that placed the city's social service slashes within the big picture of national and global restructuring. The result was a community of anti-poverty activists who are now better equipped to understand, explain and confront the corporate agenda in Canada. The strategy of using the proposed cutbacks to galvanize popular support resulted in a more broadly-based movement of women fighting poverty.

Women in the Saskatchewan Anti-Poverty Legal Rights Committee and in Saskatoon Equal Justice for All have been organizing and lobbying for many years for a more compassionate, equitable social service system. Poor women themselves are in the forefront of these organizations. From the beginning, they insisted that poor people had to drive the anti-poverty movement in Saskatchewan and made certain that only low-income members made up their steering committees. The decision to limit these committees came out of a conference in the mid-1980s. In addition, they recognize the importance of making international connections and worked with Interpares and CUSO to sponsor a tour to Canada by six women from developing countries. Theirs is the first group of poor people to organize provincially since the depression in the 1930s.

End Legislated Poverty, a Vancouver-based coalition of over twenty-two groups, works at the local level to organize low-income people. At the same time, it does extensive research on the impact of global restructuring and organizes workshops on the links between poverty in Canada and continental trade pacts. It is also working actively to raise the political issues inherent in the operation and staffing of food banks in Canada. Its recently published study, "Waste of a Nation: Poor People Speak Out About Charity," offers readers a clear account of the impact of food banks and charity drives on people who are poor. It gives people an opportunity to talk about what they experience when they are forced to use food banks. And it makes the links between charity and social control.

Organizing at the Bottom Line

> We are seeing an increased readiness to resort to heavy-handed policing methods as a means of containing the social problems that flow out of a worsening economic situation. The fact that the victims of police abuse are overwhelmingly low-income people testifies to its being a method of social regulation.
>
> *The Coalition Against Police Violence, Toronto 1992*

In Toronto there is a group of nurses who work out of street health centres, providing services to the homeless. They produced a study which exposes the level of police brutality against people forced to live on the street. The 1992 "Street Health Report" found that one in ten homeless people in Toronto had been assaulted by the police within the past year. Forty-five of 458 people described beatings by police. Citing the elimination of social programs and high unemployment, the nurses blame the collapsing social safety net for the increasing number of homeless people. Their report leaves no doubt that police assaults on the homeless are growing and becoming more brutal. Police violence is identified as an important factor in the health of homeless people. In addition, people forced to live on the street are treated with disdain by the medical profession and often turned away from hospital emergency services because many do not have health cards. Suicide, rape, violence and diseases are a way of life for Toronto's homeless.

The nurses published their report for political reasons, among others. The Liberal government of David Peterson was told about the increasing vulnerability of people living on the street. Nothing was done about it. The present (NDP) government claims there is not enough statistical evidence of the problem. The nurses have provided the statistics with this report and are waiting to see what happens.

In addition to providing valuable information about the burgeoning number of people without places to live in Toronto, the nurses have helped spearhead a coalition to stop police violence on the street. At a press conference in 1992, The Coalition Against Police Violence (CAPV) vowed "…to do all in our power to prevent police abuse in [this] community…the common targets for police violence are members of disempowered groups, the poor, the homeless and visible minorities…our goal is to alleviate problems caused by police abuse and to reduce the level of police misconduct by making known the activities which for now are carried out hidden from public view…" They plan to inform people about their rights, to confront abuses and to keep track of the patterns of abuse.

In Solidarity: Against Classism in The Women's Movement

> Reproductive choice cannot be separated from the realities…of living in poverty…the reality of not having shelter tomorrow, of not having food today, of inadequate welfare levels…poor women are always the ones who have the least control, and therefore choice is not a reality.
>
> Everywoman's Almanac 1991

Women who are poor in Canada have been organizing for a long time. These efforts, however, have remained outside the "mainstream" women's movement. The solidarity so many white, middle-class women in Canada express with such intensity for their sisters in developing countries must also find expression here at home.

The pro-choice movement remains an example of the ways poor women — Native, Black, disabled, immigrant and white — have been excluded from the mainstream concerns of white, middle-class women. The notion of "choice" for women of Colour, poor women, Native women and women with disabilities is vastly different from what it means to women who hold relative power in this society. At the same time, Native women, women of Colour and women with disabilities are the most economically vulnerable in Canada. Women who are poor are denied fundamental choices for their futures and the futures of their children. The notion of "choice," as it is applied to abortion rights, is too narrowly defined to apply to women who are poor. For women of Colour the "choice" bandwagon does not fully address the impact of birth control and sterilization on communities of Colour and the international implications of these practices. The "pro-choice" movement is primarily defined and carried out in the interests of women who can maintain some economic control over their lives and who enjoy relative freedom of choice across a wide spectrum of circumstances. The notion that the pro-choice movement will resonate with all women — whatever their race, class or culture — reflects a serious flaw in the organizing efforts of white feminists. It denies the differences and the diversity of experience among women and the intersection of race, class and gender.

Presentations of the relation between race, class and gender, carefully worked out by feminists from diverse communities, too often remain unheard or unheeded. How many of us who are white and middle-class have been asked to face our race and class biases — and failed to do so? Why do these discussions, often initiated by women of Colour and women who are poor, become polarized and contentious? Given the relative position of power we hold as a result of being white and middle-class, it stands to reason that we have a lot to unlearn.

In the current climate of accelerated change within the women's movement in Canada, it is encouraging that a more positive dialogue is emerging between and among diverse groups of women. For white middle-class feminists, giving up control of the agenda and incorporating into our analysis and practice the recognition of the equal weight of race, class and gender means being part of a representative grouping of women who are organizing and building a new political force, one that is driven by the strength of our collective anger.

Notes

1. Facts and figures come from: Barbara Blouin in "Welfare Workers and Clients: Problems of Sexism and Paternalism," Ellen Sands in "Poverty on the Reservation: One Woman's Experience," Maria Barille in "Disabled Women: An Exploited Underclass" and Pam Flemming in "Gender Bias and the Law: Is It Enough?" in *Canadian Woman Studies/ les cahiers de la femme,* Summer 1992; Carolyn Jack in "Food Banks and the Politics of Hunger" in *Canadian Forum,* December 1991; "Child Poverty in Action" (Child Poverty Action Group, 1990); the Coalition Against Police Violence; *Everywoman's Almanac* (Toronto: Women's Press, 1991); "Executive Summary: A Preliminary Study of Selected Morbidity and Mortality Indicators in Census Tracts" (Vancouver: City of Vancouver, 1986); "Fair Shares: Income, Wealth and Taxation in Canada" (Toronto: Ontario Coalition for Social Justice, 1991); *Flawline/ Action Line* (Vancouver: End Legislated Poverty, January 1992-January 1993); "The GST in the Big Tax Picture" (Ottawa: Action Canada Network, 1991); Pat Brascoupe and Georges Erasmus in "Index on Native Canadians" in *Canadian Forum,* April 1991; "Report Card on the Health of the Toronto Economy" (Toronto: Workers' Information and Action Centre of Toronto, 1992); "Street Health Report, Toronto 1992" (N.p.); "The Waste of A Nation: Poor People Speak Out About Charity" (Vancouver: End Legislated Poverty, 1992); *Wham Comix* (Ottawa: National Union of Provincial Government Employees and Public Service Alliance of Canada, 1992).

ARE THESE CLOTHES CLEAN?

The Campaign for Fair Wages and

Working Conditions for Homeworkers

Jan Borowy, Shelly Gordon, Gayle Lebans

This is a story about fighting back against forces thought to be too large and too powerful to be confronted. Canadian workers, especially women, face a changed world economy in the 1990s. It's faster, leaner and meaner than ever before. This article is a story about some of those changes, how they affect a large group of immigrant women workers in Toronto and how non-unionized workers, feminists, community groups and a union are fighting back. It is part of a larger story about how unions are reshaping themselves and their strategies to meet the challenges of the 1990s and beyond.

Twenty years ago feminists within and outside trade unions were just beginning the fight to bring women and women's issues to the fore in the labour movement. Today, instead of struggling to get trade unions to take up issues like child care, women's and community groups and trade unions are exploring new ways of working together to achieve common goals, especially the larger goals of social change outside the traditional scope of collective bargaining. The Campaign for Fair Wages and Working Conditions for Homeworkers in Toronto is one example of new forms of alliances between unions, social movements and community groups. While such a story is still not common, there are others in English-speaking Canada, in Quebec and internationally.

The drive to organize homeworkers is long-term and continuing. It requires enormous resources and patience. The objective is for homeworkers to be able to exercise the right to join a union and sign collective agreements. Until that time, however, the experience of organizing homeworkers in an association or in a pre-union formation that addresses both work and social issues offers an example of and a direction for feminists and unions as they work to protect and improve working conditions in a changing economy.

This article was written during an ongoing campaign, by women centrally involved in it, in the hope that our experience can be used by others. It is also an opportunity to reflect on the choices and decisions made during a campaign, on the various strategies for political action and on the complexities of how to assist women workers in precarious employment to organize.

The Garment Industry

Jewish women, Italian women, Chinese women, South Asian women. Greek, Caribbean, Portuguese and Polish women, Vietnamese and Eastern European women — tens of thousands of women arriving in Canada over the last century — found their first job in the immigrant job-ghetto of Canada's garment manufacturing industry, the "rag trade." The pay was low, often piece-rate. The best paying jobs went to men. The work was hard and hazardous. Employment was often seasonal. But you didn't need "Canadian experience" or "fluency in English" to get a job and be able to house and feed your family.

The garment industry plays an unique role in Canada's economy and labour market. It is often the first and only source of employment for many women, particularly immigrant women. While women make up twenty-nine percent of the workforce in the goods-producing sector as a whole, they are eighty percent of the garment manufacturing industry.[1] In Canada, sixty percent of garment production is conducted in Quebec, thirty percent in Ontario and the remaining ten percent is spread throughout the rest of the country.

In Metro Toronto,[2] in 1986, ninety-four percent of sewing machine operators were born outside of Canada, as were eighty-three percent of pattern-makers and cutters, and eighty-three percent of the employees in various textile industry occupations.[3]

Global Economic Restructuring and the Garment Industry

For the past twenty years the garment industry in Canada has been called a "sunset" industry. In an era of trade liberalization, it is seen as having little chance of survival without hefty tariffs and trade protection. Both manufacturers' associations and industry unions have focused historically on limiting imports as a way of protecting the industry in Canada. More recently, these same manufacturers and retailers have attempted to adjust to global market and labour supply changes by becoming importers themselves. The unions' strategy throughout the 1970s and 1980s consisted mainly of fighting the ever-growing number of imports, attempting to organize the ever-increasing number of small factories and providing adjustment programs for the laid-off workers.

While the policy-makers and economists argued that the garment industry was in its sunset, employment figures reveal a different story. Between 1971 and 1988 employment in the garment industry actually rose by 11,000 — at a time the industry was supposedly in decline. It was not until the late 1980s and the signing of the Free Trade Agreement that the garment industry began to face massive job loss. Employment dropped a full third from 95,800 in 1988 to an estimated 62,800 in 1992.[4] In Metro Toronto alone there were 24,711 workers in 1988, but by 1991 that number had fallen to 14,328.[5]

The thirty percent decline in the workforce in the garment industry is comparable to that in the manufacturing or goods-producing sector in general. Other industries in Metro Toronto have declined even more dramatically. For example, between 1983 and 1990 employment in the furniture, chemicals and machinery industries declined by over fifty percent. Most manufacturing in Canada, not just garment, is experiencing globalization of production and markets.

Membership in the International Ladies' Garment Workers' Union (ILGWU) Ontario District declined much faster than overall employment because of the changes in the structure of the industry. Between 1985 and 1992 union membership dropped sixty percent, almost twice the rate of the general industry decline. The overall unionization rate within the industry fell to less than twenty percent, from a high of eighty percent fifty years earlier. Faced with this picture, the union needed to evaluate what was happening in the industry. What type of restructuring was taking place? How could it so devastate union membership?

Historically, homeworking has been part of garment manufacturing. The ILGWU was founded on trying to drive illegal sweatshops out of the industry. While apparel factories have not been as large as those typical of other manufacturing industries, throughout the post-war period, most clothing production generally occurred in larger factories employing fifty or more workers. Production was contracted out to smaller firms or homeworkers only in the busiest times. A large manufacturer or "jobber" would negotiate sales with the retailer, order the fabric, then cut and sew it in the factory. When the factory was at full capacity the manufacturer would use a contractor who was sent fabric directly and who then would sew and press the pieces.

By the late 1980s there had been a significant shift in the number of homeworkers and contracting shops. In 1971 only twenty-two percent of the industry was made up of shops with less than twenty workers. By 1991 this picture had reversed so that seventy-six percent of clothing production was in shops with less than twenty workers. The number of contracting shops in Ontario grew from only four in 1971 to over 116 in 1991. There is no way of counting the number of jobs that have migrated from the factories to homeworkers.

This trend posed a direct threat to the wages and working conditions secured in unionized factories. Sporadically used, contracting shops had not competed directly with larger unionized factories. However, in the 1980s, manufacturers began to lay people off and close unionized factories completely. Quite commonly, the owner would reappear with a smaller shop under a different name and hire only a cutter.

A centrally-controlled hierarchical chain or pyramid of production began to emerge in the industry as retailers and manufacturers attempted to lower costs to compete with international suppliers. At the top of the pyramid are the huge retailers and a handful of large manufacturers with high-recognition labels like Alfred Sung. Three large retailers in Canada — the Hudson's Bay Company, Eaton's and Dylex — control access to forty percent of the clothing market.

The emerging trend in manufacturing is towards a hollow corporation, one where no actual production is done by the firm. Work is sub-contracted to contractors who employ as few as two workers or as many as thirty. These contractors then send the sewing work out to homeworkers. Homeworkers are at the bottom of the industry "pyramid."

The pyramid of production in the garment industry and the hollow manufacturing firm are a part of and a response to global economic restructuring. To lower costs, companies use new technologies to create a just-in-time production system with a just-in-time workforce. An electronic communications network — an electronic data interchange (EDI) — provides electronic hook-ups between the retailer and the jobber. When a garment is sold an electronic message is sent directly to the manufacturer or jobber ordering a new garment. Retailers carry much smaller inventories and demand production and delivery of garments with a quick turn-around time. Retailers create tighter and more direct links with fewer suppliers. To supply Eaton's, for example, a manufacturer must be linked with EDI.

The garment industry is undergoing increased concentration, with control by fewer and bigger retailers. Eaton's controls manufacturers through new technologies like EDI. According to some suppliers, the Hudson's Bay Co. exerts control throughout the entire market by the ownership of major retail chains in each price range. In addition to the Hudson's Bay stores, it owns Zellers, Simpson's, Robinsons and Fields. The Hudson's Bay Co. has recently demanded garments at the previous year's price and often on consignment. In 1991 Hudson's Bay Co. had annual sales of $4.6 billion, with profits over $158 million. Dylex dominates the shopping mall market through ownership of Fairweather, Big Steel, Tip Top Tailors, Braemar, Bi-Way, Club Monaco, Harry Rosen, Suzy Shier, Thriftys and Drug World (with combined annual sales of $1.83 billion in 1991).[6]

Manufacturers have had to make strategic choices in the face of relentless competition and increasing control and pressure from a few huge retailers. Manufacturers and jobbers could modernize production and introduce state of the art technology such as laser cutters and overhead automated bundle systems, or they could try to compete against imports by lowering labour costs — a low-wage strategy.

In general, manufacturers choose the low-wage strategy and rely on a global production system. A manufacturer may have fifty percent of production done off-shore in countries where labour costs are significantly lower. Manufacturers design the garment in Canada, buy the fabric here or abroad and (perhaps) cut the garment in their own shops. The pieces are sent to Taiwan, the Philippines, Mexico or Malaysia to be assembled and then shipped back to Canada for sale. The other half of the manufacturer's line is completed by homeworkers close to the large retailers in Canada for just-in-time production.

The shift toward homework in the garment industry is part of a larger trend toward increasingly precarious employment throughout the global economy. Precarious employment is insecure employment, including part-time, temporary, contract work or own-account self-employment. Once considered unusual or non-standard employment in Canada, it is the most rapidly expanding sector of Canada's labour market. By 1989 one-third of Canada's workers were employed in non-standard jobs. In Metro Toronto, between 1983 and 1989, part-time employment grew by ninety-nine percent. Statistics Canada reports that in July 1992, 120,000 full-time jobs were lost while 100,000 part-time jobs were created. Women are more than seventy percent of all part-time workers.[7]

Precarious employment rises due to capital's drive for a flexible workforce to reduce labour costs. The process is often called the "casualization" of work. Businesses pursue a flexible low-cost labour strategy by "reducing their fixed labour force, making payment systems more flexible and using more contract workers, temporary labour and outsourcing through the use of homeworkers, or subcontracting to small informal enterprises that are not covered by labour or other regulations and that bear the risks and uncertainties of fluctuating business."[8]

Multinational corporations first used this strategy in developing nations, using women workers in free trade or export zones. It is now being used around the world.[9]

Often the "flexibility" strategy involves three tactics: redeploying workers in new ways within a firm (for example, by "multi-skilling"), altering the size of the permanent workforce and pushing for wage concessions.[10] In the case of the garment industry, firms first altered the size of the workforce by closing down larger factories and sending work out to "flexible" contract shops which would in turn hire immigrant women (often, the same women who had worked in the factories) as homeworkers. Homeworkers are the ultimate in "just-in-time" or "flexible" workers.

The impact of this strategy on the labour force is the creation of two polar groups. A group of core factory workers maintains access to traditional collective bargaining. This group faces constant pressure for wage concessions. Surrounding this group are the peripheral "flexible" workers who have few benefits, and little or no real protection under employment law. The flexibility strategy and the "casualization" of work leaves the labour market polarized between a group of workers with higher wages, albeit under attack, and another group of workers with extremely low wages, few benefits and in a vulnerable, precarious position. This occurred in the garment industry in Ontario. It posed a tremendous challenge to the unions.

The Union Responds

The International Ladies' Garment Workers Union — Ontario District (ILGWU) had to respond to the rapid decline in membership caused by the fundamental restructuring of the industry. In 1990 two factors came together which would help set a new direction for the ILGWU Ontario District. First, the Ontario District Council (the rank-and-file representatives' council) elected as district manager a feminist who knew the fight to save the union was integrally related to the industry's restructuring and its impact on immigrant women. Second, the union successfully applied for a research grant from the Technology Adjustment Research Project, a research fund administered by the Ontario Federation of Labour for the Ministry of Labour. The researchers hired were feminists. The research project provided the resources needed to permit a closer examination of the restructuring of the industry and its impact on labour and the opportunity to work out an industrial strategy that would reverse the trends.

In 1991 the ILGWU Ontario District began to investigate the wages and working conditions of homeworkers. An information hotline was set-up. Educational pamphlets on homeworkers' rights were distributed in English and Chinese. Thirty Chinese speaking sewers were interviewed. The results were staggering. Conditions that the union had fought to eradicate at the turn of the century had re-emerged in the late twentieth century.

- Twenty-one of thirty homeworkers were not being paid the 1991 minimum wage of $5.40 per hour. One was earning as little as a dollar per hour. The average wage was $4.64. Only two highly skilled workers earned an average of seven dollars an hour.
- Only one homeworker was being paid the vacation pay to which she was entitled. None of their employers were making unemployment insurance or pension contributions. Only one employer had a permit to employ homeworkers as required by the *Employment Standards Act* in Ontario.
- Homeworkers had to buy their own equipment and cover the costs of operating expenses out of their meagre wages. Their industrial sewing machines often cost more than $3,500.
- The average work week was forty-six hours. In busy times, homeworkers worked an average of seventy hours a week. (Homeworkers are exempted from the overtime pay provisions of Ontario law.)
- Almost half of the homeworkers reported that other family members, including children, assisted them, providing unpaid labour to the contractor.
- Twenty-seven of the thirty homeworkers interviewed had health problems related to their work — often allergies to fabric dust, stress resulting from the time pressure and repetitive strain injuries or other problems associated with badly designed equipment.
- The homeworkers had no control over the scheduling of their work or the rate of pay. Twelve reported problems in getting paid for the work they had done. Twenty-one worked for sub-contractors, nine for factories and all but four worked for more than one employer.
- All but one woman reported that they had turned to homework because they could not afford child care. More than two-thirds said they would rather work outside the home. With few exceptions, their last jobs had been in garment factories and they had begun to take in homework while on maternity leave.
- Only one of the women interviewed reported that she could con-

verse in English. All but two had less than high school education, completed in their country of origin.[11]

Faced with these results, the ILGWU came to two conclusions. The union had to respond directly to the problems experienced by the homeworkers. Homeworkers were a super-exploited, flexible workforce at the bottom of the industry pyramid. This meant taking an approach that did not blame the victim but instead acknowledged the factors that oblige so many women to turn to homework.

The union understood that factory workers were being pitted against homeworkers. If the homeworkers continued to be exploited and exploitable, the union's own membership and collective agreements would be undermined. More shops would shut down and more work would be contracted out to homeworkers. During a time of high unemployment, apparel manufacturers and retailers would continue to use homeworkers.

Historically, the ILGWU fought for a ban on homework as part of its struggle for decent wages and working conditions in the industry. Trade unions in both the United States and Britain, at the turn of the century, argued it was impossible to organize homeworkers and that homework could never be regulated. In the worst cases, trade unionists blamed homework on the characteristics of women.[12]

The ILGWU in the United States won a legislated ban on homework in the garment industry. It would be completely contradictory for it to turn around and attempt to organize homeworkers — a public acknowledgement that the ban is not enforceable. To discourage homework, the ILGWU in the U.S. has in some cases levied fines against union members who performed it. In Ontario, however, homework was legal, flourishing and threatening the union's foundation.

Deciding to Organize Homeworkers — ILGWU Ontario District

The ILGWU Ontario District decided to adopt a dual strategy to organize homeworkers into their own association or "pre-union" formation; and to work with community and women's groups in a coalition to pressure for legislative changes and accessible child care and to build a public campaign to resist the impact of economic restructuring on women's work.

Organizing homeworkers poses considerable challenges. They are not at one location, such as a factory, and often work for more than one employer. The definition of bargaining units under the *Ontario Labour Relations Act* creates other problems for unionizing. And even if these difficulties are surmounted, the isolation of members and their geographic dispersal (to mention only two factors contributing to the vulnerability of homeworkers) are barriers to winning and then effectively enforcing a collective agreement. A union must be willing to commit itself to an extremely long-term and patient approach. Trade unions have been reluctant to take on this mammoth task. The resources required for organizing would have a very long-term payback, if any. However, the increasing use of just-in-time workers in non-standard forms of employment like part-time or casual work is challenging unions in the 1990s to find new ways of organizing.[13]

The homeworkers campaign provides a useful example of tactics for reaching workers in precarious employment. One of the biggest challenges in organizing homeworkers is finding them in the underground network of sub-contracting and homework. Individual homeworkers must be reached at the site of employment — their homes. One method is to hang around traditional garment district factories where contracting shops are located and follow the cars that pick up the bundles of cut garments. The ILGWU[14] tried this, but found it to be very labour-intensive, time-consuming and not particularly successful.

The union had to make stronger links with organizations and groups within the particular communities, geographic or ethnic, to which the majority of homeworkers belonged. In Toronto the ILGWU started by working with the Chinese and Vietnamese communities, increasing the profile of the union as a place to call if a worker had employment problems.

It is almost impossible for homeworkers to become union members in the traditional sense of becoming members of a bargaining unit. Labour law defines a bargaining unit as having at least two members and one employer. Yet homeworkers needed an organization in which they could break down their isolation, share experiences, work together to improve their wages and working conditions and receive some services. The history of the labour movement offers examples of other forms of associations. Industrial workers organized into Workers' Benevolent Societies, offering mutual assistance to members from the 1850s to the 1930s. There were attempts to organize homeworkers in France, Britain and (to a lesser extent) the United States in the last century. In 1894 the British Women's Industrial Council evolved from the Women's Trade Union Association and supported the Liverpool Association of Homeworkers and Outworkers. Often U.S. social reformers organized groups of homeworkers through neighbourhood settlement houses.[15]

During the mid-1980s, several U.S. unions developed "associate memberships" to maintain connections with members who had lost their jobs. The associate membership program also enabled unions to assist previously unorganized groups, which had no tradition of a union and which may not have legally had the right to sign collective agreements, to come together to form a group.

The ILGWU in the U.S. had established the AIM (Associate ILGWU Member) program. The ILGWU International office had ten AIM locals, ranging from retirees, to factory workers who hadn't (yet) been successful in organizing, to flower vendors in New York City. The ILGWU Ontario District reasoned that creating a new Associate Members local would be an appropriate way to provide an organizational structure for homeworkers. The Ontario District manager approached New York for support for the homeworker organizing drive. The International Office accepted the drive, despite its position on banning homework, recognizing that Ontario labour relations law is quite different from that of the United States. The International Office even provided funds to assist in hiring an organizer. The support from New York was significant. It had allocated a special grant on only one previous occasion.

While the move to organize homeworkers gained support in New York, there remained tension within the Ontario ILGWU. Many union members viewed homeworkers as taking their jobs away. The historical animosity towards homeworkers was deeply rooted. Members were worried that organizing homeworkers would simply allow homework to flourish. There was a lengthy debate. The argument was won when members became convinced that organizing homeworkers would help reduce the wage differential between unionized factory workers and homeworkers. In the long term, it was in the best interest of the union. One union member summed it up: "I have heard about the wages and the conditions of homeworkers. I joined this union forty-seven years ago to clean up the industry and stop this exploitation. We have to organize the homeworkers if we are really going to clean it up."

Slowly, union members began to revise their stereotypes of homeworkers. They realized that as manufacturers were restructuring their businesses they were pitting factory workers against homeworkers. Bargaining committees were being pushed to accept wage concessions, lengthened work weeks and work speed-ups at the negotiating table because employers were obliging union members to compete with the less-than-minimum wage that homeworkers could be forced to accept.

The ILGWU Ontario District attempted to introduce new collective agreement language so homeworkers would be part of the bargaining unit with a particular employer. This strategy has not yet been successful. Other ways of reaching out to homeworkers and building unity between them and factory workers had to be found.

The Homeworkers' Association

Once the ILGWU Ontario District and the Coalition for Fair Wages and Working Conditions for Homeworkers set out to create a Homeworkers' Association, they confronted the problem of actually locating potential members.

A coordinator experienced in community development and workers' rights was hired in February 1992. Importantly, the coordinator spoke Vietnamese, Mandarin and Cantonese as well as English.

The first attempt to attract women to the new organization was by contacting homeworkers who had been interviewed in the initial study and inviting them to a meeting on information about their rights as homeworkers. Only two of the forty women contacted appeared. Obviously, simply calling a meeting wasn't going to attract members to the Association.

The union and the coordinator conceived a different kind of organizing drive. They advertised the Homeworkers' Association in the Chinese and Vietnamese media, spoke about the Association at various functions and placed leaflets on Homeworkers' Rights at all community centres. The key to the drive was to convince homeworkers that there was a place they could turn to for help and counselling — the union office.

The most successful tool of the homework drive involved extending the traditional notion of organizing to include social activities, especially for families. The homeworkers had reported in the interviews that social isolation was one of their major problems. Homeworkers stay at home working all day — and often all night — long. Production schedules left no time for social activities.

This was a gap the Association could fill. The coordinator organized a series of trips for families: trips to a maple sugar bush, to Niagara Falls for the Blossom Festival, to parks outside the city and so on. The trips were advertised by leafleting factories which employ homeworkers and through media familiar to the South-East Asian community.

The response was excellent. While the focus of the trips was social, very important discussions took place on homework, the Association, the ILGWU and unionization in general. Some myths were dispelled and information on both the situation and the rights of workers exchanged. It was simply not feasible, at that stage, to limit the trips to homeworkers and their families. However, homeworkers who did attend joined the Association and the participation of other workers created opportunities for news about the Association and its activities to travel by word of mouth through the community.

Between trips, drop-in social teas and legal clinics were held on Saturday afternoons at the union office, enabling women to meet, discuss their experiences and do something about problems. The trips and teas were the most useful organizing and outreach strategies linking a woman's issues as a worker to other aspects of her day-to-day life.

In March 1992 four women joined, then two more and then another three. By the end of the first year, the Homeworkers' Association boasted over fifty members — an incredible feat in view of the obstacles faced.

In June 1992, accompanied by the coordinator, a member of the Association flew to Miami as a delegate to the first convention of the ILGWU Associate Member (AIM) locals. Mrs. Chu[17] spoke at the convention and in an organizing workshop attended by both AIM and ILGWU convention delegates about the situation of homeworkers here and the activities of the Homeworkers' Association.[18]

Another milestone was reached at an ILGWU "retreat" in August that year. The union organized an educational weekend for members of the ILGWU and the Homeworkers' Association and the Coalition at Port Elgin, a union-owned educational facility on the shores of Lake Huron.[19] People brought their families and socialized as well as engaging in some hard-hitting discussion of problems.

Each side gained a better understanding of the other's situation and of common concerns. One participant, reflecting on the retreat, says: "Two groups met at Port Elgin. But, by the end of the weekend, we were one — workers, struggling to make ends meet in an industry whose future in Toronto is uncertain. We know we have to stick together."

A few weeks later, the Homeworkers' Association and ILGWU contingents marched together in the Labour Day parade, with members of both organizations intermingled beneath the two banners.

On October 31, 1992, the Homeworkers' Association held its first annual general meeting and elected an executive from the membership to direct its affairs. The director of the ILGWU's AIM Program flew in from New York to present the homeworkers with their official union charter as AIM Local 12. It was an exhilarating moment.

Homeworkers' Association members have made presentations to provincial and federal government committees, to trade unionists and other community groups. Several are becoming experts in dealing with the media. The Association, among its other functions, provides a vehicle for women to develop and utilize strong leadership skills. Without the Association, this opportunity did not and would not exist.

Annual dues for the Association were set at twelve dollars. In addition to the life insurance which all members receive, the union has created a special health and drug benefit plan that homeworkers can purchase for themselves and their families. The union office began to function as a drop-in centre for workers in the community who come to visit for help of any sort, including personal counselling and referral to other community agencies. The Association plans to launch a Homeworkers' newsletter in Chinese script as a new outreach tool.

An example of both the exploitation which homeworkers encounter and the transformations which the Association brings is illustrated by Yen's story. Yen worked for an employer for several months. The company folded abruptly, leaving Yen with one month's wages owing, not to mention termination and vacation pay. Yen then began to do homework for another employer. She dropped off bundles of completed work, receiving in exchange only the promise of future pay. Then Yen picked up a bundle of silk blouses to sew. She was to be paid seven dollars a blouse, for a total of seventy dollars. She delivered the completed garments and requested payment for her work to date. The employer informed her that the work had been faulty (a lie) and that he could not sell the blouses. He told Yen that the selling price of the blouses was ninety dollars a piece, and that Yen's "error" had cost him nine hundred dollars. But because he was a "compassionate" man, he offered to split the loss with Yen, charging her fifty dollars for each blouse, for a total of five hundred dollars! Oddly enough, this amount was roughly equivalent to the total in wages owing to Yen. She was pounding the pavements again.

Her next employer owned a factory and retail outlets. Yen performed homework for this company until it closed up shop overnight, leaving her once again with unpaid wages. By this time Yen was a member of the Association. With the help of a legal clinic that is part of the Coalition, the Association made sure that Yen and other homeworkers received the monies owing to them. Before, the workers had said of their employers, "These people are like monsters, and I am just an ant. They can step on me easily." Now, as members of the Association, the workers had a way of fighting back.

One of the needs which the Association members identified at the August retreat was to acquire or improve English language skills. Two months later, the Association had set up classes with assistance from the Toronto Board of Education. Classes are held on Sundays, using materials developed specifically from the experiences of garment homeworkers. The Association has co-sponsored a number of workshops on workers' rights with other groups in the community.

In the first year, all the organizing was done in the South-East Asian community, where the ILGWU already had important links. Great strides have been made. The Coalition, however, is well aware that the scope of work being performed in homes is much broader than the garment trade and the workers involved are of diverse backgrounds.

When the Coalition members met with organizers from other ethno-linguistic communities, the response was always, "We're pretty sure homeworking must be happening in our community, but these workers are probably too busy, too isolated, to make contact with groups and services." Excellent suggestions and contact possibilities were shared with the Association. It has not yet, however, solved the major problem — how to find or fund the staff and resources necessary for outreach and follow-up in other communities.

Trips, socials, help with employment and other problems, English as a second language classes, health and welfare benefits — members are attracted to the Association for different reasons. Their employment remains so precarious that joining the Association is an act of bravery. But diverse motivations coalesce into a common purpose: "If we work together, we can change our situation."

The Coalition for Fair Wages and Working Conditions for Homeworkers

The second and concurrent part of the ILGWU's strategy to respond to the situation of homeworkers was to explore forming a coalition with community groups and activists. The ILGWU knew a campaign would need support beyond the union. The union had neither the resources nor the political clout to mount an effective campaign by itself. The ILGWU called people together to discuss forming such a coalition in the fall of 1991.

By the end of September the group had decided to initiate a campaign and had agreed on its major components. Active members of the Coalition have included representatives from a number of organizations: the ILGWU, the National Action Committee on the Status of Women's (NAC) Employment and Economy Committee, the Workers' Information and Action Centre of Toronto, academics who had researched and written about homeworkers in the garment industry in Canada, a member of Mujer a Mujer, a tri-national women's group that works with garment workers in U.S. border states and Mexico, a community organization working with immigrant women, a community legal clinic, the labour council, church groups and other individuals.

Building a Coalition and Launching a Campaign: September — December 1991

The principle aims of the campaign would be to win legislative changes that would offer greater protection to homeworkers and to assist in building an organization of homeworkers. In order to achieve these goals, the campaign would have to:

- Build alliances, especially a working coalition, with representation from unions, women's groups and community groups, particularly those advocating for immigrant populations;
- Educate the general public, particularly activists in the labour and women's movements, about the conditions of homeworkers, to build broad public support;
- Lay the basis for an organization of homeworkers by making contact with homeworkers, initially by re-establishing the "Homeworkers' Hotline";
- Raise the long-term global economic issues underlying the increase in homework in the garment industry.

The Coalition decided to keep its focus on garment homeworkers. Coalition members wanted to understand and to explain that what was happening to garment workers was part of broader economic and labour market trends. But they agreed that they were more likely to be effective in taking on just one sector for now.

The Coalition initially discussed whether its ultimate goal would be to make homework a reasonable alternative for women, or to see it banned. Homework, it was decided, could only be an "alternative" if women had other options. The ILGWU study had demonstrated, and subsequent experience confirmed, that women become homeworkers because they can't find decent employment outside the home. They may not have the skills required to compete successfully in the Canadian labour market and they face racial, ethnic and gender discrimination. There isn't accessible, high-quality, affordable child care, there aren't social supports that facilitate women working outside the home. Women are still almost solely responsible for the domestic sphere.

Women with whom the ILGWU spoke clearly stated that they did not want to be homeworkers. Would banning homework help to create jobs outside the home? The answer suggested by the U.S. experience was No. Such an approach could make the lives of homeworkers even more difficult by driving the work further underground, thus making homeworkers even more vulnerable to exploitation. Politically, a banning strategy could result in making women guilty by association with the illegal practices of their employers.

For these reasons, the Coalition rejected both the "reasonable alternative" and "banning" positions. Major transformations in the conditions of women's work have to be achieved for women to have real choices about where they work. Rather than trying to make homework illegal, the Coalition decided to try, through better employment legislation, stronger enforcement and through organizing, to reduce the viability of homework as an attractive low-wage alternative for labour-intensive industries.

In the fall and winter of 1991 the Coalition held a press conference and a lobby of the provincial government and opposition parties and began planning an educational conference. The Ontario Federation of Labour convention unanimously adopted a resolution in support of the campaign.

The Coalition invited the Public Service Alliance of Canada (PSAC), the union representing federal government workers, to join in sponsoring a conference on homework. The trend toward a "flexible" workforce isn't confined to the private sector. The Treasury Board was developing a pilot project that would "allow" certain federal government employees to work from home rather than in the office. PSAC had initiated a research project to prepare the union's response. It was a very exciting partnership between labour and women's movement activists and academics. It was the first time that women in Canada explored the similarities and commonalities between industrial and electronic homework — the sweat shop and the "electronic cottage."

The Campaigns for Legislative Change and "Clean Clothes"

In early 1992 political discussion and debate in Ontario centred on the provincial government's proposals for reform of the *Ontario Labour Relations Act* (later, the controversial Bill 40). The government's stated intent was to reform the *Act* to facilitate access to collective bargaining for sectors of the labour market which historically had not been unionized and were often considered unorganizable. These are sectors of the economy which are expanding — personal service, retail, finance, insurance and real estate. Women of all colours, immigrant and young workers of both sexes are concentrated in these very sectors. More heavily unionized sectors such as manufacturing are declining.

The Coalition was part of an ad-hoc group of women who organized to respond to the government's discussion paper on reform of the Labour Relations Act. Women from the trade union movement, INTERCEDE (The Toronto Organization of Domestic Workers), the retail and service sectors, the women's movement and the Coalition all agreed that the proposed reforms, while a step in the right direction, would do little to change the situation for most women. Women for Labour Law Reform met with the Minister of Labour. While generally supporting the modest amendments being proposed, the group pointed out the limited impact they would have in female-dominated sectors of the labour force. They called on the government to strengthen and enforce the *Employment Standards Act* and to establish a task force to examine the potential for sectoral or broader-based bargaining.

Homeworkers are one of the groups that cannot unionize using existing labour relations laws. The ILGWU and the Coalition had been trying to develop a model of labour relations to allow homeworkers to organize as a sector and to negotiate jointly with their employers. The issue of broader-based or sectoral bargaining became more central as the year went on.

After the launch of the Coalition late in 1991, the ILGWU focused on analysing the specific structure of the Canadian apparel industry, putting names, faces and numbers to the industry pyramid. The Coalition began discussing a campaign to pressure the three big retail firms that control the industry pyramid to take, or be held to, some responsibility for wages and working conditions down the production line. Such a campaign should continue public education, gather more public support, bring pressure to bear on the corporations to improve wages and working conditions and put pressure on the government to implement and enforce legislation to protect homeworkers.

The Coalition talked about a consumer boycott, using one of the three large retail firms that essentially control the apparel industry in Canada as a straw-dog — specifically the Hudson's Bay. The Hudson's Bay Co., Canada's "oldest corporation," presents itself as one of the founding pillars of this country. It is possibly the worst of the big retailers in terms of setting conditions for manufacturers that pressure them into using homeworkers and importing from countries where workers are paid even lower wages. But there was apprehension about the boycott strategy. How could support for the boycott be obtained from workers directly employed by the Hudson's Bay Co.? What would the concrete objectives be? How would success be defined? Most of the Coalition members had grown up with the Kraft, Nestles and green grape boycotts. While these had had some success, they required colossal effort and coordination on the part of thousands or tens of thousands of people.

Throughout the development of the Coalition there had been periodic correspondence with women in England who had been organizing and working with homeworkers throughout the 1980s. In the summer of 1992 one of the ILGWU staff went to England and met with two groups, the Leicester Outworkers' Campaign and the West Yorkshire Homeworkers' Unit. She brought back information about their "Clean Clothes Campaign."[22]

Responding to the same issues and industry structure that the Coalition faced in Canada, the Leicester Outworkers' Campaign had adopted a consumer education and preferential buying campaign directed at one large retail chain. They had drawn up a "Clean Clothes Code." Retailers who adopted it pledged to

- Buy garments from manufacturers who:
- Abide by minimum wage and employment laws ...
- Give all workers a legally-enforceable contract of employment, including homeworkers when used
- Allow free association of workers and the formation of independent worker organisations

• Do not enforce overtime
• Pay properly and promptly for all hours worked ...[23]

The retailer also pledged to ensure that their suppliers met these same standards.

The Toronto Coalition for Fair Wages and Working Conditions decided to formulate their campaign in a similar way. Rather than a boycott, there would be a campaign which asked consumers and retailers to become aware, to communicate their awareness to retailers and to make positive choices. The Coalition produced background material about the use of homeworkers, their working conditions in the garment industry and told the stories of three homeworkers who made designer-label clothes for less than the minimum wage. They created a "Clean Clothes Score Card" that shoppers could use to question retailers about their suppliers and evaluate which manufacturers they would like to buy from. They ran off tens of thousands of postcards for people to send to the presidents of Eaton's, the Hudson's Bay Co. and Dylex, demanding that they "Stop the Exploitation of Homeworkers — Buy from Manufacturers who pay Fair Wages and Working Conditions."

CLEAN CLOTHES SCORE CARD
Test your clothes: Are they clean?

The next time you buy clothes, ask the Retailer these questions:

1. Does the retailer or any of her/his suppliers use homeworkers?
2. Are they paid at least minimum wage?
3. Are homeworkers paid on time?
4. Are they paid for all hours of work?
5. Are homeworkers given reasonable turn around time to complete each job?
6. Has the original supplier registered for a Homeworkers permit, as required under the Employment Standards Act?
7. Does the original supplier/employer make contributions to Unemployment Insurance and Canada Pension Plan?
8. Were the homeworkers intimidated from joining the Homeworkers' Association?

A score of less than 8 YESes means the homeworker is not receiving fair wages and working conditions.

The Women's Committee of the Ontario Federation of Labour gave the Coalition the perfect opportunity to launch the campaign at its fall conference, "More Than A Day's Work: Women in the Union, at Home and on the Job." The focus of the conference's lobby of MPPs from the three provincial party caucuses would be homework.

The lobby was a huge success. The ILGWU presented what it had learned about the situation of homeworkers and announced the Coalition's legislative proposals to the four hundred conference delegates, assembled press and politicians.

"Kitty,"[24] a member of the Homeworkers Association, addressed the conference and each group of MPPs, opening each section of the lobby by telling her own story.

The Coalition catapulted the Clean Clothes Campaign into the public eye by releasing the names of high-profile designers whose high-priced clothes were being produced by homeworkers for less than minimum wage — Alfred Sung, Jones New York, Linda Lundstrom, Lida Baday. The *Globe and Mail* gave the story front page coverage the next day.

The Conservative and Liberal caucuses had little to say in response to the Coalition or to questions about homework from conference delegates. The minister of labour led the NDP caucus. He promised changes to the *Employment Standards Act* to protect homeworkers and the establishment of a Task Force on Broader-Based Bargaining.[25]

The apparel industry took the campaign very seriously. Big-wigs from the major firms phoned the union when they heard there might be a rally outside their stores. Dylex issued a press release detailing its response to allegations in the *Globe and Mail* article that its goods were being manufactured by homeworkers who were not receiving minimum wages. Dylex offered to participate in discussions on amendments to the *Employment Standards Act*.[26] Linda Lundstrom took out private ads claiming that homeworkers were part of her "family."[27] Articles in the manufacturers' association newspaper denounced the ILGWU's researcher. One designer threatened to sue the *Globe and Mail* reporter.

The grand finale of the Coalition's work for the year was the November conference — "From the Double Day to the Endless Day: A Conference on Homeworking for Homeworkers, Union and Community Activists and Researchers," co-sponsored by the ILGWU, PSAC and the York University Centre for Research on Work and Society.

Jane Tate and Kuldeep Bajwa came from the West Yorkshire Homeworkers' Unit to help put the situation in Toronto in its international perspective and to talk about the work they were doing. Berzabeth Corona from the executive committee of the September 19th Union in Mexico, Ligia Orozco from the Women's Secretariat of the Sandinista Workers' Central in Nicaragua and Kathleen Christensen from the United States came to talk about the situation of garment workers and homeworkers in those three countries.

Members of the Homeworkers' Association actively participated in at least part of the weekend conference.[29] Participants gave support to the United Food and Commercial Workers' Union (UFCW) Local 175. These order-takers were on strike against Pizza Pizza because it had contracted out their jobs to a non-union firm employing homeworkers using computer terminals in their residences.[30]

The 130 women and men at the conference attended workshops which put the issue of homeworking, both industrial and electronic, in the context of global economic trends and exposed the myths about homeworking. They met in smaller workshops to discuss the implications for and the links between homework and the fight against racism, the needs of immigrant workers and disabled workers, health and safety, union organizing, child care and child labour. On the final day they met to strategize about building labour-community coalitions, organizing homeworkers, working for legislative changes and enforcement and building international solidarity.

On the Saturday of the Conference the Coalition led a rally to launch the Clean Clothes Campaign outside the Eaton's Centre, handing out information to Saturday shoppers and asking people to mail postcards to the presidents of Eaton's, the Hudson's Bay and Dylex. It was attended by more than four hundred enthusiastic people, including many participants from an international feminist and anti-racism conference.[31]

Fighting for Legislative Reform

Since its formation in 1991 the Coalition has adopted a three-pronged strategy on law reform: to seek changes to the *Employment Standards Act* (ESA)[32] aimed at ensuring equitable treatment of homeworkers, to advocate effective enforcement of the *Act*, and to develop and seek implementation of broader-based bargaining mechanisms under the

Ontario Labour Relations Act[32] which would allow homeworkers to organize and act collectively in their own interests.

The *Employment Standards Act* must be amended to cover all homeworkers. Homeworkers who are involved in the production of goods are protected by the *Act*, but those engaged in the delivery of services are not necessarily. The Coalition has argued that the *Act* needs to define homework more broadly to respond to its rapid expansion into new areas, particularly electronic homework such as order-taking for fast-food chains, data-entry operations and other types of service provision.

There is a considerable promotion and romanticization of "micro-industries" and small entrepreneurs in popular currency.[34] An understanding of the real situation of homeworkers is hampered by this trend. The Coalition is aware that it will have to devote attention — soon — to developing a clearer distinction, politically and legislatively, between employees whose work is performed at home and independent contractors or small businesses. Without this, homeworkers will continue to have no, or piece-meal, eligibility for the full range of legislated programs and benefits such as unemployment insurance, the Canada Pension Plan, workers' compensation and health and safety protection.

The pyramid in the garment industry illustrates clearly that employment law also has to address the question "Who is the employer?" The Coalition has called for the *Employment Standards Act* to be amended to establish joint liability for minimum standards throughout the subcontracting pyramid.[35] If the corporations at the top of the pyramid call the shots, clearly they must be obliged to accept responsibility for ensuring adherence to minimum standards by all of the dependent sub-contractors below. This form of regulation already occurs on a sporadic basis in the United States[36] and has been legislated in the Philippines and the Netherlands. A change of this nature would mean that small sub-contractors could not try to increase their competitive advantage by violating minimum wage or other employment law. It would also give recourse up the pyramid to homeworkers who are frequently left stranded, their wages unpaid, by sub-contractors who set up and disappear with alarming rapidity.

Homeworkers must often rely on several sub-contractors for work.

They don't work enough hours or weeks for any one employer to qualify for pregnancy or parental leave, termination pay, overtime pay or unemployment insurance. The Coalition argued that homeworkers should be able to register their work for any or all related contractors in one central "account" so that it accumulates and accurately reflects their work-weeks. Where such sub-contractors are dependent upon common manufacturers, jobbers or retailers within the pyramid, joint liability could provide the basis upon which homeworkers could meet the continuity of service requirements for pregnancy and parental leave, termination pay and other provisions of the *Employment Standards* and other Acts.

While the *Employment Standards Act* recognizes that some if not all homeworkers are employees, it excludes them from maximum hours of work, overtime rates and statutory holiday provisions. This contradiction indicates the ambivalent attitude of legislators to the employment status of homeworkers. Elimination of these exemptions would allow homeworkers to curtail, or at least receive compensation for, one of the more notorious abuses associated with this form of industrial organization. Homeworkers complain of impossibly tight schedules for the delivery and completion of work and very long hours of frenzied activity, often on weekends and holidays.

Dropping these exclusions is relatively easy, as they are set out in regulations not in the law itself. Regulations do not require approval of the legislature, but may be added, deleted or revised by a Cabinet Order-in-Council. As the Coalition has pointed out to government ministers and officials for more than a year, this could be changed at any time, unilaterally, by the government of the day. The Coalition is still waiting.

The law, however, is not worth a pile of beans (or a pyramid of sweat shirts), if it is not enforced. Ontario's *Employment Standards Act* is largely not enforced. The *Act* has been called a "paper tiger" and the Employment Practices Branch a "not very effective collection agency." The most serious problem with enforcement is that the Employment Practices Branch can really do nothing when a worker is fired for filing a complaint about her or his employer. Because of the precarious nature of their employment, it is particularly difficult for homeworkers to demand the rights to which the law says they are entitled. In all of its briefs and presentations, the Coalition argues for enforcement of the *Act* before it argues for changes to the *Act,* just to make the point.

Employers hiring homeworkers in Ontario are required to hold a permit and to register the names and addresses of these employees. Only seventy-five were registered in 1991. The ILGWU estimates there are more than 2,000 garment homeworkers in Metro Toronto alone. To prod employers and the Employment Practices Branch, the Coalition and the ILGWU submitted to the Director of the Branch a list of fourteen employers that were not using permits in the spring of 1992. The response has been a game of bureaucratic hot potato. The list has been sent back and forth between regulatory agencies, employers have been given applications for permits, and nothing has been accomplished eight months later.

The Employment Practices Branch explains its inability to enforce the law by pointing to its chronic under-funding. This is a problem, of course, which is impossible for the Coalition to resolve. The only recourse is noise, action and greater pressure about the rise of precarious employment and the critical importance of employment standards in protecting vulnerable workers.

Working for better employment standards law — one that has some teeth — must be accompanied by efforts to assist homeworkers to organize in trade unions, if they so choose. As described above, the Coalition has been active in the campaign to amend the *Ontario Labour Relations Act* to allow more workers to exercise freely their right to join a union through some type of broader-based bargaining. This model would allow the extension of the benefits of collective bargaining to workers in sectors characterized by small workplaces, homework and other precarious employment which do not lend themselves to the traditional single-employer bargaining unit model of unionization.

The Coalition's three-pronged approach to legal reform has been advanced by a combined strategy of lobbying both political and bureaucratic staff, public education through workshops, conferences and the mass media, participation in other coalitions and legal casework with the Homeworkers' Association.

What Next

There is no conclusion to this story. It is part of a living campaign, one that will spread and grow in the time following the activities described here. Union organizing and negotiating, building the Coalition, lobbying government, publicizing the Clean Clothes Campaign, pressuring retailers, contacting homeworkers, fingering unlawful contractors, building the Association, increasing public awareness, learning more about homework and women's employment have all continued since this article was written.

As the Coalition headed into 1993, the campaign for legislative change was at the top of its agenda. The Ontario government had made a promise, but the Coalition was convinced that it would have to keep up the pressure to hold them to that promise.

The Clean Clothes Campaign was just beginning. More research had to be done. More education had to be done about the causes and effects of women working in isolation in their homes for abysmal wages, with no benefits and without child care.

The Coalition for Fair Wages and Working Conditions for Homeworkers[37] brought together community workers, trade unionists, religious leaders, lawyers, academics and, most importantly, homeworkers. The basis of solidarity uniting the diverse membership of the Coalition is the realization that homeworkers are on the front lines of a common struggle for decent wages and working conditions, in the face of massive economic restructuring. If we are to win, sisterhood had better be powerful.

Notes

1. Statistics Canada, 1992.
2. Census Metropolitan Area.
3. Statistics Canada as reported in *The Toronto Star*, September 21, 1992 p. A1. (Forty-three percent of the overall workforce was born outside Canada.)
4. Employment estimates from Statistics Canada's Cat. 72-002: Employment, Earnings and Hours.
5. Statistics Canada counts only workers employed in factories and shops. While employers are required to register homeworkers under permit,

enforcement is lax. Therefore no way of knowing the number of home-workers in the industry exists. Unless or until we know how many jobs have gone from factories and shops to homeworkers, we cannot know the actual job loss in the industry.

6. Hudson's Bay Co. *Annual Report, 1991*; Dylex. *Annual Report, 1991*; *The Financial Post's* "Report Card on Dylex," 1991.

7. See the Economic Council of Canada. "Good Jobs, Bad Jobs: Employment in the Service Economy" (Ottawa: Ministry of Supply and Services, 1990); A. Yalnizyan in "Full Employment Still a Viable Goal" in *Getting on Track: Social Democratic Strategies for Ontario* (Montreal: McGill-Queen's Press, 1991); H. Krahn in "Non-Standard Work Arrangements" in *Perspectives on Labour and Income* in Statistics Canada's Cat. 75-001E, Winter 1991.

8. G. Standing in "Global Feminization through Flexible Labour" in 17 *World Development* 1007 (1989) p. 1079.

9. S. Mitter. *Common Fate, Common Bond: Women in the Global Economy* (London: Pluto Press, 1986).

10. For an overview of flexibility strategies see M. Macdonald in "Post-Fordism and the Flexibility Debate" in *Studies in Political Economy*, Autumn 1992, pp. 171-201; S. Wood. *The Transformation of Work* (London: Unwin Hyman, 1989).

11. Barbara Cameron. "Chinese-Speaking Homeworkers in Toronto: Summary of Results of a Survey." Conducted by the International Ladies' Garment Workers Union (Toronto: ILGWU, 1991).

12. S. Rowbotham and S. Mitter. *Dignity and Daily Bread*. (forthcoming).

13. For more information on the history of organizing homeworkers, see E. Boris and C. Daniels. *Homework: Historical and Contemporary Perspectives on Paid Labour at Home* (Chicago: University of Illinois Press, 1989); West Yorkshire Homeworking Group. *A Penny a Bag: Campaigning on Homework* (Batley: Yorkshire and Humberside Low Pay Unit, 1990). S. Rowbotham. *Homeworkers Worldwide* (London: Merlin Press, 1993).

14. Unless otherwise specified, references to the ILGWU in the Coalition and in the organizing of homeworkers mean the ILGWU Ontario District.

15. S. Rowbotham. *Op. cit.*

16. One of the first examples was the Service Employees' International Union, which linked up with a feminist working women's group, "9 to 5," in the U.S. in an attempt to organize clerical workers into an associate member-

ship group through feminist processes such as consciousness-raising. See
K. Moddy. *An Injury to All* (London: Verso, 1989). p. 279.

17. Homeworkers' real names are not used in this article, to protect them from
retaliation by their employers.

18. The AIM convention ran concurrently with the ILGWU convention.

19. The Port Elgin Family Education Centre is a Canadian Auto Workers
facility.

20. Statisticians report that one-third of part-time workers (eight-five percent
of whom are women) are involuntary part-time workers — they want
full-time work and can't find it. They do not count or report the number of
part-time workers who would be working full-time if they had affordable,
dependable child-care, if they had enough help with domestic tasks, if the
amount of money they could earn working full-time would pay for childcare, if they could get access to training to upgrade their language or
technical skills...Twenty-nine of the thirty homeworkers surveyed by the
ILGWU would rather work outside the home but could not surmount some
or all of these barriers.

21. The press were invited to come in to the meeting with the minister but did
not. They waited for him outside to ask about business' position on Bill 40
but apparently had no interest in what a group of women thought about it.

22. The first Clean Clothes Campaign was a campaign for public health stand-
ards and enforcement at the beginning of this century. See C. Daniels in
"Between Home and Factory: Homeworkers and the State" in Boris and
Daniels, *op. cit.*, pp. 13-31.

23. Traidcraft, Kingsway, Gateshead, England.

24. Despite the Coalition's precautions, there were reprisals for "Kitty's" participation in the OFL women's conference. Her employer cut off her supply
of work. She remains active in the Homeworkers' Association.

25. The events that morning were pure theatre. The two members of the
Conservative caucus, the first to appear, had clearly not bothered to be
briefed about the issue or what to expect at the lobby. Imagine MPPs going
to a gathering of four hundred employers and not being briefed in advance!
The delegates laughed, booed and hissed as the MPPs claimed to know
nothing about the issue or what could be done about it. The three members
of the Liberal caucus were slightly better briefed but couldn't answer the
questions. They said they were sure their party would support improved

legislative protection for homeworkers, but they would have to take everything back to the Caucus. The NDP government caucus was last. Bob McKenzie, the Minister of Labour, led a delegation of thirteen MPPs, including several other cabinet ministers.

26. Dylex had participated in the public hearings on the proposed amendments to the *Ontario Labour Relations Act* in the summer. It was opposed to the government's proposals. If it participates in discussions on amendments to the *ESA* regarding homeworkers, there is some doubt it will argue the same position as the Coalition.

27. It is the Coalition's understanding that at the time Lundstrom had not obtained a permit to employ homeworkers as required by the Ontario *Employment Standards Act*.

28. Conference proceedings are available from the co-sponsors.

29. Homeworkers usually have bundles dropped off on Friday that have to be sewn by Monday, so most had to work part of the weekend.

30. The UFCW, like the ILGWU, has attempted to negotiate inclusion of the homeworkers in their collective agreement. Kentucky Fried Chicken phone orders also go to homeworkers.

31. Canadian Research Institute for the Advancement of Women international conference, "Making the Links: Feminism and Anti-racism," November 1992.

32. The *Employment Standards Act* sets out minimum employment standards for most non-unionized workers in Ontario minimum wage, hours of work, vacation pay, pregnancy and parental leave, public holidays, overtime pay and termination. While the Coalition has considered the problems associated with homeworkers' entitlement to other legislated benefits and programs such as unemployment insurance and workers' compensation, its focus to date has been on the *Employment Standards Act*.

33. The *Ontario Labour Relations Act* governs the conditions of unionization and the relations between trade unions and employers in Ontario.

34. This can be seen, for example, in recent changes to UI, allowing for receipt of benefits while setting up a small business, in the spate of laudatory articles in the media about the advantages of home-based entrepreneurship, in community legal clinics' experience of an increase in attempts by employers to designate employees as "independent contractors" and even in the transformation of erstwhile "activists" into "consultants."

35. See the Coalition for Fair Wages and Working Conditions for Homeworkers' November 1991 "Brief to the Government of Ontario" for more details about definitional change and "related employer."

36. For example, the U.S. company Guess? has agreed to work with its contractors to ensure that minimum wage, overtime and other requirements of the *Fair Labour Standards Act* are met. The agreement, a form of contract compliance between Guess? and the Department of Labour will serve as one model for enforcing the *Fair Labour Standards Act* in the garment industry. See Department of Labour Review. "Current Developments Newsletter," No. 152, 8-6-92, A-9, 1992.

37. The authors decided not to use individual names in telling the story of the Coalition as some people would get mentioned often because they were the public spokeswomen and others might not be named at all. This would not reflect the fact that everyone contributed a great deal to the work of the Coalition. Nonetheless, we think it is important to acknowledge that it takes committed individuals to work for social change, not just faceless committees. We wish to acknowledge the following individuals: Alex Dagg (Ontario district manager of the International Ladies' Garment Workers' Union), Dr. Barbara Cameron (who conducted the initial research for the ILGWU), Teresa Mak of the ILGWU, Jan Borowy (currently research coordinator of the ILGWU), Danny Sun (ILGWU organizer), Holly Du (organizer for the Homeworkers' Association), Deena Ladd (ILGWU conference organizer), Liz Fraser, Kathleen Doran and Rachel Seed (placement students at the ILGWU who assisted the Coalition), Shelly Gordon and David Kidd (Worker's Information and Action Centre of Toronto), Judy Fudge (Osgoode Hall Law School, representing NAC), Gayle Lebans, Sheila Cuthbertson, Gail Sax, Joanne Seamon, Kim Armstrong and Laryssa Holynsky (staff and students from Parkdale Community Legal Services), Barbara Paleczny (Sisters of Notre Dame and Ecumenical Coalition for Economic Justice), Linda Yanz (Mujer a Mujer), Jennifer Stephen (Metro Labour Education Centre), Carla Lipsig-Mummé (York University Centre for Research on Work and Society), Margaret Oldfield, Sue Jones and Helen Jackson (Public Service Alliance of Canada), Belinda Leach (McMaster University), Sandra Awang, Salome Loucas (Women Working with Immigrant Women), Julie Davis (secretary-treasurer of the Ontario Federation of Labour), Carrol Anne Sceviour (Ontario Federation of Labour). Even that

list leaves out others whose assistance and support have been critical and those who have begun to participate in the Coalition more recently.

V

VOICE, EMPOWERMENT
AND CHANGE

WOMEN ON THE FRONT LINE

AIDS Activists in Discussion

This discussion between
Darien Taylor, Dionne Falconer and Linda Gardner
was facilitated and edited by Martha Ayim.

Expanded from an interview prepared for the 1994 *Everywoman's Almanac* on women's resistance to state oppression, this discussion has become a dynamic coming together of women whose work is integral both to feminist AIDS (Acquired Immune Deficiency Syndrome) activism in Canada and to understanding and documenting that activism.

Interested in AIDS issues since high school, Dionne Falconer became an AIDS activist through her work in the Black Women's Collective and the Black Coalition for AIDS Prevention (Black CAP) as it started up and sought community representation on the board and in the organization.

Linda Gardner works at the Bay Centre for Birth Control as the STD (Sexually Transmitted Disease) and HIV (Human Immunodeficiency Virus) program coordinator. Her background in women's health, she began working in HIV in 1985 as a counsellor at Hassle Free Clinic. She has been active in AIDS Action Now!, Community AIDS Treatment Information Exchange, Gay Asians AIDS Project and Maggie's Prostitutes for Safer Sex Project.

In 1989 Darien Taylor joined AIDS Action Now! where she presently works with Linda. Working with the men and women at AIDS Action Now! gave her the strength, capability and political understanding to start Voices of Positive Women, an organization run by and for women living with AIDS.

Anatomy of AIDS Activism

DARIEN: I wouldn't have become an activist before finding out I was HIV positive — shamefully! I was a university student. And that would've been how I identified myself. I felt I was more connected with what was happening on the streets than some people in the academy. I marched on International Women's Day once a year but that was the extent of it. Being HIV positive has been totally transforming. When I talk about transformation, I'm not talking about it being in a necessarily positive way.

There were a whole bunch of people that I lost when I got involved with AIDS. The major complaint of friends that I keep in touch with less than I did before is: "You're always talking about AIDS." What *else* would I be talking about? Is there anything else to talk about? It's only when I'm in situations that are not AIDS-focused that I realize a lot people don't talk much about AIDS. For a couple of years, I've had relationships that are pretty stable and AIDS-oriented. Before that, though, was a terrible time. I was adjusting to a life that's centred on AIDS and I was losing friends left, right and centre. People just couldn't talk about AIDS as much as I needed to talk about it. Even now, it's important for me to be with people that I can talk to about AIDS.

I've been doing AIDS work for a long time. We're in a community where we deal with the issues that are on the edge. The people in this discussion do that kind of on-the-edge thinking. Sometimes I find it hard, working in Voices of Positive Women, because a lot of the women are new to the AIDS movement and I continually go back and cover a lot of old territory with them. And yet I have this need to be with women, with people in general, who can help me formulate the stuff that's right out there at the edge of the movement. It means I don't want to spend time with people who want to talk about something other than AIDS.

DIONNE: Definitely. When I'm in situations where people are not as close to AIDS issues as I am, I end up being teacher because they know that this is the work that Dionne does.

DARIEN: It's like: what can sustain *you* because you also want somebody to teach you or to help you move ahead, right?

DIONNE: Exactly.

DARIEN: It's a hunger to talk about these things.

DIONNE: That's why I get back to that closer bunch who know what all the issues are and who are, as you say, Darien, at the edge of the movement.

LINDA: There are a number of social events coming up for AIDS Action Now! At one of the events we will try and get people to dance. Some people have jokingly said, "Oh that's going to be really hard because all AIDS activists want to do is talk AIDS politics." While that's not exactly true, I think that's where we get our energy, though maybe we're slightly excessive.

DARIEN: There's a common patronizing attitude that it is better to regulate women around their sexuality and their HIV status than it is to give them information that will help them determine their own sexuality, determine their own behaviour. There is a real emphasis on legislation, and it particularly affects women. When Voices of Positive Women published a pamphlet on HIV-positive women's sexuality — and the context was completely about safe sex — we mentioned that it was all right to have sex without telling your partner that you were HIV-positive as long as you used safe sex. There was such outrage about that. We thought that this was a position an organization could take — that you were responsible for safe sex, not for disclosing your HIV status. The angry response to the brochure came because it was about women's sexuality and the idea that we could make decisions that couldn't be regulated by the state, that couldn't be regulated by men. It's interesting that sometimes you don't realize you are in an unsafe place until you step out of it.

LINDA: A lot of what we struggle around in our AIDS work has to do with how the state has tried to regulate and control our sexuality.

DIONNE: Another issue is legislation. Legislating disclosure is neither useful nor effective. I agree with both of you that legislation is about controlling women once again, controlling women's bodies, our sexuality, our reproduction — all aspects of our being.

DARIEN: The AIDS work we do is part of a larger struggle. But sometimes I feel a danger because there's a tendency to jump off from issues that I'm very much focused on — getting treatments for people so that they can live longer, transforming AIDS into a disease that people don't die of — and to move out to systemic health issues and social issues that we're going to have to work on for a long time to see any sort of progress. On the one hand, I feel we should think about the work that we do in the context of women's issues, social issues, issues of poverty, marginalization, race and so on. And on the other hand, I think, "No, no, no, that's work for somebody else to do. That's not my work. My work is about people with HIV. Stay focused and don't get seduced away by prevention, don't get seduced away by poverty issues, don't get seduced away by marginalization issues."

LINDA: I would echo what Darien has said, but I do believe that the very nature of our work means we are impacting on broader social and economic issues. People involved with HIV come from a wide variety of backgrounds and bring with them all of the inequities and oppressions of our society. While I'm as reluctant as Darien — because of the urgency of AIDS work — to say that we see the work that we do focuses on longer-term goals, I think that our day-to-day work is very much shaped by the need for broader societal changes. AIDS activists are forcing changes in the larger society.

DIONNE: I see AIDS activism in connection to the struggle against racism, sexism, heterosexism, marginalization and all struggles against oppression.

DARIEN: AIDS work is extremely complex. In the past six months there has been a lot of death in the community; that's really depleting, so I'm maybe feeling defeated right now. The things that I find confusing and difficult are connected to my work with HIV-positive women through Voices of Positive Women and how slow that work is. There's not a lot of support for that speed of work. Funders don't support that, other community groups don't support that. We're a group that has to work enormously slowly to keep a commitment to bringing HIV-positive women into the work that we do. There's an incredible pressure — from funders mostly — to leave HIV-positive women behind, in order to go faster, to meet deadlines, to complete the work that you're supposed to complete as a condition of funding, to be everywhere on the AIDS map that you're supposed to be as a funded organization. It's not an incredibly supportive environment.

When I go into meetings with government I'm horrified, disappointed and increasingly angry that government just does not understand the basic things that we've repeated over and over for years. They just haven't understood. It makes me cynical and angry about the process, particularly in the work that we do with AIDS Action Now! When we negotiate with government we must be increasingly tough to make sure that people hear us and know that we're going to be on the streets if they don't.

LINDA: I do think working with the government is very difficult for us in the AIDS movement. There are many different levels, departments, committees and people involved. The government does not want to address our issues. We've been successful as AIDS activists, nonetheless, and the contradiction of that is that we are asked to advise and consult on a lot of things. I think what Darien is speaking about is whether we are being co-opted in this process.

AIDS Action Now! has spent a lot of its time focusing on the provincial government. Drug funding for catastrophic illnesses, HIV/AIDS, optimal standards of care, non-coercive public health policies, adequate living conditions and support services are some policy areas. We work collaboratively with the community and AIDS service organizations whose advocacy work is sometimes hampered by their funding relationships with the government.

DIONNE: There is always the fear of being co-opted in political organizing because it happens so often. As activists we feel the responsibility to be present, in order for our issues to be raised in a concrete and supportive way that will effect change. So we don't want to be co-opted, but we also feel that we've got to let them hear us.

Even with all the work and activism that's happening, funding keeps getting cut back. Right now, there's a lot of struggle because the federal funding initiative runs out in March 1993. What does that mean for organizations who depend on that? With the expectation of funding being cut back, the tendency is to do more work, generate more things, put out more materials. We are expected to do more with less — even a fairly new organization like Black CAP. It wasn't until 1989, two years after the inception of Black CAP, that any kind of money got to the organization. What we have produced over the past three years is tremendous, given the amount of funding we've received. Now we're feeling like we need to slow down. People are going to burn out very quickly because of the speed at which we've been going. We need to cut back, but, as Darien was saying, "You've got to finish that proposal, meet that deadline, produce these materials."

LINDA: There is another aspect to burn-out that we face in the AIDS movement, an aspect that other progressive movements may not have to deal with to the same extent. There is burnout and turnover for sure. But in the AIDS movement we are faced with the loss of our community leaders and activists who are dying from the disease. I don't know how or if we are actually coming to grips with that.

At times I feel really weak emotionally because of the loss of friends and fellow activists. The very thing that is energizing about our work and keeps us going is that everyone is working together to fight this disease. The personal loss is very difficult to deal with. Then you just get angrier and angrier at government inaction and the slow response and you get even more motivated around AIDS activism.

DARIEN: I find it hard, especially when I look at the work that has to be done in Voices of Positive Women. I know this is work that is going to go on after I'm *dead*, and it's really hard to think about that. I'm not going to be here beyond even the beginnings of this organization.

There's an impression that the AIDS community is always fighting among itself and people say, "Now why is the AIDS community like that? Why is there such bitterness and conflict in this community?" And to me it's *so* obvious. It's because we're always dealing with death. We don't have to blame it on personalities, the way people often do when they ask those sorts of questions. AIDS is such a difficult area to work in. The successes that we may have with government and the successes that we may have organizationally don't begin to balance the lack of success that we've had in terms of cure for this disease or the lack of reasonable treatment.

DIONNE: Within AIDS activism, as Linda said, I don't know if we've really talked about or dealt with death. Death is a reality and when it happens we go through our emotions but then we move on. Sometimes I wonder how am I dealing with the many deaths that have occurred over the past year. It's become a part of the work. Part of my paid work is to help people prepare for death emotionally as well as practically. I help people with wills, funeral arrangements and after-death issues with their friends, families and lovers. These are very difficult things to talk about and do. I don't know if I stop to think "Dionne, what's happening for you in all of this?" because I'm so busy making sure that everything's in place. I don't have a real answer —

DARIEN: — a way of talking about it.

DIONNE: Yeah.

DARIEN: I think that's true.

DIONNE: Because I don't talk about it very often. We don't really talk about death, not in a way that we need to.

DARIEN: But people do themselves a disservice if they don't think about AIDS, don't get involved with people with AIDS or AIDS organizations because they are afraid of what death looks like. It's hard to find words for what we've learned about death, but it's not something that makes us want to run away from the work that we do.

DIONNE: If death is the reason why people don't want to get involved in AIDS, that's not good enough. Since April of 1992, I've had five people I know die. It's not that with each death it becomes easier. With each person there are different feelings. But then I look at where that person was at the time of their death. Was it for them something good or bad? Some people had come to an acceptance of their death, which made it easier to deal with.

DARIEN: On the one hand, I don't ever want to "accept" AIDS. That's why I'm working hard for a cure for AIDS. It's *not* okay to die from AIDS. But then I think the experiences that we have with people as they die are … I don't know what they are. All I can say is they're experiences that make me want to stay involved with people with AIDS.

DIONNE: Yes. Me too, definitely. I also find it interesting that AIDS has become the focal point in my life — a lot of my friends are also connected to AIDS work or to people living with HIV or AIDS. I think of it as something that's good because AIDS has a lot of challenges. I've had some really supportive friends, so when I'm tired or somebody that was close to me has died, I know that I have some place that I can go, people that I can go and talk to, sisters who will listen and be there for me.

LINDA: In the last few years, it feels as if AIDS has taken over every aspect of my life. I work and spend a lot of my personal time in this area. Like Dionne, a lot of my friends are involved in AIDS politics.

DIONNE: People I used to have connections with prior to getting involved in the work, we don't spend as much time together anymore. I get into this cycle where AIDS is in my world all the time. All of it comes home. So I don't feel a separateness between the work I do and AIDS activism generally because everything is intertwined. I think of activism in a broad sense. Sometimes when we think of activism we think of demonstrating in the streets. Activism could be socializing with people who might not be aware of all the issues; suddenly you feel you're doing this work because you're trying to get them to realize all the issues around AIDS and that they need to get involved.

DARIEN: A point to be made, though, is that most funders of our organizations don't allow us to do advocacy work. So there is a separation between the work that we're paid for — where we're not supposed to do advocacy — and activist work. Like Voices of Positive Women isn't supposed to picket in front of the —

DARIEN, DIONNE, LINDA: — Ministry of Health.

DARIEN: At its peril. There is advocacy and activist work we can do through AIDS Action Now! because it doesn't receive government funding. To that extent, there is a separation between the work we do and AIDS activism in general. But I think it's a separation that all of us try to skirt. We try to do activism in our work even though that's not what we're supposed to do.

LINDA: My paid work and AIDS activism generally are one. I don't feel any separation. There are very little resources directed to HIV/AIDS services at my workplace. I just try to inundate the place with information and affect changes in attitudes and concerns. Asking for resources and raising issues are ways to do politics in the workplace. Darien's right, though, we're not paid to be advocates, and it can be very difficult to take that on at your workplace because the employment situation right now is not good and our jobs are our livelihood. I can't always push as hard as I would like.

DIONNE: Sometimes in meetings with funders I do see political activism happening when we come in with our agendas, talking about women, Black people or any community living with HIV. It can be a real struggle, though, to do that activism in our work.

DARIEN: At Voices of Positive Women we're spending a lot of time thinking about the role of HIV-negative women in this organization because we began as an organization for HIV-positive women only. Part of that exclusivity was due to the climate we began in, which was misogynistic and sexist and saw HIV-positive women purely as patients and clients to be kept in that role.

We began Voices of Positive Women in a real sense of anger. We weren't going to put up with that patronizing attitude. Now we've been around for a year and a half. I'm beginning to think that trying to run an organization out of the skills of HIV-positive women holds us back. We're not able to bring HIV-positive women on, in terms of their skills development, fast enough. It's difficult for us to acknowledge that we can't do all of this work ourselves and to envision a way that we could continue to direct the work of the organization while involving HIV-negative women. Eventually, this will be an exciting move for the organization.

What I see among HIV-positive women that is really strong is the survival decisions that we made on our own, with no information from the medical system. Decisions like having children when you know your doctor will not to support you. At the beginning of the epidemic, the medical profession was so punitive to women. But women moved on. And these are women who in a lot of cases are critically disadvantaged.

There are a lot of different bodies wanting representation by PWAs (People with AIDS) right now. There's a real tendency to just say, "Okay HIV-positive people, come on to our boards, come on to our working groups, come on to our advisory committees." But we need skills development if we are going to participate meaningfully; people need to know how to go onto these boards and committees in ways that advance our causes as PWAs.

LINDA: When I think about the other political work I've done in the women's health movement, I am amazed at the depth, variety of and access to resources that are available within the AIDS community. This has been quite different from my experiences working in the grassroots feminist movement where these kinds of resources seemed much more limited. It was harder to get our message out, to mobilize and to get the government to recognize us. Women don't have the financial resources that men do in our society and that has affected our ability to get our message out as quickly.

DARIEN: I stay in the AIDS struggle because I can't get out. For me — being HIV-positive — AIDS activism is not something that, if you're a really good activist, you'll be rewarded by a change in your HIV status. You're just stuck with it. The only thing that makes it tolerable is working against the increasingly conservative and repressive stuff that happens around AIDS, working with friends, with people that become your friends, keeping that whole active, friendly thing happening.

AIDS activism is sophisticated work. We take on difficult issues with the government, with the pharmaceutical industry, difficult issues around organizing. It's consuming work and yet people continue. I don't know where the energy comes from but it does come — and I think it's an enormous strength.

LINDA: We've gained a lot over the years, but every time we win something, we come up with more and more issues to deal with. It's very hard at times to keep going. But we do. We do find the energy. When some of us are low, others have the energy and we just build on that. That's a positive thing.

Feminist Support

DIONNE: The feminist movement hasn't picked up AIDS in a concrete, affirming and vocal way. The movement should not just pick up AIDS as a separate issue; AIDS should be incorporated into all the issues that we struggle for as feminists. So when we talk about reproductive rights we also talk about the reproductive rights of HIV-positive women. When we talk about choice, HIV-positive women should be recognized within that. When we talk about gender inequality and patriarchy, those issues are applicable to AIDS issues. When we talk about violence against women, we can look at how violent and abusive situations affect women's risk of getting HIV. But HIV-positive women's concerns don't get addressed within the movement like that. You don't hear people talk about giving support for sisters who are HIV-positive. That's something that needs to happen because a number of the women involved in AIDS activism are feminists, and all the burden is put on our shoulders to carry the weight when the whole movement should incorporate HIV as an issue.

DARIEN: I agree.

LINDA: The movement has been slow to pick up issues that feminism needs to pick up about women living with HIV. Recently there's been a lot of activity. But early in the epidemic women were not seen to be at risk for HIV. It has been hard to get people to deal with this. The work that I am involved in now is to try and broaden the support network.

DARIEN: I support a lot of what both of you are saying I found out that I was HIV-positive about five or six years ago. It was hard finding support. But support is not enough. When I did find support, the whole model of support that was out there for women was very patronizing. It was the client and patient model: "We'll take care of you" and "Don't you worry about getting involved in the organizations that are deciding what services to deliver for you." Getting services delivered to HIV-positive women by HIV-positive women was done by a small group of HIV-positive women. It's been really hard getting other people, other women, on side. A lot of my support in the beginning came from HIV-positive men and continues to come from them. In the main, it's very hard to get women, even women who are interested in AIDS issues, to recognize that it's not only a prevention issue, it's also an issue of women *living* with AIDS.

People have never been very good about distinguishing between the needs of the general public and the needs of people living with HIV and AIDS. When feminists have taken up the issue of women and HIV, it's mostly been in terms of education and prevention. It's seldom that you see someone in touch with the needs of HIV-positive women, someone who has thought through and can articulate our needs.

Linda and I have been talking recently about contact tracing and the reportability of HIV. We know that there are feminists who argue that women want contact tracing (where public health asks you for the names of your partners when you're determined to be HIV-positive because they want to know if your partners are HIV-positive or not). But contact tracing *doesn't* work for HIV-positive women. Contact tracing for HIV-positive women is actually very dangerous because the men can figure out who of their girlfriends or sex partners supplied their name to public health. And they can harass the woman, they can be violent to her. So there is a very dangerous line being put out in government, in public health, that women want contact tracing. HIV-positive women certainly don't. And nobody's listening to that.

LINDA: In terms of feminist support, one of the first organizations that allied and worked with AIDS Action Now! was the Ontario Coalition for Abortion Clinics (OCAC). Women's control over our reproductive and sexual health is under constant threat. The experiences women with HIV in the United States were facing — coerced abortion and sterilization, lack of choice over pregnancy, violence and so on — are real possibilities for women in Canada.

AIDS Action Now! has been active in International Women's Day, where we have raised issues women with HIV are facing. But in general, AIDS Action Now! has not made woman-specific demands as visible as we could have.

DIONNE: I don't want a message to go out that it's just feminists who are not working on these issues. We need to guard against falling into that trap. Feminist support on AIDS issues needs to be looked at in perspective. Within the feminist movement there are definitely slow changes happening. Sometimes when I talk about the slowness of other feminists picking up AIDS issues, my frustration comes from the fact that I'm used to work in AIDS moving fast because of what HIV is.

DARIEN: I'm really interested in what you're saying. I ask myself why it is that there's this reluctance to pick this issue up. I've tried to puzzle this through, the reluctance to work with people who have ways of working that are slow, non-political, under-skilled. It's enormously hard. The impulse among most of us is just to run away, to run away to our friends that we have good talks with, friends that have the analysis. We leave behind those people who lack all those things.

DIONNE: I find in myself and in other people who have achieved a certain level of political consciousness that we become impatient with those who have not achieved the same level. Maybe we need to recognize that people have different styles. Where they might not have achieved a certain political consciousness about an issue that I have, in fact they might be more politically astute in other things than I am. I need to check those thoughts. I'm thinking, too, about Voices of Positive Women and realizing that it's a slower process. But then I also think about women gaining political consciousness about feminism and how that was a slow process also. People do have different speeds.

DARIEN: But Dionne, I often don't see that awareness at meetings where HIV-positive women have been encouraged to attend. We're beginning to acknowledge the problems of involving HIV-positive women, but it's been difficult for HIV-positive women — who aren't accustomed to the acronyms that we use or haven't been part of the feminist movement and haven't thought through the whole political agenda — to come out. They come to the meetings and they're at sea. That's okay if there are women there who are willing to take HIV women aside and buddy with them and say, "Look I'll explain things to you. Let's trade phone numbers." But I don't see that happening. That was disappointing to me because I know that we all went through that at one point. We weren't born with political consciousness. We've struggled so much in Voices of Positive Women. We need help, and that people didn't take on that piece of work was hurtful. Similarly, in AIDS Action Now! there's been a problem with people coming into the organization, where we just kind of said, "You either get the acronyms or you don't!" Inclusion is something that we have to work on.

Women, AIDS and Academia

DARIEN: Since many of the phone calls that we get are from students, it feels like AIDS is always an academic subject. A point that needs to be made, though, is that the insensitivity of researchers to women and AIDS has been quite astounding. Like, "Would you mind if we put a tape recorder in your support group." I mean, we've had that suggested to us!

DIONNE: Or "Can you find us somebody's who's HIV-positive for us to interview?" Totally, totally insensitive.

DARIEN: The surveys that are twenty pages long come week after week after week. That's a lot of work. HIV-positive women are expected to do this without pay, for the benefit of somebody in the academy.

DIONNE: The interest in women and AIDS feels topical. Once that paper's done, then any connection that they might have to women living with HIV just cuts off right at the end of the school session. I don't like that. If somebody is going to take the research further, get politicized around the issues and decide to get more involved, then it will feel good. If my doing on interview means another person will get involved in the work, then that will be great. But oftentimes it doesn't mean that.

LINDA: I agree that students are suddenly picking women and AIDS as a topic. But what the context for this is I don't know — is there finally a real concern women about what women with HIV are facing?

DIONNE: We need to recognize that it is academic research that the government uses to validate who they fund. For example, in Canada there aren't statistics based on race, yet they use that as a reason not to give funding to people of Colour organizations because the numbers aren't there.

I don't think that we are saying that academic research is bad and negative. The problem is that it's done in what can be a very cold, academic way — "I'm just here to get the facts." Research is not being done in a way that is in anyway supportive to people living with HIV and specifically women living with HIV. It is a depersonalized, dehumanized, "objective" study.

DARIEN: It would be great if there was someone doing research who was already engaged in issues of women and AIDS. It was interesting when Andrea Rudd and I were working on *Positive Women*,[1] we thought we would get this well-known activist academic who was working on women and AIDS to help us get in touch with women's organizations internationally. We wrote away to her, asking if she should help us by giving us her mailing list on diskette. No response. Then we asked someone we knew here at the University of Toronto, who was a friend of hers, to write on our behalf. We never heard from her. That pissed me off because to me that was just another example of people that are up there in the academy who deign to look down once in a while on the poor little people that they're writing about.

DIONNE: It's as if some people become the "expert" and the "authority" and can come in and do the research because they have those skills, but they have no real connection to the community. Nor do they *feel* like they need to have any connection to the community. And that's a piss off, I mean, straight up, that's a piss off.

Documentation has been as issue for Black CAP. In Canada there's almost nothing written on Black people and HIV. We want to have work done around that but require people who are in the work to gain that skill because they also have the analysis. This is very different from somebody who has been going to school, is not connected to the issues in any way and for whom this is just another research paper.

Communities

LINDA: Defining my community is difficult for me. I am a Chinese Canadian woman, a feminist, a pro-choice and AIDS activist. I suppose my community is composed of those who share the same ideas and who are struggling with the same issues. That includes a wide variety of people for me.

DARIEN: My community is still in the process of describing itself. I would say where I feel absolutely most comfortable is among other people who are first of all HIV-positive and second of all like-minded, because it's not like I feel instant rapport with everyone that is HIV-positive. There's a small circle of people that I would include in "my community" who are HIV-negative.

DIONNE: In terms of Black CAP and our community, the information that we put out clearly states that our target audiences are the culturally diverse Black communities. We recognize that even under the umbrella of a community there are often many communities that sometimes have sharp differences in terms of identity. Within the Black community there is the Caribbean community which is different from the continental African community or the South American Black community, just as the gay, lesbian, bisexual community is different from the heterosexual population. It's also important for us to be cohesive; ultimately we are all Black and our origins are all the same.

Within the Black community, as a diverse population, there are many challenges, particularly doing work around HIV and AIDS. The Black community has a particular history and struggle. One of the big things within the community is around the ownership of AIDS, trying to take hold of it as a disease that affects us. It's easy to understand why people might not want to own it when we look at the history of how disease has been connected to Black people. When we look at the Tuskegee syphilis experiment that happened in the United States,[2] why would we want to own HIV when we've been blamed for this other disease and how it manifests itself? Issues come up around genocide; at most workshops and forums that we run, people want to know where AIDS came from. There are many people who believe that AIDS was specifically created to annihilate the gay as well as the Black population.

Looking at gender relations, condoms don't mean much to women who don't have the power to say to their partners, "You gotta use this." Getting the community to recognize that there is gender inequality and to show ways in which that manifests itself in relationships, while at the same time dealing with homophobia and heterosexism within our community, is a challenge. We also need to say that, though we are addressing homophobia and heterosexism, the Black community isn't any more homophobic than other communities or than society in general.

There has not been within the Black community enough support around AIDS as an issue for our people. When I look at other Black community organizations and people who are considered leaders in the Black community, they do not take up AIDS as an issue for our community and do not see the connection of AIDS to other issues that the community is dealing with. Part of it is their own denial of the impact that AIDS is having on the Black community.

There has been a change within the community, though. When Black CAP first started a number of people didn't want to associate with an organization that was dealing specifically with AIDS. Now it's moved to the point where people are calling to see how they can get involved. AIDS is seen as real in our community that we have to deal with. We see more of an ownership. That's really positive.

One of the strengths I see within AIDS activism is the challenging and confronting of issues. A lot of people say, "Well, AIDS is just a medical issue." But in fact it's not. It's a political, social and cultural issue. The kind of coming together of various communities in addressing AIDS, in confronting racism, sexism, homophobia and heterosexism, has been really positive.

I think one way that community and community support break down is when someone who is part of my circle of friends or connected to my work dies. Or when I see people who are ill right now and I know that death is coming soon. I don't know if that would be considered a breakdown of support, but I feel I'm acknowledging the loss of that connection, the loss of that person.

DARIEN: Organizationally, Voices hasn't done a good job of articulating to other organizations how they can support us because of the confusion that we have about exclusion/inclusion.

I think community support breaks down a lot around burn-out. All of us are working hard to support one another and to support one another's organizations. But people are really scared of burn-out. They run from it when they see someone burning out rather than saying, "How can we help? What can we do?" Everybody sees themselves in that person and wants to stay away. It's a little bit too close to home.

It's extremely hard to continue to do good work when people are dying around you. And you don't get any time off. I mean, your

organization can support you by giving you time off, but AIDS continues. You're in the AIDS community and people continuously want your
input, even when you're supposedly taking "time off."

LINDA: It feels like there's only a small number of people at any given
time in AIDS Action Now!, although when I look at the organization as
a whole, there's a huge number of people who come and do the odd
thing once in a while. There is an expectation from agencies that have
paid staff that somehow AIDS Action Now! should be able to be as on
top, if not more on top, of the issues than they are when in fact we don't
have paid staff.

The loss of people is very difficult. We have people who are extremely active and hold a lot of information. And again, there's not a lot
of other people who want to come in to hold that amount of information.
When their health is deteriorating or when they can no longer do that,
it's a problem. How do you share? I'm sure all organizations face that
on some level, but this is particularly so with AIDS Action Now!

The Impact of AIDS Activism

LINDA: There have been results. When you look at other chronic infec-
tions, diseases or serious illnesses and the lack of organizing, you see
that the AIDS movement has been incredibly effective at raising demands and improving conditions. It doesn't mean that we've got the
cure. But in terms of getting resources and having an impact on health
care policy in general, we have been effective. It's a slow process to
change how all health care is delivered.

DIONNE: AIDS has put homophobia on the map in a big way; people talk
about it a lot more and talk about sex and sexuality a lot more. That kind
of dialogue happening in society is really positive. Ten years ago it
wasn't happening like that. I'm glad to see that there has been movement
even though it's been slow.

DARIEN: I think the AIDS movement has been enormously effective, but
sometimes it's hard for me to see what my own work has contributed. I

ask myself if Voices of Positive Women has been successful in getting HIV-positive women to organize. It's been successful in getting HIV-positive women to come together. But we are talking about political organizing; I don't think we're there yet. What we've achieved that other groups haven't achieved, or are only beginning to achieve, is a solid core of women who recognize that this is their place. But I know that many women who see Voices as their organization see it as a place for support, see it as a place where they like to hang out, see it as a place where they'd like to volunteer. Political organizing is where we go in the future. There are some women in the organization right now that are beginning to get interested in the political organizing and some women — very few women — who have an abiding interest in political organizing.

LINDA: There are many legitimate reasons for Voices to be there. But it's not easy and you can get burned out when trying to deal with the total impact of the political agenda of HIV and AIDS all the time.

DARIEN: A lot of the women that I know through Voices of Positive Women are really afraid of the word "politics." And yet the needs of the women who come to Voices of Positive Women are political. To hear at the same time that they don't want to join AIDS Action Now! because that's a political group, or they don't want Voices of Positive Women to get "too political," is very frustrating.

LINDA: I also think that the nature of our lives as women makes it very difficult to take on this added time and energy. It's not made easy for us. If we have kids we're taking major responsibility for, or we have low-paid jobs, housing problems, etc., that makes it really, really hard to put in extra energy around political organizing that for the most part is unpaid and takes up lots of time.

DIONNE: Just getting together is a political act, whether or not people want to recognize that. I agree, Darien, that the women will move from Voices as a social gathering place to Voices as a political organization that's organizing around HIV and women with HIV. Some groups that I belong to also started as informal networks. We would get together once a month and socialize, and then suddenly we had gone through that stage and we needed to do something else. But it's also a lot of self-recognition that it is time to move on.

The Future of AIDS Organizing

DARIEN: We need to stay unco-opted. As long as we're aware of that danger then we're on track. Co-optation is always looming and we really need to be careful about it.

The pace in AIDS service organizations is absolutely brutal, and somehow, somehow we have to slow down enough to support one another and to do work that doesn't see as a solution that some people burn-out and other people come on. That's not a good way to work. There should be more strategies for sustaining people and for refreshing ourselves in the work that we do. If people don't realize that they need to slow down, it's because they're so caught up in the cycle that they haven't even had time to stop and look at it.

LINDA: We should be looking at who is setting the pace and why the pace is being set.

DARIEN: Yes.

LINDA: And that connects with not being co-opted. We have to look at that very clearly. Whose agenda are we trying to follow and why? When we're doing all this extra stuff for somebody else's needs, that is when it becomes problematic.

DIONNE: We need more active involvement from women living with HIV and people of Colour living with HIV. We need to be a part of all of it, whether we hit the streets or speak on platforms. We need to be a part of the decisions that get made.

DARIEN: I think mentoring and skills development are important. If people with HIV and women with HIV are going to be involved, there has to be a very consistent development of the skills so that they can participate. Mentoring is one way to do it. But there are other simple ways. For example, if Black CAP has some computers, let's get people with HIV on them because that's how people get involved in organizations. Then they can do the minutes of meetings, or reports, or whatever. We also need to pull doctors in. Doctors are often not well connected to the HIV community and we have to continually emphasize the importance of their involvement in the community of people working around these issues.

DIONNE: We need to celebrate our victories because there have been some. It hasn't all been negative. The pace of AIDS activism is so fast we sometimes don't stop to acknowledge victories or to do some kind of real affirmation. I've always longed for affirmation and celebration in the struggle because our lives are not just about struggling. The work that we are doing as individuals, as Darien, as Linda, as Dionne, is important work that should be recognized and treated as valuable. The organizations and the groups that we belong to are important and are doing some amazing things.

DARIEN: We need a cure for AIDS.

Notes

1. Darien Taylor and Andrea Rudd, eds. *Positive Women: Voices of Women Living with AIDS* (Toronto: Second Story Press, 1992).

2. The Tuskegee Syphilis Experiment, a forty-year experiment conducted by the United States Public Health Service from 1932 to 1972, monitored the effects of syphilis when left untreated in Black men. The deaths of as many as one hundred Black men, who were mostly poor, may have directly resulted from the complications of untreated syphilis in this experiment. See James H. Jones. *Bad Blood: The Tuskegee Syphilis Experiment* (New York: The Free Press, 1981).

THE GOOD RED ROAD

Journeys of Homecoming in

Native Women's Writing

Beth Brant

"There are those who think they pay me a compliment in saying that I am just like a white woman. My aim, my joy, my pride is to sing the glories of my own people. Ours is the race that taught the world that avarice veiled by any name is crime. Ours are the people of the blue air and the green woods, and ours the faith that taught men and women to live without greed and die without fear."[1]

Those are the words of Emily Pauline Johnson, Mohawk writer and actor. Born of an English mother and Mohawk father, Pauline Johnson began a movement that to this day has proved unstoppable in its momentum — the movement of First Nations women to write down our stories of history, of revolution, of sorrow, of love.

The Song My Paddle Sings

August is laughing across the sky
Laughing while paddle, canoe and I,
Drift, drift,
Where the hills uplift
On either side of the current swift.[2]

This is the familiar poem of Pauline Johnson, the one that schoolchildren, white schoolchildren, were taught. Her love of the land made her the poet she was. Yet, in reading Johnson, a non-Native might come away with the impression that she only wrote idyllic sonnets to the glory of nature or about the "noble savage" or "vanishing redman" themes that were popular at the turn of the century. It is time to take another look at Pauline Johnson.

The Cattle Thief

How have you paid us for our game? how paid us for
our land?
By a *book*, to save our souls from the sins *you* brought
in your other hand.
Go back with you new religion, we never have understood
Your robbing an Indian's *body*, and mocking his *soul*
with food.
Go back with you new religion, and find — if find
you can —
The *honest* man you have ever made from out of a *starving*
man.
You say your cattle are not ours, your meat is not our meat;
When *you* pay for the land you live in, *we'll* pay for
the meat we eat.[3]

It is past time to recognize Johnson for the revolutionary she was. Publicized as the "Mohawk Princess" in her many tours as a recitalist, she despised the misconceptions non-Natives had about her people. Her anger and the courage to express that anger also made her the poet she was. She was determined to destroy stereotypes that categorized and diminished her people. Breaking out of the Victorian strictures of her day, she drew a map for all women to follow. She had political integrity and spiritual honesty, the true hallmarks of a revolutionary. And I think the key to understanding Native women's poetry and prose is that we love, unashamedly, our own. Pauline Johnson wrote down that love. Her short stories are filled with Native women who have dignity, pride, anger, strength and spiritual power.[4] And Pauline Johnson was a nationalist. Canada may attempt to claim her as theirs, but Johnson belonged to only one nation, the Mohawk Nation. She wrote at great length in her poems, stories and articles about this nationalism. She had a great love for Canada, the Canada of oceans, mountains, pine trees, lakes, animals and birds, not the Canada of politicians and racism that attempted the regulation of her people's lives.

In 1892 she was writing articles on cultural appropriation, and especially on the portrayal of Native women in fiction of the day. She tore apart popular white writers such as Charles Mair and Helen Hunt Jackson for their depictions of Native women as subservient, foolish in love, suicidal "squaws." Her anger is tempered with humour as she castigates these authors for their unimaginative use of language and for their insistence on naming the Native heroines "Winona" or a derivative thereof.[5]

Pauline Johnson is a spiritual grandmother to those of us who are women writers of the First Nations. She has been ignored and dismissed by present-day critics and feminists, but this is just another chapter in the long novel of dismissal of Native women's writing.

Pauline Johnson's physical body died in 1913, but her legacy to us who are Native women writers cannot be measured in any kind of human way. She walked the writing path and cleared the brush for us to follow. And the road gets wider and clearer each time a Native woman picks up her pen and puts her mark on paper.

I look on Native women's writing as a gift, a give-away of the truest meaning. Our spirit, our sweat, our tears, our laughter, our love, our anger, our bodies are distilled into words that we bead together to make power. Not power *over* anything. Power. Power that speaks to hearts as well as minds.

Land, spirit, visions of the past, the present, the future, these are expressed in sensual language. We labour with this English language that is so unlike our own. And the result of that labour has produced a new kind of writing. I sometimes think that one of the reasons our work is not reviewed or incorporated into literature courses (besides the obvious racism) is that we go against what has been considered "literature." Our work is considered "too political" and we do not stay in our place — the place that white North America deems acceptable. It is no coincidence that most Native women's work that gets published is done so by the feminist presses, the small presses, the leftist and alternative presses. These presses are moving outside the mainstream and dominant prescriptions of what constitutes good writing. The key word here is "moving." There is a movement going on that is challenging formerly-held beliefs of writing and *who* does that writing. And it is no coincidence that when our work is taught, it is being done so by women's studies instructors and those teachers who are movers and hold larger beliefs than the dominant culture would like. This is not to say that *all* women's studies are as forward-thinking as we would like. At a recent women's studies conference, the topics of discussion centered around the usual white, European precepts of theory and literature. Race and class has yet to be addressed, or if it is discussed, it is on *their* terms, rather than *ours*.

We are told by the mainstream presses that our work doesn't sell. To quote Chief Sealth, "Who can sell the sky or the wind? Who can sell the land or the Creator?" The few women of Colour who have broken through this racist system are held up as *the* spokespeople for our races. It is implied that these women are the only ones *good* enough to "make it." These women are marketed as exotic oddities (after all, we all know that women of Colour can't write or read, eh?). Pauline Johnson faced this racism constantly. The "Mohawk Princess" was considered an anomaly, and I can't say that things have changed all that much. I think of Pauline a lot, especially when I rise to read my stories. For like her, "My aim, my joy, my pride is to sing the glories of my own people."

Because of our long history of oral tradition and our short history of literacy (in the European sense), the amount of books and written material by Native people is relatively small. Yet to us, these are precious treasures carefully nurtured by our communities. And the numbers of Native women who are writing and publishing is growing. Like all growing things, there is a need and desire for assuring the flowering of this growth. You see, these fruits feed our communities. These flowers give us survival tools. I would say that Native women's writing is the Good Medicine that can heal us as a human people. When we hold up the mirror to our lives, we are also reflecting what has been done to us by the culture that lives outside that mirror. It is possible for all of us to learn the way to healing and self-love. It is so obvious to me that Native women's writing is a generous sharing of our history and our dreams of the future. That generosity is a collective experience. And perhaps this is the major difference between Aboriginal writing and that of European-based "literature." We do not write as individuals communing with a muse. We write as members of an ancient, cultural consciousness. Our "muse" is *us*. Our "muse" is our ancestors. Our "muse" is our children, our grandchildren, our partners, our lovers. Our "muse" is the Earth and the stories She holds in the rocks, the trees, the birds, the fish, the animals, the waters. Our words come from the very place of all life, the spirits who swirl around us, teaching us, cajoling us, chastising us, loving us.

The first novel written by a Native woman was *Cogewea — the Half-Blood*.[6] Written by Hum-Ishu-Ma, an Okanagan Nation woman, this novel depicts the difficult circumstances surrounding that state of being called half-breed. Probably autobiographical, Hum-Isha-Ma concentrates on the relationship the female protagonist has with her Indian grandmother and how Cogewea does not turn her back on her people, although she is courted and temporarily seduced by the white world. Again, I am reminded of Pauline Johnson and her Indian women who remain steadfast in their Aboriginal beliefs and spiritual connections to their land and people.

Fifty years later, Maria Campbell wrote her ground-breaking *Half-breed*,[7] taking up the theme of despair that comes as a result of the imbalance that racism and poverty create in a people. Maria has a grandmother whose words and strength give her nurturance and hope and a way back to the Good Red Road. The Good Red Road is a way of life among Native peoples that is one of balance and continuity. Again, this seems to be the overwhelming message that Native women bring to writing. Creating a balance in their protagonists' worlds, remembering what the Elders taught, recovering from the effects of colonialism. This is not to say that Native women's writing contains "happy" endings or resolutions. In fact, to wrap things up in a tidy package is not following the Good Red Road — it's a falsehood. Perhaps this is what irritates white critics — our work is said to have no plots! If we won't conform, how can these conformist reviewers write reviews?! Perhaps the questions should be, Why are critics so unimaginative in *their* writing? Why are they so ignorant of what is being written by my sisters?

Why is a white-European standard still being held up as the criteria for all writing? Why is racism still so rampant in the arts?

Leslie Marmon Silko published her novel, *Ceremony*,[8] in 1976. In 1992 *Almanac of the Dead*,[9] by the same author, was published. In between those years, Paula Gunn Allen, Louise Erdrich, Jeannette Armstrong, Anna Lee Walters, Ella Deloria, Beatrice Culleton, Ruby Slipperjack, Cyndy Baskin and Linda Hogan also published novels.[10]

In the field of autobiographical works, the number of Native women's books is outstanding. Minnie Freeman, Maria Campbell, Ruby Slipperjack, Minnie Aodala, Alice French, Ignatia Broker, Lee Maracle, Madeline Katt, Florence Davidson, Mary John, Gertrude Bonnin, Verna Johnson and others[11] tell their stories for all to hear, and we become witness to the truth of Native lives. Throughout these writings, strong female images and personas are evident. The Cheyenne saying, "A Nation is not conquered until it's women's hearts are on the ground," becomes a prophecy about Native women's writing. First Nations women's hearts are not on the ground. We soar with the birds and our writing soars with us because it contains the essence of our hearts.

Deep connections with our female Elders and ancestors is another truth that we witness. Grandmothers, mothers, aunties all abound in our writing. This respect for female wisdom is manifested in our lives, therefore, in our writing.

Poetry seems to be the choice of telling for many Native women. In our capable hands, poetry is torn from the elitist enclave of intellectuals and white, male posturing and returned to the lyrical singing of the drum, the turtle rattle, the continuation of the Good Red Road and the balance of the Earth. We write poems of pain and power, of ancient beliefs, of sexual love, of broken treaties, of despoiled beauty. We write with our human souls and voices. We write songs that honour those who came before us and those in our present lives and those who will carry on the work of our Nations. We write songs that honour the every-day. We write songs to food, we even incorporate recipes into our work. Chrystos, Mary Tall Mountain, Nora Dauenhauer, Mary Moran,[12] are just a few who write about the joys of fry bread, salmon, corn soup and whale blubber, then turn around and give instructions for preparing these treats! To me, this is so ineffably Indian. Mouth salivating with the descriptions of our basic foods, the readers are then generously offered the gift of how to do this for ourselves. No wonder the critics have so much trouble with us! How could food possibly be art?! How can art remain for the elite, if these Native women are going to be writing recipes in poems? What will the world come to when food is glorified in the same way Titian glorified red hair?

There are numerous books of poetry written by Native women.[13] We are getting our poems published in forward-thinking journals and magazines, although there are still the literary journals that wish to ghettoize our work into "special" issues, which, if you will notice, happen about every ten years or so. And the editors are usually white and educated in the mainstream constructs of European sensibility. When I was asked in 1983 to edit a Native women's issue of the feminist journal, *Sinister Wisdom,* I did not expect the earthquake *A Gathering of Spirit* would cause. Eventually, this work became a book, published in 1984, then re-issued by Women's Press in 1989.[14] Perhaps there is a lesson here. When Natives have the opportunities to do *our own* editing and writing a remarkable thing can happen. This thing is called "telling the truth for ourselves" — a novel idea to be sure and one that is essential to the nurturance of new voices in our communities. I do writing workshops with Native women around North America, and the over-riding desire present in these workshops is to heal. Not just the individual, but to heal the broken circles that have occurred in our Nations. So writing does become the Good Medicine that is necessary to our continuation into wholeness. And when we are whole our voices sail into the lake of *all* human experience. And the ripple-effect is inevitable, vast and transcendent.

There are those women who are writing bilingually. Salli Benedict, Lenore Keeshig-Tobias, Rita Joe, Beatrice Medicine, Ana Lee Walters, Luci Tapahonso, Mary Tall Mountain, Nia Francisco, Ofelia Zepeda, Donna Goodleaf[15] are just some of the Native women who are choosing to use their Nation's languages when English won't suffice or convey the integrity of the meaning. I find this an exciting movement within our movement. And an exciting consequence would be the development of *our own* critics and of publishing houses that do bilingual work. Our languages are rich, full of metaphor, nuance and life. Our languages are not dead or conquered — like women's hearts, they are soaring and spreading the culture to our youth and our unborn. Pauline Johnson must be smiling. She was fluent in Mohawk but unable to publish those poems that contained her language. There is a story that on one of her tours she attempted to do a reading in Mohawk. She was booed off the stage. Keeping her dignity, she reminded members of the audience that she had to learn *their* language, wouldn't it be polite to hear hers? Needless to say, impoliteness won the day.

From Pauline Johnson to Margaret Sam-Cromarty,[16] Native women write about the land, the land, the land. This land that brought us into existence, this land that houses the bones of our ancestors, this land that was stolen, this land that withers without our love and care. This land that calls us in our dreams and visions, this land that bleeds and cries, this land that runs through our bodies.

From Pauline Johnson to Marie Baker, Native women write with humour. Even in our grief, we find laughter. Laughter at our human failings, laughter with our Tricksters, laughter at the stereotypes presented about us. In her play *Princess Pocahontas and the Blue Spots*,[17] Monique Mojica, Kuna/Rappahannock, lays bare the lies perpetrated against Native women. And she does it with laughter *and* anger — a potent combination in the hands of a Native woman. Marie Baker, Anishanabe, has written a play that takes place on the set of an Indian soap opera, "As the Bannock Burns." Baker's characters are few — the Native star of the soap, and the new co-star, a Native woman who gives shaman lessons to wannabes. In the course of the one-act play, the star shows the would-be shaman the error of her ways under the watchful eyes of a chorus of women of Colour. Not only does Baker poke fun at the Greek chorus concept in theatre, she turns this European device to her own and *our* amusement in a gentle, loving way to bring the would-be shaman to a solid understanding of herself and her own tradition.

Sarah Winnemucca, Suzette La Flesch,[18] Pauline Johnson also left them laughing as they took their work on the road. To tell a good story, one has to be good actor. I remember my granddad telling me stories when I was little and punctuating the sentences with movement and grand gestures, changing his facial expressions and voice. It was such a treat. I think we are likely to witness more Native women writing for the theatre. Margo Kane has ventured into that place with her play *Moon Lodge*. Vera Manuel has written a play, *The Spirit in the Circle*, that addresses the painful past of residential schools and the painful present of alcoholism and family dysfunctions. But she posits a vision for the future out of these violent truths. The women of Spider Woman's Theatre have been writing, producing and acting in plays for a number of years now. And Muriel Miguel, one of the Spiders, has done a one-woman show incorporating lesbian humour, Native Tricksters and female history. Native women are writing the scripts for their videos and directing and producing these films. How Pauline Johnson would have loved video!

As Native women writers, we have formed our own circles of support. At least once a week, I get poems and stories in the mail, sent to me by Native women I know and some I have never met. It thrills me to read the words brought forth by my sisters. And this is another form our writing takes — being responsible and supportive to our sisters who are struggling to begin the journey of writing truth. The WordCraft Circle, a mentoring program that matches up more experienced writers with our younger brothers and sisters, was born out of a Native writer's gathering held in 1992 in Oklahoma. I am currently working with a young, Native lesbian, and it moves my heart that it is now possible for lesbian Natives to give voice to *all* of who we are. Keeping ourselves secret, separating parts of ourselves in order to get heard or published has been detrimental to our communities and to our younger sisters and brothers who long for gay and lesbian role models. I am proud of the burgeoning Native lesbian writing that is expanding the idea of what constitutes Native women's writing. There are my sisters who have internalized the homophobia that is so rampant in the dominant culture and has found its way into our own territories and homes. These sisters are afraid and I understand that fear. Yet I ask for a courage greater than fear: the courage to be who we are for the sake of our young and to honour those who have come before us. Courage of the kind that Connie Fife, Chrystos, Barbara Cameron, Sharon Day, Susan Beaver, Nicole Tanguay, Two Feathers, Donna Goodleaf, Janice Gould, Vickie Sears, Donna Marchand, Mary Moran, Elaine Hall, Lena ManyArrows and

many others have displayed.[19] Writing with our *whole* selves is an act
that can re-vision our world. The use of erotic imaging in Native lesbian
work becomes a tool by which we heal ourselves. This tool is powerfully
and deftly evident in the hands of these writers, especially the poems of
Janice Gould and Chrystos. In my own work, I have explored such
themes as self-lovemaking, and the act of love between two women[20] as
a way to remake the broken circles of my own life and hopefully to give
sustenance to other women who are searching for new maps to their
lives. But Native lesbian writing is not only about sex or sexuality. A
broader cultural definition of sexuality is at work here. Strong bonds to
the Earth and Her inhabitants serve as a pivotal edge to our most sensual
writing. Like our heterosexual sisters, Native lesbians who write are
swift to call out the oppressions that are at work in our lives. Homophobia is the eldest son of racism — they work in concert with each other —
whether externally or internally. Native lesbian writing *names* those
twin evils that would cause destruction to us.

A major theme in the work of Vickie Sears, Cherokee Nation, is the
power over children's bodies by the state.[21] Sexual abuse, physical abuse,
emotional abuse are "normal" occurrences to the girl-children in
Vickie's short stories. Herself a survivor of the foster-care system, she
finds her solace and power through the things of the Earth and the love
between women. Her short stories emphasize these possibilities of
self-recovery. Indeed, one could say that much of the Native lesbian
writing of today celebrates the Earth as woman, as lover, as companion.
And woman, lover, companion being celebrated as Earth. Two-Spirit
writers are merging the selves that colonialism splits apart.

Recovery writing is another component in the movement of Native
women writers. Recovery from substance abuse as well as from racism,
sexism and homophobia. Two Feathers, Cayuga Nation, is a wonderful
example of this kind of recovery writing, as is Sharon Day of the Ojibway
Nation.[22] Again, Chrystos, a Menominee poet, excels in naming what it
feels like to be hooked, a slave to the substances that deaden the pain of
being Native in the twentieth century. Highly charged with anger, this
recovery writing is, at the same time, gentle with the knowing of how
difficult the path is toward the Good Red Road. There is empathy and
compassion in the telling of our people's struggle to stay clean and sober

— there is rage against the state that employed *and* employs addiction to attempt our cultural annihilation. Many of my short stories focus on that moment between staying sober and taking "just one" drink. The characters are caught in that timescape of traditional Native "seeing" and the unnatural landscape of colonization through addiction. In my stories as in my life, Creator brings gifts of the natural to "speak" to these characters. It then becomes a choice to live on the Good Red Road or to die the death of being out of balance — a kind of "virtual reality," as opposed to the real, the natural. Pauline Johnson knew first-hand the effects of these attempts at annihilation. Her father, a Chief of the Mohawk Nation, was a political activist against the rum-runners who would have weakened his people. Severely beaten many times by these smugglers and murderers, his life was considerably shortened. Many of Pauline's stories are filled with righteous anger against the whiteman who wished to rape our land, using alcohol as a weapon to confuse and subjugate us. I think she would applaud recovery writing and name it for what it is — an Indian war cry against the assassination of our culture.

Oral tradition requires a telling and a listening that is intense and intentional. Giving, receiving, giving — it makes a complete circle of Indigenous truth. First Nations writing utilizes the power and gift of story, like oral tradition, to convey history, lessons, culture and spirit. And perhaps the overwhelming instinct in our spirit is to love. I would say that Native writing gives the gift of love. And love is a word that is abused and made empty by the dominant culture. In fact, the letters L O V E have become just that, blank cyphers used frivolously to cover up deep places of the spirit.

I began writing when I turned forty, twelve years ago. I imagine the spirits knew I wasn't ready to receive that gift until I was mature enough and open enough to understand the natural meaning of love. I believe that the writing being created by First Nations women is writing done with a community consciousness. Individuality is a concept and philosophy that has little meaning for us. Even while being torn from our spiritual home, having our ancestors' names stolen and used to sell sports teams or automobiles or articles of clothing, having our languages beaten out of us through residential school systems, even while having our spirits defiled and blasphemed, our families torn apart by institutionalized violence and genocide, even after this long war, we still remain connected to our own.

And that connection takes many forms. I, as a Mohawk, feel deep spiritual bonds towards many who do not come from my Nation. These people — Carrier, Menominee, Cree, Cherokee, Lakota, Inuit, Abenaki and many others — are like the threads in a weaving. This Mohawk and the people of many Nations are warp and woof to each other. While the colour and beauty of each thread is unique and important, together they make a communal material of strength and durability. Such is our writing because such is our belief-system. Writing is an act that can take place in physical aloneness, but the memory of history, of culture, of land, of Nation is always present, like another being. And that is how we create. Writing with all senses, and with the ones that have not been named or colonized, we create.

Janice Gould, Maidu Nation, has written, "I would like to believe there are vast reserves of silences that can never be *forced* to speak, that remain sacred and safe from violation."[23] I feel that these sacred silences are the places *from* which we write. That place that has not been touched or stained by imperialism and hatred. That sacred place. That place.

Like Pauline Johnson, mixed-blood writers find those sacred places in the blood that courses through our bodies, whispering, "Come home, come home." Although we have never left that home, in a sense we have been pulled and pushed into accepting the lies told about our Indian selves. For those of us who do not conform to a stereotype of what Native people "look like," claiming our identities as Native people becomes an exercise in racism. "Gee, you don't look like an Indian." "Gee, I didn't know Indians had blue eyes." "My great-great-grandmother was a Cherokee princess, does that make me an Indian too?" After a while it becomes humourous, even while it's tiresome. Perhaps the feeling is that we're getting away with something, that we are tapping into unknown strengths to which we are not entitled. And how the dominant culture loves to quantify suffering and pain! And how well it has worked to divide us from each other and from our self. Colourism is another face of racism. And we write about that — exposing our fears of abandonment by the people we love, the people whose opinion matters, the very people who in our dreams whisper, "Come home, come home." Yet mixed-blood writing is also what I have been examining, for most of us are bloods of many mixes and Nations. Linda Hogan, Chickasaw Nation, calls us "New People." New People are the survivors of five hundred years of colonial rule. Our grandmothers bodies were appropriated by the conquerors, but the New People have not forgotten that grandmother nor the legacy she carried in her womb.

In Mexico a story is told of La Llorona. It is told that she wanders throughout the land, looking for her lost children. Her voice is the wind. She weeps and moans and calls to the children of her blood. She is the Indian, the mother of our blood, the grandmother of our hearts. She calls to us. "Come home, come home." She whispers, she cries, she calls to us. She comes into that sacred place we hold inviolate. She is birthing us in that sacred place. "Come home, come home," the voice of the umbilical, the whisper of the placenta. "Come home, come home" And we listen. And we write.

Notes

1. E. Pauline Johnson as quoted in Betty Keller. *Pauline: A Biography of Pauline Johnson* (Vancouver: Douglas & McIntyre, 1981), page 5.
2. E. Pauline Johnson. "The Song My Paddle Sings" in *Flint & Feather* (Toronto: Hodder & Stoughton, 1931).
3. E. Pauline Johnson. "The Cattle Thief" in *Flint & Feather*.
4. E. Pauline Johnson. *The Moccasin Maker* (Tucson: University of Arizona, 1987).
5. E. Pauline Johnson. "A Strong Race Opinion on the Indian Girl in Modern Fiction" originally published in the *Toronto Sunday Globe*, 22 May 1892, reprinted in Betty Keller, *op. cit.*
6. Hum-Ishu-Ma (Mourning Dove). *Cogewea, The Half-Blood* (Lincoln: University of Nebraska, 1981). Hum-Ishu-Ma's mentor was a white man. My reading of *Cogewea* is that much of it was more influenced by his perceptions than Hum-Ishu-Ma's.
7. Maria Campbell. *Halfbreed* (Toronto: McClelland & Stewart, 1973).
8. Leslie Marmon Silko. *Ceremony* (New York: Viking Press, 1977).
9. Leslie Marmon Silko. *Almanac of The Dead* (New York, Toronto: Simon & Schuster, 1991).
10. Paula Gunn Allen. *The Woman Who Owned The Shadows* (San Francisco:

Spinsters/Aunt Lute, 1983); Louise Erdrich. *The Beet Queen* (Boston: Bantam, 1987); Louise Erdrich. *Love Medicine* (Toronto, New York: Bantam, 1989); Louise Erdrich. *Tracks* (New York: Henry Holt, 1988); Jeanette Armstrong. *Slash* (Penticton: Theytus, 1986); Anna Lee Walters. *Ghost-Singer* (Flagstaff: Northland, 1988); Ella Deloria. *Water Lily* (Lincoln: University of Nebraska, 1988); Beatrice Culleton. *In Search of April Raintree* (Winnipeg: Pemmican, 1983); Ruby Slipperjack. *Honour The Sun* (Winnipeg; Pemmican, 1987); Ruby Slipperjack. *Silent Words* (Saskatoon: Fifth House, 1992); Cyndy Baskin. *The Invitation* (Toronto: Sister Vision, 1993). Linda Hogan. *Mean Spirit* (New York: Atheneum, Toronto: Collier McMillan, 1990).

11. Minnie Freeman. *Life Among the Qallunaat* (Edmonton: Hurtig, 1978); Ignatia Broker. *Night Flying Woman: an Ojibway Narrative* (St. Paul; Minnesota Historical Society, 1983); Mary Crow Dog. *Lakota Woman* (New York: Harper Perennial, 1990).

12. Chrystos. "I Am Not Your Princess" in *Not Vanishing* (Vancouver: Press Gang, 1988); Mary Tall Mountain. "Good Grease" in *The Light on the Tent Wall: A Bridging* (Los Angeles: University of California at Los Angeles, 1990); Nora Marks Dauenhauer. "How to Make Good Baked Salmon" in *The Droning Shaman* (Haines: The Black Currant, 1985); Mary Moran. *Métisse Patchwork*, unpublished manuscript.

13. Published poets include Beth Cuthand, Joy Harjo, Marie Baker (Annharte), Chrystos and Janice Gould.

14. Beth Brant, ed. *A Gathering of Spirit* (Sinister Wisdom Books, 1984/Ithaca: Firebrand, 1988/Toronto: Women's Press, 1989).

15. Lenore-Keeshig Tobias. *Bird-Talk* (Toronto: Sister Vision, 1992). Rita Joe. *Poems of Rita Joe* (Halifax: Abenaki, 1978). Beatrice (Bea) Medicine. "Ina, 1979" in Beth Brant, ed. *A Gathering of Spirit*. Anna Lee Walters. *Talking Indian: Reflections on Survival and Writing* (Ithaca: Firebrand, 1992); Nia Francisco. *Blue Horses for Navajo Women* (Greenfield Center: Greenfield Review, 1988); Ofelia Zepeda. Unpublished manuscript; Donna Goodleaf. Unpublished manuscript.

16. Margaret Sam-Cromarty. *This Land I Love*. Chapbook.

17. Monique Mojica. *Princess Pocahontas and The Blue Spots* (Toronto: Women's Press, 1991).

18. Sarah Winnemucca and Suzette La Flesch travelled and performed in the

United States, talking about their people in poetry and stories, at about the same time as Pauline Johnson did.

19. Makeda Silvera, ed. *Piece of My Heart* (Toronto: Sister Vision, 1991) and Will Roscoe, ed. *Living The Spirit: A Gay American Indian Anthology* (New York: St. Martin's, 1988) are two collections with Native lesbian writing.

20. Beth Brant. *Mohawk Trail* (Ithaca: Firebrand, 1985/Toronto: Women's Press, 1990) and Beth Brant. *Food and Spirits* (Ithaca: Firebrand Vancouver: Press Gang, 1991).

21. Vickie Sears. *Simple Songs* (Ithaca: Firebrand, 1990).

22. Sharon Day. *The Winds*. Chapbook.

23. Janice Gould. "Disobedience (in Language): Texts by Lesbian Natives." Unpublished speech to the Modern Language Association (New York, 1990).

WHAT ABOUT US?

Organizing Inclusively in the
National Action Committee
on the Status of Women

A roundtable discussion facilitated
by Maureen FitzGerald and Alice de Wolff
Edited by Amy Gottlieb

Ⅰn 1972 the National Action Committee on the Status of Women
formed as an umbrella group for women's organizations in Canada.
Today it represents over five hundred groups, with a membership of
over three million. NAC became a household word in Canada in 1992
by supporting the No vote in the Canadian referendum. The referendum
itself, about whether and how to restructure the Canadian federation,
was preceded by an unprecedented and unexpected amount of popular
debate — debate in which both the No forces and the Yes forces claimed
that a vote against their position was likely to lead to a breakup of
Canada. In that debate Judy Rebick, the president of NAC, became
recognized as a forceful media presence who carved out a unique
position for NAC. In this discussion four members of the twenty-three-
member NAC executive and the executive coordinator discuss some of
the changes in NAC that led it to take a position that separated the
organization from its traditional allies in the three major parties of
Canada (the Conservative Party, the Liberal Party and the New Democratic Party) *and* from most of organized labour outside Quebec.

   Canadian federal state-building has, both currently and historically,
pirouetted precariously on the twin points of regional equalization
payments and a mystique of two–founding–nations. The success of the
No vote in the referendum was at least partly a rejection of the exclusiv-

ity of the two founding nations rhetoric. Led by the example of the Native Women's Association of Canada, groups like NAC spoke up and said, "What about us?" In so doing, they were able to keep the debate from being solely framed by the male politicians who had drafted the Charlottetown Accord, the blueprint of a changed federal system on which Canadians voted. NAC was able to bring to the country's attention, among other things, the way that the Charlottetown Accord failed constitutionally to protect the rights of women, people of Colour, immigrants, gays and lesbians and the elderly.

Those of us who have been friendly bystanders to NAC should not have been so surprised by NAC taking what was initially an unpopular position. Aside from its annual "rite" of lobbying parliamentarians on the many issues that concern women, NAC had already garnered media attention in 1992 when it, along with the National Organization of Immigrant and Visible Minority Women, the Congress of Black Women and the DisAbled Women's Network broke from the Federal Panel on Violence Against Women. All of these groups charged that the panel was not inclusive of women of Colour. Could it be that NAC, the largest women's group in the land, was changing? That it was beginning to take a clear anti-racist stance in its positions and in how it was constituted? To find out what changes were happening in NAC, Alice de Wolff and I interviewed as many NAC executive members as we could assemble after an exhausting board meeting in Toronto in November of 1992. The following is an edited transcript of that interview. Beverly Bain, a Black women who became the executive director in 1992, spoke first followed by three white women, Maureen Leyland, Shelagh Day and Judy Rebick.

Maureen FitzGerald

BEVERLY: I see the process of inclusiveness and anti-racism in its initial stages at NAC. I don't see rapid movement. NAC has non-white representation on its executive and has more non-white representation in its membership. I also see a shift in terms of class representation. NAC has moved from being a very middle-upper-class organization, in the nature of its politics, to more of a middle-working-class representation in the way in which issues are put forward.

I do have problems with the way issues are being presented in the briefs, mailings and materials that go out to the public. NAC is still presenting a very white perspective, devoid of an analysis which integrates the perspectives of women of Colour and Aboriginal women. I don't see the materials trying to make those links yet.

In terms of anti-racism, NAC now has within its constitution an employment equity policy that ensures representation on its executive. I see NAC attempting to make the links to ensure that we are working towards inclusiveness and working towards some kind of perspective on what anti-racism is all about. I see it as a process.

In examining the Constitutional referendum that took place October 1992, in terms of perspective, in terms of opinion, in terms of politics, we probably have made some connection with non-white, progressive communities which felt this referendum was not in their interest. We couldn't claim any kind of success in terms of actual participation from the non-white communities. But I certainly think the minds of many people were with us, primarily because of the position we had taken. We were heard by more people because of the issues that we put forward about concerns and issues of women of Colour and Aboriginal women. I think we have to do a lot of work in terms of how we make those links.

It's really important how we understand the communities which have traditionally been marginalized within NAC and how we start verbalizing, how we start writing. The language we start using as an organization will also determine how we're able to bring those communities together. We need a language that's really reflective. I don't think we have actually started that process yet, in terms of really examining the way in which we articulate, write and the way we send messages across. We have a lot of work to do to make the process complete.

MAUREEN: It has become clearer and clearer in the past few years that if NAC were to become a women's movement in Canada that was a real force, we would have had to be inclusive. We had to look at the diversity among women and make that diversity a strength and not a weakness and a division. To pursue objectives on the basis of a single issue with a single community group was not going to bring about any major change in terms of social change, in terms of equity and equality.

I became aware that as a white woman I always thought I was fighting for women's issues that included everybody but realized that no, in the hierarchy of oppressions I was probably more at the top than I was at the bottom. How were we going to deal with the problem of hierarchies of oppression? Essentially what we have to do is change the whole social domain, the way we organize ourselves and the way we relate to each other. The only way we could really do that with any great effect was to change things for the most disadvantaged people.

JUDY: I agree with Bev — we're at the initial stages of transformation in terms of women of Colour and even more initial in terms of women with disabilities — we haven't figured that one out at all. What Bev said is very instructive: we have changed NAC enough for it to be attractive to women of Colour for the first time, at the level of the membership. In the last two or three years, we've had strong participation from women of Colour. It's four years now that we've had strong women of Colour caucuses. Before that the women of Colour on the executive were token. There were one or two and they were not able to have a big leadership role inside the executive because there wasn't the overall consciousness or commitment to anti-racist issues and to inclusion. I remember the annual general meeting (AGM), I think it was four or five years ago, where the resolutions of "visible minority" women got dropped from the agenda because resolutions were in alphabetical order by category!

What I'm learning, particularly in the last year, is how important it is for women of Colour to provide leadership to the feminist movement. The whole issue around the Federal Panel on Violence was important because there was a change in how NAC responded. We followed the leadership coming from women of Colour on how to proceed in relation to the panel. I didn't initially agree with the rejection of the panel. One executive member, Sunera Thobani,[1] knew at a very early stage what was going to happen and argued that NAC shouldn't support the panel. She was outvoted on the NAC executive in the initial stages. Pretty well everything she predicted came true. I think the same was true for women in Toronto like Beverly and others who saw the problems with the panel from the beginning. I think that I didn't see it because I was looking at the issue as a white woman. I wanted to believe in the panel even though I knew there would be problems. We wanted to believe that it was going to work out.

Listening and following the leadership that women of Colour were providing was a major change. The second element was being willing to stick our necks out. I mean we really stuck our necks out on this one and it was a test of NAC. We tried to work out an agreement, a compromise with the panel, so it could continue and maybe be useful. When we couldn't come to a compromise, when the demands of front-line workers and women of Colour were not met, then it was a test. Were we willing to take the blows we knew would come if we withdrew? Could we also get other women's groups to withdraw? We've paid heavily in public opinion for what we did. I'm still getting attacked about it. But on the other side, we gained tremendously in terms of building unity based on solidarity, which means you're willing to stick your neck out and give up your privilege in a certain way to support a fight. In a sense, for everybody to be mad at you is a very minimal way you give up your privilege. You have to share the risk as well as share the power. It was NAC's pulling out that was the public perception of what was important. If the National Organization of Immigrant and Visible Minority Women and the DisAbled Women's Network and the Congress of Black Women had pulled out alone, it wouldn't have had the same impact. It would have had an impact, but it wouldn't have had anywhere near the impact of NAC pulling out. That was sharing power to do that. But it was also sharing risk.

My experience around the Federal Panel on Violence was that we could have explained it better. I feel responsible around that, but the reality is that people didn't want to hear what we had to say about the panel. They didn't want to hear it. They didn't want to believe it was an important issue. But that's the resistance — there is a notion of democracy which is really the rule of elites. We're challenging that notion of democracy and it's a very profound thing. We are developing a collective understanding of the needs of the group, and then people are doing what they're good at doing in leading that. That's a very radical notion and one that's extremely threatening to the status quo and to anybody who buys into the status quo.

SHELAGH: NAC is becoming representative. It's only beginning. The encouraging thing for me is that we seem to have said Yes, this is a task and it's one that we're taking on, and that women are inside NAC working together to figure out how to do it.

During the last five years, I've seen a change in the composition of NAC in a very visual way. I came onto the NAC executive in 1990, precisely because NAC seemed like an attractive place. I have spent a good part of the last ten years working on coalition-building and working on equality questions which have to do with the intersection of different kinds of discrimination. When I first came to work with NAC that was precisely where NAC was — it was beginning to take the coalition work inside the organization itself. Now it seems to me that NAC has tried to internalize coalition work into its membership and into its vision.

I think the message that NAC is now putting across about the intersection of gender, race, disability and so on, is a very profound one. Our society is used to having us all divided up into boxes and divided from each other.

I came onto the executive at the same time as the resolutions about representation within NAC got put in place. Those things are very important in ensuring that there will be a permanent presence of women of Colour. Again, I think we're at the very beginning and that we've a long way to go in terms of the executive and table officers and regional organizations and incorporating work on racism into everything that we do. The thing that has changed is that NAC can go out in public now and speak about race, disability and sexual orientation and have credibility. NAC gets a lot of respect from the public for being something more than a white, middle class organization.

Inside NAC, as in many women's organizations, there have been lesbians working on the front lines since the beginning. But lesbians have not been visible. At the 1990 AGM, many women were wearing purple dots as a way of declaring the visibility of lesbians inside the organization. I still don't think that this is an issue on which NAC always does its best or that we have lesbian issues incorporated into all our public work. Nonetheless, in the last couple of years NAC has done some extraordinarily important things on that front. It has taken a role with a coalition of intervenors in the Mossop case, that was just recently heard by the Supreme Court.[2] And in the referendum debate the lesbian and gay community felt as though NAC had spoken up for lesbians and gay men when nobody else would.

On the issue of disability we have a lot of work to do. The diversity of the disability community and incorporating all of that diversity into the functioning of our organization is a major piece of work. We have more consciousness about disability issues now than five years ago, but still there's a very long way to go.

MAUREEN: There has been a noticeable shift in NAC, which is not to say that we can rest on our laurels. We've only just begun to change. But the fact that there are these very definite manifestations of change means that there has not just been a noticeable shift, but a dramatic shift, around the composition of the national executive, the nature of the membership, the issues that are taken up, how the issues are pursued and the analysis of the issues. However, inclusivity doesn't just mean having different people representing different groups as members or on the executive; it means that you're connecting the issues. You're forming a much more cohesive and comprehensive analysis. You play a much more inclusive role around particular issues. I don't think that happened by chance. There was a change in consciousness.

I've come out of a white background, first of all poor working class and then middle class. I bring that with me. What I see has happened in NAC and what happened for me primarily in the labour movement, working for women in the labour movement, was an opportunity to listen to other people, to hear other people's experiences. I think NAC has moved to that openness. We have to constantly struggle to under-stand the oppression of different kinds of people and the different places they've been. The struggle doesn't end. Not for white women who are trying to get a grasp on all this stuff.

BEVERLY: When NAC decided to withdraw from the Federal Panel on

Violence last year, that was when I began to notice the changes taking place within NAC. NAC was actually demonstrating inclusiveness. It was critical of the panel because of how it was set up in the first place, which wasn't inclusive of women of Colour. It was critical of the process because women's groups were not a part of the consultation process and there were implications for women coming forward and giving testimonies. That's where I began to notice NAC as an organization where the process had begun to take place.

JUDY: There have been a couple of complete transformations of NAC. One is on the regional level. NAC is no longer a Toronto-dominated organization, especially in the last two years. We have a much bigger presence across the country, as big as we have in Ontario. Certainly that is true out west. The participation of women in NAC is not primarily from Toronto any more. That's a huge transformation from what NAC was ten years ago or even five years ago. We are working with national campaign committees rather than Toronto-based committees. (On the other hand, it makes doing some of the work very difficult because we haven't figured out a way for a committee outside Toronto to lead a national campaign in a very effective way.)

The negative side is that NAC used to have much more participation of Francophones at the membership level. That's a big step backwards, unless Francophone women decide that they want an independent relationship. When I first started to come around NAC, a third to a quarter of the annual general meeting were Francophone women; now it is a handful. The decrease in the number of active Francophone women has a lot to do with the overall political tensions in the country, but we're working on it.

The second thing is the membership of NAC has completely transformed in the last ten years from primarily professional, middle-class women to grassroots activists in the women's movement. What was really clear in our discussion on what position to take in the referendum was the extent to which our executive is now made up of grassroots activists. All of them are active in various aspects of the women's movement.

The other big change that has happened in NAC is how we function.

That has probably been the most dramatic change: NAC is a much more functional organization. NAC used to function through faction fights and a lot of back room manouvering. There was a lot of bitterness, there were a lot of people hating each other on the executive. You'd ask somebody after two years of being on the executive if they would continue and they wouldn't if their life depended on it. There was a lot of division both at the AGM and on the executive. There was very little political debate on the executive, most of it was on organizational issues. Now we deal with politics and we have campaigns which we didn't have five years ago.

In terms of the issue of inclusion, there is a big change in terms of trade union women; most people don't notice, but there has been a big change in how trade union women see NAC, although trade union women have always been involved in NAC. There's much more support from the trade union movement now, financially and in terms of invitations to speak and to work in coalitions around particular issues.

BEVERLY: Where we take this, where we move with NAC as an organization and the decisions that we make in terms of policies and campaigns are going to be really important. We have garnered support from a certain population, but we can lose that depending on where we continue to go. So the issue for us is to really pay attention to how we started that process and to continue to build on that. Every task and activity must be done with that in mind, to continue to build, to expand, to ensure that we are reaching women of Colour, women with disabilities, lesbians, etc.

JUDY: I've always believed that the most oppressed women will be the best and the strongest fighters for women's equality. In the Referendum Campaign we saw that happen again. Aboriginal women led the struggle on the constitution. NAC had an analysis of the issues, but the Native Women's Association of Canada (NWAC) was prepared to push the issues much further than we were initially. NAC was into the lobbying mode on the constitution. We developed a very sophisticated analysis and we did our education. But in the end, if it hadn't been for NWAC, I'm not sure we would have come out for the No side. It was NWAC that was willing to go to the wall. Their example of demanding all of what they wanted, not just a little part of it, really pushed us. They took enormous risks, way more than any risk we took. They provided the leadership. In addition, the Native women within NAC contributed to our ability to take the No position. They assured us that there was a lot of opposition to the Charlottetown Accord among grassroots Aboriginal people. Sandra Delaronde, a Métis woman who is vice-president of NAC, assured us of the support of the elders of her community for our deliberations. That gave us a lot of strength.

Even if there was no other reason to say No in the Referendum, I think that the issue of Charter protection for Aboriginal women should have been enough.[3] Because a group of women standing up for equality inside their community is probably the toughest thing that a women's group can do. If the mainstream women's movement didn't support them, we would just abandon them to total isolation.

Aboriginal women have always participated in the NAC executive. There has always been a pretty good relationship between NAC and Aboriginal women. So that's not new for NAC. What's new is the way Aboriginal women are affecting our politics. That's the key. Women of Colour and Aboriginal women are affecting how we see everything politically. And that influence is challenging the idea that little steps forward are really what we're fighting for. The participation of women of Colour and Aboriginal women pushes us to understand that the struggle for equality is a revolutionary struggle.

NAC has never had the level of public support that we have today. And we've never had the level of attack we've had. Why? Because we're getting more and more radical. That's occurring because of the participation and the leadership of women of Colour and Aboriginal women and grassroots activists.

What's changed in the last year is that the consequence of that participation is starting to show, in terms of the political positions we have been taking. That's what's getting some of these white upper-middle-class feminists so uptight. They feel challenged.

SHELAGH: NAC is taking up a much bigger political space than it ever has before, and the Constitutional Referendum is one of the places where you can see that. Essentially, what's happened is that NAC has become the extra-parliamentary opposition. There is an identification with NAC that goes beyond women. I think the politicians who were involved in drafting the Charlottetown Accord made the traditional error; they assumed that we would go on functioning like a lobby group does. We would lobby like hell and if we didn't win we would still want to stay friends. They thought we really didn't count. But because of the position we took during the Referendum NAC isn't viewed as a bunch of self-interested white middle-class women. It takes up a bigger space because people see NAC as representing a big swath of the society's interests.

JUDY: NAC has changed fundamentally from a lobby group to a group that in a way structures the women's movement — attempting to be a national representation of the women's movement in its broadest sense. A lobby group tries to sway government and pushes on particular issues, sometimes even going as far as to organize on issues. A lobby group has to maintain its ties with people in power at a certain level. What we did in the Referendum, and one reason why people in power got so mad at us, was that we broke that rule. They responded so viciously to NAC taking a high profile No position because we were breaking a taboo. We were standing up and declaring that we couldn't accept the deal. And we were taking a strong position on something that wasn't traditionally considered our issue. We're allowed to own only certain issues, like abortion. But this was on *their* agenda. The impact of that is enormous. We knew people in power would be mad at us. But we also made a lot of women in positions of influence very uncomfortable because our position was very challenging.

SHELAGH: I had a conversation with a woman who invited me to come and talk to her class at one of the community colleges during the Referendum period. She teaches women's studies and considers herself to be someone who has been in the women's movement for a long time. She said, "You know, I just don't know how to relate to the women's movement any more. For a long time there I felt that it was all about lesbians. And now I feel like it's all about women of Colour, and I think that's probably a good thing. But you know, I just don't know what it has to do with me." I didn't know what to say to her because my own sense is that it's now that the women's movement, or at least NAC, feels like a place that I'm really interested in and feels comfortable to me. But I think what she expressed is felt by many (straight, white women).

BEVERLY: We do hear from some white women their perception that suddenly Black women's or non-white women's issues are becoming important. These women are seeing that what they define as their issues aren't always given priority and they're not seeing the connection between Black women and white women's issues. Some white women are recognizing that non-white women are no longer content to be represented in terms of Colour or numbers or shades; we will not be content without our voices being heard equally. I think we can see much more of a force coming from non-white women not to compromise any more. It's very clear that Aboriginal women's voices are no longer going to be compromised. "You hear us and you listen." From some white women there is also a sense that finally, yes, they do have to give way, they do have to make some room. We've spent a lot of time talking about it, and I've found that lots of white women are able to intellectualize what you say. "Yes, I understand what you're saying, it makes perfect sense." But when it comes down to actually *doing* something, that is where the difficulty arises. That's where we are seeing some of the difficulties, the defensive reaction. White women have to show that it's no longer words.

JUDY: There's huge resistance from all sides. And what we found is that on women's issues which can be defined as pure gender issues we can make gains. But when we start fighting, taking up specific issues around racism, we're not making gains. Look at the Federal Panel on Violence. They would agree to an accountability to thirteen women's groups, but they wouldn't agree to adding women of Colour to the panel. With the rape law, we couldn't get the amendment on women of Colour, Aboriginal women, women with disabilities and prostitutes.[4] That was the only thing we couldn't get them to budge on, in terms of what we wanted in the rape law. It's much harder to fight on those issues.

MAUREEN: We knew we were taking a big risk when we made the decision to come out for the No side in the Referendum. We could even articulate some of the risks we were taking, including the fact that we would be challenging our traditional allies and friends and there would be repercussions. We felt energized by the unanimity we reached in making our decision on the Referendum. The campaign took a tremendous amount of effort and we were all physically and mentally exhausted after it was over. What happened after that was a sense of deflation — we were pariahs. We took a position with a great deal of integrity and we knew we were opposing our traditional allies. But what I feel very desperate about is that we can't reconnect. Maybe it just takes a bit of time for that to happen, but it's very depressing. Then when I look at the battles that are ahead, particularly the campaign to defeat the North American Free Trade Deal, I know we will work with our allies to try to sink the deal, but I don't honestly feel that we're going to get a tremendous amount of support from them for anything else.

JUDY: It's the loyalty stuff. It's also the male thing. It's like sports and war. You have to be loyal to your side or your family. We're breaking that down too. We tried very consciously in the Referendum Campaign and with the Panel not to trash individuals. We chose not to do that. But we got trashed as a result of pulling out of the panel and the same in the Referendum Campaign. We didn't trash the NDP or anybody else, but some of them trashed us. And it's very hard to keep that up, because part of what we're doing is fighting for a different kind of process. It feels a lot better than trashing everybody in sight. But we've had to take a lot of shit.

Beverly said that NAC's image in racial minority communities has changed because of our position in the referendum. I've experienced that with racial minority women. But what's much more visible to me is the support we have from racial minority men and gay men. I don't get into a taxi cab or get served in a restaurant without a racial minority man saying how great NAC was in the referendum, and how much they think that the struggles of women and the struggle against racism are linked. Whereas five years ago we were getting the opposite feedback — that white women were getting all the privilege and taking away from minorities.

BEVERLY: When I decided to come and work for NAC I had a couple of people ask me, Do you think you'll survive? I said to them that a lot of it would also depend on them. If you're just going to leave me there hanging by myself, no, I won't survive. I know you're concerned and that means you need to be there for me. It's part of your responsibility to make sure that I survive. It was very good for me to throw that back at them. These are people from my community, people who I have worked with, people who have always said if I can do anything just let me know. It's my sense that women of Colour who are struggling within NAC have community support backing them.

JUDY: The women's movement, not just NAC, is way ahead of everybody else in society in dealing with issues of inclusion. We're breaking new ground for an organization like NAC. Nobody else is doing it to the same degree and most institutions aren't doing it at all. Or if they're doing it, they're doing it through tokenism. It's the same way they do it with women: you get the tame, safe women, or you get the tame, safe people of Colour who aren't going to challenge anything and you include them. We're not doing it that way. I think what we're doing is real.

There's also a lot of pressure on NAC right now to do everything because there's a lack of leadership of progressive forces in this country. People see us as one of the only progressive voices that has any power. And they want us to do everything, not just focus on women's issues. They want us to act like a political party. One of the reasons for this crisis of leadership among progressive forces is the failure of the Left to deal with representing our diversity as oppressed peoples. It's only in the women's movement where we've begun to deal with transforming our narrow and privileged notions of democracy. The Left has been as patriarchal and as racist as the rest of society. We must learn how to deal with difference, with power and privilege. The women's movement is just beginning to learn.

Notes

1. At NAC's May 1993 Annual General Meeting, Sunera Thobani was elected president. She is the first woman of Colour to hold that position.

2. Brian Mossop, a translator with the federal civil service, was refused bereavement leave when his lover's father died. His case was heard by the Supreme Court in February 1993 but was again rejected.

3. The process of negotiating Aboriginal self-government included in the Charlottetown Accord would have superseded all other legislation, including the *Indian Act* and the Charter of Rights. Aboriginal women's rights would not necessarily be protected in a transfer of governance to First Nations with political structures dominated by men.

4. In 1992 the Canadian government passed a new rape law, popularly known as the "No Means No" law. Under the old rape shield law, which was struck down by the Supreme Court, a woman's sexual history could, and often was, entered as evidence against her. Leading up to the new legislation, a coalition of women's groups consulted with then Justice Minister Kim Campbell and had a hand in drafting the new law. However, NAC's proposal for a preamble that pointed out the differential vulnerability and access to the criminal justice system of women of Colour, women with disabilities and prostitutes, was flatly turned down by the justice minister.

POWER OR EMPOWERMENT

Questions of Agency in the Shelter Movement

Rita Kohli

Prologue

Hatred I have known as a child
A girl child at that
When males both boys and men
Played predator games
On I a defenceless girl

Repeated assaults on my body
Hands raised
Words that destroyed my psyche
Looks and gestures
Fear instilled I froze in my head

Betrayed

Didn't anybody see
Didn't anybody hear
Betrayal steadfast
Betrayed by my body
I abandoned myself

One ...
I must have caused it

Two ...
I must have deserved it

Three ...
Counts of sexual assault
I must have asked for it
I must enjoy it

Severed from my neck
Too much the loathing
Walls after walls resurrected
I left myself behind
Perched somewhere on a wall a roof
So much the hatred and the pain

Bonded with men
Sister outsider I
Illusively hoping the pain would go

It has been a long journey of
Remembering
Rejoicing
Reclaiming
Returning
Finally
To the circle of women

The circle complete, I thought I had a home-coming when I started to work with women in the anti-violence movement. I thought at last I will not be objectified, infantalized or exoticized. Six months into working in shelters I came face to face with a strange kind of warfare, "Oh, she is demanding, she is manipulative," as poor women and women of Colour asked for what was theirs to ask. Collective members mimicking immigrant women, collective meetings with co-workers saying, "Not another refugee woman to take in again .... We can't take her because she is too old ... We do not want to create dependencies, so say no to an interpreter" ... A woman of Colour is suddenly noticed because she cooked curry for the staff ... Children of Colour ignored ... Intakes not done for three weeks ... Now familiar with the territory, I questioned the difference in treatment of white women and women of Colour ...

My first mistake and last. Gone the multiculturalism rhetoric, the pretence gone ... "She is argumentative, others are scared of her" ... So is the white woman, why are the women of Colour being punished? ... to rolling of eyes ... It then became about me ...

I started a project with another white woman. "What a wonderful report, they said to her," while throughout it was, "We don't understand your work." No amount of explaining enlightened the collective and now all waited for me to fall flat on my face, with a strange kind of anticipation, almost one of pleasure ... I didn't ... The cold war stopped momentarily ... to maintain the social facade, all is well in our house for the public to see ... The count down began for my exit ... Too much the sabotage ... Too much the punishment for women from our communities ... Too much the confusion at the silences and silencing ...

Amid the chaos I came out ... "I am not going to kiss you, I don't want to get cooties (joke, joke) ... I am too big for my boots and fly on the tail of my lover's political work" ... I finally succumbed and said I would leave ... to myself, leave quietly ... Personnel committee agreed I could do relief ... I began to wind up the work, waiting to hear about possible jobs, only to find it would not be so easy ... The grapevine had been busy. Amazed at being turned down at other jobs ... A new experience ... Suspicious to say the least, I asked at a collective meeting, "Is somebody giving references about me without my permission? ..." Silence ... I repeat my question, "Is somebody giving references for me other than those members I had specified? ..." "Yes, I am and you cannot stop me," piped a white woman who had worked but a shift, perhaps two, with me ... "You cannot do this ... You do not know my work" ... "Yes, I can," she says, "and you can't stop me" ... I look in astonishment at dozen faces around me ... I particularly look with dismay and amazement at the Brown and Black faces and the face of the Jewish woman ... No response. The bell had tolled ... The message clear for others like me ... I squared my shoulders ... I have only a few weeks to go ... My fundamental rights have been violated, I could sue ... Just let it be stated for the record that only three women can give a reference for me and I will be gone in weeks to come ...

I left to go to another shelter, amid much resistance and controversy ... The previous shelter sends a Black messenger (what a set-up) "She

cannot do relief ... the white staff would not know what to say to her"
... Suffering amnesia about the excellent work I did ... I tell my sister,
You know your hands are dirty as well and your time will come too ...
Ain't going to be no one but the likes of us to pick up the pieces ... But,
of course, she did give me a good reference, so I could go on and not
shake the boat ... So here I was at another shelter ... CAS being called
right left and centre on Black women. Why is this white working-class
woman being penalized for going out to help another woman, must we
police the women? ... Must this South Asian woman wait for six weeks
before her abscessed tooth will be attended to? ... It once again became
about us ... the Black woman and South Asian woman always creating
trouble ... the Black woman walked out ... Since the last time the bell
tolled for me I could not say my piece, I decided I to say my piece and
demand accountability ...

Several rounds of futile discussions with both the collective and the
board, finally the consultants arrived ... Outsiders to validate the insid-
ers ... It was not me, they said, but the collective that needs to do some
work ... well, you cannot say that to a collective without repercussions
... The punishment began in full swing ... She and she does not want to
work on shift with me ... Particularly this one who three weeks ago told
me it would be a loss to the counselling program and I should reconsider
not applying for the follow-up worker's position ... A resignation ...
With two months to go to wrap up ... A collective meeting my turn to
update ... Laughter, giggles I stop, Lets share the joke ... finally a
semblance of order I open my mouth to speak. Laughter, footsie, eyes
derisive ... I stop and say, As my work is to fight abuse, I was not going
to be part of a disrespectful and abusive process ... this would be the last
meeting I would attend ... much to the chagrin of personnel members
(collective), I let board members on personnel know my status in the
collective meetings and how I will make up my time ... three weeks still
to go. The erasure began, "No there is nobody by the name of Rode, Rode
who? No, she does not work here" ... The second last day of my work
... I have a dental crisis ... Weeks of "go ahead and do your surgery" ...
3,000 dollars debt incurred for surgery, that neither the shelter nor the
insurance would pick up the tab ... Seventy-five hours still due to me in
overtime ... I lay stunned, looking at myself ... Raw without a skin ...

The hatred and the punishment followed long after ... I, a South Asian lesbian whose work was impeccable, could not be called for relief ... I have an attitude ... We cannot work with her ... Ensuring that I could not get work in other organizations ... Such hatred and cruelty ... I remained silent and silenced my rage ... thinking at least an assaulted immigrant woman, woman of Colour could have a roof over her head ... My silence coerced and completed by the incestuous grapevine ... "This is a troublemaking woman of Colour ... No job ... No options ... I finally succumbed and internalized the hatred ... I became silenced ... attempts of sabotage still continue ...

Yesterday I got a call, "Can you help this woman of Colour kicked out of the shelter, the other day it was a Black woman ... CAS called" ... neither my silence nor that of others meant a let-up in the hatred and the cruelty ... so after much thought I said, I will speak ... break the silence, I will and make sense of a different kind of war on women of Colour, Jewish and immigrant women, different from the daily violence waged on women by men ... are there any survivors? Are their any walking wounded of the shelter movement? ...

Introduction

In many parts of the world "empowerment" is integral to popular social change movements which promote social justice for oppressed people by changing the existing social order. Although initially relevant to exploited peoples in countries under the influence of dictatorships, capitalism, colonialism, neo-colonialism and imperialism, "empower- ment" has also become a commonplace phrase in the feminist move- ment in North America.

The feminist movement of the early 1970s not only led to the emer- gence of the anti-rape/sexual assault and anti-child abuse movement but also to the battered women's movement, enabling the emergence of the "battered woman" from the family closet. Consequently, the chal- lenges posed to the ideology of male supremacy/patriarchy have brought the private (personal) domain — the mythical safety of the home — into the public (political) realm and have centred the issue of the *empowerment* of assaulted women in existing struggles for equality for women.

391

Since the establishment of the first battered women's shelter in Alberta in 1972, wife/woman assault has become recognized as a social problem of epidemic proportions. The last two decades have seen the emergence of increased services for assaulted women. Valuable analysis of wife/woman assault has occurred through the careful documentation and analysis of testimonies of assaulted women by shelter workers and feminist academics. The lobbying efforts of women's organizations at the grassroots and national level and the hiatus of Royal Commissions and Enquiries on the Status of Women have led to the transformation of grassroots services into a network of state-funded shelters and related services for assaulted women and their children. Some will argue that increments in state funding have co-opted and diffused the political power of the shelter movement by creating a middle-class social service network.

Today "Wife/Woman Assault is a Crime" has become a familiar slogan, even in the men's movement against violence against women. Police have state directives to lay charges in incidents of "domestic disputes," however violence against women remains unabated. The Montreal Massacre of fourteen women and the continued high rates of femicide in the family (sixty-two percent) seem to indicate that freedom from violence for women is remote, leaving little room for complacency in the movement to end violence against women.

While the feminist movement has succeeded in putting gender-based violence on the national agenda, the anti-racist movement has gained momentum as well. Organizing efforts of the latter have resulted not only in the federal government's implementation of the multicultural policy of 1971 but, as well, the affirmative action and employment equity policies and initiatives by the state. Access to services by immigrants and members of diverse racial, ethnic and religious groups has attained prominence, necessitating many community consultations to bridge gaps in services.

In the context of shelters for battered women, the push for affirmative action by community activists has led to increased ethno-racial representation among staff counsellors, boards and volunteer workers. Moreover, the educational activities of immigrant and women of Colour shelter workers have not only resulted in demands for anti-racist service delivery but also in a notable increase in assaulted immigrant women and women of diverse racial backgrounds using shelter services. The latter is by no means indicative of increased violence in ethno-racial communities. Wife/woman assault transcends all boundaries of race, class, culture, religion and ability. Yet it has certainly challenged the white middle-class stranglehold on the social service sector. Demands for anti-racist service delivery have resulted in the mushrooming of the anti-racist and intercultural sensitivity training industry.

Where I enter ...

Toward the end of 1986 I joined the rank and file of front line workers at the Emily Stowe Shelter, then the only shelter in the region of Scarborough assisting assaulted women and their children. Having worked in traditional hierarchies of "malestream" services, this was an exciting move for me. I was coming into the work with a very grounded analysis of violence against women and a sensibility of myself as a downwardly mobile woman of Colour. Needless to say, the contradictions of feminism as an ideology and of feminist collectives in terms of race, class and lesbianism have left me, like others before me, politically squeezed because I refused to be tokenized or exoticized and resisted working just enough to get by. Among much sabotage of any anti-racist organizational change initiatives coming from women of Colour and in spite of willful slander directed at me, I joined the North York Women's Shelter in 1988 only to be politically squeezed again.

After approximately four years of full-time employment as a counsellor and a cultural interpreter — whose work was "impeccable" but who others "couldn't work with" — two years as a relief worker, two years of "recovery," I envisaged a journey to find other walking-wounded of the shelter movement, if there were any. I decided to document the experiences of immigrant, Jewish and women of Colour shelter workers, with the intent of exploring the notion of empowerment within various Metropolitan Toronto shelters and the implications therein for other feminist organizations.

I had believed that since shelter work is about empowerment — women experiencing male violence saying no to violence and taking control of their lives — the notion of empowerment was not removed from the workers' sense of their own empowerment. Is the motivation for working in feminist collectives not informed by the framework that all women are susceptible to male violence? The nature of our work demands elimination of any form of violence. Is the notion of power-sharing as opposed to power over — characteristic of malestream organizations — not the founding basis of feminist collectives? For that matter, are feminist collectives not oppositional models to hierarchies in society at large, which, in the first place, perpetuates violence against women? If the answer to the above is yes, as was constantly reiterated in the shelters where I worked, then certainly my experiences must be an abberation. Confusion and chaos became my companions, arising from the dissonance between what was professed about empowerment in shelters and what I carried in my body. To make sense of my experiences and the ensuing sense of craziness, as a South Asian worker who came out while working in shelters, I could only rely on my own inner wisdom. No, I was not insane ... my experiences in working in shelters were not empowering.

This is not to say that there was no inspiration, encouragement, or optimism and learning for me. But the only empowerment I experienced was vicariously attained through working with the women residing in shelters, who left violent situations or even returned to violent homes, more empowered and less isolated. After all, knowledge is power. To a marginal extent I was empowered by the camaraderie and solidarity of a few women of Colour, Jewish women and immigrant workers who refused to comply with the status quo, the mediocrity, rhetoric and hypocracy of shelters. On rare occasions after my exit and erasure, I encountered the occasional walking-wounded of the shelter movement. Past shelter workers who gave the sense of having left frustrated, powerless and wounded in the unstated power and control games inherent in the white, middle-class, heterosexual, able-bodied norms of feminist collectives. We would bump into one another, and say, "Let's get together and talk." But we never did.

For some of us, including myself, speaking of those experiences has not been possible until now. But contradictions of empowerment, confidentiality and secrecy, of silence and silencing, remain no more our burden to carry. We will not remain the walking-wounded of the shelter movement. Thus, though erased, I wish to reclaim and give voice to those experiences, with the intent of evolving a discourse and a political debate that is inclusive of the reality of *all* women.

Amidst the paucity of research on the experiences of shelter workers, particularly women of Colour, Jewish women and immigrant women, this article explores the issue of empowerment as relevant to the experiences of racially, ethnically and religiously diverse shelter workers. It will also examines whether multiculturalism and its concomitant affirmative action give authentic or token representation to women marginalized by race. Lastly, the article unravels who determines voice in shelters, and why, as well as the impact of this voice on service delivery. Here voice poses the question, Do women of Colour, Jewish women and immigrant women have a sense of agency in shelters? Are they agents of transformations in service delivery, policy and structures, or are they simply tokens?

A Note on Biases, Beliefs, Assumptions and Implications

Women all over the world face some form of oppression or exploitation, but women's experience of this oppression differs according to their race, class, culture, religion, ability, etc., in addition to gender. Issues of power and powerlessness based in race, class, sexuality, etc., are integral to empowerment.

The assumption of equality in feminist collectives is an end to achieve, not a given. Furthermore, the fallacious assumption of equality in feminist collectives denies and by denying exacerbates the inequities in power and privilege based on members' differential socio-political identities.

Multiculturalism perpetuates the very oppression it seeks to eliminate, by denying the power differential based on race and culture in a white supremacist society. Shelters are no exceptions to this.

The presence of assaulted immigrant and racially diverse women in shelters occasions the necessity for counsellors from similar backgrounds. This points to the feeling of powerlessness that assaulted immigrant women and women of diverse racial and cultural background feel within shelters.

If racially and ethnically diverse shelter workers feel disempowered in their work, immigrant, Jewish and women of Colour service recipients will experience disempowerment as well.

Since the "personal is political," an analysis of "empowerment" must emerge from the experiences of shelter workers who are not from the dominant group, for evaluations by service recipients are necessarily contaminated by their dependence on shelters for post-shelter support.

A Note on Language, History and Political Correctness

In as much as gender, race, class, sexuality, etc., are not neutral, the language needed to explicate these constructs is not neutral. Historically, the term "wife battering" spoke to the reality of legally married women who found themselves in violent homes. Given that "wife" excludes women who are living common-law or perhaps not even residing together and are experiencing violence from their male partner, the term "woman" as opposed to "wife" seems more useful. Furthermore, since "battering" is limited to physical assaults and ignores the psychological, emotional, sexual, economic abuse that are a part and parcel of violent heterosexual relations, "battering" is not a useful term. The term "assault" speaks to the criminal and chargeable nature of the act. Hence the usage of the term "woman assault" instead of wife battering.

Non-white/Women of Colour/Visible Minority Women

"Non-white" and "visible minority" women are terms used to indicate women whose racial-cultural identity is not white Anglo-Saxon and who, in addition to experiencing sexism, suffer the added oppression of racism in particular. Though "non-white" describes those without white skin privilege, politically it is not viable because of the negative connotation of "non" in non-white and the implied superiority of white.

"Visible minority" is problematic because people of Colour form nine-tenths of the world's population; however, they exercise less power than the minority whites in the world. It is the ideology of white supremacy and the power and privilege based on being white which underpin the oppression of people of Colour and that needs to be deconstructed in all institutions. Often we are invisible or homogenized within white liberalism, thus denying critical differences in power and privilege. "Oh, but first and foremost we are women" and the debate goes no further. To that my response is, "I just ain't a woman." More than anything, the invisibility of colour and its associated lack of privilege engenders further hatred of people of Colour, besides masking our diversity. The forementioned, however, still continue to be used.

"Women of Colour" was coined to bring to the forefront the denied added discrimination based on race. To address the particular needs of assaulted immigrant and women of Colour, especially to address racism, the term "women of Colour" is politically significant.

Sexuality

Lesbians have given tremendous leadership to various social change movements and there is an erasure of this herstory. It is imperative therefore that the term "lesbianism" be used. Also, lesbophobia and heterosexism are flip sides of the same coin. A thorough analysis of heterosexism is critical to understanding sexism, misogyny and the underpinning of violence against women generated through the institution of marriage.

A Note on the Actual Process

Seven shelter workers of diverse racial and religious backgrounds, ages, and current status in shelters participated in the interviews. Two group interviews comprising three and two women respectively were conducted and two women were individually interviewed because of time constraints and for safety reasons.

The racial mix of the group was Vietnamese, Black — from Jamaica and Trinidad — Jewish, European immigrant and South Asian women. Among these women, one was a lesbian and another bi-sexual; the remainder were heterosexual. The women were largely single mothers. There was some variation in age, ranging from the late-twenties to late-thirties. Four of the women had left shelters (one to three years) and the remaining were working in shelters (one to four years).

All participants were informed that this article will be exploring empowerment in the context of racially diverse shelter workers and the issue of multiculturalism.

Given the political nature of voice, I have decided to present a collage of comments from four women, as well as the three-women interview, to illustrate in tangible terms the experiences of the participants in their own voices. Furthermore, in addition to the analysis by the participants, I use the literature on race, class, gender, sexuality, etc., to inform the data analysis.

Four Voices

Following are some excerpts from interviews with four women. The initials are simply to differentiate between speakers and bear no relation to identity.

Y: Collective is very good for feminists ... We can prove our value as women working together. But it must be based in respect and sharing power and not control of power. But because of the imbalance of power women hurt women, just because they want to control power.

Y: Why have I been treated like a dog? ... It makes me crazy, crazy. I could not find an answer. But first I look at myself like an abused wife. You blame yourself first ... You question yourself, whether I did something wrong, or I am not sufficiently qualified, or my English is not as fluent as theirs or I don't have enough knowledge.

Y: I decided not to speak in the group because I don't feel safe from my situation ... The shelter community is small, most workers know each other and who knows if what I am going to talk about will be kept confidential or not. I was afraid that what I am talking about will turn back on me and my job will be jeopardized, which has already been hell for me.

N: In terms of the shelter movement ... I don't know what "empowerment" is supposed to mean because when women do take on the situation for self-power, self-strength and self-expression they are punished.

N: In terms of working within differences and different expressions, we take it issue by issue and we do not make the links.

N: In terms of the shelter, I bring in the issues of anti-Jewish racism, etc. They hired me because of my qualifications, but in the package they got a "Jew" which they didn't bargain for. I am a *good* Jew if I am what my résumé says and I am a *bad* Jew if I talk about anti-Jewish racism. Because it is not mentioned. I am the one who mentions it. Then I become a *single issue worker*, which I am not and nor do I want to be.... This is where my gut goes into my heart and my heart into my throat. I have been personally hurt at the shelter ... I am supposedly given a platform or space to speak from but no platform from which to speak from, so every time I speak, I am out of line ... it's just so painful as a shelter worker.

N: I have seen Jewish women's needs obliterated, actually stamped out in the shelter ... If I was to talk about it, and in naming anti-Jewish racism, if I get angry at the omission or invisibility, that anger is seen as more powerful and manipulating than what is actually being done by others... Actually, it's the manipulation of power, where the power in the world lies is being used to silence me.

N: I see state funding as a huge restriction on the shelters ... We are not as political as we would like to be, or as some of us would like to be ... We don't look at the fact that we are employees of the government...

C: Looking at representation and voice, as a Black woman there is a certain amount of silencing that I experienced from white women. I think that if you are above that silencing or you challenge the lack of support and acceptance that I expect from white women, you are perceived as *aggressive and controlling* ... If I go back to my experience, I can only say that it was *pathetic*. I get very emotional about it, so bear with me.

C: My pain is from both white women and immigrant women who have been silenced by white women ... The fact that immigrant women were not there for me was not a direct intent on their part. I relate that to their need to survive in the shelter movement as it is. But if we begin to understand the purpose of the shelter, I don't think that should be the situation, where so many immigrant women have to move away and experience so much bitterness — bitterness in the sense that the valued contributions made by them to expand the services ... there has been no validation or appreciation for that.

C: Multicultural services are a myth because immigrant women are further traumatized as there is a total lack of sensitivity to their needs.

C: I think if you truly understand what abuse does to women ... I think it is impossible for you to be able to deliver service to minority groups without understanding what racism does to oppressed people ... I think if you cannot understand the impact that society has on your life, you cannot truly understand violence against women. I think that is the first analysis that we have to have to begin to understand ... otherwise you can forget service delivery.

C: To work in a women's organization and be abused by women ... it is worse than that from men ... The abuse is intense. How can you be a feminist and be racist! This disdain for those endeavouring to unlearn racism and denial has to change and white women have to be accountable for their racism ... White women have to relinquish the control and power-share.

Y: I remember leaving the shelter feeling really battered ... bitter. And if I had not done the work on my self-esteem for a number of years, I would have felt totally worthless. This is the first time I am speaking publicly ... I feel really emotional ... I remember I just bled for three months straight — a direct result of being at the shelter, the stress level.

Three Voices

M: When I was working in the shelter there were two other non-white women. They had been there longer than I. When we had our staff meeting once every week and we used to go for lunch, I felt basically that it was totally impossible for me to socialize in any kind of relaxed way. It was just impossible. Never in all the time that I was there did I feel relaxed in a social gathering within the collective.

Not only as a woman of Colour, I was also isolated because my political position was not a hot favourite in that collective. In the staff meetings we were fighting and arguing, and sometimes it was only me who was fighting all the time over political issues. I think this made it much more difficult for me. The other thing was that because most of the women were white their socialization was very different from mine. Let me give an example, I did not even know how to say "quiche," which is a kind of food, and nobody told me what it was. The movies they would like or the music I would hear were different. There was no common ground. The only common ground I had with those women was the shelter.

Regarding the shelter, I was taking positions that did not make anyone comfortable. There was this poor white women. She did not have enough education, she did not have a job, she did not qualify for a good job and she was not in the position then to be entitled for Ontario housing. The shelter came to have a unit in a cooperative and they would not give it to her. They wanted to give it to someone who had a job, who qualified for Ontario housing, who had education and who was earning when she was living in the shelter. I have nothing against the [second] woman, but the only thing is that when you compare it with the situation of the other woman — who did not have nothing and she had a child to look after also — I could not believe how they could give that unit to the [second] woman and not to the poor woman. That was totally inconceivable. Can you believe it? I had to fight three months, every week, for that woman, that poor white woman to have that bloody unit. Can you believe that I am saying this now? And even now I can't believe it.

M: When I went into the shelter that was my second job in Canada. All my past experience was working very closely with women who had gone through different kinds of abuse. That was something that you almost naturally did. It is not that you are appointed a counsellor that you do it, but you do it because you are living in the community. I mean, I don't think it was a conscious decision to do that. I had experience of working with women who were abused for maybe ten years or so.

Until I came into the shelter I had not worked in a collective structure, but I knew what it was because that was how we were used to working in an informal situation. Now I think I took the mandate of the shelter, the commitment to the issue of abuse of women, and the structure of the collective very idealistically. I took everything to mean what it said, so I could not see that in the collective structure some women can practically cut each other's throat just because they want more power. I felt that this was not in the structure that I am going into.

D: But you have internalized it. So many people seem to have internalized these outside structures. Whether you set up a collective or not, inherently there is something in them that they have to put in place these structures. I had been working in collectives before and I have had bad experiences of collectives before, but I went back thinking this is going to be good. This is a ... women's shelter. We can all work together, we all know what the issues are, there is going to be something in common around here — and I rapidly found it just drifting away. Until in the last year and a half it disappeared in the issues of race and power itself. It is sad ... it is like losing this idealism about what you could have had.

M: Definitely, it is a loss of trust, it is a breach of trust.

B: My issues with the collective started when I got hired. When I went into this particular shelter they had never ever hired a Black woman as a full-time staff, and they were getting a lot of pressure from outside the community to hire a full-time Black worker. They had previously promised a white woman the position, but because of the political pressures they had to hire a Black woman, and I did not know all this dirt when I applied. I was the most qualified among those who applied for the position. Once I got hired, one white woman quit. It was really odd that in one evening she quit and became a part-time worker. Within days, she said to me, "You were hired as a token."

So I went back to the collective and I said, What is happening here? I mean, as far as I know, my work is excellent and I am highly qualified for this position, so why is this worker saying that I was hired based on my race? It was pushed under the rug. Two white women said, We will talk to the person about that, but that you were hired based on your skills. I said, What about my qualifications? I was the most qualified person who applied. They said, Well, we are not into qualifications. I thought that was really weird because as a Black woman you know that if you are not qualified, you do not get the job. Usually you get told that you are over-qualified and you do not get the job. So it started there. And then I never felt safe again.

Shortly after, they were going to hire again, and the same white woman they had promised the position to before was once again applying for the job. There was also another woman of Colour who out-qualified her in all aspects of the role that was required and that became a really big thing. We had to have a retreat. To make a decision, we had to leave Toronto. As to what that was doing to me as a Black woman in all this ... Anyway, they wanted this wonderful kind of retreat, a lot of food and having a really nice time and nobody could make a decision and so I thought I have to take a stand as the only Black woman there. I threw out the question in terms of, If this was a white woman applying for this position, would we need a retreat to make a decision? I also had to share with them my own responsibilities as a woman of Colour and the responsibilities to my communities to see some fair process because I live out there with these people and these are my people. So that was to be strike two because now I had caught them red-handed and people started to cry right, left and centre. So, of course, now I am the bitch. I mean victims cry, right!

Through my years there, I have seen significant amount of violence against women of Colour. Children were treated in a discriminatory manner, women were treated in a very patronizing manner, women were ignored, children were being treated with immense violence. I remember in particular — this was what tripped my resignation — an Asian child being asked to leave the playroom by a placement student, while white children could stay. I called the collective on it and it became really a big thing. I did not want to see any child experiencing that violence inside the shelter. I could not keep quiet about that. So my role out there in many ways was really service and challenging the racism that was embedded in there.

Because I am an excellent worker, I have very high expectations. So it was like, How dare you, a Black woman, challenge me? All that I was asking for was *accountability* because as a Black woman you have to be

highly accountable, you know, to survive. That's where I share something with you, M. Maybe similar to you in that I did not know the
culture, did not know how to go in and play the game. I went into work
and that was a major crime and I was highly punished for that one, too.

M: The collective members had a lot of power over the residents. Any
attempt to reduce that control of the collective over the residents was
not welcomed very much.

D: The residents who have challenged that power structure, who do not
fit into how they are supposed to be, seemed to be put down very quickly
and told, This is your place, this is who we are, and this is what we do.

M: I think this thing disturbed me very deeply. I think that I could not
believe it … The structure was there to heal women, not to control
women in this manner. My biggest issue was that the collective was
having discussions to have some kind of policy for penalties for residents for coming in late, etc. They had to sign a piece of paper saying
they are not going to do it again. It was just the formalizing of a penalty
structure. Now to my understanding, women do not come late every
night. But they are human beings and they are in crisis. What the heck
if they can't come right at 12:00 a.m. It is fine with me if they come at
12:00 or if they come at 2:00 a.m. They are feeling good and they have
drunk a bit, I don't mind. At night, I drink a bit, too, at home and
everybody in the collective did something of that sort. They made this
formalized structure of penalizing women for small things like not
doing chores, etc. That was formalized totally against my will. I really
fought it but every one seemed to want it and so …

I think it was just a formalization of the power they had. There is
power, but it is not formalized. But after some time the people who have
power they want it formalized because otherwise they do not feel
satisfied, maybe. I think power is a very greedy thing: you have a little
and you want to have more, especially if you are not political and not
consciously thinking about the process and how this is affecting you.
And if you are not doing that, then you keep on going deeper into it.
And I think it was totally unnecessary.

M: The thing is in that particular shelter, it had got to a stage where people wanted to formalize structures of power in order to feel safe. When I came in I was totally for dissolving that power because I was not with them in that greed. I was not conscious, though, at the time that I was going against their vested interest. What I was thinking was that they are not thinking straight.

D: It is almost as if people see power so finite that they have to have it to reassure themselves. As if to feel that they have to enforce it over other people. The paradoxical thing to me is that the more you have to enforce it the less you have, that if you have to make such an issue of it you don't have it. If I am secure in what I am doing and what I know, as I acknowledge the power that I have, I do not need to penalize a woman because she is coming an hour later or four. I don't need to say to somebody else, You didn't do your chore, so I give you this warning point.

We put a system of warnings, and I posted it at first, and I thought, Okay, I am tired of fighting this issue. Fine, you want me to give them warnings, I will play the game with you. But I realized very quickly that those warnings were used only with women we didn't like much, or to get rid off women, and not for the women who break the house rules. For example, we had this woman who smoked in her bed, came in drunk repeatedly. One time, her son came and helped her up the stairs because she was too drunk to walk and the other women were afraid of her. It did not matter how many warnings she got because she had friends who could keep her. Whereas with the other women who one night didn't come home until three or four in the morning, well, that was a major issue.

So it is interesting that they put a system of warnings to increase their own power base, to use those structures to get rid of the undesirable elements ... I think both among the staff and the residents they don't want.

M: I noticed that the people who were most hard in terms of these bureaucratic structures were also the people who did not do the actual counselling.

405

D: Exactly, absolutely. It is nine times out of ten. The people who have no contact with the women, who don't do counselling, who have no context except with the women that they choose to work with or their favourite persons.

M: There is another thing about the women — the kind of women that we are talking about. That is that they have become too comfortable in that job because they are not doing real counselling. They are not healing anybody. It really becomes like the skills they are using are not demanding on them, so they really become very comfortable in the job and they don't want to leave it because they might feel that in the competition out there — in terms of actual skills of counselling and other things — they cannot compete. So it just becomes like another job. It is not about a collective, it is not about the shelter, it is not about the abuse of women — it is just a job and all the struggle is about keeping the job. For some women I think it might be that simple.

B: Yeah, but I think it goes much deeper then that. I think it goes with this whole notion of feminism and that feminism means that you no longer have to be accountable. If feminism means that you cannot challenge, because if I love women then I will not challenge them based on this construction ...

B: I don't want to look at this really superficially. I think that it goes more deeply. I don't think anybody should work in a shelter full-time for more than two years in front-line work. I think after two years there is no way you can on a daily basis see women hurting, see women powerless in terms of housing and the health system, the court system and everything else and still continue to do good work.

D: No. You are absolutely right.

B: I think there has got to come a time when your body is going to close down and you are going to miss cues around you. You can no longer key into the pains because ... you will die. You have to block ... you must block ...

D: What you do is set up limits and you start setting up limits around how you work, where you work, who you work for and I realized that…

B: But also, the whole powerlessness that comes with being a shelter worker. I mean shelter workers are not considered professionals. They are not acknowledged. They are not seen as being qualified. This is where women of Colour are still more disadvantaged. For example, our case and the issues we were raising in terms of race and class in service delivery … We practically ran the shelter's programming. So they have experts coming into the collective with their ideas and not one person in the collective can say, But now is not that what R. was talking about?

M: Most of the fights that I started I won, but they were for the rights of the residents. Racism or the bureaucratic formalization of the issue, for example, of being ignored, or why someone's work was being ignored and not the other's, was never seen as important. It was just passed over to another meeting because it involved too much work and the staff would say, We have to discuss it some other time. We do not have enough time. You know, that was passed over definitely in different ways.

B: Like M., I really believed my voice was heard and I quite often felt they were respecting what I was saying on the condition that it was unrelated to race. If I raised something on race, my personality would be attacked and I would be told that I am too angry or what I said was not said in an appropriate way, that is, not using the rape crisis model of communication the right way — "When you say this, I felt that…" This is without any cultural analysis that a Jamaican Black woman does not speak like that. If you stepped on my foot and you hurt me, I say, You stepped on my foot … stop it. Not like, When you said or did, I feel … Which is *objectifying* me because I feel it, you know. So there is so much work that needs to be done.

M: I think there is very much a link between the shelter movement and the larger movement. I think that in the larger feminist movement it is much more deadly because it is affecting more woman than it is in the shelter movement. I think a lot of the issues related to race and class are not seen or acknowledged in the feminist movement, they are not seen and acknowledged in the shelter movement and that is my experience.

D: We can add sexual orientation to that. I am probably the only lesbian in the collective or in that shelter. I don't exist, my issues are non-issues. When I bring up issues around lesbianism, it doesn't matter. "We are not like that ... those issues don't affect us, we are good people, we would not treat you that way. We want to do a workshop on lesbian sexuality, so we are good people." You get really tired of talking and talking and fighting and fighting and being silenced. It is not even that you are silenced, it is as if you are speaking, but your voice has no sound. The movement ignores you, you do not exist.

D: We have had lesbian women in the shelters, but it is not acknowledged that they are lesbians in the shelter. In the shelter they basically come out to me and I know they are lesbians. I will have done the work with them, but otherwise no one else does any work with them. Lesbianism is not seen as a choice. For example, if a woman starts talking about building a relationship again and says she is not quite ready, first thing that is said is, Well, you will find a man who will be real nice to you. No one says, Maybe you will find a woman who would be really nice. It doesn't exist, it is not a choice. Oh! You are again rendered invisible. We do not deal with lesbian residents. If a resident makes homophobic comments, it is dismissed as a cultural thing, that there aren't any lesbians in India, so we do not have to worry about that.

You are faced with these comments like, Its okay. It is part of their culture to make homophobic comments like that. It shouldn't be part of anybody's culture to make homophobic comments. It is like saying, It is part of my culture to make racist comments, and it isn't. And it shouldn't be part of anybody's culture because then there is something wrong. It should not happen ... you need to call people on it and not say it is okay and make excuses for it. But that happens in the shelter every time.

B: In the shelter we used to talk about sex and sexuality a lot and they looked at us as if we were sick. I mean, as if once you came through the door you were *no longer sexual.*

M: You lose it.

D: Yeah! You become the vestal virgin service.

D: Nobody talks about sexuality. They want to talk about husbands, boyfriends, or it is always my children … Children is a real big topic because it is really a safe topic. People feel really uncomfortable with residents talking about their sexuality. They are uncomfortable when residents are going out on a date. Some of them go out and see their husbands once a week and get laid and come home, and it is like a real bad thing because she went out with her husband, or she went out with her boyfriend. So what is the big deal? You know there is a woman right now who talks about going out and getting her bananas and people talk about it as "not appropriate."

D: Abortion counselling is usually done by a few counsellors and the others tip-toe around the topic. Counselling on abortion issues is usually done as, Well, it is the woman's choice to choose what ever she wants to choose. I will never influence her in any way. Although I think the life that she carries within her is sacred, I would support her on any choice she makes. I am standing there thinking, You have already made a stand and there is no way on earth that you are going to be able to support this woman. I mean, we have been told that we cannot ask women applying to work about their stance on the issue of choice. I won't say that there is no place for pro-life in the feminist movement, but what happens within the shelter is that people put their issues on women and so sexuality and safe sex is not an issue, sex is not an issue, birth control is not an issue.

We had a woman, a resident, who was working as an escort, but she did not feel comfortable saying, This is my job. That was fine with me. But she told a resident she was working in it and anyways we eventually found out and people said we have to ask her to leave because she works at night. Well, I said, If you had a woman who worked night shifts or in a factory you would not tell her to quit her job because she worked at night. They just did not want her there. There is something wrong with a woman working at night as an escort. She was seen as a prostitute, she was seen as a lesser being.

M: I had a similar experience with a woman who was dancing in a night club. Most of the counsellors would not say anything openly, but she knew they were putting her down.

I want to go back to another issue. It seems like the concept of the "victim" is perpetuated in the shelter. They feel that they [women residents]do not have the right to enjoy, they do not have right to go out, they do not have right to have sex. It seems like an assaulted woman is like a sacred woman and she has to remain in that sacredness.

D: She is a martyr. I imagine this idea of woman as a martyr who must suffer and through her suffering she becomes saint-like and pure. There is this whole concept ... A woman comes into the shelter to heal and healing is a serious business which does not include going out or dancing or going out with a partner and having a drink.

M: And if someone is doing that they are not serious about the crisis.

D: I think we should be paid well. I think what's happening, though, is the money is not going to front-line work. I think the money is going into building bigger and better new shelters, more conveniences and better appliances — you know, new photocopier machines, two new computers instead of one. I look at our shelter, when we started we had really good benefits and over the years we were cut down. Everything that has been eroded has a direct impact on the counsellor and the front-line workers, while the hierarchy is getting stronger and more entrenched. As the funding is more secure, those at the top get more, those in the bottom get less of things.

M: We need to include the invisibility of women of Colour's work and that we feel we cannot go back to the shelter.

B: It reminds me of the political parties in Jamaica — if Manley, say, started to build a school now and he went out of power and the other party came into power, then Siago would come in and destroy that school from the foundation, or just leave it unfinished, or it would be completed and Manley would get no credit.

M: I just don't want to go back to it because I suffered a lot of emotional abuse in that shelter. Besides, maybe I have not dealt with it because I don't have time to do it. But the pain is still there. I don't want to go through it again. The other reason is that I did not develop any relations in that shelter with any one who was working at that time which would make me go back to it. I think that was because I was a Brown woman.

B: Initially, I was doing some relief work and that was even worse because people would come in and not see me. I think that I did about six shifts and felt that I had done enough self-abuse and being abused, I felt that there was no way that I could go in and do healing work if I was being abusive to myself, so I finally stopped. But one thing dawned on me ... because I work close by the shelter, that I would not drive close to it even. If I was going a block away, I would go south or north. I will not put myself in that position again ... I guess I am afraid. Also, I guess like M., I didn't build any alliances. The only alliance I built left with me. So I am very angry at the women who saw my work and destroyed it ... the women who didn't acknowledge it. I really think they are irresponsible and I don't want to be their friend. I'm very clear that I have no respect for the quality of their work because they can't do four full-time jobs and work for the shelter and do quality work.

You see women who are survivors, like Black people, when somebody said, You going to be okay? I say, Oh! If my people have had four hundred years of slavery, it is proof enough that I must have inherited that survival ability, you know. So women who go into the shelter will survive it. My major concern is that I am not sure I want to send any woman of Colour into the shelter, so that is certainly a dilemma.

B: Within this context, I think that the George Brown training program could play a critical inter-cultural part and make the attempt to make the connections of all these "isms." But the contradiction is that we are working with women who are wounded. In other words, they are not coming from a space where they can heal and do the work and move on because raising the "isms" means raising their own abusive histories. It is not happening. As long as we are divided, we won't have any power.

B: They have just started a white women's group and Black women's caucus separately. I don't know if it is happening in other shelters. I don't think they have the space yet. Women are now going in for therapy from the collective and they say it openly, so there is some long-term gain from that. I don't think caucuses work until people are educated about the context of women going into the shelter ... That kind of education is not happening.

M: There is another factor that we are totally forgetting because we were concentrating in a minute way on the shelter movement and our experiences in them, and that is the kind of society this feminist movement and the shelter movement is in. I think it is a very competitive and demanding society for individuals like us. It is cut-throat in terms of simple economic survival and I think we cannot ignore factors such as the economic system. That is, how people have to fight for employment and fight for an apartment. So race and class and sexuality have to be defined within that context.

I think what you were saying, D., in terms of your shelter, actually cannot be explained just in terms of race. It is more in terms of class, the economic condition that we are living in.

D: I think that there are many more issues where I work which you don't have in other shelters. I mean I am their token white woman, which I am not, and yet that is how they view me. It is funny because they view me as that when it is convenient and they view me as an immigrant woman also when it is convenient to them.

D: I refer to myself as the token white woman although I am not Anglo-Saxon. That's the bottom line. I am an immigrant child and I grew up in a different culture. Yet I am seen as being white when they want something from me or part of the privilege. For example, if grant proposals or blurbs for the funders are to be written, I will be asked to do so because "you write so well, you are so good with your language." I keep saying why doesn't somebody else write, and if there are problems, then I can sit down with the woman and maybe we can work out something together and I can teach them, I can help them. But I'm not going to be doing this and then when it comes to presenting it: "you tell me just stay at the shelter because they don't want to see a white woman appearing." I said, Wait a minute I'm an immigrant woman too. Sometimes I don't understand that, sometimes I feel caught because one day I am this and the next day I am that and it all depends upon what people want from me.

D: In my experience, alliances are made on class issues and various class levels but the over-riding thing is … I don't know … I can't find the commonality between the power. Like I said, there is a break in power and … there is a hierarchical structure. There are four people in power and the rest of the people are on their own. When I look at the commonalities that the woman have, it is not class, for the power they keep to themselves; it is not race, so the only thing I can say is, it must be politics or it must be the ….

M: The right-wing kind of politics.

D: Yeah!

M: I know what you are saying. Is it that there is a group of immigrant women who are forming an elite group on the basis of colour?

D: The situation is really complicated. I have spent a lot of time looking at it. It is a power elite that is based in right-wing politics, which is self-perpetuating … "We are only out for ourselves and our friends" type of politics and keep the jobs going. Then they have attempted to make alliances on race and class, but I don't think that has worked, so it has come down to power.

Actually, there is a conservative elite that cuts across class and colour that wants to maintain the status quo. I think it sort of typifies what you see almost in any country. Looking at Canada, you have a conservative elite that you have members from all cultural groups and it is the desire to keep power in one's own conservative hands and anybody who does not fit into it no matter what your class or colour, maybe ... Under "normal" (oops!) different circumstances there would be a break down into class and culture, it hasn't happened because when I look at it, the conservative elite represents members of all classes and cultures at that point, except Vietnamese, or Portuguese or Eastern European women...

M: Yeah! Just got me thinking about it just by listening to what I was hearing today and corroborating it with my experiences.

Certainly "racialism" is a very big issue that is not acknowledged.

D: Racialism is not acknowledged. I mean the theory is that we are all happy immigrants working together. I think I find that offensive. You just cannot assume that just because there are two Egyptian women they are going to be friends? How dare you assume that because they are Vietnamese they are going to become bosom buddies? They are setting up the ghetto and there is a real reinforcement of stereotypes. I mean, there is a lot of work that needs to be done in terms of racialism from resident to resident. For example, if somebody calls another "nigger" or "paki," then it is recognized as racism, but there is a lot that is not acknowledged. Say, if a South Asian woman goes to give a West Indian woman's child a cookie and the woman keeps saying, No you cannot give the child the cookie or food. But, if a Spanish woman gives that child something, and it is okay, then I say, Wait a minute, there has got to be an underlying issue here. That child isn't going to be full, twenty-four hours a day, every time one women gives her something to eat and it is not the same with another ... So there is so much work that needs to be done ... It is quite overwhelming.

Discussion

If "empowerment" is by definition "power from within" rather than "power over," if "empowerment" gives a sense of "personal and political control,"[1] then certainly the experiences as described by immigrant, Jewish and women of Colour, past and present shelter workers, have not been *empowering*. The silencing, invisibility, fear of reprisals, the greater demand for accountability, profound sense of betrayal, powerlessness, implicit coercion and punishment speak of grievous contradictions between the feminist mandates of shelters and the actual practices therein. In the same way that the notion of personal control can help us to define empowerment, so can the concepts of powerlessness and dependency help us to understand what it means not to be empowered. This section explores the disempowering experiences described and offers an analysis that may promote changes in the prevailing climates of shelters.

Participants have described their experiences in shelters as anything but empowering. The descriptions of the experiences and reactions of past workers — "pathetic," "feeling really bitter and battered," "punished," "whipped," "I guess slavery still exists" — by no means indicate empowerment. For those participants who have left the shelter movement, in spite of their continued involvement in struggles on women's issues, the thought of returning to shelter work as "frightening" is therefore not surprising but certainly disturbing.

For participants still working in the shelters, the hope of building bridges (not unlike their predecessors) encourages them to continue the struggle. Or as another participant states, "I still keep going ... It's like everyday I just survived another day." These comments from front-line workers display a deep sense of confusion that comes with a lack of control, a loss of power and agency. They, however, continue to engage themselves,in the hope that things might change. It is the seduction of possibilities that keeps them going. However, ironically enough, the struggles of both categories of participants show the hopefulness and the loss of hope for the desired absence of violence that characterizes the process, not unlike that of assaulted women leaving violent relationships.

Both categories of participants — those currently working and those who have left — display a profound sense of loss and demoralization stemming from a knowledge of the repercussions for pushing against the status quo. The process of healing has been long and the injuries still linger, as evidenced in the participants need to block the experiences, or as evidenced in the comment of one participant, "You just made me relive everything again ... I thought I had flushed it out."

More significant, perhaps, is that none of the participants had formally spoken about their experiences until the interviews. That one woman didn't feel safe even to do an interview with others present speaks volumes in itself about the terror that women of Colour experience in the workplace, shelters being no exception.

Though generally there was scepticism, the women felt relieved by giving voice to their experiences. Emotions ranged from a deep sense of isolation, fear of not being believed, fear of reprisals, denial and finally relief at giving voice to their experiences.

Two sources of considerable distress and anger for both the women of Colour and the Jewish woman were the sense of erasure/invalidation of their work and the fear that others like them would not be hired. Their statements are testimony to their frustrations at the resistance of the workers from the dominant culture to addressing and redressing racism, anti-semitism and class in the shelters. All participants attributed their pain to a part of their entity being rendered invisible.

The astonishment and outrage at the treatment meted out to working-class women testify to the invisibility of class issues. Furthermore, the formalization of power and control over women through the use of penalties speaks to contradictions. Women residing in shelters are infantilized, not regarded as responsible adults who make informed choices. To maintain control over women — not from the perspective of safety in the real sense of the word — policies of moving women to another shelter or warnings leading to discharge are implemented. This is borne out by the participants' accounts of constantly fighting for the rights of marginalized women and children. These accounts support the assumption that if immigrant, Jewish and women of Colour shelter workers feel disempowered, then all residents, particularly those from diverse ethno-racial backgrounds, will be correspondingly more vulnerable to similar disempowerment.

That women residents are often manipulated for the self-serving ends of staff or fall as pawns in power struggles within dysfunctional collectives or hierarchies is amply evident. Furthermore, that resident women are not allowed to have fun is indicative of a growing coercive morality and an alarming fundamentalism in shelters.

The responses of participants to the manner in which prostitutes, lesbians, and the issues of sex, abortion, sexuality are treated are frightening in their implications. The same manner in which issues of race, class are dealt or not dealt with, seems to be true for sex, sexuality and power. Sex and sexuality, if not taboo, are seen from a heterosexual framework, as evidenced in "Once you come through the door you were no longer sexual." Thus it comes as no surprise that prostitutes are dealt with disregard and contempt, while abortion is dealt with a repressive and insidious and dangerous liberalism. Often these issues get used to divide and conquer the progressive element.

In one shelter the historical existence of lesbians was negated. This erasure is no accident. Lesbians have been in the forefront of radical grassroots organizing on many social ills. As in other movements, once the transition towards "mainstreaming" commences, the lesbians are coerced out of the rank and file.

Though shelters may be empowering for some battered women and may enable them to leave violent relationships, the participants' responses indicate that it might not always be so. It is equally possible that many a woman residing in a shelter may simply endure her stay. Tiding her over in this temporary, though disempowering state, may well be the woman's own strength, fortitude and creativity. That this aspect of battered women is (mis)appropriated by the shelter workers is evident in the comment of a participant who states, "It seems that a victim mentality is perpetuated in shelters." This trend is reflective of, on one hand, the middle-class white cathartic feminist therapy industry and on the other, fosters subservient behaviour on the part of workers and also on resident women who do not fit the mythical norm. It perpetuates a benevolent tyranny in shelters where the "good girls" are rewarded and the "bad girls" are punished.

In a sense then, Jewish, women of Colour, immigrant or Canadian-born workers either do not have a voice or have a voice to the extent that it does not challenge the status quo. That their work was not equally valued, and at best was rendered invisible, speaks further to the tokenism and exploitation of the work of racially and ethnically diverse workers.

The participants identified their exclusion, marginalization and silencing to the predominance of the issue of gender. Due to the predominance of gender, any analysis of race, class, sexuality and ability get relegated to secondary importance. According to the participants, this state of affairs reflects the politics of the wider women's movement. Consequently, when these issues are raised they become "single worker's issues." Persistence in bringing visibility to these issues typically meets with resistance in the form of either denial or attack on the personality of the woman raising the issues. As a result, few alliances were made and if any were made, those alliances usually were with other racialized workers, who left in quick succession.

The regressive politics in shelters are seen in part as being linked to state funding. This trend leads to the growth of a "right-wing kind of politics" or "a conservative elite." Any attempt to address the depolitization of the shelter movement is not welcome and meet with reprisals.

Multiculturalism, by not recognizing colour and the related issues of power and privilege, perpetuates the very oppression it claims to undo. If there is a recognition of colour then it is tokenistic. Also, multiculturalism simply means hiring women who do not pose a threat to the status quo. This is evident in the struggles around hiring the woman of Colour who became a contentious candidate because of her political track record in another shelter. Typically, a collective crisis resulted when the racism was challenged by a women of Colour and the resolution of the crisis necessitated a retreat — a middle-class indulgence.

The result of these power struggles, the contradictions and a high level of accountability demanded of women of Colour and Jewish women workers adversely affected their health and well-being. The same was true of residents.

Resistance to empowerment work was attributed also to shelter workers' extended tenures in shelters and to their working four jobs at the same time. According to another shelter worker, the ensuing powerlessness becomes further aggravated when "shelter workers are not considered professionals." In spite of these struggles, these women felt some sense of empowerment through the bonding that evolved with assaulted women staying in the shelters.

Solidarity, Sisterhood and Alliances

Given that historically, race, class and sexuality and the implicit issues of power and powerlessness have prevented alliances across diversity/differences, a discussion on solidarity, sisterhood and alliances is merited both in the context of shelter collectives and collective struggles in the feminist movement.

Beginning with collective structures of shelters, the accounts cited indicate support in principle for a collective way of working with battered women. This belief has merit, given that a collective structure, with its theoretical emphasis on horizontal inter-relations, is critical to a feminist framework since it aims at eliminating the hierarchies of the traditional work milieus.

More fundamentally, collectives imply power-sharing, the repudiating of the one-up-one-down patriarchal relations central to the widespread violence against women by men. Moreover, collectives can provide the opportunity for forming alliances between all feminists from a place of mutuality and respect.

For collectives to be truly empowering, however, the taboo against confronting power and powerlessness based on race, class, sexuality, etc. — in addition to gender — must be eliminated. This was clearly evident in the analysis brought to bear by the participants as they told their experiences. Collectives can become the groundswell of alliances only if there is a political will to examine *power*, not only as it resides in patriarchal institutions, but in the political processes of collectives and in each of us. It is critical that power be made visible, if we are to shed the distortions of power and thereby eliminate the cultural patterns of domination and submission so "all women are free." As it stands, not only are women who do not meet the requisites of "the mythical norm" excluded from the wider women's movement, they are also marginalized, silenced and punished for challenging the status quo in the shelter movement. The process to end this state of affairs, although not an easy one, must be embarked upon.

To begin with, the pretence "to a homogeneity of experience covered by the word sisterhood"[2] must be forsaken. The subsumed equality in collectives must be challenged.

It is not surprising, given the facade of equality that the participants found, that in collectives "naming power is taboo [for] to raise the question of power is to threaten the freedom of those who have it," power obtained, of course, at the expense of others.[3] The backlash to challenging the status quo by raising the issues of power was resplendent with fears of reprisals in the responses of all participants.

Secondly, this state of affairs is indicative "that [not only do] white women ignore their in-built privilege of whiteness and define women in terms of their own experience alone, [but make] the Women of Colour become [the] other, the outsider whose experience and tradition is too 'alien' to comprehend."[4] Even more importantly, this reinforces the fear of difference invoked by the ideology of patriarchy and white supremacy at the outset. In a sense, having internalized "the dynamic of domination,"[5] many white women have internalized the "oppressor" to maintain a semblance of power and privilege. On the other hand, many women of Colour have internalized the "dynamic of oppression." For alliances to occur in shelter collectives or in the wider women's movement, "the identification and interruption of internalized oppression and internalized domination is, thus, seen as necessary."[6]

Immigrant and racialized women may align themselves with white women — "the same white women, who in the first place silence them" — to survive. This speaks of the powerlessness of women of Colour and their subsequent internalized racism, which further alienates them from others like them. This is but one example of how solidarity fails to occur between the oppressed groups in collectives. On the other hand, white members of collectives bond together on the basis of the power to dominate others, rather than out of respect for one another, and this prevents them from making alliances with women of Colour. Thus an environment is created in collectives where power, privilege and leadership cannot be challenged without bringing forth the divisive reactions of guilt, denial and over-personalization.[7]

One way to make visible and to deal with internalized oppression and domination is the use of caucuses. However, participants cautioned that caucuses are doomed to fail if they are unable to move women beyond catharsis. This is a must for translating anti-racist intent into action. Otherwise, one's sense of personal power continues to be perceived as a threat and repeatedly diminished by those entrenched in maintaining the status quo, as shown in the accounts of participants who felt battered or excluded and finally coerced to leave shelters.

Aside from internalized oppression and domination, "the contradictions of race, class and sexuality have made it clear that sisterhood in not enough."[8] "Common oppression" is not as "common" as we would like to believe. Thus "common oppression needs to be replaced by the recognition of our similarities as much as our differences." Alliances across differences demand that white feminists no longer give "lip service to women's diversity,"[9] that the racism, anti-semitism, classism and lesbophobia of the white women's movement not be swept under the rug and that white feminists definition of "gender as narrowly defined as the white woman's experience"[10] has to be eliminated. Failure to do so will not only block our vision and paralyze our creativity as diverse women but will create divisions which will play into the hands of our oppressors. This need is well-demonstrated in the accounts of the women, who found the definitions and mandates of shelters problematic when based on gender alone.

The homogeneity assumed by white middle-class feminists and the assimilationist and culturally pluralist strategies of multiculturalism are extremely palatable to the status quo since both fail to recognise "differences" in power and privilege. In failing to do so, both make invisible the power differentials based on race, class, sexuality, religion, ability, etc., and thereby perpetuate existing institutionalized subordination and domination. An interactive analysis of oppression is critical in disrupting the illusion of unity and equality that the state and the bourgeois feminist movement perpetuate. If the competition, hostility, perpetual disagreement and abusive criticism — trashing — that is the norm of feminist groups (shelter collectives being no exception) are to be eliminated, then an interactive analysis must inform any alliances made between diverse feminists.

The mythical dictates of the "unconditional" love offered by a homogenous feminism needs to be eliminated and a feminism rooted in knowledge of, respect for and commitment among women who are in essential ways different but whose interests are in essential ways akin must emerge. This transition is essential to power sharing.

In the process, then, the indignation and anger of both constituencies would be mobilized to dismantle the institutionalized inequities that account for the lack of control in the lives of all women. Further still, the internalized misogyny of women will be appropriately rectified and the emotion of anger rightfully politicized for the empowerment of all women, by directing it towards dismantling white supremacy and patriarchy.

The discussion has so far focused on issues largely pertinent to racially mixed collectives and alliances; however, these issues apply as well to predominantly women of Colour collectives and alliances. As we have seen in the interviews, internalized racism and other oppressions are issues here too. However, it is imperative to acknowledge that it is white women who are *racist*. While women of Colour can and do display prejudices against the dominant whites, they cannot be racist per se because they lack institutional power. This is not to say that women of Colour cannot oppress white women, but this needs to be seen in terms of class, sexuality, etc., where women of Colour in a given context exercise power. Furthermore, women of Colour may be racialist, nationalist and ethno-centric among their own kind. However, these need to be understood as by-products of the divide-and-conquer tactics of colonialism and imperialism. Without doubt, both internalized racism and racialism are companions, breeders of hatred of others and of self. Where white-skin-privileged immigrant women experience the traumas of displacement and settlement, their experiences are markedly different from the experiences of immigrant women of Colour.

Also worth cautionary attention are the male values that might inform alternative structures such as collectives: the creation of a conservative elite, the bureaucratization of state funding and the issue of the proverbial "healer ... heal thyself first" not being given attention in shelter work.

I believe that once our politics are truly politicized to be equally relevant to all women's realities, not only will we not be entrapped by bureaucracy, but we will be accountable to one another. The opportunism, oppression and the lack of humanity and empathy often seen in collectives and in larger alliances will be ended. Until then we will continue to co-opt and be co-opted, selling out the opportunity to heal ourselves and the planet.

Conclusion

Writing this article was extremely difficult, not only because of the difficulties in conducting the interviews, integrating the information gathered but also because of my own inability to stay present. The inconsistency in interview formats may be viewed as a shortcoming. However, it was imperative to respect participants' unwillingness to speak in individual or group interviews because of their fears of reprisal. The sample, though small, is fairly diverse across demographic lines. First Nations Women were not interviewed because of the time constraints and this is acknowledged as a limitation.

On discovering the similarities between the participants' experiences and the issues confronting them, and finding that none had formally spoken about their experiences, I decided that the only way to give voice and visibility to their shared experience was to present them in this format. Perhaps unusual, but minimally contaminated by even the flexible structures of qualitative feminist research. I wanted the participants to "live the words and the silence fully," or as the Chilean poet, Pablo Neruda, says, "Let me speak with your silence / Clear as a lamp / Simple as a ring."

For me, this writing also entailed recovering the words and the silence, enabling me, to become a subject in the transformation that comes from naming and reclaiming a voice ... for I too had been muted, trashed and exiled as a shelter worker, ironically enough, in the name of empowerment and feminism.

Epilogue

I learned while working in shelters that there is a cost to speaking out critically, and even though it is several years since leaving the shelters I still pay that price. The incestuous trashing network not only blocks and undermines any progressive discourse but also makes survival impossible. The experiences that had left me skinless also became the source of my strength and further strengthened an integrated anti-racist politic. I do know that I cannot remain silent. Silence will mean I, too, have participated and been complicit in the silencing and destruction of many women of Colour and Jewish women and therefore the decision to write. I appreciate the risks that the other participants have taken in speaking out and their desire to remain unnamed for fear of a backlash that comes from male-identified women. Also, it needs to be noted that this article is a work-in-progress for a thesis and is not intended to discount male violence. Violence against women as perpetuated by abusive men is not the same as that discussed by the women participants. Power differentials exist between women but are not based on gender. Given that when it suits men they appropriate the work of feminists they also undermine women's collectivity by using such writing to undermine the lethality of male violence towards women, a word of caution for the well-intentioned, and not so well-intentioned, men — do not misrepresent or (mis)appropriate. This writing was pursued with the intention of evolving an analysis of empowerment for all women, by bringing forward glaringly difficult issues of difference among women.

I wish to express my profound gratitude, respect and acknowledgement of the courage of the seven women who spoke out about their past and present struggles in the shelter movement. The participants once again court the risk of being trashed, minimized and trivialized, but speak we must. To remain silent would be to court death. This is our collective piece of resistance, opposition and protest, as we still rise with the courage of our conviction and are no longer held hostage by fear.

I want to reiterate that it is possible that other immigrant, Jewish or women of Colour may have empowering experiences while working in shelters. In such instances, the likelihood of alliances across differences has been possible, I assume, on the basis of political will and mutual respect. However, it has not been the case with the women I interviewed and no others that I know of.

The research was conducted for a term paper for the course, "Seminar in Community Psychology and Community Development" offered at the Ontario Institute for Studies in Education and is preliminary to a thesis.

Notes

1. D. Farlow and J. Lord. *A Study of Personal Empowerment: Implications for Health Promotion* (Kitchener: Department of Human Services, Centre for Research and Education, n.d.), p. 2.

2. Audre Lorde. *Sister Outsider: Essays and Speeches* (New York: The Crossing Press Feminist Series, 1984), p. 116.

3. Margaret Adair and Sandra Howell. *The Subjective Side of Politics* (California: Tools for Change, 1989), p. 6.

4. Lorde. *Op. cit.*, p. 117.

5. Charlotte Bunch in "Bringing the Global Home" in C. Bunch. *Passionate Politics: Feminist Theory In Action* (New York: St. Martin's Press, 1987), p. 329.

6. G. Pheterson in "Alliances Between Women: Overcoming Internalised Oppression and Internalized Domination" in Lisa Albrecht and Rose. M. Brewer, eds. *Bridges of Power: Women's Multicultural Alliances* (London: New Society Publishers, 1990), p. 37.

7. bell hooks. *Feminist Theory Margin to Center* (Boston: South End Press, 1984); Lorde, *op. cit.*; Bunch in "Making Common Cause Diversity of Coalitions" in Albrecht and Brewer, *op. cit.*

Bibliography

Books

Abdo, Nahla. *Family, Women and Social Change in the Middle East: The Palestinian Case.* Toronto: Canadian Scholars' Press, 1987.

Abo-Jaber, F. *et. al. Conditions of Some Working Women in Jordan.* Amman: UN-ECWA Publication, 1978.

Abu-Ghazaleh, Elham. *Ana...Anta wa-l Thawrah: Women's Poetry in the Third World.* Jerusalem: Ittihad al-Kuttab al-Falastiniyeen (Union of Palestinian Writers), Second Printing 1990.

Abu-Laban, B and S. McIrvin Abu-Laban, eds. *The Arab World: Dynamics of Development.* The Netherlands: E. J. Brill, 1987.

Abu-Lughod, Leila. *Veiled Sentiments: Honour and Poetry in a Bedouin Society.* Berkeley: University of California Press, 1986.

Acton, Janice *et al.*, eds. *Women Unite! An Anthology of the Canadian Women's Movement.* Toronto: Canadian Women's Educational Press, 1972.

Adair, M. and S. Howell, S. *The Subjective Side of Politics.* California: Tools for Change, 1989.

Adamson, Nancy, Linda Briskin and Margaret McPhail. *Feminists Organizing for Change: The Contemporary Women's Movement in Canada.* Toronto: Oxford University Press, 1988.

Afshar, Haleh. *Women, State, and Ideology: Studies from Africa and Asia.* Hong Kong: State University Press, 1987.

al Farouqi, Lois Lamya. *Women, Muslim Society and Islam.* Indianapolis: American Trust Publication, 1988.

al-Naqeeb, Khaldoun Hasan. *Society and State in the Gulf and Arab Peninsula: A Different Perspective.* London and N.Y.: Centre for Arab Unity Studies, 1990.

Albrecht, L. and Rose M. Brewer, eds. *Bridges of Power: Women's Multicultural Alliances for Social Change.* London: New Society Publishers. 1990.

Allen, S. and C. Wolkowitz. *Homeworking: Myths and Realities.* Houndsmills, Basingstoke: Macmillan Educational Press, 1987.

Alloula, Malek. *The Colonial Harem.* Minneapolis: University of Minnesota Press, 1986.

Altorki, Soraya. *Women in Saudi Arabia: Ideology and Behaviour Among the Elites.* New York: Columbia University Press, 1986.

Anzaldua, Gloria, ed. *Making Face, Making Soul: Haciendo Caras.* San Francisco: Aunt Lute Foundation Books, 1990.

Armstrong, Jeanette. *Slash*. Penticton: Theytus, 1986.

Azari, Farah. *Women of Iran: the Conflict with Fundamentalist Islam*. London: Ithaca Press, 1983.

Backhouse, Constance. *Petticoats & Prejudice: Women and Law in Nineteenth-Century Canada*. Toronto: Women's Press, 1991.

Barakat, Halim. *Visions of Social Reality in the Contemporary Arab Novel*. Washington, D.C.: Georgetown University Centre for Contemporary Arab Studies, 1977.

——. *Al Mujtama' al-Arabi al Mua'sir (Contemporary Arab Society)*. Beirut: Markaz Dirasat al-Wihdah al-Arabiyyah, 1984.

Baskin, Cyndy. *The Invitation*. Toronto: Sister Vision, 1993.

Bendt, Ingela and James Downing. *We Shall Return: Women of Palestine*. London: Zed Books, 1980.

Bernal, Martin. *Black Athena: The Afroasiatic Roots of Classical Civilization. Vol. 1: The Fabrication of Ancient Greece 1785-1985*. London: Free Association Books, 1987.

Best, Carrie M. *That Lonesome Road: The Autobiography of Carrie M. Best*. New Glasgow: The Clarion Publishing Company, 1977.

Blanchard, David. *Seven Generations: A History of the Kanienkehaka*. Kahnawake: Kahnawake Survival School, 1980.

Boris, E. and C. Daniels. *Homework: Historical and Contemporary Perspectives on Paid Labor at Home*. Urbana: University of Illinois Press, 1989.

Bowles, S. and H. Gintis. *Democracy and Capitalism*. New York: Basic Books, 1986.

Boylan, Esther. *Women and Disability*. London and New Jersey: Zed Press, 1991.

Braithwaite, Rella and Tessa Benn-Ireland. *Some Black Women*. Toronto: Sister Vision Press, 1993.

Brand, Dionne. *No Burden to Carry: Narratives of Black Working Women in Ontario, 1920s to 1950s*. Toronto: Women's Press, 1991.

Brant, Beth, ed. *A Gathering of the Spirit*. N.p.: Sinister Wisdom Books, 1984/ Ithaca: Firebrand, 1988/ Toronto: Women's Press, 1989.

——. *Mohawk Trail*. Ithaca: Firebrand, 1985/ Toronto: Women's Press, 1990.

——. *Food and Spirits*. Ithaca: Firebrand, 1991/ Vancouver: Press Gang, 1991.

Broker, Ignatia. *Night Flying Woman: An Ojibway Narrative*. St. Paul: Minnesota Historical Society, 1983.

Browne, Susan E., Debra Connors and Nanci Stern, eds. *With the Power of Each Breath: A Disabled Women's Anthology*. Pittsburgh: Cleis Press, 1986.

Bulkin, Elly, Minnie Bruce Pratt and Barbara Smith. *Yours in Struggle: Three Feminist Perspective on Anti-Semitism and Racism.* Brooklyn: Long Haul Press, 1984.

Burstow, Bonnie and Don Weitz, eds. *Shrink Resistant: The Struggle Against Psychiatry in Canada.* Vancouver: New Star Books, 1988.

Campbell, Maria. *Halfbreed.* Toronto: McClelland & Stewart, 1973.

Campling, Jo. *Images of Ourselves: Women with Disabilities Talking.* London: Routledge and Kegan Paul, 1981.

Carillo, Ann Cupolo, Catherine Corbett and Victoria Lewis. *No More Stares.* Berkeley: Disability Rights Education and Defense Fund, 1982.

Carnoy, Martin. *Education As Cultural Imperialism.* New York: David McKay Company, Inc., 1974.

Christensen, K. *Women and Home-based Work: the Unspoken Contract.* Westview Press: 1988.

Clarke, George Elliott. *Fire on the Water: An Anthology of Black Nova Scotian Writing.* Vols. I and II. Lawrencetown Beach, Nova Scotia: Pottersfield Press, 1991.

Commemorative Booklet. Amherstburg: The North American Black Historical Museum, 1984.

Conrad, Earle. *Harriet Tubman: Negro Soldier and Abolitionist.* New York: International Publishers, 1942.

Cornell, Drucilla. *Beyond Accommodation: Ethical Feminism, Deconstruction and the Law.* New York: Routledge, 1991.

Crow Dog, Mary. *Lakota Woman.* New York: Harper Perennial, 1990.

Culleton, Beatrice. *In Search of April Raintree.* Winnipeg: Pemmican, 1983.

Cuneo, C. *Pay Equity: The Labour-Feminist Challenge.* Toronto: Oxford University Press, 1990.

D'Aubin, April, ed. *Breaking the Silence.* Winnipeg: Coalition of Provincial Organizations of the Handicapped, 1988.

Dauenhauer, Nora Marks. "How to Make Good Baked Salmon" in *The Droning Shaman.* Haines: The Black Current, 1985.

Day, Sharon. *The Winds.* Chapbook

D'Oyle, Enid F. and Rella Braithwaite. *Women of Our Times.* Toronto: Self-Published, 1977.

Das Gupta, Tania. *Learning from Our History: Community Development with Immigrant Women, 1958-1986.* Toronto: Cross Cultural Communication Centre, 1986.

Davis, Angela. *Women, Race and Class.* New York: Vintage Books, 1981.

Dearden, A., ed. *Arab Women.* London: Minority Rights Group, 1983.

Deeb Jabbour, Hala. *A Woman of Nazareth*. New York: Olive Branch Press, 1989.

Deegan, Mary Jo and Nancy A. Brooks, eds. *Women and Disability: the Double Handicap*. Rutgers: Rutgers University Transaction Books, 1985.

Degener, Theresa *et. al.*, eds. *Geschlecht: behindertBesonderes Merkmal: Frau. Ein Buch von behinderten Frauen*. (*Sex: Disabled Significant Feature: Female. A Book by Disabled Women*). Munich: AG SPAK M68, 1985.

DeKeseredy, Walter and Ronald Hinch. *Woman Abuse: Sociological Perspectives*. Toronto: Thompson, 1991.

Deloria, Ella. *Water Lily*. Lincoln, University of Nebraska, 1988.

Doucette, Joanne. *Violent Acts Against Disabled Women*. Toronto: DisAbled Women's Network Toronto, 1986.

Driedger, Diane. *The Last Civil Rights Movement: Disabled Peoples' International*. London and New York: C. Hurst & Co. and St. Martin's Press, 1989.

—— and Susan Gray, eds. *Imprinting Our Image: An International Anthology by Women with Disabilities*. Charlottetown: gynergy books, 1992.

Duffy, Yvonne. *All Things Are Possible*. Ann Arbor: A.J. Garvin and Associates, 1981.

Eickelman, Christine. *Women and Community in Oman*. New York: New York University Press, 1984.

Ellis, Marc. *Beyond Innocence and Redemption: Confronting the Holocaust and Israeli Power*. New York: Harper & Row, 1990.

Eposito, John L. *Women in Muslim Family Law*. New York: Syracuse University Press, 1982.

Erdrich, Louise. *Love Medicine*. New York and Toronto: Bantam, 1989.

——. *Tracks*. New York: Henry Holt, 1988.

——. *The Beet Queen*. Boston: Bantam, 1987.

Falbel, Rita, Irena Klepfisz and Donna Nevel. *Jewish Women's Call for Peace: A Handbook for Jewish Women in the Israeli/Palestinian Conflict*. Ithaca: Firebrand Books. 1990.

Fine, Michelle and Adrienne Asch, eds. *Women with Disabilities: Essays in Psychiatry, Culture and Politics*. Philadelphia: Temple University Press, 1988.

FitzGerald, Maureen *et al.*, eds. *Still Ain't Satisfied! Canadian Feminism Today*. Toronto: Women's Press, 1982.

Francisco, Nia. *Blue Horses for Navajo Women*. Greenfield Centre: Greenfield Review, 1988.

Freire, Paulo. *Pedagogy of the Oppressed*. New York: Seabury Press, 1970.

Freeman, Minnie. *Life Among the Qallunaat*. Edmonton: Hurtig, 1978.

Fudge, J. and P. McDermott, eds. *Just Wages: A Feminist Assessment of Pay Equity*. Toronto: University of Toronto Press, 1991.

Fuss, Diana. *Essentially Speaking: Feminism, Nature, and Difference*. New York: Routledge, 1989.

Gadant, Monique, ed. *Women of the Mediterranean*. Zed Press: London, 1986.

Ghallem, Ali. *A Wife for My Son*. Chicago: Banner Press, 1984.

Gajerski-Cauley, Anne, ed. *Women, Development and Disability*. 2nd ed. Winnipeg: Coalition of Provincial Organizations of the Handicapped, 1989.

Ghallem, Ali. *A Wife for My Son*. Chicago: Banner Press, 1984.

Giddings, Paula. *When and Where I Enter: The Impact of Black Women on Race and Sex in America*. New York: William Morrow & Company, 1984.

Gordon, Linda. *Heroes of Their Own Lives*. New York: Viking, 1988.

Grant, John N. *The Immigration and Settlement of the Black Refugees of the War of 1812 in Nova Scotia and New Brunswick*. Hansport: Lancelot Press Ltd., 1990.

Gunn Allen, Paula. *The Woman Who Owned the Shadows*. San Francisco: Spinsters/Aunt Lute, 1983.

Hijab, Nadia. *Women's Power: the Arab Debate on Women at Work*. London: Cambridge University Press, 1988.

Hill Collins, Patricia. *Black Feminist Thought: Knowledge, Consciousness and the Politics of Empowerment*. New York and London: Routledge, 1990.

Hill, Daniel G. *The Freedom-Seekers: Blacks in Early Canada*. Agincourt: The Book Society of Canada Ltd., 1981.

Hine Clark, Darlene. *Black Women in White: Racial Conflict and Cooperation in the Nursing Profession, 1890-1950*. Bloomington: Indiana University Press, 1989.

hooks, bell. *Ain't I a Woman: Black Women and Feminism*. Boston: South End Press, 1981.

——. *Feminist Theory: From Margin to Center*. Boston: South End Press, 1984.

——. Yearning: Race, Gender and Cultural Politics. Toronto: Between the Lines, 1990.

—— and Cornel West. *Breaking Bread: Insurgent Black Intellectual Life*. Toronto: Between the Lines, 1991.

Hogan, Linda. *Mean Spirit.* New York: Antheneum/ Toronto: Collier McMillan, 1990.

Hum-Ishu-Ma (Mourning Dove). *Cogewea, The Half-Blood.* Lincoln: University of Nebraska, 1981.

Jaimes, Annette M. *The State of Native America: Genocide, Colonization, and Resistance.* Boston: South End Press, 1992.

Joe, Rita. *Poems of Rita Joe.* Halifax: Abenaki, 1978.

Johnson, E. Pauline. *Flint & Feather.* Toronto: Hodder & Stoughton, 1931.

———. *The Moccasin Maker.* Tuscon: University of Arizona, 1987.

Johnson, L. C. with R. E. Johnson. *The Seam Allowance: Industrial Home Sewing in Canada.* Toronto: Women's Press, 1982.

Jones, James H. *Bad Blood: The Tuskegee Syphilis Experiment.* New York: The Free Press, 1981.

Jones, Jacqueline. *Labor of Love, Labor of Sorrow: Black Women, Work and the Family from Slavery to the Present.* New York: Basic Books, 1985.

Kabbani, Rana. *Europe's Myth of the Orient.* Bloomington: Indiana University Press, 1986.

Kandiyoti, Deniz, ed. *Women, Islam and the State.* Philadelphia: Temple University Press, 1991.

Kanienkehaka Solidarity Group. *Bridges & Barricades: In Defense of Mohawk Land.* Montreal: McGill University, 1991.

Kaye/Kantrowitz, Melanie. *The Issue is Power.* San Francisco: Aunt Lute. 1992.

——— and Irena Klepfisz. *The Tribe of Dina: A Jewish Women's Anthology.* Vermont: Sinister Wisdom Books, 1986.

Keddie, Nikkie R. and Beth Baron, eds. *Women in Middle Eastern History: Shifting Boundaries in Sex and Gender.* New Haven: Yale University Press, 1991.

Keller, Betty. *Pauline: A Biography of Pauline Johnson.* Vancouver: Douglas & McIntyre, 1981.

Kelly, Liz. *Surviving Sexual Violence.* Minneapolis: University of Minneapolis Press, 1988.

Klepfisz, Irena. *Dreams of an Insomniac: Jewish Feminist Essays, Speeches and Diatribes.* Oregon: Eighth Mountain Press. 1990.

Lewis, D., with J. Barnsley. *Strategies for Change.* Vancouver: Women's Research Centre, 1990.

Lewis, D. et. al. *Just Give Us the Money: A Discussion of Wage Discrimination in Canada.* Toronto: McGraw-Hill Ryerson Limited, 1988.

Lind, Loren and Susan Prentice. *Their Rightful Place: An Essay on Children,*

Families and Childcare in Canada. Toronto: Our Schools/Our Selves, 1992.

Lockman, Zachary and Joel Benin, eds. *Intifada: The Palestinian Uprising Against Israeli Occupation.* Boston: South End Press and Toronto: Between the Lines, 1989.

Lorde, Audre. *Sister Outsider: Essays and Speeches.* New York: The Crossing Press Feminist Series, 1984.

Lowman, John *et. al.,* eds. *Regulating Sex.* Burnaby: Simon Fraser University School of Criminology, 1986.

Maclain, Craig and Michael Baxendale. *This Land Is Ours: The Mohawk Revolt At Oka.* Toronto: Optimum Publishers International Inc., 1990.

Mairs, Nancy. *Plaintext: Deciphering a Woman's Life.* New York: Harper & Row, 1987.

Matthews, Gwyneth Ferguson. *Voices From the Shadows: Women with Disabilities Speak Out.* Toronto: Women's Press, 1983.

McLaren, Angus and Arlene Tigar McLaren. *The Bedroom and the State: The Changing Practices and Politics of Contraception and Abortion in Canada, 1880-1980.* Toronto: McClelland and Stewart, 1986.

Mernissi, Fatima. *The Veil and the Male Elite.* Reading, Massachusetts: Addison-Wesley Publishing Company, 1992.

——. *Beyond the Veil: Male-Female Dynamics in Modern Muslim Society.* London: al-Saqi Books, 1985.

Milani, Farzaneh. *Veils and Words: the Emerging Voices of Iranian Women Writers.* Syracuse: Syracuse University Press, 1992.

Mitter, S. *Common Fate, Common Bond: Women in the Global Economy.* London: Pluto Press, 1986.

Morris, Jenny, ed. *Able Lives: Women's Experience of Paralysis.* London: The Women's Press, 1989.

Mumtaz, Khawar, and Farida Shaheed. *Women of Pakistan.* London: Zed Press, 1987.

Ng, Roxana. *The Politics of Community Services.* Toronto: Garamond Press, 1988.

Oliver, Pearleen. *A Brief History of the Colored Baptists of Nova Scotia, 1782-1953.* Halifax: n.p., 1953.

Pachai, Bridglal. *Beneath the Clouds of the Promised Land: The Survival of Nova Scotia's Blacks.* Vol. 2, 1800-1989. Halifax: Lancelot Press Ltd., 1990.

Parker, Arthur C. *The Constitution of The Five Nations or The Iroquois Book of The Great Law.* Albany: New York State Museum Bulletin, 1916.

Patton, Cindy. *Sex and Germs: The Politics of AIDS*. Boston: South End Press, 1985.

——. *Inventing AIDS*. New York: Routledge, 1990.

Phillips, Anne. *Engendering Democracy*. University Park: Pennsylvania State University Press and Cambridge: Polity Press, 1991.

Phillips, P. and E. Phillips. *Women and Work: Inequality in the Labour Market*. Toronto: James Lorimer and Co., 1983.

Phizacklea, A. *Unpacking the Fashion Industry: Gender, Racism and Class in Production*. London: Routledge, 1990.

Pierson, Ruth Roach. *"They're Still Women After All": The Second World War and Canadian Womanhood*. Toronto: McClelland and Stewart, 1986.

Rassam, Amal. *Social Science Research on Arab Women*. London: Frances Pinter, 1984.

Riley, Denise. *Am I That Name?* Minneapolis: University of Minnesota Press, 1988.

Ripley, C. Peter, ed. *The Black Abolitionist Papers, Vol. II* Chapel Hill and London: University of North Carolina Press, 1985.

Robinson, Gwendolyn and John W. Robinson. *Seek the Truth: A Story of Chatham's Black Community*. Canada: Self-Published, 1989.

Rodinson, Maxime. *Israel: A Colonial Settler State?* New York: Monad Press, 1973.

Roscoe, Will, ed. *Living the Spirit: A Gay American Indian Anthology*. New York: St. Martin's, 1988.

Rousso, Harilyn, with Susan Gushee and Mary Severance. *Disabled, Female and Proud! Stories of Ten Women with Disabilities*. Boston: Exceptional Parent Press, 1988.

Rush, Florence. *The Best Kept Secret*. New Jersey: Prentice Hall, 1980.

Saadai, Nawal. *Women at Point Zero*. London: Zed Press, 1983.

Said, Edward. *Orientalism*. New York: Vintage Books, 1979.

—— with Jean Mohr. *After the Last Sky: Palestinian Lives*. New York: Pantheon. 1985.

Sam-Comarty, Margaret. *This Land I Love*. Chapbook.

San Juan, Jr., E. *Racial Formations/Critical Transformations: Articulations of Power in Ethnic and Racial Studies in the United States*. London and New Jersey: Humanities Press, 1992.

Saxton, Marsha and Florence Howe, eds. *With Wings: An Anthology of Literature By and About Women with Disabilities*. New York: The Women's Press of the City University of New York, 1987.

Sayigh, Rosemary. *Palestinians: From Peasants to Revolutionaries*. London: Zed Press, 1979.

Sears, Vickie. *Simple Songs*. Ithaca: Firebrand, 1990.

Shaaban, Bouthaina. *Both Right and Left Handed: Arab Women Talk About Their Lives*. London: The Women's Press, 1988.

Shaarawi, Huda. *Harem Years: The Memoirs of an Egyptian Feminist* (Margot Badran, trans.). London: Virago Press, 1986.

Shadd Shreve, Dorothy. *The AfriCanadian Church: A Stabilizer*. Ontario: Paideia Press, 1983.

Sharabi, Hisham, ed. *Theory, Politics and the Arab World in Critical Perspective*. London: Routledge, 1990.

Silko, Leslie Marmon. *Almanac of The Dead*. New York and Toronto: Simon & Shuster, 1991.

—— *Ceremony*. New York: Viking Press, 1977.

Silvera, Makeda. *Silenced*. Toronto: Williams-Wallace, 1983.

——. *Piece of My Heart*. Toronto: Sister Vision, 1991.

Slipperjack, Ruby. *Honour The Sun*. Winnipeg: Pemmican, 1987.

——. *Silent Words*. Saskatoon: Fifth House, 1992.

Smith, Barbara, ed. *Homegirls: A Black Feminist Anthology*. New York: Kitchen Table Women of Color Press, 1983.

Spelman, Elizabeth. *Inessential Woman: Problems of Exclusion in Feminist Thought*. Boston: Beacon Press, 1988; London: The Women's Press, 1990.

Sterling, Dorothy. *We Are Your Sisters*. New York: W.W. Norton & Company, 1984.

Stewart, Houston, Beth Percival and Elizabeth R. Epperly, eds. *The More We Get Together*. Charlottetown: gynergy books, 1992.

Swirski, Barbara and Marilyn P. Safir, eds. *Calling the Equality Bluff: Women in Israel*. Tarrytown, New York: Pergamon Press, 1991.

Talbot, Carol. *Growing Up Black in Canada*. Toronto: Williams Wallace, 1984.

Talpade Mohanty, Chandra *et. al.*, eds. *Third World Women and the Politics of Feminism*. Bloomington: Indiana University Press, 1991.

Taylor, Darien and Andrea Rudd, eds. *Positive Women: Voices of Women Living with AIDS*. Toronto: Second Story Press, 1992.

Tibi, Bassam. *Islam and the Cultural Accommodation of Social Change* (Clare Krojzl, trans.). Boulder: Westview Press, 1990.

Tobias, Lenore-Keeshig. *Bird Talk*. Toronto: Sister Vision, 1992.

Tucker, Judith. *Women in 19th Century Egypt*. Cambridge: Cambridge University Press, 1985.

Walker, Gillian. *Family Violence and the Women's Movement.* Toronto: University of Toronto Press, 1990.

Walker, James W. St. G. *A History of Blacks in Canada: A Study Guide for Teachers and Students.* Hull: Ministry of Supply and Services Canada, 1980.

———. The Black Loyalists: The Search for a Promised Land in Nova Scotia and Sierra Leone 1783-1870. New York: Africana Pub. Co. and Halifax: Dalhousie University Press, 1976.

Walters, Anna Lee. *Ghost-Singer.* Flagstaff, Arizona: Northland, 1988.

———. *Talking Indian: Reflections on Survival and Writing.* Ithaca: Firebrand, 1992.

Ward, K., ed. *Women Workers and Global Restructuring.* Ithaca: ILR Press, 1990.

Warnock, Kitty. *Land Before Honour: Palestinian Women in the Occupied Territories.* New York: Monthly Review Press. 1990.

Wheeler, Kelly and Gem Wirszilas, eds. *Visions of Flight: A Journey of Positive Thought By and About Women With Disabilities.* Surrey: Self-Published, 1991.

White, J. *Mail and Female.* Toronto: Thompson Press, 1990.

Winks, Robin. *The Blacks in Canada.* New Haven: Yale University Press, 1971.

Women with Disabilities Feminist Collective. *Women and Disability: An Issue.* Melbourne: Women with Disabilities Feminist Collective, 1987.

Wood, S. *The Transformation of Work.* London: Unwin Hyman, 1989.

York, Geoffrey and Loreen Pindera. *Peoples of the Pines: The Warriors and the Legacy of Oka.* Toronto: Little, Brown & Company, 1991.

Yuval-Davis, Nira and Floya Anthias, eds. *Woman-Nation-State.* London: Macmillan, 1989.

Chapters in Books

Accad, Evelyn. "The Theme of Sexual Oppression in North African Novel" in Lois Beck and Nikki Keddie, eds. *Women in the Muslim World.* Cambridge: Harvard University Press, 1980.

Acker J. "Sex Bias in Job Evaluation: A Comparable Worth Issue" in C. Bose and G. Spitze, eds. *Ingredients for Women's Employment Policy.* Albany: State University of New York, 1987.

Ahmad, Leila. "Feminism and Feminist Movements in the Middle East" in Aziza al-Hibri, ed. *Women and Islam.* Tarrytown, New York: Pergamon Press, 1982.

Azzam, Henry. "Al-Mar'ah al-Arabiyyah wa Musharakatuha fi amaliyyat al-Tanmiyah (The Arab Woman and Her Participation in the Development Process)" in *The Arab Woman and Her Role in the Arab Unity Movement.* Beirut: Markaz Dirasat al-Wihda al-Arabiyyah, 1982.

Bakker I. "Women's Employment in Comparative Perspective" in J. Jenson *et. al.*, eds. *Feminization of the Labor Force.* Toronto: Oxford University Press, 1988.

Barakat, Halim. "The Challenge of Social Transformation" in Elizabeth Warnock Fernea, ed. *Women and the Family in the Middle East.* Austin: University of Texas Press, 1985.

Brand, Dionne. "Bread Out of Stone" in Libby Scheier, Sarah Sheard and Eleanor Wachtel, eds. *Language in Her Eye: Writing and Gender by Canadian Women Writing in English.* Toronto: Coach House Press, 1990.

Briskin, L. "Feminist Practice: A New Approach to Evaluating Feminist Strategy" in Jeri Wine and Janice Ristock, eds. *Women and Social Change: Feminist Activism in Canada.* Toronto: James Lorimer and Company, 1991.

Brooks-Higginbottam, Evelyn. "The Problem of Race in Women's History" in Elizabeth Weed, ed. *Coming to Terms: Feminism, Theory, Politics.* New York: Routledge, 1989.

Bunch, Charlotte. "Bringing the Global Home" in Charlotte Bunch. *Passionate Politics: Feminist Theory in Action.* New York: St. Martin's Press. 1987.

Calliste, Agnes. "Canada's Immigration Policy and Domestics from the Caribbean: The Second Domestic Scheme" in Jesse Vorst, ed. *Race, Class, Gender: Bonds and Barriers.* Toronto: Between the Lines, 1989.

Carty, Linda. "African Canadian Women and the State: Labour Only Please" in *We Are Rooted Here, And They Can't Pull Us Up: Essays in African Canadian Women's History.* Toronto: University of Toronto Press, Forthcoming 1994.

Chrystos. "I Am Not Your Princess" in *Not Vanishing.* Vancouver: Press Gang, 1988.

Danforth, Pat. "Women with Disabilities" in McDonnell, Kathleen and Mariana Valverde, eds. *The Healthsharing Book: Resources for Canadian Women.* Toronto: Women's Press, 1985.

Dobash, Russell P. and R.E. Dobash. "The Response of the British and American Women's Movements to Violence Against Women" in Jalna Halmer and Mary Maynard, eds. *Women, Violence and Social Control.* Atlantic Highlands, New Jersey: Humanities Press International Inc. 1987

Dworkin, Andrea and Catherine MacKinnon. "Whose Freedom of Speech?"

in *Pornography and Civil Rights: A New Day for Women's Equality.*
Minneapolis: Organizing Against Pornography, 1988.

Egan, Carolyn *et. al.* "The Politics of Transformation" in Frank Cunningham *et. al.,* eds. *Social Movements/Social Change.* Toronto: Between the Lines, 1988.

Findlay, Sue. "Democratizing the Local State: Issues for Feminist Practice and the Representation of 'Women'" in Greg Albo *et. al.,* eds. *A Different Kind of State.* Toronto: Oxford University Press, 1993.

———. "Making Sense of Pay Equity: Issues for Feminist Political Practice" in Judy Fudge and Patricia McDermott, eds. *Just Wages.* Toronto: University of Toronto Press, 1991.

———. "Facing the State: The Politics of the Women's Movement Reconsidered" in Heather Jon Maroney and Meg Luxton, eds. *Feminism and Political Economy: Women's Work, Women's Struggles.* Toronto: Methuen, 1987.

Freccero, Carla. "Notes of a Post-Sex Wars Theorizer" in Marianne Hirsch and Evelyn Fox Keller, eds. *Conflicts in Feminism* (New York: Routledge, 1990.

Freeman, Jo. "The Tyranny of Structurelessness" in Jane Jaquette, ed. *Women in Politics.* New York: John Wiley & Sons, 1974.

Giacaman Rita and Penny Johnson. "Palestinian Women: Building Barricades and Breaking Barriers" in Zachary Lockman and Joel Benin, eds. *Intifada: The Palestinian Uprising Against Israeli Occupation.* Boston: South End Press and Toronto: Between the Lines, 1989.

Hamilton, Sylvia. "Naming Names, Naming Ourselves" in *We Are Rooted Here, And They Can't Pull Us Up: Essays in African Canadian Women's History.* Toronto: University of Toronto Press, Forthcoming Spring 1994.

Hernandez, Carmencita. "The Coalition of Visible Minority Women" in Frank Cunningham *et. al.,* eds. *Social Movements/Social Change.* Toronto: Between the Lines, 1988.

LaDuke, Winona. "Natural to Synthetic And Back Again" in Ward Churchill, ed. *Marxism and Native Americans.* Boston: South End Press, 1982.

Leslie, Genevieve. "Domestic Service in Canada, 1880-1920" in Janice Acton, *et. al.,* eds. *Women at Work: Ontario, 1850-1950.* Toronto: Canadian Women's Educational Press, 1974.

McKay, Nellie Y. "Race, Gender and Cultural Context in Zora Neale Hurston's Dust Tracks on a Road" in Bella Brokzki and Celeste Schenck, eds. *Life/Lines: Theorizing Women's Autobiography.* Ithaca: Cornell University Press, 1988.

Najmabadi, Afsaneh. "Hazards of Modernity and Morality: Women, State and Ideology in Contemporary Iran" in Deniz Kandiyoti, ed. *Women, Islam and the State*. Philadelphia: Temple University Press, 1991.

Ng, Roxana. "State Funding to a Community Employment Centre: Implications for Working with Immigrant Women" in Jacob Mueller *et. al.*, eds. *Community Organization and the Canadian State*. Toronto: Garamond Press, 1990.

Phillips, Susan. "How Ottawa Blends: Shifting Government Relationships with Interest Groups" in Frances Abele, ed. *How Ottawa Spends: The Politics of Fragmentation*. Ottawa: Carleton University Press, 1991.

Prentice, Susan. "'Kids are Not for Profit': The Politics of Childcare" in Frank Cunningham *et. al.*, eds. *Social Movements/Social Change: The Politics and Practice of Organizing*. al. Toronto: Between the Lines, 1988.

Ristock, Janice and Jeri Wine. "Feminist Activism in Canada" in Jeri Wine and Janice Ristock, eds. *Women and Social Change: Feminist Activism in Canada*. Toronto: Lorimer: 1991.

Roberts, Barbara. "'A Work of Empire': Canada Reformers and British Female Immigration" in Linda Kealy, ed. *A Not Unreasonable Claim: Women and Reform in Canada: 1880s-1920s*. Toronto: Women's Press, 1979.

Savanah Williams in "The Role of the African United Baptist Association in the Development of Indigenous Afro-Canadians in Nova Scotia, 1782-1978" in Barry Moody, ed. *Repent and Believe: The Baptist Experience in Maritime Canada*. Hansport: Lancelot Press Ltd. for Acadia Divinity College, 1980.

Schecter, S. "Building Bridges Between Activists, Professionals and Researchers" in Kersti Yllö and Michele Bograd. *Feminist Perspectives on Wife Abuse*. Newbury Park, California: Sage Publications, 1988.

Stasiulis, Daiva. "The Politics of Minority Resistance Against Racism in the Local State" in Jacob Mueller *et. al.*, eds. *Community Organization and the Canadian State*. Toronto: University of Toronto Press, 1990.

Stone, Sharon D. and Joanne Doucette. "Organizing the Marginalized: The DisAbled Women's Network" Frank Cunningham *et al.*, eds. *Social Movements/Social Change*. Toronto: Between the Lines, 1988.

Tall Mountain, Mary. "Good Grease" in *The Light on the Tent Wall: A Bridging*. Los Angeles: UCLA, 1990.

Thompson, D. "Bureaucracy and Democracy" in *Democratic Theory and Practice*. Cambridge: Cambridge University Press, 1983.

Thornton, Bonnie Dill. "Race, Class and Gender: Prospects for an All-Inclusive Sisterhood" in Mary Jo Deegan and Michael Hill, eds. *Women and Symbolic Interaction*. Boston: Allen & Unwin Inc. 1987.

Valverde, Mariana. "When the Mother of the Race is Free: Race, Reproduction, and Sexuality in First-Wave Feminism" in Franca Iacovetta and Mariana Valverde, eds. *Gender Conflicts: New Essays in Women's History*. Toronto: University of Toronto Press, 1992.

Wainwright, Hilary. "The State and Society: Reflections of a Western Experience" in Kaldor, M. and G. Holden and R. Falk, eds. *The New Detente*. London: Verso, 1989.

Walby, S. "Flexibility and the Changing Sexual Division of Labour in S. Wood, ed. *The Transformation of Work*. London: Unwin Hyman, 1989.

Yalnizyan, A. "Full Employment — Still a Viable Goal" in *Getting on Track: Social Democratic Strategies for Ontario*. Montreal: McGill-Queen's Press, 1991.

Young, Iris Marion. "Social Movements and the Politics of Difference" in *Justice and the Politics of Difference*. Princeton: Princeton University Press, 1990.

Articles

Abdo, Nahla. "Middle East Politics Through Feminist Lenses: Negotiating the Terms of Solidarity" in *Alternatives*, No. 18, 1993.

——. "Racism, Zionism and the Palestinian Working Class, 1920-1947" in *Studies in Political Economy*, No. 37, Spring 1992.

——. "Women of the Intifada: Gender, Class and National Liberation" in *Race and Class*, Vol. 32, No. 4, 1991.

Adams, Mary Louise. "There's No Place Like Home" in *Feminist Review*, No. 31, Spring 1989.

Ahmad, Leila. "Western Ethnocentrism and Perceptions of the Harem" in *Feminist Studies*, Vol. 8, No. 3, Fall 1982.

Amos, Valerie and Pratiba Parmar in "Challenging Imperial Feminism" in *Feminist Review*, No. 17, 1984.

Antonius, Soraya. "Fighting on Two Fronts: Conversation with Palestinian Women" in the *Journal of Palestine Studies*, Vol. VIII, No. 3, 1979.

Armstrong, P. and H. "Lessons from Pay Equity" in *Studies in Political Economy*, No. 32, Summer 1990.

Aswad, Barbara. "Key and Peripheral Roles of Noble Women in a Middle East Plains Village" (Margot Badran, trans.) in the *Anthropological Quarterly*, Vol. 40, No. 3, 1967.

Azzam, Henry. "Analysis of Fertility and Labour force differentials in the Arab World" in the *Population Bulletin of the United Nations Economic Commission for Western Asia*, No. 16, June 1979.

Badran, Margot. "Dual Liberation: Feminism and Nationalism in Egypt, 1870s-1925" in *Feminist Issues*, Spring 1988.

Bannerji, Himani. "Re:Turning the Gaze" in *RFR/DRF,* Vol. 20, Nos. 3-4.

Barille, Maria. "Disabled Women: An Exploited Underclass" in *Canadian Woman Studies/les cahiers de la femme,* Summer 1992.

——. "A New Voice in the Women's Community" in *Communiqu'ELLES,* September 1986.

Barret, S. "Paths Towards Diversity: An Intrapsychic Perspective" in *Women and Therapy,* Vol. 9, 1993.

Barrett, Michell and Mary McIntosh. "Ethnocentrism in Socialist Feminist Theory" in *Feminist Review,* No. 20, 1985.

Beach, Jane. "The Only Answer for Child Care" in *Canadian Woman Studies/les cahiers de la femme,* Vol. 12, No. 3, 1992.

Black, Ayanna. "Working with Collectives" in *Tiger Lily,* Vol. I, No. 2.

Blouin, Barbara. "Welfare Workers and Clients: Problems of Sexism and Paternalism." *Canadian Woman Studies/les cahiers de la femme,* Summer 1992.

Bogle, Marlene T. "Brixton Black Women's Centre Organizing on Child Sexual Abuse" in *Feminist Review,* No. 28, January 1988.

Bourne, Jenny. "Homelands of the Mind: Jewish Feminism and Identity Politics" in *Race and Class,* Vol. 29, No. 1, Summer 1987.

Brascoupe, Pat and Georges Erasmus. "Index on Native Canadians" in *Canadian Forum,* April 1991.

Briskin, Linda. "Feminism: From Standpoint to Practice" in *Studies in Political Economy,* No. 30, Autumn 1989.

Brown, Louise. "The Personal is Apolitical" in the *Women's Review of Books,* Vol. VII, No. 6, March 1990.

Cantarow, Ellen. "Zionism, Anti-Semitism and Jewish Identity in the Women's Movement" in *Middle East Reports (MERIP),* September-October 1988.

Carty, Linda. "Women's Studies in Canada: A Discourse and Praxis of Exclusion" in *RFR/DRF,* Vol. 20, Nos. 3-4.

Cole, Juan Ricardo. "Feminism, Class and Islam at the Turn-of-the-Century Egypt" in the *International Journal of Middle East Studies,* Vol. 13, No. 4, 1979.

COPOH. "An Interview with Joan Meister" in *Compass,* No. 1, Summer 1988.

Cornelius Mohawk, Carol. "Native Women: Working For The Survival of Our People" in *Akwesasne Notes,* Late Fall, 1982.

D'Aubin, April and Paula Keirstead. "An Emerging Movement" in *Compass,* No. 1, Summer 1988.

Darweish, Marwan. "The Intifada: Social Change" in *Race and Class*, Volume 31, No. 2, October-December 1989.

Doucette, Joanne. "Disabled Women and Poverty: Double Oppression" in *Just Cause: A Journal of Law and People with Disabilities*, No. 5, Fall 1987.

—— and Dawn Heiden. "White Feminist Racism in the March 8th Coalition" in *Cayenne*, Vol. 2, June-July 1986.

Driedger, Diane. "Speaking for Ourselves: A History of COPOH on Its 10th Anniversary" in *Caliper*, Vol. XLI, December 1986.

——. "Women with Disabilities in Developing Countries" in the *Association for Women and Development Newsletter*, No. 5, Summer 1991.

——. "Women with Disabilities: Naming Oppression" in *RFR/DRF*, Vol. 20, Summer 1991.

——. "Discarding the Shroud of Silence: An International Perspective on Violence, Women and Disability" in *Canadian Woman Studies/les cahiers de la femme*, No. 12, Fall 1991.

——. "From Artisan to CEO: Women with Disabilities Take on the Global Challenge" in *MATCH News*, Spring 1991.

——. "Literacy for Whom? Women with Disabilities Marginalized" in *Women's Education des femmes*, No. 8, Winter 1991.

——. "Women with Disabilities Challenge the Body Beautiful" in *Healthsharing*, Vol. 12, Winter-Spring 1992.

—— and April D'Aubin. "Disabled Women: International Profiles" in *Caliper*, Vol. XLI, March 1986.

Dueck, Susan Gray. "Stepping Stones to the Land of the Living" in *Women's Education des femmes*, No. 9, Spring 1992.

Ellinger, Nina. "Forum 1985 in Retrospect" in *Disabled Women's International Newsletter*, No. 1, June 1986.

Fine, Michelle and Adrienne Asch. "Disabled Women: Sexism Without the Pedestal" in the *Journal of Sociology and Social Welfare*, Vol. VIII, July 1981.

Fleming, Pam. "Gender Bias and the Law: Is It Enough?" in *Canadian Woman Studies/les cahiers de la femme*, Summer 1992.

Franklin, Kris. "A Family Like Any Other Family: Alternative Methods of Defining Family in Law" in the *New York University Review of Law and Social Change*, Vol. 18, 1990-1991.

Ghossoub, Mai. "A Reply to Hammami and Rieker" in *New Left Review*, No. 120, 1988.

Giron, Eileen. As told to Diane Driedger and April D'Aubin in "Women and

Disability in El Salvador: An Uphill Fight for Rights and Visibility" in *Kinesis*, September 1991.

Gomez, Jewelle. "Repeat After Me: We Are Different, We Are The Same" in the *New York University Review of Law and Social Change*, Vol. 14, 1986.

Gran, Judith. "The Impact of the World Market on Egyptian Women" in, *MERIP*, No. 57, 1977.

Hale, Sandra. "The Wing of the Patriarch: Sudanese Women and Revolutionary Parties" in *MERIP*, January-February 1986.

Hamilton, Sylvia. "Our Mothers Grand and Great: Black Women of Nova Scotia" in *Canadian Woman Studies/les cahiers de la femme*, Vol. 4. No. 2, 1982.

Hammami, Reza. "Women, the Hijab and the Intifada" in *MERIP*, Nos. 164-165, May-August, 1990.

—— and Martina Rieker. "Feminist Orientalism or Orientalist Marxism" in *New Left Review*, No. 120, 1988.

Harris, Angela. "Race and Essentialism in Feminist Legal Theory" in the *Stanford Law Review*, Vol. 42, February 1990.

Hatem, Mervat. "The Enduring Alliance of Nationalism and Patriarchy in Muslim Personal Status Laws" in *Feminist Issues*, Vol. 6, No. 1, 1986.

Hegland, Mary Elaine. "Political Roles of Iranian Village Women" in *MERIP*, January-February 1986.

Herman, Didi. "Are We Family? Lesbian Rights And Women's Liberation" in the *Osgoode Hall Law Journal*, Vol. 28, 1990.

International Labour Organization. *Conditions of Work Digest*, Vol 8, Homework. Geneva: ILO, 1990.

Israel, Pat. "Editorial" in Women and Disability Issue, *RFR/DRF*, No. 14, March 1985.

Jack, Carolyn. "Food Banks and the Politics of Hunger" in *Canadian Forum*, December 1991.

Joseph, Souad. "Women and Politics in the Middle East" in *MERIP*, January-February 1986.

Kelly, Liz. "What's in a Name? Defining Child Sexual Abuse" in *Feminist Review*, No. 28, January 1988.

Khater, Akram and Cynthia Nelson. "Al-Haraka al- Nissa'iyyah: The Women's Movement and Political Participation in Modern Egypt" in *Women's Studies International Forum*, Vol. 11, No. 5, 1988.

Lazreg, Marnia. "Feminism and Difference: the Perils of Writing as a Woman on Women in Algeria" in *Feminist Studies*, Vol. 14, No. 1, Spring 1988.

Lipsig-Mummé, C. "The Renaissance of Homeworking in Developed Economies" in *Industrial Relations*, No. 38, 1983.

"Women in the Clothing Trades" in *Studies in Political Economy*, No. 22, 1987.

Macdonald, M. "Post-Fordism and the Flexibility Debate" in *Studies in Political Economy*, No. 36, 1991.

MacLeod, Mary and Esther Saraga. "Challenging the Orthodoxy: Towards and Feminist Theory and Practice" in *Feminist Review*, No. 28, January 1988.

Magar, Michele. "Disabled Women Organize" in *MS.*, January 1986.

Mama, Amina. *Feminist Review*, No. 17, 1984.

——. *Feminist Review*, No. 20, 1985.

Martin, Ged. "British Officials and Their Attitudes to the Negro Community in Canada, 1833-1861" in *Ontario History*, Vol. LXVI, No. 2, June 1974.

Martin, Susan and the Women of DAWN. "Disabled Women and Sex: 'We have successes and failures'" in *Kinesis*, October 1986.

McPherson, Cathy. "Tackling Violence Against Women with Disabilities" in *Canadian Woman Studies/les cahiers de la femme*, Vol. 12, Fall 1991.

——. "Vulnerable Victims of Assault" in *Archetype*, 1987.

Meister, Joan. "DAWN Is Rising" in *Herizons*, Vol. 3, October-November 1985.

——. "DisAbled Women Win NAC Support" in *Kinesis*, July-August 1986.

Mernissi, Fatima. "Muslim Women and Fundamentalism" in *MERIP*, July-August 1988.

Miller, Jean B. and J. Surrey. "Revisioning Women's Anger: The Personal and the Global" in *Work In Progress*, Vol. 43, 1990.

Moghadam, Valentine. "Islamist Movements and Women's Responses in the Middle East" in *Gender and History*, Vol. 3, No.3, 1991.

Mytelka, L. "Global Shifts in the Textile and Clothing Industries" in *Studies in Political Economy*, No. 36, 1991.

Nelson, Cynthia. "Public and Private Politics: Women in the Middle Eastern World" in the *American Ethnologist*, Vol. 1, No. 3, 1974.

——. "The Voices of Doria Shafik: Feminist Consciousness in Egypt 1940-1960" in *Feminist Issues*, Vol. 6, No. 2, 1986.

—— and Virginia Olsen. "The Veil of Illusion: A Critique of the Concept Equality in Western Feminist Thought" in *Catalyst*, Nos. 10-11, Summer 1977.

Ng, Roxana. "Sexism, Racism and Canadian Nationalism" in *Socialist Studies*, No. 5, 1990.

Peteet, Julie. "Women and the Palestinian Movement: NO GOING BACK?" in *MERIP*, January-February 1986.

Philip, Marlene Nourbese. "The Disappearing Debate: Racism and Censorship" in *This Magazine*, Vol. 23, No. 2, 1989.

Rockwell, Susan. "Palestinian Women Workers in the Israeli-Occupied Gaza Strip" in the *Journal of Palestine Studies*, Vol. XIV, No. 2, Winter 1985.

Ross, Becki. "Heterosexuals Only Need Apply: The Secretary of State's Regulation of Lesbian Existence" in Special Issue on Feminist Perspectives on the Canadian State, *RFR/DRF*, Vol. 17, No. 3, September 1988.

Ryan, Sheila. "The Israeli Economic Policy in the Occupied Areas: Foundations of a New Imperialism" in *MERIP*, No. 24, 1974.

Said, Edward. "Representing the Colonized: Anthropology's Interlocutors" in *Critical Inquiry*, Nos. 19-20, Fall 1989.

Sands, Ellen. "Poverty on the Reservation: One Woman's Experience" in *Canadian Woman Studies/les cahiers de la femme*, Summer 1992.

Sayigh, Rosemary. "Roles and Functions of Arab Women" in the *Arab Studies Quarterly*, Vol. 3, No. 3, Summer 1981.

Shohat, Ella. "Gender in Hollywood's Orient" in *MERIP*, No. 162, January-February, 1990.

———. "Sephardim in Israel: Zionism from the Standpoint of its Jewish Victims" in *Social Text.* Nos. 19-20, Fall 1988.

"Statement of the Black Women's Collective, Presented to the Coalition on February 5, 1986" in *Our Lives*, Vol. 1, No. 1, March 1986. Reprinted in *Cayenne*, Vol. 2, Toronto, June-July 1986.

Strom, Ann. "FFO's [Norway] Group of Disabled Women" in *DPI Calling*, Vol. 6, March 1990.

Stuart, Meryn and Glynis Ellerington. "Unequal Access: Disabled Women's Exclusion from the Mainstream Women's Movement" in *Women and Environments*, Vol. 12, Spring 1990.

Tate, Denise and Nancy Hanlan Weston. "Women with Disabilities: An International Perspective" in *Rehabilitation Literature*, Vol. 43, July-August 1982.

Thomas, B. " The Fourth R?: Racism and Education" in *Currents: Readings in Race Relations*, Vol. 2. No. 3, 1984.

Toews, Charlynn. "Feika Makes Women a Priority" in *Herizons*, Vol. 5, March 1987.

Troper, Harold Martin. "The Creek-Negro of Oklahoma and Canadian Immigration, 1909-11" in the *Canadian Historical Review*, Vol. 53, 1972.

Warskett, R. "Wage Solidarity and Equal Value" in *Studies in Political Economy*, No. 32, Summer 1990.

Wood, Chris *et. al.* "Sending in The Troops" in *Maclean's,* September 3, 1990.

Yuval-Davis, Nira. "Front and Rear: Sexual Division of Labour in the Israeli Military" in H. Afshar, ed., *Women, State and Ideology.* London: Macmillan, 1986.

Zaremba, Eve. "Collective Trouble" in *Broadside,* Vol. 10, No. 1, October 1988.

"Basic Call to Consciousness" in *Akwesasne Notes.* Via Rooseveltown, New York: the Mohawk Nation, 1986.

"Cayenne Takes Up the Debate" in *Cayenne,* Vol. 2, No. 2-3, June-July 1986.

"Kahnawake" in *Tribune Juive — Magazine d'actualité culturelle,* janvier-fevrier, 1989.

"Violence Against Women: Strategies for Change." Special Issue of *Canadian Woman Studies/les cahiers de la femme,* Vol. 12, No. 1, Fall 1991.

"Women and Disability Project in Sweden" in *DPI Calling,* Vol. 6, March 1990.

DIVA: A Quarterly Journal on South Asian Women. Special Issue on Violence Against South Asian Women, Vol. 3, No. 2, March 1992.

Fireweed — A Feminist Quarterly. Special Issue. No. 16, 1983.

Fireweed — A Feminist Quarterly. Special Issue. No. 26, 1988.

Ms., Vol. II, No. 5, March-April 1992.

Papers

Canadian Disability Rights Council and DisAbled Women's Network. "Four Discussion Papers on New Reproductive Technologies." Winnipeg: CDRC and DAWN, 1990.

Cleveland, Gordon. "Provincial Day Care Subsidy Systems in Canada." A background document produced for the House of Commons Special Committee on Child Care, 1987. Photocopied.

D'Aubin, April. "Disabled Women's Issues: A COPOH Discussion Paper." Winnipeg: COPOH, 1986.

Derksen, Jim. "The Disabled Consumer Movement: Implications for Rehabilitation Service Provision." Winnipeg: COPOH, 1980.

Friendly, Martha, Laurel Rothman and Mab Oloman. "Child Care for Canadian Children and Families: A Discussion Paper." Ottawa, 1991. Photocopied.

Gould, Janice. "Disobedience (in Language): Texts by Lesbian Natives." Unpublished speech to the Modern Language Association. New York, 1990.

Heumann, Judith E. "Acquiring a Voice of Our Own: Women with Disabilities Advance into the Mainstream of Society." Presented at the United

Nations Seminar on Women with Disabilities, Vienna, Austria, August 20-24, 1990.

MacIntosh, Peggy. "White Privilege and Male Privilege: A Personal Account of Coming to See Correspondence Through Work in Women's Studies." *Working Paper No. 189.* Wellesley: Wellesley College Centre for Research on Women, 1988.

Ontario Coalition for Better Child Care. "Commercial Child Care Fact Sheets." March 1991. Photocopied.

——. "Draft Response to Setting the Stage: A Public Consultation Paper on Child Care Reform in Ontario." Toronto: 1992. Photocopied.

Ontario Ministry of Community and Social Services. "The Parents Newspaper." Toronto: COMSOC, 1992.

——. "Setting the Stage: A Public Consultation Paper on Child Care Reform in Ontario." Toronto: COMSOC, 1992.

——. "Summary of Consultations on Child Care Reform." Toronto: COMSOC, 1992.

Ridington, Jillian. "Beating the 'Odds': Violence and Women with Disabilities." Position Paper 2. Vancouver: DisAbled Women's Network Canada, 1989.

——. "Different Therefore Unequal: Employment and Women with Disabilities." Position Paper 4. Vancouver: DisAbled Women's Network Canada, 1989.

——. "The Only Parent in the Neighbourhood: Mothering and Women with Disabilities." Position Paper 3. Vancouver: DisAbled Women's Network Canada, 1989.

——. "Who Do We Think We Are: Self-Image and Women with Disabilities." Position Paper 1. Vancouver: DisAbled Women's Network Canada, 1989.

Panitch, Leo. "Address on Democratic Administration." Toronto: Ministry of the Attorney General, November 1990. Photocopy.

Conference Papers and Proceedings

D'Aubin, April, ed. "Proceedings of COPOH's Workshop on Disabled Women's Issues." Winnipeg: COPOH, 1987.

DAWN Canada. "National Organizing Meeting of the DisAbled Women's Network, March 26-29, 1987." Winnipeg: DAWN Canada, 1987.

Driedger, Diane, ed. "Aim At the Sky: Report of the Disabled Peoples' International North American and Caribbean Region — Disabled Women in Development Seminar — Roseau, Dominica, July 18-22, 1988." Kingston, Jamaica: DPI North American and Caribbean Regional Secretariat, 1989.

Heumann, Judith E. "Acquiring a Voice of Our Own: Women with Disabilities Advance into the Mainstream of Society." Presented at the United Nations Seminar on Women with Disabilities, Vienna, Austria, August 20-24, 1990.

Morris, Cleata. *Impetus — The Black Woman.* Address to the Fourth National Congress of Black Women of Canada. Windor: Proceedings of the National Congress of Black Women of Canada, 1977.

Oldfield, M. "The Electronic Cottage — Boon or Bane for Mothers? in A.M. Letito and I. Ericsson, eds. Proceedings of the Conference on Women, Work and Computerization, Helsinki, Finland, 1991.

Pike, Lois. "A Selective History of Feminist Presses and Periodicals in English Canada." A. Dybikowski *et al.*, eds. *The Feminine: Women and Words: Conference Proceedings 1983.* Edmonton: LongSpoon Press, 1985.

Ridington, Jillian. "Beating the 'Odds': Violence and Women with Disabilities." Position Paper 2. Vancouver: DisAbled Women's Network Canada, 1989.

———. "Different Therefore Unequal: Employment and Women with Disabilities." Position Paper 4. Vancouver: DisAbled Women's Network Canada, 1989.

———. "The Only Parent in the Neighbourhood: Mothering and Women with Disabilities." Position Paper 3. Vancouver: DisAbled Women's Network Canada, 1989.

———. "Who Do We Think We Are: Self-Image and Women with Disabilities." Position Paper 1. Vancouver: DisAbled Women's Network Canada, 1989.

Shah, Dr. Fatima. "Right to Equality of Women with Disability." Presented at the Disabled Peoples' International Symposium, Ottawa, Ontario, Canada, 1986.

United Nations. "Seminar on Disabled WomenVienna20-24 August 1990." Draft Report released August 1990.

"COPOH Fifth National ForumEdmonton, Alberta, 1983." Conference Report. Winnipeg: COPOH, 1984.

"Echange Entre Femmes." Conference Report. Montreal: Action des Femmes Mtl., c. 1989.

Reports

Ambrosio, E. *et. al.* "Street Health Report: A Study of the Health Status & Barriers to Health Care of Homeless Women & Men in the City of Toronto." Toronto: N.p, n.d.

Bisset, L. and U. Huws. "Sweated Labour: Homework in Britain." London: London Low Pay Unit, 1985.

City of Vancouver. "Executive Summary: A Preliminary Study of Selected

Morbidity and Mortality Indicators in Census Tracts." Vancouver: City of Vancouver, 1986.

Coalition for Fair Wages and Working Conditions for Homeworkers. "Brief to the Government of Ontario." Toronto: CFWWC: 1991.

Committee on Sexual Offences Against Children and Youth. "Sexual Offences Against Children." Ottawa: Department of Supply and Services, 1984.

Economic Council of Canada. "Good Jobs, Bad Jobs." Ottawa: Ministry of Supply and Services, 1990.

Farlow, D. and J. Lord. "A Study of Personal Empowerment: Implications for Health Promotion." Kitchener: Department of Human Services, Centre for Research and Education, n.d.

Gunderson, M. et. al. "Women and Labour Market Poverty." Ottawa: Canadian Advisory Council on the Status of Women, CACSW, June 1990.

Huws, U. "The New Homeworkers, New Technology and the Changing Location of White-collar Work." London: London Low Pay Unit, 1984.

International Ladies' Garment Workers' Union. "Study of Thirty Chinese-Speaking Homeworkers." Toronto: ILGWU, 1991.

Mukherjee, A. "From Racist to Anti-Racist Education: A Synoptic View." Toronto: Toronto Board of Education's Department of Race Relations, 1988.

National Action Committee on the Status of Women. "Review of the Situation of Women 1992." Toronto: NAC, 1992.

Ontario Native Women's Association. "Final Study Report on Aboriginal Family Violence." Thunder Bay: Ontario Native Women's Association, 1989.

Participatory Research Group. "Women on the Global Assembly Line." Toronto: PRG, 1985.

Rochon, Monique and Pierre Lepage. "Oka-KanehsatakeSummer 1990: A Collective Shock." Montreal, Commission des droits de la personne du Quebec, April: 1991.

Social Planning Council of Metro Toronto. "Electronic Homework Research Project." Toronto: SPC: 1984.

Werkerle, Gerda and Sylvia Novac. "Gender and Housing in Toronto." Toronto: Women and Work Institute of the City of Toronto, June 1991.

West Yorkshire Homeworking Group. "A Penny A Bag: Campaigning on Homework." Batley: Yorkshire and Humberside Low Pay Unit, 1990.

White, J. "Women and Unions." Ottawa: Canadian Advisory Council on the Status of Women, 1980.

"Child Poverty in Action." N.p.: Child Poverty Action Group. 1990.

"Equal Opportunity Corporate Review 1986-1990." Toronto: City of Toronto Management Services Department, 1991.

"Fair Shares: Income, Wealth and Taxation in Canada." Toronto: The Workers' Information and Action Centre, 1991.

"The GST in The Big Tax Picture." Ottawa: Action Canada Network, 1991.

"Report Card on the Health of the Toronto Economy." Toronto: The Workers' Information and Action Centre, 1992.

"Report of the Coalition Against Police Violence." Toronto: Coalition Against Police Violence, 1992.

"The Waste of a Nation: Poor People Speak Out About Charity." Vancouver: End Legislated Poverty, 1992.

House of Commons Proceedings

"Minutes, Proceedings and Evidence of the Standing Committee on Aboriginal Affairs — House of Commons — Ottawa, March 12, 1991.

Material in Archives

Brown, Rosemary. Keynote Speech to the National Congress of Black Women, April 1973. Ottawa: Daniel Hill Papers, National Archives of Canada.

Head, Edmund. Letter to Lord Grey. CO42/167, PRO, London.

History of the Hour-A-Day Study Club History. The North American Black Historical Museum Papers, Amherstburg, Ontario, n.d.

McCurdy, Alvin. Letter written on behalf of the Amherstburg Community Club to the NAACP in Detroit, June 1934. Alvin D. McCurdy Papers.

The *Provincial Freeman* (1855). Ontario Provincial Archives.

Stratton, H.E., Letter to the Amherstburg Community Club. Ontario Provincial Archives, *Alvin D. McCurdy PapersReference F 2076.*

Press Releases

B.C. Union of Chiefs. "B.C. Chiefs Call For Immediate Action in B.C. to Save Lives and Protect Rights at Oka," September 3, 1990.

Grandmothers in Solidarity with Mohawk Clan Mothers, September 2, 1990.

Mohawk Women of Kahnawake. August 31, 1990.

Manifestos

"The Feminist Manifesto." Prepared for a National Action Committee on the

Status of Women annual general meeting. Vancouver: Working Group on Sexual Violence, 1985.

Newsletters and Pamphlets

Flawline, Action Line. Vancouver: End Legislated Poverty, January 1992-January 1993.

Wham Comix. National Union of Provincial Government Employees and the Public Service Alliance of Canada, Ottawa: NUPGE and PSAC, January 1992.

Kits

Marshall, J. "Training for Empowerment: A Kit of Materials Based on an Exchange among Educators from Mozambique, Nicaragua and Brazil." Toronto: The Moment Project, 1990.

Bibliographies

Bibliography on Violence and Sexual Abuse, May 1991. (Available at Parentbooks, 201 Harbord Street, Toronto, Ontario, M5S 1H6.)

Unpublished

Abdo, Nahla. "Colonial Capitalism and Rural Class Formation." University of Toronto Ph.D. diss., 1989.

Cassin, M. "Women, Work, Jobs and Value: The Routine Production of Inequality — A Report with Special Reference to Consumer's Gas." Dalhousie University, 1990.

Goodleaf, Donna. Unpublished manuscript, n.d.

Moran, Mary. *Métisse Patchwork.* Unpublished manuscript, n.d.

"Oscroft Manifesto," 1972.

Rowbotham, S. "Strategies Against Sweating: Experiences of Organizing Against the Casualization of Women's Work in Nineteenth- and Early Twentieth-Century Europe and the United States." 1992.

Zepeda, Ofelia. Unpublished manuscript, n.d.

Contributors

Nahla Abdo is an Assistant Professor in the Department of Sociology and Anthropology at Carleton University, Ottawa. She specializes in the Middle East, particularly in gender issues. Active in the feminist and anti-racist movements, she has published extensively on gender, race, nationality, class and the state. She is currently editing *Who Silences Palestinians?: A Feminist Critique of Racial, National, and State Oppression*. The book embraces the voices of Palestinian women, Arab and Eastern Jewish women, and European Jewish women.

Carol Allen is a Black lesbian feminist who graduated from law school in 1992. Her background includes working with The Women's Legal Education and Action Fund (LEAF) on its subcommittees for cases involving lesbian and race equality issues. She is a frequent speaker on lesbian equality and on the intersection of race, gender and lesbian identity. At press time, she is articling at the law firm Sack, Goldblatt and Mitchell in Toronto.

Martha Ayim is a short story writer and editor who joined Women's Press in 1991. She has been co-managing editor since February 1993.

Jan Borowy is a community activist and Research Coordinator for the International Ladies' Garment Workers' Union Ontario District.

Peggy Bristow is one of a group of Black women excavating the history of Black women in Canada. She is particularly interested in how Black women have organized, often in ways not conventionally seen as political. She is a contributing author of the forthcoming book, *We Are Rooted Here, And They Can't Pull Us Up: Essays in African Canadian Women's History*. She is also a researcher at the Centre for Women's Studies at the Ontario Institute for Studies in Education.

Beth Brant is a Mohawk writer, editor and teacher, a grandmother and a lesbian. She is the author of two collections of short stories, *Food & Spirits* (Press Gang/Firebrand) and *Mohawk Trail* (Women's Press /Firebrand),

and the editor of *A Gathering of Spirit,* the first collection of writing by Indigenous North American women. Her work on and off the page has been essential to the development of First Nations writers in Canada and the United States.

Debi Brock is a Toronto-based socialist feminist. She teaches sociology at Ryerson Polytechnical Institute in Toronto.

Ann Decter is a feminist writer and editor living in Toronto. She is author of the novel, *Paper, Scissors, Rock* (Press Gang Publishers, 1992) and has been a co-managing editor of Women's Press since 1990.

Diane Driedger has worked in the disabled people's movement for thirteen years at the local, provincial, national and international levels. She was involved in the founding of Disabled Peoples' International and currently works with the Coalition of Provincial Organizations of the Handicapped (COPOH) as its International Development Officer. Her most recent book is *Imprinting Our Image: An International Anthology by Women with Disabilities,* co-edited with Susan Gray. Until a recent brush with a back disability, Diane was a non-disabled ally in the disabled persons' movement.

Sue Findlay is a white feminist living in Toronto who writes about the relation between women and the state as it has been reorganized since the Report of Canada's Royal Commission on the Status of Women in 1970. Working from her experiences over the last three decades with federal, provincial and municipal governments and her participation in feminist organizations in Ottawa and Toronto, she has published articles in anthologies such as *Feminism and Political Economy, Just Wages* and *A Different Kind of State.*

Maureen FitzGerald teaches in an access program at the University of Toronto and is active in Lesbians Making History, an oral history project. She works on the social issues manuscript group at Women's Press and also expresses her passion for publishing as the managing editor of Well Versed Publishing.

Chris Gabriel is a member of Women's Press and a graduate student at York University, Toronto. Her doctoral dissertation focuses on how the struggles of Third World women in Canada are mediated by the the politics of official multiculturalism.

Donna Kahenrakwas Goodleaf is a citizen of the Kanienkehaka Nation, Kahnawake Territory, Quebec, Canada. She is a political activist and scholar and teaches women's studies at the University of Massachusetts, Amherst.

Shelly Gordon has been active in the women's movement and in solidarity with the labour movement for almost twenty years. She is the Coordinator of the City of Toronto Workers' Information and Action Centre of Toronto.

Amy Gottlieb is an artist, a lesbian and feminist activist and part of the Jewish resistance to the occupation of Palestinian land and history. She teaches photography to community activists, helping to develop new visual languages for transforming women's lives.

Daina Green is an educator and equity advocate who became active in the Ontario Public Service Employees Union more than ten years ago. She went on to be the union's Equal Opportunities Coordinator and now works independently, developing educational programs on equity issues for unions and other groups. She is an executive member of the Ontario Alliance for Employment Equity and a long-time member of the Equal Pay Coalition.

Sylvia Hamilton is a filmmaker, writer and researcher who lives in Halifax, Nova Scotia. Her primary area of interest is the social and cultural history of people of African descent in Nova Scotia, with a focus on the history of African Nova Scotian women. She researched, wrote and co-directed *Black Mother, Black Daughter* (1989) for the National Film Board. The film explores the experiences of Black women in Nova Scotia. Her most recent film, *Speak It! From the Heart of Black Nova Scotia,* (1993) also for the National Film Board, focuses on contemporary issues facing African Nova Scotian youth. Her writings on history and literature have appeared in anthologies, newspapers and journals

Lois Harder is a doctoral candidate in political science at York University, Toronto. Her research focuses on the translation of "family values" into public policy. She is the co-editor of the graduate student journal *Problematique* and is an active member of the Women's Caucus in Political Science.

Jennifer Keck is a feminist and community activist living in Sudbury, Ontario. She is a founding member of the Sudbury Women's Centre and a past executive member of the National Action Committee on the Status of Women. She teaches at the School of Social Work at Laurentian University.

Rita Kohli is a Toronto-based South Asian lesbian educator and activist. For the last decade she has worked extensively in the anti-violence against women and anti-racism movement. She was the coordinator of Making The Links, the 1992 Canadian Research Institute for the Advancement of Women/Institut Canadien Recherche de Femmes (CRIAW/ICREF) conference on anti-racism and feminism. Rita is currently finishing her M.Ed. in community psychology at the Ontario Institute for Studies in Education.

Gayle Lebans is a community worker with Parkdale Community Legal Services in the Workers' Rights Group. She has been involved in the trade union movement, workers' rights and community development for a number of years. She is a steward with the Ontario Public Service Employees Union.

Katherine Scott is a doctoral student in political science at York University in Toronto. She has also worked for the Ontario government as a policy analyst for the past three years. She is conducting research for her dissertation in Stockholm, Sweden, on women and welfare state restructuring. She has been active in the women's movement since 1982 and a member of Women's Press since 1985.

Naomi Binder Wall is an adult educator, writer and community activist. She was one of the founding organizers of CUPE Local 3452, the first union in Canada for teachers of English as an adult second language and for literacy instructors. She has coordinated literacy programs in Regent Park, a Toronto public housing development. She is on the Board of Directors at Central Neighbourhood House, a Toronto-based community centre, facilitates workshops on the labelling and streaming of poor children in the Metro Toronto school system and acts as an advocate for women.

Photo by Ann Decter

LINDA CARTY is a sociologist who teaches at University of Michigan, Flint Campus. She spent twenty years in Toronto as an activist in the feminist community, completing her Ph.D. at University of Toronto, where she specialized in international development and in the sociology of education. Linda Carty has taught in women's studies programs at the University of Toronto and at Oberlin College in Ohio. A number of her publications address the structural location of women of Colour in advanced capitalist countries and Third World countries, the state and economic development in the Caribbean, and the historical significance of colonialism and imperialism to the international division of labour. Recent publications include "Women's Studies in Canada: A Discourse and Praxis of Exclusion" in *Resources for Feminist Research* and "Black Women in Academia: A Statement from the Periphery" in *Unsettling Relations* (Women's Press/South End). Linda Carty is working on a book on the work histories of Caribbean domestics in Canada and the United States.